DEVELOPING INTERCULTURAL
COMPETENCE AND TRANSFORMATION

DEVELOPING INTERCULTURAL COMPETENCE AND TRANSFORMATION

Theory, Research, and Application
in International Education

Edited by

Victor Savicki

STERLING, VIRGINIA

Sty/us

COPYRIGHT © 2008 BY STYLUS PUBLISHING, LLC.

Published by Stylus Publishing, LLC
22883 Quicksilver Drive
Sterling, Virginia 20166–2102

Library of Congress Cataloging-in-Publication Data
Developing intercultural competence and transformation :
theory, research, and application in international
education / edited by Victor Savicki.—1st ed.
    p.   cm.
    Includes bibliographical references and index.
    ISBN 978–1-57922–265–9 (cloth : alk. paper)—
    ISBN 978–1-57922–266–6 (pbk. : alk. paper)
    1. International education.   2. Foreign study.
    I. Savicki, Victor.
LC1090.D43   2008
370.116—dc22   2007048782

ISBN: 978–1-57922–265–9 (cloth)
ISBN: 978–1-57922–266–6 (paper)

Printed in the United States of America

All first editions printed on acid free paper
that meets the American National Standards Institute
Z39–48 Standard.

Bulk Purchases

Quantity discounts are available for use in workshops
and for staff development.
Call 1–800–232–0223

First Edition, 2008

10   9   8   7   6   5   4

To all our students past, present, and future—interculturally competent global citizens—and to all their teachers—in the classroom and in life.

CONTENTS

SECTION TWO
RESEARCH ON THE PROCESSES OF
INTERCULTURAL COMPETENCE AND
TRANSFORMATION

SECTION THREE
APPLICATIONS TO ENHANCE INTERCULTURAL
GROWTH AND TRANSFORMATION

ACKNOWLEDGMENTS

S pecial thanks to AHA International for its support and encouragement for research, for conference presentations, and for dropping this book into the center of the expanding pool that is international education. The ripples will roll outward to touch many beyond the bounds of our initial vision.

PREFACE

International education is changing in many ways. What used to be a rare experience reserved for few students has grown and expanded. Some institutions of higher learning are promoting study abroad as a de facto requirement for the liberally and professionally educated graduate. The Lincoln Report recommends that by the 2016–2017 academic year the United States send one million students each year to participate in some form of study abroad program (Commission on the Abraham Lincoln Study Abroad Fellowship Program, 2005). More students are heeding the call.

The variety of study abroad options has expanded dramatically. The "traditional" junior year abroad has been augmented by semester-long, month-long, weeklong experiences hosted by a variety of institutions, and taught by a variety of educators with a variety of experience in international education. While this expansion of options may be beneficial for the goal of sending a million students abroad, it does raise important questions about the quality of study abroad outcomes and how those outcomes may be accomplished. We must look to the "high road" for study abroad experiences that emphasize predictable, planful, progressive, and positive intercultural outcomes (Wineberg, 2007). This book attempts to address some of those objectives.

The onus is on study abroad educators and administrators to meet the challenges that arise from both growing numbers of students and the growing variety of formats for study abroad experience. We cannot pitch students into a "trial by ordeal" and hope for the best. We need to be more specific about what we want students to look like when they emerge from their study abroad. We also need to be more systematic about how we aid students in attaining those outcomes.

The goal of this book is to help international educators create study abroad experiences that reach their goals by design, not chance. In order to help educators move beyond the trial-and-error approach to instructional design, it seems that we need to offer not only ideas for curriculum but also the theory and research that backs them up. Merely picking and choosing from a cookbook of topics and classroom exercises may be expedient, but it is not necessarily effective, nor does it automatically move toward the positive outcomes we want for students.

It is our belief that a balance of theory, research, and application best serves the needs of study abroad educators facing the coming challenges. These are the threads that run through the chapters of this book. Section one, "Theories for Intercultural Growth and Transformation," sets the stage by describing the international education context and by identifying "what" the specific desirable study abroad outcomes are. What does a culturally competent person look like? What aspects of learning reflect those outcomes? The section on theory also addresses the questions of "how" to help students attain life-changing outcomes. How can we mobilize educational processes that are likely to encourage such outcomes? How can we set the stage for transformation?

Section two, "Research on the Processes of Intercultural Competence and Transformation," shows how some of these outcomes and processes can be measured and assessed. What psychological and educational processes impact intercultural adjustment? What aspects of these processes are teachable? learnable? What is the relationship between characteristics of home and host cultures and positive study abroad outcomes?

Section three, "Applications to Enhance Intercultural Growth and Transformation," addresses applications and offers a number of proven study abroad education structures, processes, and expressions. How do you help students to think about rather than just react to culture clashes? What principles are involved in sequencing exposure to cultural issues? What is the role of the instructor in helping students process their experiences in the most beneficial way? How do the external words of the students reflect the internal competence and transformation that emerge from the study abroad experience? Each thread is intertwined with the others.

In a more general sense, the pattern of the threads woven into this book is captured by its title, *Developing Intercultural Competence and Transformation.* We are interested in both "competence" and "transformation," and see them as different from more traditional emphases in international education. In standard academic settings emphasis is usually placed on learning specific content, be it the date of the Norman Invasion or the difference between impressionism and cubism. International education certainly has content, and students usually attend content courses during their sojourns. However, study abroad offers explorations above and beyond the standard classroom experience. These differences are the *raison d'etre* for promoting intercultural encounters. Otherwise, what would be the advantage of shipping students off to a different country with all of its attendant expense and disruption? Students who return from a study abroad experience often say that it has transformed their lives. By and large, they do not attribute this change to learning to conjugate verbs in a foreign language or to visiting an art museum. Rather, they focus on interactions with host nationals, the shock of confronting a different set of values and attitudes, and their ability to sort through the myriad of cultural differences and not only survive but thrive. These are growth experiences. They engage the whole person: thinking, feeling, and behaving. It is the whole person whom we address. The task of international educators is to set the stage for students to learn competencies and to make the shift of perception that leads to transformation. As with all other learning, we can only create favorable conditions for growth and transformation. The spark, the click of a light flooding on, the "Ah ha!" remains within the minds of our students.

Study abroad outcomes that focus on personal competence and transformation have become more mainstream, yet they remain somewhat elusive in terms of assessment and curriculum. How do you design a course to increase a student's world-mindedness, or intercultural sensitivity, or coping abilities, or life satisfaction? Though difficult to measure and instruct, it is just these aspects of the study abroad experience that demand our attention. It is these features that compose the "transformation" aspect mentioned in this book's title. It is these outcomes that form the core of this book. Measuring aspects of international education just because they are easy to count (e.g., number of students sent, grades attained, credit hours completed) does not address the heart of the study abroad experience. Just because an outcome is difficult to assess doesn't mean that it should be glossed over.

This book attempts to shed light on the issues facing study abroad educators and administrators in the coming years. The introductory chapter, Chapter 1, "Designing Transformation in International Education," makes the case for emphasizing personal transformation as a stated goal for study abroad. Rather than relying on serendipity, international educators can state objectives clearly and design curricula to achieve them. Such an approach has clear implications for educators given the evolving study abroad context. In section one, "Theories for Intercultural Growth and Transformation," several issues critical to study abroad are addressed from a broad perspective. These chapters set the framework for the personal competence and transformation approach to international education. They also speak to not only the "what" but also the "how" of this approach. Chapter 2, "On Becoming a Global Soul: A Path to Engagement During Study Abroad," suggests a perspective in which an intercultural competence is based on cognitive learning (mindset), behavioral development (skillset), and clarification of affect and values (heartset). These areas of personal change are at the core of study abroad, which is in turn the centerpiece of liberal education. It discusses a selection of intercultural competencies particularly critical to international education and suggests a perspective for placing the global soul at the heart of education. This chapter describes important assumptions and trends for those participating in study abroad programs whether as administrators, teachers, or students. Chapter 3, "Intercultural Competence: A Definition, Model, and Implications for Education Abroad," describes the target international educators and administrators should aim toward. Based on a comprehensive research project, it gives flesh to the elusive construct of intercultural competence, as well as describing some of the processes involved in helping students attain both internal and external shifts of behavior and perception. The study abroad field needs a consistent, coherent model to work toward. This chapter proposes such a model. Chapter 4, "Growth and Transformation Outcomes in International Education," is a review of the current research literature that speaks to the personal competence and transformation approach. Key concepts such as self and cultural awareness, cross-cultural adaptability, interpersonal flexibility, autonomy in cross-cultural learning, etc., are difficult to operationalize; yet these are core to the growth of study abroad students. A mounting body of literature now focuses on these issues, and this chapter reviews their current status. Chapter 5, "Experiential and Affective Education for International Educators," takes the position that study abroad is an ultimate expression of experiential and affective learning. By virtue of being thrust into a foreign culture, the encounters that students experience are fodder for the holistic reflection and processing that is the centerpiece of experiential learning. Likewise, affect, in the form of feelings, attitudes, and values, becomes content and can be examined and evaluated to help students move to positive outcomes. Chapter 6, "Transformative Learning in International Education," gives voice to the common student perception that "my study abroad experience changed my life." How those changes occur and what educators can do to facilitate those changes are discussed in this chapter, particularly with regard to the study abroad context. Transformative Learning Theory has substance that applies well to international education. Knowledge of this theory advances the goal of reaching positive student outcomes by design. It provides the theoretical foundation for the concept of "transformation" as it is used in this book.

In section two, "Research on the Processes of Intercultural Competence and Transformation," the chapters address different aspects of study abroad using a variety of methods. All of the studies reported here were conducted with students who were enrolled in one of the international education programs described in the applications section of this book. There is a bridge between research and application. Chapter 7, "Contrasts and Changes in Potential and Actual Psychological Intercultural Adjustment," looks at student adjustment five times over a 9-month period. Surprising relationships between intercultural adjustment potential and actual adjustment forms the message of this study. Though it is not easy, study abroad is satisfying, and it produces positive outcomes. Chapter 8, "Tuscan Dreams: Study Abroad Student Expectation and Experience in Siena," takes an anthropological look at the goals, self-articulated motivations, and assessments that students make. These reveal the explicit and tacit values that structure student overseas experiences, as well as the reactions and learning patterns that develop. It is a peek into student thinking and feeling. Student and program sides of the study abroad equation are found to be equally relevant parts of the same process. Practical recommendations are offered regarding optimal program structure, emphasis, and design drawn from participant observation and student responses. Chapter 9, "Intercultural Development: Topics and Sequences," is a qualitative analysis of the kinds of events and encounters that seem important to study abroad students over a 12-week study abroad sojourn. Some issues stand out as more frustrating/engaging than others. There seems to be a predictable sequence in which many of these 23 issues emerge that bears a relationship to existing developmental theories of intercultural adjustment. Not all issues are equally salient, nor do they each follow the same pattern. Finally, Chapter 10, "Acculturative Stress, Appraisal, Coping and Intercultural Adjustment," assesses how strategies of psychological appraisal and coping are related to both the mental and emotional well-being of students, and to their ability to fit in with their study abroad culture. The relationships between ways of viewing and dealing with cultural clashes, on the one hand, and adjustment, on the other, follow distinct patterns. Cultural distance emerges as a key feature defining how adjustment occurs on the psychological, sociocultural, and acculturative levels.

In section three, "Applications to Enhance Intercultural Growth and Transformation," the chapters illustrate methods and approaches to study abroad instructional design and students' reactions to it. The authors in this part have made special efforts to share the actual words of their students to reveal the processes of thinking, feeling, and behaving that form the substance of change in the study abroad experience. Chapter 11, "Action Methods for Integration of Experience and Understanding," emphasizes the experiential, and transformational learning opportunities that may be organized for students while in the study abroad setting. The experience of daily living and structured classroom activities are both reviewed. Specific exercises are listed, but more important, the role of the instructor and the manner of delivery are explained, so that the experiential and transformational learning processes can proceed. Chapter 12, "Italy: Everyday Another Soulful Experience to Bring Back Home," illustrates an on-site curriculum to help students adjust to living in Italy. Both cultural content and intercultural processes are taught. Student reports demonstrate not only the unique aspects of Italian culture, through students' eyes, but also their reactions to it. These reports form an on-the-ground, student perspective that may be valuable for prospective study abroad students. Chapter 13, "The Eye of the Beholder: Study Abroad in Spain Viewed Through Multi-Cultural Lenses," also examines an on-site, intercultural communication course, with a unique, Spanish flourish. The cultural issues identified in the course set the stage for cultural observations, comparisons, discussions, and self-examination. Values and attitudes that form the core of cultural identity become overt, not hidden. American students who feel like they have no culture discover that indeed they do. Student reports document their struggles with the cultural clashes they encounter. Chapter 14, "Case Studies for Integration of Experience and Understanding While Studying in Vienna," is the final on-site course in this book, set in Vienna, Austria. It is an especially vivid demonstration of how to incorporate and deal with emotionally laden topics that may arise in any culture. Feelings and emotions are a valuable part of the human condition. Acknowledging and incorporating them into the intercultural curriculum addresses the whole person. The instructor's role in this process is well illustrated in this chapter. Student reports document the effective manner in which students can integrate these sometimes intense reactions to enhance their intercultural understanding. Chapter 15, "Dynamics of Cultural Contexts: Meta-Level Intervention in the Study Abroad Experience," illustrates an innovative design to support students before, during, and after their sojourn by means of both face-to-face activities and computer-based interaction. Email and online discussions not only raise issues that students must contend with while in their individual placements but also allow comparison of the several different cultures in which students may be studying. Students learn from each other's intercultural trials and celebrations, and get a meta-perspective on culture not available through an only two-culture comparison. Chapter 16, "Reflection, Reciprocity, Responsibility, and Committed Relativism: Intercultural Development Through International Service-Learning," explores a rapidly growing form of study abroad that incorporates service activities and intercultural learning as a dual emphases. The opportunities for immersion and meaningful contributions to the foreign community are immense; yet, so too are the potential issues. The chapter illustrates methods that can be mobilized to help students structure, interpret, and integrate their service experiences. It also articulates the responsibilities of such programs to establish mutually enhancing partnerships with the communities that they serve. Chapter 17, "Narratives of Intercultural Transformation: Student Perspective Transition," is a series of student narratives focusing on key issues in intercultural adjustment that have been identified through research, as reported in section two of this book. Students find these key issues compelling, and they tell us why. Both prospective students and international educators will find the content revealing. Forewarned is forearmed. The specificity and detail of student response helps put these important issues in a positive frame.

Finally, chapter 18, "Synthesis and Conclusions," attempts both to highlight the threads running through the preceding chapters and also to put words to the emerging patterns arising from them. With the notion that the whole is greater than the sum of the parts, we believe that the book content has important insights for the international education community.

We hope that you will find both affirmation and new possibilities between the covers of this book. There are many good things now happening in the study abroad setting, from orientation to on-site teaching and coaching to reentry and follow-up. However, many of these approaches are not now systematic, and it remains to be seen if international education approaches of the past will be effective in dealing with future changes in study abroad. It is the combination of understanding the rationale, seeing the research connections between theory and outcomes, and utilizing the rationale and connections in program design that develops the most potent results. In designing international education strategies, we believe that it is the combination of theory, research, and application that will help educators and administrators to weave a rich fabric with the disparate threads of student intercultural experience. The patterns may differ, but the resulting outcomes will be realized effectively by well-considered design.

References

Commission on the Abraham Lincoln Study Abroad Fellowship Program (2005). *Global competence and national needs: One million Americans studying abroad.* Retrieved May 9, 2007 from http://www.culturalinsurance.com/pdf/lincoln_final_report.pdf

Wineberg, A. (2007). Quantity or quality in study abroad? *Inside Higher Ed.* Retrieved May 9, 2007 from http://www.insidehighered.com/views/2007/05/08/weinberg

DESIGNING TRANSFORMATION IN INTERNATIONAL EDUCATION

Robert Selby

I t has become cliché to promote study abroad as a "life-transforming" experience. I am genuinely glad that my colleagues embrace the life-changing potential of international study. I still remember when, less than two decades ago, many of us denied that we, as educators, bore any responsibility for student personal development. Nevertheless, I am not sure any of us understands what we mean by the expression "life-transforming," or even if students know what they intend. If we are going to make such claims, then we should be certain there is empirical substance to back them, and if substantive, then find a way to describe what occurs. That is the objective of this book: to validate that study abroad students experience something that is truly *transformational* and, in so doing, to cast light on objectives for designing international study programs.

What and How Do Students Learn by Studying Abroad?

I have long been impressed by the different manners in which colleagues describe their objectives for study abroad. Many, faculty members in particular, tend to be very narrow and specific, using the same terminology and concepts they employ when writing a course syllabus. Indeed, many faculty members who teach abroad think of student learning as being primarily associated with their teaching. Learning, at this level, is linked to a familiar didactic process with the same evaluation procedures used on campus. In fact, any deviation from traditional *academic* practice is viewed askance, with suspicion that study abroad is simply a "blow-off" semester, giving students the chance to raise their GPAs while avoiding the rigors of campus instruction.

International educators and less traditional faculty cite the *experiential* value of study abroad. But even here, the tendency is to emphasize how the experience of being somewhere will bolster only the objectives of academic coursework. It is easy to justify that, for example, soaking up something of the local color and sensory feel of the place where Jane Austen wrote her novels or where Dante composed his poetry will give students additional perspective on their works. Being surrounded by, preferably immersed in, another language is assumed to accelerate linguistic skills. But many of my colleagues get skittish if the experiential dimension is pressed too strongly. Observe the reaction of language departments when students gain proficiency in colorful colloquialisms and you have a metaphor for experiential learning in general—it is valued as long as it reinforces our original academic objectives; it is decidedly devalued when it leads students in unanticipated directions. I have always been curious how it is that we educators can observe and comment on the value students take from incidents of getting lost or having to cope with difficult experiences, but are nonetheless loathe to build these serendipitous elements into curricular plans, much less to evaluate students on how they handle such ordeals. Fortunately, activities like "service learning" are becoming more common elements in many study abroad curricula. Nevertheless, even these are often approached without clear, consistently agreed-upon objectives for what students should take from the experience.

International educators are becoming increasingly comfortable these days with the *developmental* dimension of study abroad, acknowledging that student maturation accelerates abroad as learners are surrounded by other points of view and have to come to terms with their own core values and identity. As is evident in chapters in this book, some study abroad programs make this self-reflection an explicit part of the curriculum by requiring students to analyze both observed local patterns of behavior and their own reaction to those patterns. But this necessitates specialized pedagogical skills as well as a foundation in intercultural and developmental theory—expertise that is difficult to find anywhere but is especially scarce in many study abroad locations. I suspect that focus on developmental learning is much more talked about in our profession than practiced in the field. Nevertheless, many of my colleagues and I believe that this is precisely the domain in which students intuit that they have changed as a result of living abroad.

Study Abroad: The Educator's Dilemma

This, then, is our profession's dilemma: students describe the benefits of study abroad in terms of life-changing impact, while faculty, by and large, evaluate it in terms of specifically stated learning outcomes; international educators all too often leave it to serendipity to bridge the two. This is not mere sophistry. It is at the heart of how we design, develop, and evaluate study abroad. If the objectives for sending students abroad are contained on a course syllabus much like the one used on campus, administrators are correct to question the additional cost/loss of revenue. If students gain significantly from the experience of being abroad but the benefit cannot be described or validated, then most program evaluations are really little more than measures of customer satisfaction. In fact, if we are unable to define what we want students to take from study abroad generally, then we lack clear objectives and are, consequently, unable to evaluate our—or students'—achievement. In my career I have frequently been disappointed to note how many of my colleagues have institutional objectives in mind for study abroad, mere percentages in some cases; if our profession cannot agree on what students should take from the experience, it is natural to think in terms of how international study fits into strategic planning on campus rather than how it shapes individual development.

This becomes all the more critically important given two current trends in study abroad: short-term programs and faculty-led programs. If the intercultural-developmental-maturational aspects of international study are significant objectives for sending students abroad, then longer sojourns are better than shorter ones. And (only now that I am retired dare I say this) the criteria necessary for selecting faculty to lead programs may differ widely from those employed by most departments. Based on studies included in this text, I think our profession must be prepared either to challenge these trends or, conversely, to be very clear, intentional, and prescriptive with regard to structuring curricula for international study. I will return to this theme.

Intercultural Education

In oversimplified terms, *international* education leads students to learn about the objective, material culture of others—their political and social institutions, their language, art, and literature—while *intercultural* education leads students to learn about the subjective meaning people ascribe to events and relationships with institutions and other people, and ultimately to themselves. Didactic instruction is very effective for teaching about material culture. It is not necessarily the best means to stimulate interactive relational or reflective thinking. Experiential learning, on the other hand, tends to ground one's perspective somewhere else and provide external feedback, enabling one to see things, even oneself, through the eyes of others. Given time and feedback, one may eventually perceive one's own self and culture with the same objectivity usually reserved for others. It can be incredibly unsettling to discover that nothing one knows, not even oneself, is what one imagines it to be when seen through the eyes of another. That is, experiential learning may lead to total confusion—"the ideal state of learning," as one of my undergraduate professors was fond of saying. I vividly recall my epiphanic incident.

I was teaching in Mexico at the time. I worked up courage to go on what, as an American, I understood to be a *date*. I had already lived in Mexico for a year, had seen much of the Republic, was able to converse in Spanish, enjoyed many friends, and felt reasonably at home there. Indeed, from the day I arrived I had fallen in love with Mexico and its diverse traditions, gregarious people, the ubiquitous cacophony of noises, chaotic traffic, riotous colors, and apparent lack of restrictive rules. I knew corporate CEOs and daily laborers, ate in open village markets and French restaurants in Mexico City. Mexico, compared to my narrow life in the States, was a limitless cornucopia of contrasting experiences. I had, as part of my self-education, read Andrew Whiteford's *Two Cities of Latin America* (1964), one of which cities was the place I was living. So I knew Mexico, and Querétaro in particular, had a stratified social structure. And I knew from reading Octavio Paz (1950) that Mexicans could lead isolated lives. But Mexico, as I knew and experienced it, was open, fluid, gregarious, congenial, intensely interpersonal. Indeed, I knew this *because* I experienced it personally.

Anyway, I was on a date driving to a nice restaurant on a Sunday evening, passing the plaza just as groups of young ladies were heading home from their *vuelta al jardin*. Hoping to set a light tone I jestingly asked my date: "So, what's a nice girl like you doing going out with a Gringo at this time of night?" "*Bueno, Señor Selby,*" she formally replied, "since you are an outsider without status, you don't elevate my position, but you don't endanger it either." I didn't matter socially! That was the only reason she went out with me.

Over dinner, I learned that my date was one of the local "bluebloods" described by Whiteford as deriving her heritage from an ancient Spanish coat of arms. She had last dated a fellow 7 years previously; he went off to study in England and never returned. There was no other male of similar status in the city (of over 250,000) she could date until a statusless Gringo showed up with a casual dinner and glass of wine in mind.

Setting aside the unknowable significance of the situation in which I found myself, what I realized in an instant was that I had never, until that moment, really experienced Mexico. The Mexico I knew existed only in the imagination of a foreigner, an outsider left on his own to observe and interpret an apparently convivial Mexico without ever sensing its rigid social norms that isolated class from class, family from family, coworker from colleague. In an instant my perceived Mexico vanished and I was confronted with a clear choice: I could either continue to enjoy my social fluidity as an outsider, or I must become a Querétaro, ascribed to whatever status and social circle the community would accord me. Eventually, I learned to my surprise that I was ascribed relatively high status, but having it and being expected to use it was a burden—until I later became a post-graduate student back in the States and had to adjust to being an American in America without status, a far worse cultural shock.

I had dedicated myself to learn about Mexico, reading its literature and visiting its museums, discovering how to obtain medical care and a driver's license, getting to know along the way its material culture. Slowly I began to discover its invisible culture, the lines that separated classes and neighborhoods, the unwritten expectations of each, who pays and when, when and how to shift from *usted* to *tu*, when to be punctual and when to arrive an hour "late"—the level of culture anthropologists study. But in the end, what I really learned from Mexico was that I could not be comfortable with ascribed status, even high status, and preferred a society in which I and most others have to earn our social positions. I returned home prepared to earn mine. What started out as an international experience became, at some point, an intercultural experience. Ultimately, it turned into an *existential* experience, leaving me to wonder if I mattered or, if I did, if I mattered in a manner that mattered to me. I had to reconstruct and affirm my new identities.

When students show up exhilarated from the experience of having been lost in a strange place, they have, of course, learned something about their new environs, but more important, they have learned something about themselves and their own abilities. Hopefully, they will have gained confidence, too, in the kindness of strangers. Conversely, students who are reprimanded by the homestay mother for taking food from the refrigerator enjoy a great intercultural learning moment, as well: that different societies give different ascriptions to what is public or private, so that in navigating through someone else's house, or transportation system, or healthcare facility, one is traveling through a different universe of meanings than back home. Given enough time and feedback, students will eventually figure out the meanings others ascribe to things, including outsiders. What hope is there, however, for students to make sense of their host culture, much less their place in it, within the scope of a 10- to 15-week study abroad program? What if their professor knows all about local architecture or the political system but little of the host culture?

Transformation as Content

My fundamental hypothesis, as should be apparent by now, is that what students describe as "life-transforming" is, at root, the experience of seeing themselves, their culture and values, in some new way, as perceived through the lens—that is, feedback—of the host culture. They are, perhaps for the only time in their lives, the existential outsider. At one level, students acquire knowledge about limited aspects of their new surroundings. At a more profound level, they begin to compare their heritage to that of others and to doubt the superiority of their own cultural values. But at a still more transformative level, the possibilities of their own existence, as they have imagined them, are challenged. The letdown of "reentry shock" is not mere reverse culture shock, but rather the tedious task of having to question all one's prior experience, including the reconstruction of one's own self-image, within the context of multiple new insights but now without the sharp contrast of a "foreign" culture to define it for one.

If this hypothesis is true, the obvious question becomes, As internationalists, do we explicitly want study abroad to be life changing? If not, then it seems to me that we define ourselves only as administrators—not as international *educators*, but as professionals limited to the budgets and logistics of sending students overseas. On the other hand, if we buy into the notion that study abroad is truly transformative beyond the scope of course syllabi, then we need to think of ourselves as being true educators, making certain that program curricula contain elements specifically designed to include intercultural embarrassment and ambiguity that find release, even resolution, through analysis and reflection.

In short, the whole experience of study abroad should be comprehensible to students. I have been much impressed over the years by Janet Bennett's musings regarding the all-too-often polar contrasts in how we approach on-campus curricula versus international study (see chapter 2 of this book). At home we start students in 101 overview courses and guide them logically and methodically into deeper, more specific coursework. We do not begin math instruction with algorithms employed by programmers, nor do we teach Spanish by assigning students to translate *Don Quixote*. Nevertheless, we think it is fine to encourage students who have never traveled abroad to do an independent internship in some exotic corner of the world. Indeed, some educators seem to doubt students have an "authentic" experience unless they are overwhelmed in their new environment, a "throw them in the deep end to see if they can swim" approach. Professors who jealously protect traditional pedagogical practice on campus seem curiously to swing to the opposite extreme when advising students to go abroad. Students who have never even encountered another Western culture may be directed to Asia, for example. Just as beginning Spanish students handed *Don Quixote* may acquire some unique vocabulary or expressions without being able to use the language effectively to order a taco, students placed in extremely different circumstances may gain from unique personal tests but not acquire significant insights into their host culture, much less transferable intercultural skills. We should prepare students to learn other cultures by employing the same principles we use to teach them how to appreciate art or how to acquire another language. Otherwise, they return with rich experience and increased confidence but with limited transferable skills.

In my ideal world of international study, every study abroad experience—regardless of whether it is a direct-enroll, exchange, island, hybrid, or any other structure—should involve these elements:

1. *A stated set of objectives that include academic learning, intercultural analysis, and personal development.* Academic objectives should be every bit as rigorous as those employed on campus but should also acknowledge that students are engaged in multisensory learning and most require contextual frameworks within which to process new information; therefore, courses need to be structured with greater attention to interdisciplinary and analytical processes.

Intercultural analysis involves either adding a new dimension to all courses or adding a new course that enables students to report on, discuss, and analyze daily incidents they find frustrating, amusing, or merely curious. These personal incidents and observations should be considered within the context of the host culture and extrapolated to reveal larger patterns of attitudes and beliefs. Is limited access to the family refrigerator a case of stinginess, or is it a window on ideas of public–private domains? If the latter, how do these domains affect behaviors more generally, and how can one learn to navigate successfully through them? After students have applied their own interpretations to observed events, they need to hear how native peers would interpret them. By learning to doubt their own ascription of significance to events, students should return, for example, from Italy much better prepared to anticipate and work through cultural differences in China, and vice versa.

It is all well and good to ask students to write down a statement of personal objectives or even to draft a "learning contract" for themselves. But it is absurd to expect students to define on their own a personal objective that they cannot begin to anticipate and may not be able to explain even years later. If we expect students to be changed, we need to ensure that students are put in situations in which they are confused and challenged, but have the opportunity to make sense of what occurs so they meet future frustrations with increasing confidence. That is, we must believe that students gain from embracing ambiguity, even if their normal reflex is to avoid or resolve it.

2. *Sufficient time to realize the stated objectives.* The more time students are immersed in another culture, the more time they have to figure things out for themselves through random experience and local feedback. A shorter time frame means that the structure must be manipulated to result in intended experiences and analysis within the time available. That is, curricular intentionality must increase as the period abroad decreases.

One way to alter the structure is to require prerequisite intercultural orientation and coursework. It is highly unlikely that a program in marine biology being developed for Costa Rica, for example, would not require students to have some foundational knowledge of biology or oceanography, hopefully even Spanish; the same should hold for intercultural knowledge. Indeed, the shorter the time abroad, the more prior preparation is needed.

3. *Staff who are proficient and qualified with respect to all the stated objectives.* In the case of direct-enroll and exchange programs, there need to be local staff at host institutions who understand the overall objectives for sending students abroad and who are capable of providing learning structures that support those objectives.

Faculty led programs should be led by professors who, in addition to being qualified in their own discipline, are specifically trained to facilitate intercultural and developmental learning. Otherwise, additional coursework and staff need to be built into the program structure.

In many cases, this will require universities to provide or cooperate with international infrastructures that can support reasonably uniform instructional methodologies wherever students are headed.

4. *Reentry reflection and analysis.* Confusion is the ideal state of learning—but only if meaningful learning results from it. Some kind of follow-up seminar must ensure that students do not return home without gaining closure on their experience. "Closure" should involve the ability to describe how international experience will be integrated into future life goals.

A successful study abroad experience involves choices about retaining what one has learned in another culture while reaffirming things one appreciates in one's own culture. This process of selection results in personal "re-engineering," that is, the reconstruction of one's identity, something made possible because now there are new elements one can draw into the conception of self.

I do not have illusions that campuses have resources to achieve all this, nor do I want to downplay the absolutely obvious importance of the "international" dimension in international academic study. I am confident, nevertheless, that students gain far more from study abroad than we dare state in our program objectives. I hope that the impacts on student lives documented in this book will inspire our profession to look beyond the academic dimension, confident that, with increased intentionality, we can expand learning outcomes to include significantly higher levels of abstraction and critical analysis.

References

Paz, O. (1950). *El Laberinto de la soledad.* Mexico, D.F.: Fomento de la Cultura e Educación.

Whiteford, A. H. (1964). *Two cities of Latin America: A comparative description of social classes.* Garden City, NY: Doubleday.

SECTION ONE

THEORIES FOR INTERCULTURAL GROWTH AND TRANSFORMATION

"There is nothing so practical as a good theory," goes the old saying. This is especially true with international education. Although there may be many perspectives on the study abroad experience, a consistent theoretical approach will help international educators organize themselves to deliver the best quality service to their students. The chapters in this part of the book address several issues in a way that provides some of this consistency of approach. First, what is the place of study abroad within the higher education system? Clearly, change is afoot. How should we approach this change? A focus on interculturalism aims to prepare students not only to succeed in the country in which they study but also to be prepared to succeed better in any culture. There is a generalization that is embedded in the intercultural approach that has special meaning for international educators. Second, there are identifiable, specifiable outcomes toward which international educators can strive. Intercultural competence can be defined. These are the goals toward which international educators can aim. The emphasis in section one, and in this book as a whole, is on the "growth and transformation" aspect of intercultural education. Initial findings in the literature of the field help to describe some of the growth and transformation aspects more clearly. Finally, there are processes of education and learning that are more likely to help international educators and their students achieve these goals. Experiential education, transformative learning, and systematic attention to affective outcomes all increase the likelihood that study abroad students will attain those life-changing experiences that we wish for them. The hope is that one's study abroad not only provides intense growth experiences in the present, but also that it teaches lifelong patterns of understanding that will incubate to bestow students with meaningful insights about themselves and others in the future, from a global viewpoint. Understanding the broad sweep of theory helps to put the day-to-day minutia of dealing with study abroad students into a consistent conceptual framework. It pays to rise up from focusing on the trees to see the forest. From that angle the trees gain a new clarity.

2

ON BECOMING
A GLOBAL SOUL
A Path to Engagement During Study Abroad

Janet M. Bennett

> The man who finds his homeland sweet is still a tender beginner; he
> to whom every soil is as his native one is already strong; but he is
> perfect to whom the entire world is a foreign land.
> —Hugo of St. Victor as quoted in *Global Soul* (Iyer, 2000)

B eing "global souls"—seeing ourselves as members of a world community, knowing that we share the future with others—requires not only intercultural experience but also the capacity to engage that experience transformatively.

For the international educator, being interculturally competent and facilitating the development of competence in others supports and exemplifies the transformative nature of studying abroad. This chapter will suggest a perspective in which an intercultural mindset, skillset, and heartset are at the core of study abroad, which is in turn the centerpiece of liberal education. It will discuss a selection of intercultural competencies particularly critical to international education, and suggest a perspective for placing the global soul at the heart of education.

Interculturalizing the New American Campus: A Place for International Education

After decades of being housed in the basements of student unions or in small bungalows just around the corner, international education is taking its rightful place at the center of liberal learning. The widely discussed report from the Lincoln Commission (Commission on the Abraham Lincoln Study Abroad Fellowship Program, 2005) stated, "What nations don't know can hurt them. The stakes involved in study abroad are that simple, that straightforward, and that important. For their own future and that of the nation, college graduates today must be internationally competent" (p. iv).

Current research in a variety of academic disciplines is unequivocally endorsing precisely the outcomes that study abroad can provide. There is widespread acknowledgment of the need for intercultural competence, and growing recognition that sojourning abroad can be transformative. Although the majority of learners are pursuing academic and cultural outcomes, we are facing for the first time new agendas for study abroad, including corporate and healthcare internships, service learning, scientific research, and even humanitarian relief. While international educators have long argued for the intercultural perspective (Mestenhauser & Ellingboe, 1998; Paige, 2004), they have more recently been supported by other disciplines and, indeed, the academy as a whole.

In higher education, researchers have explored the interface of global citizenship, democracy, and liberal learning (Cornwell & Stoddard, 1999, 2001; Deardorff, 2005, 2006; Hovland, 2006; Meacham & Gaff, 2006; Stoddard & Cornwell, 2003) and have concluded that culture matters. According to McTighe Musil (2006),

> The Association of American Colleges and Universities Greater Expectations Project on Accreditation and Assessment reported that global knowledge and engagement, along with intercultural knowledge and competence, have been identified as essential learning outcomes for all fields of concentration and for all majors. (p. 1)

From executive leadership studies to pragmatic applications, the research on corporate globalization also continues to emphasize core intercultural competencies (Boyacigiller, Beechler, Taylor, & Levy, 2004; Mendenhall, Kuhlmann, & Stahl, 2001; Osland, Bird, Mendenhall, & Osland, 2006). A recent Council on International Educational Exchange survey of over 300 employers concluded that employers value study abroad and overseas internships to a greater extent than any other form of education except foreign language learning (and, of course, the students' majors) (Vande Berg, 2007a). Summarizing the necessity of intercultural learning for future leaders, an amicus brief (Supreme Court, 2003) was presented on behalf of 65 major U.S. businesses in the University of Michigan affirmative action case. It argued:

> The students of today are this country's corporate and community leaders of the next half century. For these students to realize their potential as leaders, it is essential that they be educated in an environment where they are exposed to diverse ideas, perspectives, and interactions. Today's global marketplace and the increasing diversity in the American population demand the cross-cultural experience and understanding gained from such an education. (p. 2)

Finally, in the related field of language learning, culture has finally found its place "as the core" (Paige, Lange, & Yershova, 1999). The student guide *Maximizing Study Abroad* was designed for facilitating language acquisition in tandem with intercultural skills (Paige, Cohen, Kappler, Chi, & Lassegard, 2002). Its emphasis on predeparture, in-country and post-study-abroad self-guided observation, reflection, and practice illustrates both best practices of transformative learning and the integration of culture in language acquisition.

Across campuses, and across the world, there is an unmistakable conne that what international educators assumed was important the rest of the academy now recognizes.

Perspectives on Intercultural Competence

Often in the past, describing intercultural competence has been not unlike recognizing pornography, famously described by Justice Potter Stewart (1964) as hard to define, but "I know it when I see it."

In terms of intercultural competence, for many decades intercultural educators have known it and seen it. Ask nearly anyone in the field and she or he will regale you for hours with tales of students transformed by their overseas experiences, wise lessons learned, maturity gained, and worldviews expanded.

Times have changed. While the stories will forever thrive, now accreditation agencies are requiring more substantive attention to intercultural competence and its definition and measurement. Granting agencies are calling for greater accountability (Clayton-Pedersen, Parker, Smith, Moreno, &

Teraguchi, 2007). Organizations are developing benchmarks and scorecards by which to judge progress on diversity issues (O'Mara & Richter, 2006). Increasingly, institutions of higher learning are including in their mission statements such competences as "appreciating diversity," "building communities that acknowledge and respect difference," and "international and global understanding" (Meacham & Gaff, 2006, p. 9).

In addition, as education becomes more consumer oriented and the Ivory Tower is replaced by the student fitness center, the customers and their parents want a clear statement of outcomes and a specific return on investment: "If we underwrite our daughter's trip to Brazil, what outcomes can we expect? How will we know?"

With accountability and assessment comes a need for clarity of purpose. To measure intercultural competence, we must know what it is.

Intercultural Competence

Intercultural competence has been variously related to "global competence/ global mindset" (Bird & Osland, 2004), "global learning" (Hovland, 2006; McTighe Musil, 2006), "culture learning" (Paige et al., 2002), "education for democracy" (Cornwell & Stoddard, 2001), "cosmopolitan citizenship" (Stoddard & Cornwell, 2003), and "globalizing knowledge" (Cornwell & Stoddard, 1999), among others, no doubt.

However, despite the breadth of the disciplines examining the nature of intercultural competence (Deardorff, 2006), there is an "emerging consensus around what constitutes intercultural competence, which is most often viewed as a set of cognitive, affective, and behavioral skills and characteristics that support effective and appropriate interaction in a variety of cultural contexts" (Bennett, in press).

Five Foundation Principles

There are five principles for developing intercultural competence that provide a foundation for our examination of this process.

I recall a study abroad advisor who, when asked what he was doing to prepare students joining him on a program in Hong Kong, noted that intercultural preparation was not necessary, since they were going to study geology, and English is commonly spoken. His lack of understanding revealed two principles central to intercultural competence.

First, cultural knowledge does not equal cultural competence. Learners can be knowledgeable about objective culture (history, politics, geography, literature, etc.) and still be unsuccessful in their daily interactions. The learners in Hong Kong may very well have been able to identify streambeds and cliff formations but unable to navigate appropriate social interactions to discuss their discoveries. Such effectiveness requires attention to subjective culture, the learned and shared values, beliefs, and behaviors of a community of interacting people.

Second, language learning may not be sufficient for culture learning. If learners concentrate only on learning language and fail to learn the culture, they may become fluent fools, able to insult people at ever-higher levels of sophistication. When individuals are articulately rude, it is often an unrecoverable error.

A third principle of culture learning suggests that disequilibrium need not lead to dissatisfaction. Disequilibration, upsetting the balance, "results from the experience of differences that causes cognitive irritation, emotional imbalance, and a disruption of one's own worldview" (Otten, 2003, p. 15). The resulting teachable moments, or trigger events, are often the stimuli for developing intercultural competence. Well facilitated, such events can turn culture shock into culture learning.

A fourth principle notes that cultural contact does not necessarily lead to competence. The mere intermingling of individuals in intercultural contexts is not likely to produce, in itself, intercultural learning. Bennett and Salonen (2007), citing psychologist George Kelly, note, "learning from experience requires more than being in the vicinity of events when they occur. Learning emerges from our capacity to construe those events and then to reconstrue them in transformative ways" (p. 46). In the study abroad context, learners may be in the vicinity of Asian events when they occur but be having an American experience. It becomes the educator's task to facilitate reconstruing those events as *Asian*.

The fifth principle is that cultural contact does not always lead to a significant reduction of stereotypes. The well-known contact hypothesis (Allport, 1954; Amir, 1969) and the meta-analysis of 50 years of subsequent research (Pettigrew & Tropp, 2000) suggest key conditions for intercultural contact to reduce stereotypes and prejudice, and note that international contact (apart from limited tourism) and optimally structured programs typically have larger effects than domestic contact. Once again, "intervention strategies are required to achieve these outcomes" (Ward, 2001, p. 27).

Defining the Illusive Intercultural Competencies

Frequently, researchers have enumerated lengthy lists of knowledge, attitudes, and skills that constitute intercultural competence. (For a comprehensive examination of this research, see Deardorff, 2006.) However, for purposes of centering international education at the heart of liberal education, this discussion will review those core competencies only briefly, instead concentrating on the unique educational potential of the intercultural encounter.

The Mindset: Cognitive Competencies

The most commonly cited knowledge areas within the cognitive dimension, or *mindset*, include culture-general knowledge, culture-specific knowledge, identity development patterns, cultural adaptation processes, and the first priority: cultural self-awareness.

When we talk of culture-general knowledge in study abroad, we mean more than knowing anthropological systems for analyzing culture, more than research on values. Instead, we refer to culture frameworks that are also contexted in awareness of the cultural filters we use, as well as the filters used by others. Viewing truth as a "collaborative project" (Stoddard & Cornwell, 2003, p. 4) and using the contemporary metaphor of a Global Positioning System (GPS), Stoddard and Cornwell observe,

> A GPS is not reliable when it is trying to position one on the globe through information from only one satellite. In fact, a GPS determines one's position by reconciling information from multiple sources; it works on an epistemology of triangulation. The more satellites used as sources of information, the more certain the location is. This serves as a model for the way one needs to collect perspectives from differently situated knowers and citizens around the world in order to be able to make informed judgments, to have a sufficient base for knowledge. (p. 5)

Consistent with the Stoddard and Cornwell metaphor, Paige (2004) describes necessary "positioning" competencies that include, among other cognitive tasks, "exploring alternative and sometimes contradictory theories" (p. 89) as well as seeing various disciplines and their origins, perspectives, and practices as culturally influenced.

While not often noted in the international education literature, the domestic concerns about cultural and racial identity and privilege are also essential constructs in the international arena as offered by McTighe Musil (2006), who urges an examination of "privilege, power, democratic opportunity, and patterned stratifications" (p. 11).

The Skillset: Behavioral Competencies

The behavioral dimension, or *skillset*, typically includes such characteristics and skills as the ability to empathize, gather appropriate information, listen, perceive accurately, adapt, initiate and maintain relationships, resolve conflict, and manage social interactions and anxiety.

For the learners on study abroad the ability to gather appropriate information entails not only reading, researching, and experiential learning but also the use of cultural mentors (Osland & Bird, 2000), those precious individuals who are able and willing to use awareness of their own culture for enlightening visitors, interpreting the local culture, and alerting them to the realities they have missed. In return, the learner has to be willing to apply new insights in ways that take cultural values, beliefs, and behaviors into account.

Daloz's (2000) work on transformative learning investigated individuals' experiences with someone they viewed as different. He entitled this experience "constructive engagement with otherness," and goes on to relate this to empathy:

> For the experience to be more than simply an encounter, for it to be a constructive engagement, there had to be some sense of empathic connection with people different from themselves. In some significant way the inner experience of the other was engaged, a bond was formed, and some deep lesson about connection across differences was learned. (p. 110)

It is from such trigger events that transformative intercultural learning can take place. Daloz (2000) defines the condition on which engagement with otherness can lead to greater social responsibility: the presence of difference where "the encounter crossed some earlier boundary between 'us' and 'them,' and made available an alternative way of being, a different voice that challenged the earlier assumptions about how life is and made possible the construction of a new 'we'" (p. 113).

In addition, transformative learning includes the opportunity for reflective discourse, in a climate of safety, within a mentoring community with the possibility of forming durable commitments and acting on them. His recommendations are echoed in the study abroad literature, where the necessity of processing critical incidents and facilitating intercultural experiences—rather than just *having* them—is well-recognized.

The Heartset: Affective Competencies

The affective dimension, or *heartset*, of attitudes and motivations includes, first and foremost, curiosity, as well as initiative, risk taking, suspension of judgment, cognitive flexibility, tolerance of ambiguity, cultural humility, and resourcefulness.

Curiosity is often cited as the key to intercultural competence. Gregersen, Morrison, and Black (1998) described global leaders who "stated repeatedly that inquisitiveness is the fuel for increasing their global savvy, enhancing their ability to understand people and maintain integrity, and augmenting their capacity for dealing with uncertainty and managing tension" (p. 23).

As the keystone of intercultural competence, curiosity shapes the study abroad experience as no other skill or characteristic does. Whether exploring the unique perspective of a host family, confronting poverty—and sophistication—never imagined, or simply learning to slow down and smell the curry, the sojourner is best served and educated by engaging with curiosity. Opdal (2001) describes curiosity as a sense of wonder:

> Wonder . . . always points to something beyond the accepted rules. Because of this, the feeling of being overwhelmed, or the experience of humbleness and even awe could accompany it. Wonder is the state of mind that signals we have reached the limits of our present understanding, and that things may be different from how they look. (p. 331)

Reaching that learning edge where things *certainly* are different than they seem is facilitated by cultural humility, wherein we question the primacy of our worldview and accept—or even enjoy—the creative tension of holding multiple perspectives (Guskin, 1991).

Cultural humility also provides a foundation for the capacity to suspend judgments and competitiveness. Stoddard and Cornwell (2003) describe this as a disposition not to meet differences with a desire to win, to have one's own point of view triumph over others, but instead to meet differences as a project, a sign that power and point of view are likely in play. Intercultural communication skills emerge by this analysis not simply as useful in getting by in a diverse world, but as capacities essential to build a complex account of what is the case and what is important to do. (p. 5)

The Future of Intercultural Competence, Study Abroad, and the New American Campus

As sojourners master the intercultural competencies suggested previously and the particular competencies emphasized for study abroad, they are also fulfilling part of the mission of higher education. As we contemplate the future of international education, there are encouraging trends that the properly designed, thoroughly processed, and responsibly assessed international programs will flourish.

When interculturalists look forward, there is a temptation to create an idyllic vision of how we might thrive on campus. Perhaps all students will go on study abroad in a well-funded department where colleagues collaborate in designing innovative, interdisciplinary programs. Perhaps all students will seek in-depth, transformative experiences, where they achieve fluency in a second language, master the objective and subjective cultures, develop the described competencies, and become global souls. Perhaps the professional study abroad office will be perceived as offering valuable expertise to campus initiatives on intercultural learning. Perhaps the world will take a turn for the better, and risk-management need not be our pervasive daily burden.

Tempting though such comprehensive dreams may be, the realistic future suggests that while we cannot control all the variables there are several promising trends we *can* impact.

Trend #1: Campuses are recognizing that a bridge can be built between domestic diversity and global learning. Cornwell and Stoddard's (1999) seminal monograph *Globalizing Knowledge: Connecting International and Intercultural Studies*, offers the notion of "reconceptualizing identities and location . . . [through] new ways of charting the relationships between geographical territories and human belongings" (p. 10). Their carefully drawn consideration of global learning suggests that the field of intercultural communication can provide a bridge "to signify a merger of 'multicultural' and 'international'

. . . [hence] emphasiz[ing] the interaction between and mutual influences of cultural forms and practices on each other" (p. 17).

They recommend four interconnected goals for the new American campus, all of which relate directly to international education: "understanding diverse cultures and understanding cultures as diverse, developing intercultural skills, understanding global processes, and preparing for citizenship, both local and global" (p. 21).

By combining the interdisciplinary perspectives offered in intercultural communication, international studies, language, and education, an effective approach to intercultural learning readily emerges.

Cornwell and Stoddard are not alone in offering a path for reconciling intersections in the sometimes contentious debates between domestic diversity and globalization (Bennett & Bennett, 2004; Gardenswartz, Rowe, Digh, & Bennett, 2003; Hovland, 2006). While it is not the purpose of this chapter to resolve the complex questions that inevitably arise around such a challenging topic, it is worth noting a few of the difficult dialogues as they relate to international education.

1. Are interculturalists merely "exotifying" international cultures and ignoring the issues of power and racism at home? "If we think globally, do we oppress locally?" (Bennett & Salonen, 2007)
2. Are interculturalists educating patriots or cosmopolites? (Cornwell & Stoddard, 1999)
3. Is "cultural relativism" in conflict with universal human rights? (Stoddard & Cornwell, 2003)
4. Is culture constructed and dynamic or knowable and measurable? Are interculturalists reifying culture?

As professionals in international education creating bridges, not barriers, among worldviews, these are questions we had best be prepared to address.

Trend #2: International education is recognizing that comprehensive design is essential. In some ways, international education has developed through experiential learning; not just the students' learning but also the educators' learning. For decades, administrators, faculty, and study abroad professionals have in essence developed grounded theory, generating models from the qualitative data of observing successful and not-so-successful programs, and now from the quantitative studies that examine outcomes and impacts.

What was obvious ("I'll know it when I see it") to early international educators has now become consolidated through research and theory into standards such as *NAFSA's Principles for U.S. Study Abroad* (2001), which suggest intercultural approaches to study abroad. The principles state:

> The program should include an orientation, both predeparture and ongoing, which assists participants in making appropriate personal, social, and academic adjustments. Programs maintaining centers abroad should provide counseling and supervisory services . . . with special attention to the problems peculiar to the location and nature of the program. (Administration of Study Abroad Programs, principle #6)

The five principles described previously reflect the perspective that unfacilitated intercultural interaction without preparation and debriefing often fails to foster intercultural competence, decrease stereotypes, or engender learning. Indeed, luck prefers the prepared mind. In the context of study abroad, this preparation does not stand alone but is part of a systematically constructed sequence of predeparture preparation, in-country facilitation of critical incidents, and cognitive, affective, and behavioral reintegration upon return.

Bruce La Brack, a long-term advocate for such a comprehensive design, offered the following comment on this framework:

> While it is possible for individuals to cross cultural boundaries without adequate preparation, the question is why would they want to? More importantly, why would sponsoring institutions choose not to offer the tools we know could contribute to making the sojourns successful? Everything we know about culture learning and intercultural sojourns suggests that the most effective and appropriate way to accomplish this is with an integrated approach that combines pre-departure orientation with in-country support and instruction and includes opportunities for post-return discussion and analysis. (personal communication, August 15, 2007)

Furthermore, recent research has suggested that both predeparture preparation and mentoring students while they are overseas affect their intercultural development in significant ways (Vande Berg, 2007b).

Perhaps it is only through the commitment to comprehensive design that transformative learning can take place.

Trend #3: Study abroad programs must be intentionally developmentally designed. Perry's landmark research on cognitive development (1970) inspired many educators to examine their curricula through the lens of a developmental perspective. Models that sequence objectives (Bloom, Engelhart, Furst, Hill, & Krathwohl, 1956) or address learning styles or cognitive styles (Claxton & Ralston, 1978; Kolb, 1984) and identity (Cross, 1995; Evans, Forney, & Guido-DiBrito, 1998; Sabnani, Ponterotto, & Borodosky, 1991) have all been employed to provide a theoretical rationale for program design. For instance, Immelman and Schneider (1998) researched study abroad students using Bloom's Taxonomy (Bloom et al., 1956) and Erikson's Eight Stages of Psychosocial Development (1998). The Intercultural Communicative Competence Task Force at World Learning created a set of competencies based on four levels of development: the educational traveler, the sojourner, the professional, and the intercultural/multicultural specialist. Competencies were developed in the "domains of cognitive, attitude, skills, awareness, and language" for each of the four levels (World Learning, 1994, p. 6).

While many filters can be layered in creating effective intercultural learning, the Developmental Model of Intercultural Sensitivity (DMIS) (Bennett, 1993) provides particularly useful grounding for the intentional balancing of optimal learning in stressful contexts. Proposing a framework for moving learners from stages of ethnocentrism to greater intercultural competence at ethnorelativism, the DMIS has been elaborated for educators and trainers with detailed recommendations for activities and design. For language teaching, the cultural competencies have been matched with levels of language proficiency and with pedagogy for limited proficiency at the earlier stages, progressing to more complicated cultural interventions when language sophistication permits (Bennett, Bennett, & Allen, 1999). For use in intercultural training for international education or other contexts (Bennett & Bennett, 2004) or management education (Bennett, 2003; Bennett, in press; Bennett, 2001), the model and stage-appropriate design and activities have been detailed. In addition, Paige (2004) has developed a set of objectives for cognitive, affective, and behavioral measurement carefully sequenced on the DMIS, based on developmental readiness.

Trend #4: The assessment of intercultural competence is part of our developmental work. Assessment of the development of students who study abroad has been a source of curiosity in international education since the earlier impact studies at the American Field Service (Hansel & Grove, 1984) and Youth for Understanding (Hopkins, 1982). No longer merely a curiosity, assessment of the outcomes of all campus learning has become routine (at least in the United States), and international education is no exception. The assessment of global learning or campus internationalization must inevitably include the experience of studying in and about other cultures (Deardorff, 2006). Educational outcomes must address the institutions' educational mission statements, and as noted earlier, intercultural competence is core to these statements (Meacham & Gaff, 2006).

Current research reflects both qualitative and quantitative methods, short- and long-term sojourns, and a variety of programs from business to service learning (Anderson, Lawton, Rexeisen, & Hubbard, 2006; Jackson, 2005; Paige, Cohen, & Shively, 2004; Tonkin & Quiroga, 2004; Vande Berg, 2007b). Using a variety of instruments to conduct pre- and post-study-abroad assessments, the research can now quantify what administrators knew in their hearts: well-designed study abroad makes a difference, and we can prove it with numbers.

Trend #5: International education will assume its rightful place at the core of global learning. In a recent debate in the letters to the editor in the *New York Times*, a reader observed that "study abroad is the best way I know to reconcile the competing agendas of the traditional broad liberal arts education and the more narrowly focused pre-professional curriculum" (Brown, 2007).

He is not alone, nor is this true only in preprofessional curricula. In the last decade of the twentieth century, Barbara Burn (1991) and her colleagues examined two issues that are ultimately being addressed on campuses of the twenty-first century. They sought "(1) to identify factors, circumstances, and attitudes that prevent study abroad . . . from being an important and integral part of their degree program . . . and (2) to identify and encourage institutional strategies and policies aimed at eliminating or at least reducing these obstacles" (p. vii). This Study Abroad Articulation Project was a pioneering effort to place study abroad where it is now centered.

In numerous monographs on global learning, the Association of American Colleges and Universities has recognized the role of international education for interculturalizing the campus (Cornwell & Stoddard, 1999; Hovland, 2006; McTighe Musil, 2006).

Furthermore, the recent funding of the Study Abroad for Global Engagement (SAGE) project suggests that international education is now linked in important ways to the academic agenda. The SAGE research study connects the recent explorations of social capital (Putnam, 2007) with study abroad. Focused on long-term impact, the study (now in the data-gathering stage) explores a connection between "personal, professional, and social capital outcomes associated with study abroad experiences that occurred during the college years" (Fry & Paige, 2007, project background section).

Clearly, there is a case building for well-designed, well-assessed, well-integrated international experience in the hallowed halls of the academy, where dozens of languages are spoken, multiple cultures are recognized and honored, and curiosity guides the acquisition of intercultural competence.

Conclusion

As we justify our accomplishments with learners, collect our data, and assess our outcomes, we need not lose the spirit that engulfed the field many decades ago. We can be of two spirits, knowing that our work matters in countless important ways yet taking our professional role with all the necessary seriousness that the current climate demands. As we do so, Daloz (2000) offers some gentle advice to us:

> Provide at least some opportunities for students to come together to hold the ambiguity, to reflect on the mystery of their lives and commitments—to practice holding their lives and convictions against the backdrop of both radical doubt and unshakeable faith. (p. 118)

This is the space where the global soul flourishes. While curriculum committees throughout the world struggle with how to achieve "constructive engagement with otherness" (Daloz, 2000, p. 110), international educators can foster intercultural competence at the intersection of what philosopher Maxine Green (1988) has called "a world lived in common with others" (p. 4).

References

Allport, G. W. (1954). *The nature of prejudice*. Cambridge, MA: Addison-Wesley.
Amir, Y. (1969). Contact hypothesis in ethnic relations. *Psychological Bulletin, 71*, 319–342.

Anderson, P. H., Lawton, L., Rexeisen, R. J., & Hubbard, A. C. (2006). Short-term study abroad and intercultural sensitivity: A pilot study. *International Journal of Intercultural Relations, 30,* 457–469.

Bennett, J. M. (2003). Turning frogs into interculturalists: A student-centered development approach to teaching intercultural competence. In N. A. Boyacigiller, R. A. Goodman, & M. E. Phillips (Eds.), *Crossing cultures: Insights from master teachers* (pp. 157–170). New York: Taylor & Francis.

Bennett, J. M. (in press). Transformative training: Designing programs for culture learning. In M. A. Moodian (Ed.), *Contemporary leadership and intercultural competence: Understanding and utilizing cultural diversity to build successful organizations.* Thousand Oaks, CA: Sage.

Bennett, J. M., & Bennett, M. J. (2004). Developing intercultural sensitivity: An integrative approach to global and domestic diversity. In D. Landis, J. M. Bennett, & M. J. Bennett (Eds.), *Handbook of intercultural training* (3rd ed., pp. 147–165). Thousand Oaks, CA: Sage.

Bennett, J. M., Bennett, M. J., & Allen, W. (1999). Developing intercultural competence in the language classroom. In R. M. Paige, D. L. Lange, & Y. A. Yershova (Eds.), *Culture as the core: Integrating culture into the language curriculum* (pp. 13–45). Minneapolis: Center for Advanced Research on Language Acquisition, University of Minnesota.

Bennett, J. M., & Salonen, R. (2007). Intercultural communication and the new American campus. *Change: The Magazine of Higher Learning, 39*(2), 46–50.

Bennett, M. J. (1993). Towards ethnorelativism: A developmental model of intercultural sensitivity. In R. M. Paige (Ed.), *Education for the intercultural experience* (2nd ed., pp. 21–71). Yarmouth, ME: Intercultural Press.

Bennett, M. J. (2001). Developing intercultural competence for global leadership. In R. Reineke & C. Fussinger (Eds.), *Interkulturelles management: Konzeption—beratung—training* (pp. 207–226). Germany: Gabler.

Bird, A., & Osland, J. S. (2004). Global competencies: An introduction. In H. W. Lane, M. L. Maznevski, M. Mendenhall, & J. McNett (Eds.), *Blackwell handbook of global management: A guide to managing complexity* (pp. 57–79). Malden, MA: Blackwell.

Bloom, B. S., Engelhart, M. D., Furst, E. J., Hill, W. H., & Krathwohl, D. R. (1956). *Taxonomy of educational objectives: The classification of educational goals, Handbook I: Cognitive domain.* New York: Longmans, Green.

Boyacigiller, N., Beechler, S., Taylor, S., & Levy, O. (2004). The crucial yet illusive global mindset. In H. W. Lane, M. L. Maznevski, M. E. Mendenhall, & J. McNett, *The Blackwell handbook of global management: A guide to managing complexity* (pp. 81–93). Malden, MA: Blackwell.

Brown, W. C. (2007, August 18). When students go abroad, follow the money [Letter to the editor]. *New York Times*, p. A12.

Burn, B. B. (1991). The study abroad articulation project: Introduction. In B. B. Burn (Ed.), *Integrating study abroad into the undergraduate liberal arts curriculum: Eight institutional case studies* (pp. vi–x). Westport, CT: Greenwood.

Claxton, C. S., & Ralston, Y. (1978). *Learning styles: Their impact on teaching and administration* (Report No. 10). AAHE-ERIC/Higher Education Research. (ERIC No. ED167065)

Clayton-Pedersen, A. R., Parker, S., Smith, D. G., Moreno, J. F., & Teraguchi, H. (2007). *Making a real difference with diversity: A guide to institutional change.* Washington, DC: Association of American Colleges and Universities.

Commission on the Abraham Lincoln Study Abroad Fellowship Program. (2005). *Global competence and national needs: One million Americans studying abroad.* Retrieved March 21, 2007, from http://www.nafsa.org/public_policy.sec/ public_policy_document/study_abroad_1/lincoln_commission_report

Cornwell, G. H., & Stoddard, E. W. (1999). *Globalizing knowledge: Connecting international and intercultural studies.* Washington, DC: Association of American Colleges and Universities.

Cornwell, G. H., & Stoddard, E. W. (2001). The future of liberal education and the hegemony of market values: Privilege, practicality, and citizenship. *Liberal Education, 87*(3), 6–15.

Cross, W. E. (1995). The psychology of nigrescence: Revising the Cross model. In J. G. Ponterotto, J. M. Casa, L. A. Suzuki, & L. M. Alexander (Eds.), *Handbook of multicultural counseling* (pp. 92–122). Newbury Park, CA: Sage.

Daloz, L. A. P. (2000). Transformative learning for the common good. In J. Mezirow & Associates (Eds.), *Learning as transformation: Critical perspectives on a theory in progress* (pp. 103–123). San Francisco: Jossey-Bass.

Deardorff, D. K. (2005). A matter of logic? *International Educator, XIV*(3), 26–31.

Deardorff, D. K. (2006). Identification and assessment of intercultural competence as a student outcome of internationalization. *Journal of Studies in International Education, 10*(3), 241–266.

Erikson, E. H. (1998). *Identity and the life cycle.* New York: W. W. Norton.

Evans, N. J., Forney, D. S., & Guido-DiBrito, F. (1998). Gay, lesbian, and bisexual identity development. *Student development in college: Theory, research, and practice* (pp. 89–106). San Francisco: Jossey-Bass.

Fry, G. W., & Paige, R. M. (2007). *Beyond immediate impact: Study abroad for global engagement (SAGE).* Retrieved August 15, 2007, from University of Minnesota, College of Education and Human Development website: http://www.education .umn.edu/projects/SAGE/

Gardenswartz, L., Rowe, A., Digh, P., & Bennett, M. (2003). *The global diversity desk reference: Managing an international workforce*. San Francisco: Jossey-Bass.

Green, M. (1988). *Dialectic of Freedom*. New York: Teachers College Press.

Gregersen, H. B., Morrison, A. J., & Black J. S. (1998). Developing leaders for the global frontier. *Sloan Management Review, 40*(1), 21–32.

Guskin, A. (1991). Cultural humility: A way of being in the world. *Antioch Notes, 59*(1). Yellow Springs, OH: Antioch Publications Office.

Hansel, B., & Grove, N. (1984). *Why an AFS experience accelerates learning and the growth of competence* (Report No. 25, Revised and Expanded). (ERIC Document Reproduction Service No. ED257732)

Hopkins, R. (1982). *Defining and predicting overseas effectiveness for adolescent exchange students*. Washington, DC: Youth for Understanding.

Hovland, K. (2006). *Shared futures: Global learning and liberal education*. Washington, DC: Association of American Colleges and Universities.

Immelman, A., & Schneider, P. (1998). Assessing student learning in study-abroad programs: A conceptual framework and methodology for assessing student learning in study-abroad programs. *Journal of Studies in International Education, 9*, 59–79.

Iyer, P. (2000). *The global soul: Jet lag, shopping malls, and the search for home*. New York: Knopf.

Jackson, J. (2005). Assessing intercultural learning through introspective accounts. *Frontiers, The Interdisciplinary Journal of Study Abroad, XI*, 165–186.

Kolb, D. A. (1984). *Experiential learning: Experience as the source of learning and development*. Englewood Cliffs, NJ: Prentice Hall.

McTighe Musil, C. (2006). *Assessing global learning: Matching good intentions with good practice*. Washington, DC: Association of American Colleges and Universities.

Meacham, J., & Gaff, J. G. (2006). Learning goals in mission statements. *Liberal Education, 92*(1), 6–13.

Mendenhall, M. E., Kuhlmann, T. M., & Stahl, G. K. (Eds.). (2001). *Developing global business leaders: Policies, processes, and innovations*. Westport, CT: Greenwood.

Mestenhauser, J. A., & Ellingboe, B. J. (1998). *Reforming the higher education curriculum: Internationalizing the campus*. Phoenix, AZ: American Council on Education/Oryx Press.

NAFSA: An Association of International Educators. (2001). *NAFSA's principles for U.S. study abroad*. Retrieved on March 21, 2007, from http://www.nafsa.org/about.sec/governance_leadership/ethics_standards/nafsa_s_principles_for_5

O'Mara, J., & Richter, A. (2006). *Global diversity and inclusion benchmarks.* Retrieved January 4, 2008, from www.diversityresources.com/rc42e/GDIBench marksOct06.pdf

Opdal, P. M. (2001). Curiosity, wonder and education seen as perspective. *Studies in Philosophy and Education, 20,* 331–344.

Osland, J. S., & Bird, A. (2000). Beyond sophisticated stereotyping: Cultural sensemaking in context. *Academy of Management Executive, 14,* 65–79.

Osland, J. S., Bird, A., Mendenhall, M., & Osland, A. (2006). Developing global leadership capabilities and global mindset. In G. Stahl & I. Bjorkman (Eds.), *Handbook of international human resource management research* (pp. 197–222). London: Elgar.

Otten, M. (2003). Intercultural learning and diversity in higher education. *Journal of Studies in International Education, 7,* 12–26.

Paige, R. M. (2004, July 21). The intercultural in teaching and learning: A developmental perspective. *Models of intercultural learning and development.* Paper presented at a seminar: The Intercultural in Teaching and Learning at the University of South Australia. Retrieved November 28, 2006, from http://www.unisanet .unisa.edu.au/learningconnection/staff/practice/internationalisation/documents/ models.pdf

Paige, R. M., Cohen, A. D., Kappler, B., Chi, J. C., & Lassegard, J. P. (2002). *Maximizing study abroad: A students' guide to strategies for language and culture learning and use.* Minneapolis: University of Minnesota.

Paige, R. M., Cohen, A. D., & Shively, R. L. (2004). Assessing the impact of a strategies-based curriculum on language and culture learning abroad. *Frontiers, The Interdisciplinary Journal of Study Abroad, X,* 253–276.

Paige, R. M., Lange, D. L., & Yershova, Y. A. (Eds.). (1999). *Culture as the core: Integrating culture into the language curriculum* (pp. 13–45). Minneapolis: Center for Advanced Research on Language Acquisition, University of Minnesota.

Perry, W. G., Jr. (1970). *Forms of intellectual and ethical development in the college years: A scheme.* New York: Holt, Rinehart, and Winston.

Pettigrew, T. F., & Tropp, L. R. (2000). Does intergroup contact reduce prejudice? Recent meta-analytic findings. In S. Oskamp (Ed.), *Reducing prejudice and discrimination* (pp. 93–114). Mahwah, NJ: Lawrence Erlbaum.

Putnam, R. D. (2007). *E pluribus unum:* Diversity and community in the twenty-first century. The 2006 Johan Skytte Prize lecture. *Scandinavian Political Studies, 30*(2), 137–174.

Sabnani, H. B., Ponterotto, J. G., & Borodosky, L. G. (1991). White racial identity development and cross-cultural counselor training: A stage model. *The Counseling Psychologist, 19,* 76–102.

Stewart, P. (1964). *Jacobellis v. Ohio*. Retrieved September 14, 2007, from http://caselaw.lp.findlaw.com/scripts/getcase.pl?court = US&vol = 378&invol = 184

Stoddard, E. W., & Cornwell, G. H. (2003). Peripheral visions: Toward a geoethics of citizenship-perspectives. *Liberal Education*. Retrieved January 29, 2008, from http://www.aacu.org/liberaleducation/le-su03/le-su3fperspective.cfm

Supreme Court of the United States. (2003). *Brief for* amici curiae *65 businesses in support of respondents*. Nos. 02–241 and 02–516. Retrieved June 24, 2007, from http://chronicle.com/indepth/michigan/documents/briefs/respondent/Fortune 500.pdf

Tonkin, H., & Quiroga, D. (2004). A qualitative approach to the assessment of international service-learning. *Frontiers, The Interdisciplinary Journal of Study Abroad, X,* 131–150.

Vande Berg, M. (2007a, February). *It's not all about the numbers: Maximizing student learning abroad*. Paper presented at the meeting of the Association of International Education Administrators, Washington, DC.

Vande Berg, M. (2007b, July). *Intervening in student learning: The Georgetown consortium study*. Paper presented at the Summer Institute for Intercultural Communication, Portland, OR.

Ward, C. (2001). *The impact of international students on domestic students and host institutions*. Report prepared for the Export Education Policy Project of the New Zealand Ministry of Education. Retrieved February 2, 2006, from http://www.minedu.govt.nz/index.cfm?layout = document&documentId = 5643&CFID = 10520007&CFTOKEN = 80025650

World Learning. (1994). *Competencies required for intercultural competence: (FY94)*. A report by the Intercultural Communicative Competence Task Force at World Learning. Brattleboro, VT: Author.

3

INTERCULTURAL COMPETENCE

A Definition, Model, and Implications for Education Abroad

Darla K. Deardorff

I nterest in intercultural competence has greatly increased in recent years, with institutions seeking ways to develop "global-ready students"—whether through study abroad, service learning, integrated curriculum, or extracurricular activities. Arguably, intercultural competence development is central to students' education abroad experiences. Numerous studies, articles, and conference presentations in recent years have discussed the centrality of intercultural competence to education abroad. And despite over 30 years of scholarly work on the meaning of intercultural competence, there has not been consensus on a definition. This chapter proposes a definition and a model of intercultural competence, developed from the first study that documents consensus among leading intercultural experts on key elements of this construct. The intercultural competence model is then discussed with regard to its implications for education abroad administrators, educators, and students.

Research Source for the Intercultural Competence Model

With the goal of developing a consensual definition of intercultural competence, Deardorff (2004) constructed a panel of 23 internationally known intercultural scholars, including two of the three most influential authors in the field (Hart, 1999). These experts participated in an iterative Delphi study through electronic mail (Linstone & Turoff, 1975), in which a series of three rounds of questions prompted them to generate definitions of intercultural competence, refine those definitions, and ultimately reach agreement on key characteristics as well as appropriate assessment methods of this concept. In addition, administrators in international higher education participated in the final round of the Delphi study to indicate their acceptance or rejection of the data developed by the intercultural experts. (For further details on this study, see Deardorff, 2004, 2006.)

The first phase of the study, consisting of the key question "What is intercultural competence?" generated a great breadth of definitions among the intercultural experts. The top-rated definition described intercultural competence as "the ability to communicate effectively and appropriately in intercultural situations based on one's intercultural knowledge, skills, and attitudes." There were numerous other statements developed by the experts regarding intercultural competence that received 85% or higher agreement, including the ability to shift one's frame of reference appropriately, the ability to achieve one's goals to some degree, and the ability to behave appropriately and effectively in intercultural situations. Most of these definitions focus primarily on issues of communication and behavior in intercultural situations.

With regard to specific components of intercultural competence, the experts seemed to feel strongly that one component alone is not enough to ensure competence, i.e., either cultural knowledge or language by itself. In fact, all of the items shown in Table 1 received 80% or higher acceptance by the top intercultural experts in this study. These results are quite noteworthy, since previously there had been no consensus among experts as to what constitutes intercultural competence.

Several surprises emerged from the results of this study. Only one element received 100% agreement from the intercultural expert, that of "the understanding of others' worldviews." This finding substantiates other literature that upholds respect for other cultural perspectives as essential to intercultural competence, in which "worldview" is described as basic perceptions and understandings of the world (Fong & Furuto, 2001; Ibrahim, 1985; Sue & Sue, 1990). Another surprise is that the intercultural experts did not reach consensus on the role of language in intercultural competence: some felt that it was an essential component while others did not, citing that one may be fluent in a language but still not be interculturally competent. This

TABLE 1
Intercultural Competence Elements With 80–100% Agreement
Among Top Intercultural Experts

Accept	Reject	Mean	SD	Components of Intercultural Competence
20	0	3.4	0.7	Understanding others' worldviews
19	1	3.8	0.6	Cultural self-awareness and capacity for self-assessment
19	1	3.7	0.6	Adaptability—adjustment to new cultural environment
19	1	3.5	0.6	Skills to listen and observe
19	1	3.4	0.8	General openness toward intercultural learning and to people from other cultures
19	1	3.4	0.8	Ability to adapt to varying intercultural communication and learning styles
18	2	3.8	0.4	Flexibility
18	2	3.8	0.4	Skills to analyze, interpret, and relate
18	2	3.7	0.6	Tolerating and engaging ambiguity
18	2	3.6	0.6	Deep knowledge and understanding of culture (one's own and others')
18	2	3.5	0.8	Respect for other cultures
17	3	3.5	0.9	Cross-cultural empathy
17	3	3.4	1.0	Understanding the value of cultural diversity
17	3	3.3	0.9	Understanding the role and impact of culture and the impact of situational, social, and historical contexts involved
17	3	3.2	1.0	Cognitive flexibility—ability to switch frames from etic to emic and back again
17	3	3.0	0.8	Sociolinguistic competence (awareness of relation between language and meaning in societal context)
17	3	3.0	1.1	Mindfulness
16	4	3.6	0.8	Withholding judgment
16	4	3.4	0.8	Curiosity and discovery
16	4	3.2	0.9	Learning through interaction
16	4	3.1	1.2	Ethnorelative view
16	4	2.9	0.9	Culture-specific knowledge/understanding of host culture's traditions

finding is substantiated through another, similar study on global competence (Hunter, 2004) in which business experts could not reach consensus on the role of language in global competence. Further, it was surprising to observe that specific cross-cultural skills did not make the final list, but rather, the more general skills of analyzing, interpreting, and relating, as well as listening and observing, emerged, which points to the importance of going beyond knowledge acquisition to knowledge processing and application. Derek Bok (2006) affirms this by stating, "Undergraduates cannot possibly amass all the information they would need to know about even the most important foreign cultures with which they might come in contact . . . As a result (institutions) must be chiefly concerned with teaching students to think interculturally . . ." (p. 249).

From the outset of this study, there was the question of whether the intercultural experts would even reach consensus on a definition and components of intercultural competence. As can be seen in Table 1, consensus was indeed reached, albeit with a few surprising results, providing international educators and students with a common foundation from which to approach and assess intercultural competence.

A Model of Intercultural Competence Development

In much of the literature on intercultural competence, scholars and researchers provide lists of what comprises this concept, often with little guidance as to which elements are most crucial or their relation to each other. Often, assessment tools may claim to assess intercultural competence without taking into account the many complexities of measuring this construct. In an effort to provide a framework within which to develop and assess intercultural competence, the researcher took the items in Table 1 and categorized them into knowledge, skills, and attitudes. Other elements clearly fit more naturally into two additional categories, internal and external outcomes, which can then lead to further assessment. These categories, when placed within a visual framework or model, lead to more nuanced development and assessment of individuals' intercultural competence.

Description of the Model

There are many ways in which the items in Table 1 could be grouped. Figure 1 eliminates long, fragmented lists by placing these components of intercultural competence within a cyclical framework.

FIGURE 1
Process model of intercultural competence.

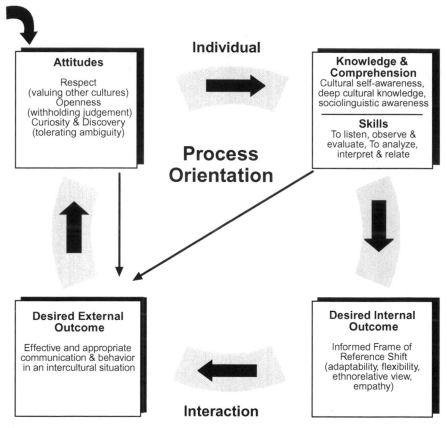

Notes:
- Begin with attitudes; move from individual level (attitudes) to interaction level (outcomes)
- Degree of intercultural competence depends on degree of attitudes, knowledge/comprehension, and skills

From *The identification and assessment of intercultural competence as a student outcome of internationalization at institutions of higher education in the United States* by D. K. Deardorff, 2004. Unpublished doctoral dissertation, North Carolina State University, Raleigh. Printed with permission.

Attitudes

Though individuals can enter this process at any particular point, attitude is a fundamental place to start (Byram, 1997), as illustrated by an arrow in this visual representation. Lynch and Hanson (1998) highlight the fundamental role of attitude in the development of intercultural competence:

> After all the books have been read and the skills learned and practiced, the cross-cultural effectiveness of each of us will vary. And it will vary more by [the attitudes] we bring to the learning than by what we have learned. (p. 510)

Similarly, Okayama, Furuto, and Edmondson (2001) reinforce the foundational importance of attitude by stating that

> What may be most important is . . . to maintain culturally competent attitudes as we continue to attain new knowledge and skills while building new relationships. Awareness, the valuing of all cultures, and a willingness to make changes are underlying attitudes that support everything that can be taught or learned. (p. 97)

The model in Figure 1 concurs with these scholars in emphasizing the importance of attitude to the learning that follows. Specifically, the attitudes of openness (withholding judgment), respect (valuing all cultures), and curiosity and discovery (tolerating ambiguity) are viewed as fundamental to the acquisition of the knowledge and skills that will lead to both the conceptual shifts and the behavioral changes needed to increase intercultural competence. As respect, openness, and cultural curiosity increase, so does capacity to acquire cultural knowledge.

Knowledge

Knowledge areas that emerged from this research focused on both awareness of one's own cultural norms and sensitivity to those of other cultures. Cultural self-awareness could arguably be considered the essence of cross-cultural knowledge in that it is crucial for individuals to be aware of the way in which they view the world. Often this self-awareness is difficult to gain without moving beyond one's own culture, whether through education abroad experiences or cultural immersion experiences within one's home country. However, cultural self-awareness is indeed key, since experiences of others are often measured against one's own cultural conditioning.

While there have long been discussions about what constitutes "global knowledge," the knowledge needed for intercultural competence extends to a deep understanding of other cultures, including a thorough understanding of other worldviews, influences on cultural development, and the role and impact of specific cultures in the world. Culture-specific knowledge such as underlying cultural values and communication styles is essential in understanding behaviors that are encountered. And while there was not consensus on the role of language in intercultural competence, experts did agree on the role of sociolinguistic awareness—of how one uses language within a societal and social context. One might argue that language itself becomes a window through which to understand another culture's worldview and thus remains a key knowledge component.

Skills

As Table 1 indicates, the experts also agreed on the importance of cognitive skills, including comparative thinking and cognitive flexibility. This strong emphasis on analytical abilities and critical thinking skills points to the importance of *process* in acquiring intercultural competence and the attention that needs to be paid to developing these key academic skills that enable individuals to process the knowledge they acquire about other cultures. Yershova, DeJeagbere, and Mestenhauser (2000) concur with this finding in arguing that the intercultural perspective, along with intellectual competencies, is integral to developing intercultural competence.

As the model emphasizes, awareness and cultural knowledge are gained through the development of key communicative and cognitive skills. Specifically, those skills include listening, observing, evaluating, analyzing, interpreting, and relating. Knowledge, which is constantly changing, is not sufficient in the development of intercultural competence, and it is important for individuals to use these necessary cognitive skills to be able to acquire and apply cultural knowledge on an ongoing basis. These skills also illuminate the importance of reflection and of being aware of the *process* of acquiring intercultural competence.

Internal outcomes

Such skills, in combination with the prerequisite attitudes and the resulting knowledge gains, ideally lead to an internal "frame of reference shift" in which adaptability and flexibility play a central role. One's adaptability is manifested not only in one's adjustment to different cultural environments but also in switching between communication styles, much in the way someone would switch between languages. Flexibility, for example, is demonstrated through the use of different behavioral styles in various intercultural contexts and in being able to switch between various worldviews when interacting with those from different cultural backgrounds. Empathy plays a key role in these internal outcomes. One way to operationalize empathy is to employ the "platinum rule," which is to "do unto others as they would have done unto them." This assumes deep cultural knowledge and the ability to see from the other's perspective.

External outcomes

This mental shift ultimately manifests itself in the observable (and thus assessable) "external outcome" of effective and appropriate communication and behavior in intercultural situations. Definitions of *appropriate* and *effective* are taken from Spitzberg's (1989) work, by which appropriateness is the avoidance of violating valued rules and effectiveness is the achievement of valued objectives. These behaviors and communication form the basis of intercultural interactions and are ultimately greatly impacted by the attitudes, knowledge, and skills one brings to each interaction.

Further discussion of the intercultural competence model

While the model clearly depicts through its circular design that attitudes lead to acquisition of knowledge and skills, which helps to reshape internal frames of reference that then influence external behaviors, it is important to notice that each part of the model can impact the others directly as well. For example, new knowledge can directly impact observable behavior, or a shift in internal frame of reference can influence attitudes by increasing curiosity, openness, and/or respect. The nonlinear nature of the model emphasizes the ongoing nature of the process, implying that one never reaches the pinnacle of intercultural competence. External outcomes—i.e., increasingly appropriate and effective communication and behavior—serve to promote further respect, openness, and curiosity, attitudes that enhance the continuation of the cycle and the ongoing development of intercultural competence. This in turn reinforces the ongoing process of acquiring and honing one's intercultural competence. In essence, the development of intercultural competence becomes a lifelong journey.

Advantages of the Model

There are a number of advantages to conceptualizing the development of intercultural competence as a dynamic process. First, this model provides a structured way of understanding the experts' consensual definition of intercultural competence, illuminating the complexity of the construct. Given the complex nature of the concept, the model allows for degrees of competence. As the number and degree of acquired competency elements increases, so does the probability of a greater degree of intercultural competence as an external outcome. The anticipated outcomes of intercultural competence development progress logically from the individual level of attitudes and personal attributes to the interactive cultural level. Moreover, the specific skills delineated in this model are useful for acquiring and processing knowledge not only about one's own culture but about other cultures as well. Identifying specific skills and outcomes allows for the development of context-specific assessment indicators, which again reflect the complexity of the concept. In these ways, this model emphasizes not only the necessary attitudes, knowledge, and skills but also the expected internal and the external outcomes of intercultural competence.

Limitations of the Model

One caution about this intercultural competence model is the Western bias inherent in the model, given that the intercultural experts involved in the study were predominantly from the United States. See Table 2 for a list of participants. Other limitations of the study include the reliance on expert opinion and the forced consensus of the Delphi technique.

Description of an Interculturally Competent Student

So, according to this model, what would an interculturally competent student look like, keeping in mind that such competence is a lifelong endeavor? Let's take a look at Pangea, an interculturally competent college student who is curious to learn about other cultures—in fact, she regularly looks for opportunities to meet those from different cultures, seeking out students, and even faculty, from different cultures on campus and engaging them in conversation. As a result, she has numerous friends from different cultural backgrounds. As she interacts with those from different cultural backgrounds, she accepts them without judging their external features, habits, or decisions,

TABLE 2
Intercultural Scholars* Participating in the Delphi Study

Janet Bennett, Intercultural Communication Institute, Oregon
Michael Byram, University of Durham, England
Guo-ming Chen, University of Rhode Island
Mary Jane Collier, University of Denver
Mitchell Hammer, American University
Daniel J. Kealey, Centre for Intercultural Learning, Canadian Foreign Service
     Institute, Canada
Jolene Koester, California State University–Northridge
L. Robert Kohls, Institute for Intercultural Leadership, California
Bruce La Brack, University of the Pacific
Josef Mestenhauser, University of Minnesota
Robert Moran, Thunderbird, American Graduate School of International
     Management
R. Michael Paige, University of Minnesota
Paul Pedersen, Syracuse University
Margaret Pusch, Intercultural Communication Institute, Oregon
Brian Spitzberg, San Diego State University
Craig Storti, Craig Storti & Associates, Maryland
Harry Triandis, University of Illinois
Gary Weaver, American University
Richard Wiseman, California State University–Fullerton
. . . and four other intercultural scholars who served on the panel but did not wish
     to be acknowledged

*We gratefully acknowledge the intercultural scholars who graciously shared their time and
expertise as expert members of the Delphi panel.

realizing that acceptance does not necessarily mean approval. In her acceptance of others, she makes them feel valued and respected, largely by showing
an interest in them along with a willingness to learn from them. Pangea, who
has spent time reflecting on her own cultural conditioning about what she
believes and values, frequently reads about other cultures and stays abreast
of news on world events, seeking to understand the contexts in which others
live. Pangea regularly visits local ethnic grocery stores and restaurants and
enjoys attending and participating in events of local ethnic groups (concerts,
festivals, and so on), even if it means she will feel uncomfortable as a minority. As she meets others and participates in cultural events, she strives hard to
have an open mind and refrains from making judgments. In her interactions,

Pangea is aware of how her responses may be interpreted by others and adapts her responses to appropriately interact within each context, thinking about how the other person may wish to be treated rather than how she herself would want to be treated. During and after the interactions, she is aware of not just what was said but how it was said. She reflects on what went well, what she learned from the interaction, and what she could improve as she interacts the next time. Pangea realizes that learning about cultures is a never-ending process and she must continually strive for an intercultural lifestyle, one in which she seeks to see from others' viewpoints and not just her own. Admittedly, Pangea is an idealized example who embodies intercultural competence to a high degree. She illustrates a combination of aspects that may be seen in more piecemeal fashion in our actual, nonidealized students. Recognizing such aspects in our students and encouraging them to move toward her model can be helpful for both students and international educators.

Implications for International Educators

Given this framework for addressing intercultural competence in education abroad, what are the implications of this model for international educators? There is no singular way for developing intercultural competence (Brustein, 2006), and this model provides a holistic framework for intercultural competence development and assessment. In applying this model to education abroad programs, administrators can discern the importance of designing experiences and curricula that focus on the whole of intercultural competence—not only on knowledge or skill acquisition, for example, but also on attitudes and observable behaviors that can be assessed. Five specific implications will be discussed in this section: the importance of preparation, skills development, reflection, meaningful intercultural interactions, and assessment.

Importance of Preparation and Support: A Framework

Adequate preparation and support is vital for students to begin developing their intercultural competence, in part with the goal of students being able to articulate the learning outcomes they obtain while abroad. This means that education abroad programs must substantively and intentionally address intercultural competence before students go abroad, as well as while they are abroad. Too often, predeparture orientations tend to give short shrift to the intercultural piece, focusing more on logistics. Even when intercultural issues are addressed in predeparture orientations, too little time is often spent on only a very few random aspects of intercultural communication or cultural adjustment. The intercultural competence model discussed earlier provides a framework for designing predeparture preparation, perhaps even for developing a course or series of workshops in a coherent, intentional manner, in which intercultural activities fit into the larger whole of intercultural competence. Even in short-term study abroad experiences, programs can be designed to focus on essential aspects such as cultural self-awareness or being able to see from others' perspectives. One example of such short-term preparation is the University of Pennsylvania's Lauder Institute, which provides one month of preparation for an eight-week immersion experience and five pre-trip sessions for a four-week study tour, with two of the goals being to provide an understanding of the region's cultural environment and to promote intercultural awareness (Lauder Institute, 2007).

Additionally, it is incumbent upon faculty leading study abroad programs to be prepared interculturally so that they themselves are interculturally competent to lead students through intercultural competence development. Such preparation may take the form of a faculty development workshop or dialogue/reading discussion; more programs are now seeking ways to prepare faculty as well as students. Administrators are also beginning to move beyond solely pre-experience preparation and are building in ways to support student and faculty learning during the time abroad and after their return (see the following discussion on the importance of reflection). This support of intercultural learning, not only before one leaves, but throughout the entire experience is essential and it behooves administrators to be intentional about the learning support given to pre, during and post experiences abroad.

Importance of Skills Development

One of the vital skills that emerged from this study is observation, coupled with the skills of analyzing and evaluating. Of the main knowledge components to emerge, the only item upon which all the intercultural experts agreed is the ability to see from others' perspectives. And in order to change attitudes, the assumptions underlying attitudes must be challenged. A tool that addresses these essential elements of intercultural competence is called the OSEE Tool (Deardorff & Deardorff, 2000), which not only allows students to challenge their assumptions but also moves them to explore other perspectives through observation and analysis. Initially developed in 2000 and based on the scientific method, it has been used in cross-cultural training programs and courses as well as in predeparture programs.

O—Observe what is happening
S—State objectively what is happening
E—Explore different explanations for what is happening
E—Evaluate which explanation is the most likely one
(copyright Deardorff & Deardorff, 2000)

OSEE starts with the basics of observation, and listening—of really being aware of what is occurring in intercultural situations. As noted in the intercultural competence model discussed in this chapter, this is an essential skill and a key starting point. The next step is to state as *objectively* as possible what is happening. This is much more difficult than it sounds given the ease in which judgment can enter into observation. There are a variety of activities that can be used to help students practice the development of objective statements, including viewing brief film clips and writing about them. The next step, of exploring different explanations, addresses the need to see from others' perspectives. It also allows one to begin to move beyond initial assumptions that may have been made inadvertently. Different explanations could include personal and cultural explanations, the latter of which necessitates the need to know culture-specific information. The last step, evaluation, is the most difficult, since it is often challenging to know which explanation(s) is the most likely one(s) for the situation that is occurring. There are a number of different ways to evaluate the likely explanations, including collecting further information through conversations with others and through asking questions. When these steps are followed, one is able to view and understand behaviors more objectively, thus achieving a measure of intercultural competence.

In using the OSEE Tool with students, there are a number of activities that can be employed, including brief film clips, photos, critical incidents, and role plays. Exposing students to the OSEE Tool can aid them in developing intercultural competence and will hopefully result in students beginning to move beyond cultural assumptions to realizing a fundamental lesson in cross-cultural understanding: most people do behave rationally; you just have to discover their rationale (Storti, 1997). The OSEE Tool helps students begin to understand the rationales behind the behaviors they encounter in intercultural situations, thus increasing their intercultural competence.

Importance of Reflection

It is also essential to note that mindfulness permeates the model, which implies that participants in education abroad experiences must be aware of the learning that takes place at each point, especially during the actual time abroad, and must be given the process skills necessary to analyze their development of intercultural competence. This may include reflections on their own cultural identity as well as reflections on their interactions with those in the host culture. Journals, blogs, and reflection papers have been used successfully in study abroad programs to encourage students' mindfulness and process orientation needed for intercultural competence development. Furthermore, such reflection activities can help hone the necessary critical thinking skills of relating, evaluating, and synthesizing. This reflection is especially important while the student is abroad; including a more structured, intentional "abroad component" in the overall program can be quite helpful in aiding this reflection (see section three of this book for examples of such programs). In addition, it is helpful for programs to include a significant reflection component on the student's reentry and even again after the initial reentry when possible.

Importance of Meaningful Intercultural Interactions

One way that intercultural competence is developed is through meaningful interactions with those from different cultures. Thus, it becomes crucial for study abroad programs to incorporate ways in which students can engage in such meaningful interactions with host nationals while abroad, beyond brief interactions with those in the service industries, for example. Meaningful interactions are the first step in building real relationships with others. Such meaningful intercultural interactions result when both persons are able to engage at a deeper level, beyond the perfunctory surface-level engagement (note that this description of "meaningful" and "engagement" will vary by culture and involves necessary preparation as discussed previously). This deeper-level engagement often requires a degree of risk taking, of trust building, of being able to see from the other's perspective, and a willingness to reach out. The greater the understanding of the host culture, the increased likelihood for meaningful communication and beneficial exchange (which emphasizes the importance of preparation). Meaningful interactions, given appropriate preparation, can occur through service learning, homestays, volunteering in the community, involvement in local groups (such as religious groups or clubs), and through student interactions in courses, to name a few examples.

Importance of Assessment

Assessment of intercultural competence as a learning outcome of study abroad experiences has been generating an increased amount of attention in recent years (Bolen, 2007). Over 85 intercultural competence assessment tools are available to assess various aspects of intercultural competence (Fantini, 2006). There is no one tool or method that can assess the whole of intercultural competence. From the Deardorff (2004) research study with leading intercultural experts, however, several common themes emerge that are necessary for administrators to keep in mind when engaging in such assessment. As indicated in Table 3, intercultural experts agreed that it is important to use a variety of assessment methods in measuring intercultural competence. The highest-rated methods include the use of case studies and interviews. These techniques are perhaps best incorporated into coursework, both at home and overseas.

Other methods preferred by the experts include analysis of narrative diaries, self-report instruments, and observation. It is interesting to compare these recommendations from the intercultural experts with the actual assessment practices reported by the university administrators who also participated in the study. According to their responses, summarized in Table 4, administrators largely agree with the intercultural experts that interviews and observations are among the most valuable methods of assessing progress toward intercultural competence. Other top methods currently in use include student presentations, portfolios, and professor evaluations.

One surprising finding is that there was not agreement among the experts on the use of pre- and post-testing, a technique that is commonly used by institutions in conjunction with measuring the effectiveness of study abroad programs. Given the process orientation of the model described here,

TABLE 3
Assessment Items With 80–100% Agreement Among Top Intercultural Experts

Accept	Reject	Mean	SD	Ways to Assess Intercultural Competence
18	2	3.2	0.9	Case studies
18	2	2.9	1.0	Interviews
17	3	3.7	0.8	Mix of quantitative and qualitative measures
17	3	3.4	0.7	Qualitative measures
17	3	3.2	0.9	Analysis of narrative diaries
17	3	3.2	0.9	Self-report instruments
17	3	3.2	0.9	Observation by others/host culture
17	3	3.1	1.0	Judgment by self and others
16	4	3.1	1.1	Developing specific indicators for each component/dimension of ICC and evidence of each indicator
16	4	3.0	1.2	Triangulation (use of multiple data collection efforts as corroborative evidence for validity of qualitative research findings)
19	1	3.6	0.5	ICC assessment involves more than just observable performance.
19	1	3.4	0.6	It is important to consider the cultural and social implications of assessing ICC.
17	3	3.6	0.6	It is important to determine who measures ICC, who is the locus of evaluation, in what context, for what purpose, to what benefit, the time frame involved, the level of cooperation, and the level of abstraction.
16	4	3.2	0.9	It is important to measure the degrees of ICC.
16	4	3.1	0.7	When assessing ICC, it is important to analyze the impact of situational, social, and historical contexts involved.

educators may do well to reconsider current assessment practices, which often seem less likely to tap into key elements within intercultural competence, elements that simply cannot be covered adequately by a pre-post self-report instrument. Further, satisfaction surveys completed at the end of the study abroad experience can be honed to incorporate more substantive

TABLE 4
Expert and Administrator Accept/Reject Rate on Methods to Assess
Intercultural Competence

Expert % Acceptance	Administrator % Acceptance	Assessment Methods
85%	95%	Mix of quantitative and qualitative measures
85%	81%	Qualitative measures
90%	100%	Case studies
85%	95%	Analysis of narrative diaries
85%	95%	Self-report instruments
85%	100%	Observation by others/host culture
65%	70%	Quantitative measures
65%	90%	Critical incidents
65%	85%	Critical essays
70%	95%	Other-report measures
85%	100%	Judgment by self and others
80%	90%	Developing specific indicators for each component/dimension of ICC and evidence of each indicator
75%	85%	Inventory combined with qualitative measure
80%	95%	Triangulation
90%	100%	Interviews
79%	95%	Bottom-up approach (focus groups, workshops, dialogues, open-ended surveys)
50%	75%	Satisfaction ratings with all involved in interaction
65%	90%	Pre-post test

assessment. In sum, the key aspects of intercultural competence include assessment that is multi-perspective, multi-method, intentional, ongoing, and integrated.

Based on the data collected from this study, the guide to intercultural competence assessment shown in Figure 2 was developed. (For further elaboration on assessment, please see Deardorff, 2005, 2007.)

Conclusion

This chapter presents a comprehensive model of intercultural competence, developed from the first study that documented consensus from leading intercultural experts on a definition of this concept. It is useful for international educators and administrators, especially those interested in more

FIGURE 2
Assessment guide for intercultural competence.

Based on the research and findings from The Identification and Assessment of Intercultural Competence as a Student Outcome of Internationalization at Institutions of Higher Education in the United States *(Deardorff, 2004), the following questions can be used in assessing intercultural competence:*

1. Has intercultural competence been defined using existing definitions in the literature?
2. From whose perspective is intercultural competence being assessed? What are the cultural biases of the evaluator?
3. Who is the locus of the evaluation?
4. What is the context of the intercultural competence assessment?
5. What is the purpose of the intercultural competence assessment?
6. How will the assessment results be used? Who will benefit from the assessment?
7. What is the time frame of the assessment (i.e., one point, ongoing, etc.)?
8. What is the level of abstraction, or in other words, will the assessment be more general, or will it assess more specific components of intercultural competence?
9. Do the assessment methods match the working definition and stated objectives of intercultural competence?
10. Have specific indicators been developed for the intercultural competence assessment?
11. Is more than one method being used to assess intercultural competence? Do the methods involve more than one evaluator's perspective?
12. Are the degrees of intercultural competence being assessed? What is to be done with those not meeting the minimal level of intercultural competence?
13. Does the assessment account for multiple competencies and multiple cultural identities?
14. Has the impact of situational, social, and historical contexts been analyzed in the assessment of intercultural competence?
15. How do the assessment methods impact the measurement outcomes? Have the limits of the instruments/measures been accounted for?
16. Have student/participant goals been considered when assessing intercultural competence?

intentional assessment of student outcomes, to have a well-defined goal to aim toward. Helping students acquire intercultural competence presumes that we know what the concept is. This model provides a clearer picture of the end goal. The model can be used as a framework in preparing study abroad participants—students and faculty—to engage meaningfully, intentionally, and mindfully in their education abroad experiences, with the goal of developing interculturally competent individuals through skills development, reflection, and significant interactions with host nationals. Through the utilization of this model, international educators and administrators can design programs in a more systematic manner, with clearly stated goals that achieve the desired outcomes related to intercultural competence. And through the assessment of students' intercultural competence, postsecondary institutions will be able not only to document the effectiveness of their education abroad programs but also to provide students with valuable feedback that will foster students' lifelong intercultural journeys.

This model attempts to make understandable an exceedingly complex phenomenon. Each student will have unique readiness, unique exposure to intercultural events, and unique skills to move them through the process leading to intercultural competence. Individual expressions of this competence will vary. Yet, there are generalizations captured by the model, and it is hoped that in using this model as a framework international educators will be able not only to design programs that will help students in their intercultural competence development but also to utilize this model in constructing assessment that measures students' intercultural learning through education abroad experiences. Ultimately, effective education abroad experiences that intentionally support, hone, and assess students' intercultural competence improve international education and, more important, transform lives.

References

Bok, D. (2006). *Our underachieving colleges: A candid look at how much students learn and why they should be learning more.* Princeton, NJ: Princeton University Press.

Bolen, M. C. (Ed.). (2007). *A guide to outcomes assessment in education abroad.* Carlisle, PA: Forum on Education Abroad.

Brustein, W. (2006, Spring). Paths to global competence: Preparing American college students to meet the world. *IIENetworker,* Spring, 23–25.

Byram, M. (1997). *Teaching and assessing intercultural communicative competence.* Clevedon, England: Multilingual Matters.

Deardorff, D. K. (2004). *The identification and assessment of intercultural competence as a student outcome of internationalization at institutions of higher education in the United States.* Unpublished doctoral dissertation, North Carolina State University, Raleigh.

Deardorff, D. K. (2005). A matter of logic. *International Educator, 14*(3), 26–31.

Deardorff, D. K. (2006). The identification and assessment of intercultural competence as a student outcome of internationalization. *Journal of Studies in International Education, 10,* 241–266.

Deardorff, D. K. (2007, Spring). Principles of international education assessment. *IIENetworker,* 51–52.

Deardorff, D. K., & Deardorff, D. L. (2000). *Crossing cultures course material.* Unpublished manuscript, Duke University.

Fantini, A. (2006). *Exploring and assessing intercultural competence: Final report of a research project conducted by the Federation of the Experiment in International Living.* Brattleboro, VT: Federation of the Experiment in International Living.

Fong, R., & Furuto, S. (Eds.). (2001). *Culturally competent social work practice: Skills, interventions and evaluation.* Boston: Allyn & Bacon.

Hart, W. B. (1999). Interdisciplinary influences in the study of intercultural relations: A citation analysis of the *International Journal of Intercultural Relations. International Journal of Intercultural Relations, 23,* 575–589.

Hunter, W. (2004). *Knowledge, skills, attitudes, and experiences necessary to become globally competent.* Unpublished dissertation, Lehigh University, Bethlehem, PA.

Ibrahim, F. A. (1985). Effective cross-cultural counseling and psychotherapy: A framework. *The Counseling Psychologist, 13,* 625–638.

Lauder Institute. (2007). The Lauder Institute, Wharton Arts and Sciences, University of Pennsylvania. Retrieved August, 2007, from http://lauder.wharton.upenn.edu/

Linstone, H. A., & Turoff, M. (1975). *The Delphi method: Techniques and applications.* London: Addison-Wesley.

Lynch, E. W., & Hanson, M. J. (1998). *Developing cross-cultural competence: A guide for working with children and families.* Pacific Grove, CA: Brooks/Cole.

Okayama, C. M., Furuto, S. B., & Edmondson, J. (2001). Components of cultural competence: Attitudes, knowledge, and skills. In R. Fong & S. B. Furuto (Eds.), *Culturally competent practice: Skills, interventions, and evaluations* (pp. 89–100). Boston: Allyn & Bacon.

Spitzberg, B. H. (1989). Issues in the development of a theory of interpersonal competence in the intercultural context. *International Journal of Intercultural Relations, 13,* 241–268.

Storti, C. (1997). *Culture matters: The Peace Corps cross-cultural workbook.* Washington, DC: Peace Corps Information Collection and Exchange.

Sue, D. W., & Sue, D. (1990). *Counseling the culturally different: Theory and practice.* New York: Wiley.

Yershova, Y., DeJeagbere, J., & Mestenhauser, J. (2000). Thinking not as usual: Adding the intercultural perspective. *Journal of Studies in International Education, 4,* 59–78.

4

GROWTH AND TRANSFORMATION OUTCOMES IN INTERNATIONAL EDUCATION

Joseph G. Hoff

T he number of students studying abroad from U.S. higher education institutions continues to increase annually, as does the number of international students coming to the United States. According to the Institute of International Education (IIE), in the 2005/2006 academic year the number of study abroad students increased to 205,983, an 8% increase from the previous year (IIE, 2006). More students are also studying in less traditional destinations outside of Western Europe than in previous years (IIE, 2006). Many higher education institutions have established the goal that the number of study abroad students equal 10% of the overall undergraduate student body (Laubscher, 1994). Given the rise in the overall number of study abroad students and the establishment of institutional goals for study abroad, attention is now focusing on the outcomes of the study abroad experience and ways to assist our students in attaining global or intercultural competence. The goal of this chapter is to provide an overview of the current personal development and non-foreign-language study outcomes of the study abroad experience as described in the major research studies of the education abroad field. Research on these types of outcomes is in its infancy, yet the emphasis on personal growth is increasing. The studies reviewed here represent the emerging, solid research base supporting this trend.

Table 1 lists terms related to study abroad outcomes that are of interest in this type of research in international education.

Study Abroad Learning Outcomes

Study abroad learning outcomes can be divided into two areas: nonacademic (affective and attitudinal, personal development, awareness) and academic (knowledge and skill development) (Rubin & Sutton, 2001). The variables influencing study abroad learning outcomes have been classified in a variety of ways. Engle and Engle (2003) classify the influencing variables in the following manner:

1. Duration of program (e.g., three-week, semester, academic year)
2. Amount of earlier target language for each student
3. Extent to which target language is used in coursework on-site
4. Context of academic work (students enrolled in courses in one of four ways: home institution courses taught by accompanying home institution faculty, specially arranged host university courses taught by host institution faculty, regular university courses taught by host institution faculty, or a combination of these)
5. Type of housing for each student (e.g., homestay, apartment with other U.S. students, etc.)
6. Whether students participate in structured cultural/experiential learning
7. Whether students receive on-site mentoring that asks them to reflect on learning. (p. 8)

Medina-Lopez-Portillo (2004) focuses on external and internal variables referent to the student by classifying the variables in the following manner:

Internal: Student backgrounds, characteristics, and personal circumstances (including student language proficiency prior to departure, student intercultural sensitivity level, previous experience abroad, previous exposure to cultural differences, and academic discipline)

External—Program: Choice about the experience made by the study abroad office (including length and location of the program, content

TABLE 1
Definition of Terms in the International Education Field

Term	Definition
Study abroad	"Credit-bearing [overseas] study programs for undergraduates" (Hoffa & Pearson, 1997, p. xiii). For the purposes of this chapter, "study abroad" refers to at least three months or a semester abroad, which is considered to be the minimal time in which significant culture learning may take place (Martin, 1987). "Study abroad experience" refers to events or actions that take place during study abroad including culture learning.
Global competence	The ability of faculty, staff, and students not only to contribute to knowledge but also to comprehend, analyze, and evaluate its meaning in the context of an increasingly globalized world (NASULGC, 2004).
Culture-general learning	As defined by Lustig and Koester (1993), culture general learning, also referred to as "culture learning" (Paige, Cohen, Kappler, Chi, & Lassegard, 2002), refers to generic skills for developing intercultural competence, as opposed to "culture-specific learning," which refers to learning perceptions and behaviors that are unique to specific cultures. Although I do not refer specifically to language as part of culture learning, it is implied that learning a language is considered a part of the culture learning process.
Intercultural competence	Sometimes referred to as "intercultural communication competence," it is defined as "the ability to relate and communicate effectively when individuals involved in the interaction do not share the same culture, ethnicity, language, or other salient variables" (Milagros & Reese, 1999, p. 3).
Intercultural training	"The purpose of a cross-cultural training program is to provide a *functional awareness* of the cultural dynamic present in intercultural relations and assist trainees in becoming more *effective* in cross-cultural situations" (Pusch et al., as cited in Paige, 1993, p. 171).
Ethnocentric	"assuming that the world view of one's own culture is central to all reality" (Bennett, 1993, p. 30)
Ethnorelative	"cultures can only be understood relative to one another and particular behavior can only be understood within a cultural context" (Bennett, 1993, p. 46)
Intercultural sensitivity	"the construction of reality as increasingly capable of accommodating cultural difference that constitutes development" (Bennett, 1993, p. 24)
Worldview	"A comprehensive conception or apprehension of the world, especially from a specific standpoint" (Woolf, 1977, p. 1331)

of study, predeparture and on-site orientation programs, reentry activities, the availability of an on-site study abroad faculty director, and
internships and service learning opportunities)

External—Student: Choices made by the students (including housing arrangements, independent travel, and amount of contact with hosts
and target-language friends). (p. 192)

Clearly, each of these influencing factors will play a part in a student's
quality of experience while abroad. The mix of factors makes it likely that
study abroad programs, and study abroad students, will be difficult to categorize precisely.

Study Abroad Outcomes Studies

Given that there are many variables related to the study abroad experience,
one would expect to find a variety of research that mirrors the field. Research
in study abroad outcomes spans a period of more than forty years but only
recently has become prevalent. The variety of study abroad outcome studies
focuses on both qualitative and quantitative data. The majority of the studies
focus on pre- and posttests of the effect of the study abroad experience on
the growth of intercultural sensitivity or attitudinal change in study abroad
students. Some qualitative studies of the study abroad experience also focus
on the process involved in culture learning. Little research has been undertaken, however, on the effect of study abroad on discipline-specific learning
outcomes.

Pre- and Postsojourn Change-Focused Studies

In an early study for the field, Yachimowicz (1987) concluded there are four
independent variables important to sojourn research: age, academic status,
gender, and sponsorship. Sponsorship refers to the type of program a study
abroad student attends—whether it be direct enrollment in a foreign university where the student is more or less on his or her own or an organized study
abroad program. Yachimowicz referenced Adler's (cited in Yachimowicz,
1987) social learning theory as an experiential model that describes culture
shock and cultural adjustment. The model consists of five stages of growth:
contact, characterized by excitement and euphoria; disintegration, characterized by tension, confusion, and alienation; reintegration, characterized by

strong rejection of the foreign culture; autonomy, characterized by increased understanding of the host culture; and independence, characterized by increased self- and cultural awareness (Adler as cited in Yachimowicz, 1987).

Yachimowicz (1987) also used Piaget's (cited in Yachimowicz, 1987) model of "decentration" to describe the change in perspective gained from a sojourn abroad for international understanding. The model includes three stages: unconscious egocentricity, in which individuals assume that their attitudes applied to their cultural context are the only valid ones; transitional beliefs, in which individuals' beliefs are transitional and beginning to change to accept more of the other culture's value system; and reciprocity, in which individuals achieve "intellectual and ethical 'reciprocity,'" which is defined as a "faculty for social awareness and international understanding" (Piaget as cited in Yachimowicz, 1987, p. 19).

Yachimowicz's (1987) study using a quasi-experimental pre-post design revealed that there was little change in international understanding among study abroad students. He interpreted his results by noting that study abroad students are self-selected and already hold a large interest in international affairs. He also stated that his findings found that study abroad students increased their knowledge of the host culture but expressed more negative feelings toward the host culture as well. His theory on why this occurred is that it is possible that "students have overly optimistic feelings toward other cultures before going abroad, but after study abroad their attitude reflects a more realistic perspective and comparison to their own culture" (p. 100).

In a frequently cited resource on study abroad outcomes entitled *Study Abroad: The Experience of American Undergraduates* (SAEP), Carlson, Burn, Useem, and Yachimowicz (1990) examined the following facets of the study abroad experience: the type of student who studies abroad, the changes that occur due to the study abroad experience, the aspects of the individual that might affect study abroad outcomes, and the long-term effects of the study abroad experience. The study also examined gains in language skills by using a self-appraisal method developed by the Educational Testing Service and the language proficiency oral interview developed by the American Council on Teaching of Foreign Languages.

The results of SAEP demonstrated "[that] students who study abroad are much more interested in international affairs after this [study abroad] experience than before and that their knowledge of their host country increased dramatically" (Carlson et al., 1990, p. 116). The study also found that, at the time, those who sought to undertake a year abroad were not reflective of the general higher education population. One of the implications of the results of the study includes the acknowledgment of the influence of a variety of variables on creating a successful study abroad experience.

Sutton and Rubin (2004) discuss initial results of an attempt by the University of Georgia system to compare the learning outcomes of students who study abroad and those who do not. The scope of the research project involves six phases, which focus on the following: (1) comparison of study abroad participants and nonparticipants on self-reported learning outcomes, (2) comparison of predeparture and postdeparture self-reported learning outcomes, (3) comparison of study abroad participants and nonparticipants on course-specific examinations, (4) comparison of study abroad participants and nonparticipants on academic performance measures, (5) correlation of learning outcomes with program design features, and (6) comparison of study abroad alumni and nonparticipation cohort on self-reported learning outcomes, career paths, and other factors two to five years after graduation. The paper cited reports specifically on phase 1 of the project: comparison of study abroad participants and nonparticipants on self-reported learning outcomes.

Phase 1 of the project was intended to investigate the difference in self-reported learning outcomes between students who had studied abroad and those of a control group who did not study abroad. In four of the factors, functional knowledge, knowledge of global interdependence, knowledge of cultural relativism, and knowledge of world geography, there was a statistical difference in favor of the study abroad participants. According to the authors, the other factors—relating to verbal acumen, knowledge of interpersonal accommodation, and knowledge of cultural sensitivity—not affected by study abroad or by academic major share a "direct linkage to knowledge of interpersonal communication skills, especially an emphasis on interpersonal flexibility" (Sutton & Rubin, 2004, p. 78). The authors suggest that further research occur in this area, especially involving behavioral and affective effects of study abroad on communication competence.

In a similar study conducted by Michigan State University (Ingraham & Peterson, 2004), the university created a three-phase project currently in progress. Phase I, completed in May 2001, assessed the impact of study abroad on students by focusing on their personal growth, intercultural awareness, and professional development.

The study surveyed 1,104 study abroad students both before and after study abroad using a 33-question instrument focusing on outcomes and expectations of the study abroad experience. Factor analysis yielded five factors related to study abroad outcomes for students: personal growth, intellectual growth, career development, language learning, and academic performance. The project also sought qualitative data in the form of student journals, focus groups of study abroad returnees, and articles written by study abroad returnees.

The quantitative results indicated a strong postmeasure response, with moderate to high growth among the five factors. The five factors highly correlated with each other. Another finding showed a correlation between program length and three of the factors: personal growth, intellectual growth, and academic performance—the longer the sojourn abroad, the higher the mean for these factors. Winter break scored higher for language learning and career development than a summer session but lower than a semester or academic-year program.

The main qualitative result that is related to this study focuses on intercultural awareness. One student was quoted as saying, "Cultural immersion takes effort . . . in order to gain the most from the experience you should attempt to learn the language, the history and other aspects of the culture that are important to the people" (Ingraham & Peterson, 2004, p. 95). This statement can be interpreted as the student's need for culture learning, whether it is culture-general or culture-specific, and the need for intercultural training such as that called for by La Brack (1993) and Paige, Cohen, Kappler, Chi, & Lassegard (2002) to maximize the learning of students.

Erwin and Coleman (1998) examined the influence of a variety of intercultural experiences and second language proficiency on college students' cross-cultural sensibility using the Cross-Cultural Adaptability Inventory (CCAI) (Kelley & Meyers, 2005) as a measurement tool. Cross-cultural adaptability as measured by the CCAI refers to the ability of an individual to adjust to a new culture or environment (Kelley & Meyers, 2005). The results suggested various differences in CCAI scores based on language acquisition and travel abroad. First, the results showed that college student competence in a second language was related to an increase in cross-cultural adaptability. The results also showed that students who spent a longer amount of time abroad demonstrated an increase in cross-cultural adaptability. Short-term study abroad for a summer or a month did not increase cross-cultural adaptability.

The authors discussed the limitations of the study, including the causal-comparative design of the study rather than a pre-post design. They also listed the number of variables that may influence the responses, including parental socio-demographic factors, quality of secondary education, and developmental timing of the participants in the study. The study suggested that "residing in a foreign country and travel with family members abroad were found to be more consistently related to differential levels of cross-cultural adaptability than academic-related experiences abroad" (p. 8). The study further suggests that, because there may be more contact with host nationals in other types of intercultural experiences than when learning abroad, study abroad programming should include different opportunities for meeting host nationals, such as "buddy programs." The more intercultural experiences students undergo, the higher the score they will receive on the CCAI.

An empirical study that examines students' expectations of the study abroad experience and related outcomes was conducted by Martin, Bradford, and Rohrlich (1995). The study is based on expectancy theory (Feather, 1967; Feather & Newton, 1982), which suggests that "it is the fulfillment of expectations about the sojourn that leads to positive evaluations and ultimately to satisfactory sojourner expectations" (Martin et al., 1995, p. 88). On the contrary, violations of expectations may lead to negative evaluations of the sojourn and to problems with adaptation.

The results of the study showed that the location of the sojourn had the strongest effect on violations of expectations. An interesting sideline to this point is that students who attended programs in England tended to have their expectations violated negatively, affecting their adaptation. As Martin et al. (1995) state, "this calls into question an assumption in the literature that the more similar the host and native culture, the less difficulty experienced by sojourners" (p. 103). Gender was considered to somewhat affect violations of expectations in the case of language learning, "where males' expectations seemed to be more negatively violated and females' expectations more positively violated" (p. 103). Previous domestic relocations were found to have little effect on the violation of expectations. According to Martin et al. (1995) there exists an overall positive correlation between expectation violation and positive evaluation of the sojourn.

Martin et al. (1995) conclude the study by calling for future research to identify additional variables that may have an effect on the fulfillment/violation of expectations of the sojourn. Martin et al. (1995) state that the study has implications for cross-cultural training in that it supports previous research that demonstrates the importance of intercultural training for preparing sojourners, to avoid unrealistic expectations and subsequent negative violations of these expectations. Martin et al. (1995) concur with La Brack (1993) as to the importance of orientation to give students a more realistic view of the experience, since most students lack a good understanding of what to expect.

Savicki, Downing-Burnette, Heller, Binder, and Suntinger (2004) investigated personality traits such as "emotional regulation" and "satisfaction with life" as possible measures of intercultural adjustment, in a study that compared a control group in the United States and a group of study abroad students. In addition, discussion focuses on key features that may enhance both actual and potential intercultural adjustment.

Savicki et al. (2004) tested both groups using the Intercultural Adjustment Potential Scale (ICAPS) (Matsumoto et al., 2001) as the basis of examining how students will function successfully in intercultural contexts. In addition, the groups were tested on various personality traits using instruments that measured emotional regulation, personality, optimism/pessimism, hope, and coping skills. The study abroad group of 19 students was tested on all measures during four stages: predeparture and at the beginning, middle, and end of the study abroad experience. The control group consisted of 46 students who were enrolled in a social psychology class for the same semester at a U.S. university. According to Savicki et al. (2004), "the social psychology class dealt in a didactic manner with some of the same concepts that the SA students were actually experiencing by virtue of their study abroad placement; such as stereotyping, in-group-out-group labeling, individualism-collectivism, etc." (p. 316). The control group was tested with the same measures at the beginning and end of the semester.

Results demonstrated that overall the study abroad (SA) group came out higher on intercultural adjustment potential at the beginning of the semester than did the control group, but there was no difference of statistical significance between the two groups at the end of the semester. Personality traits tested showed that SA students came out higher for emotional regulation, critical thinking, and satisfaction with life at the end of the semester and that emotional regulation in particular may be correlated with intercultural adjustment potential.

Given that intercultural adjustment potential was tested throughout the study abroad experience and both groups had undergone training (an intercultural communication class abroad and a regular social psychology class at home) to assist in managing different cross-cultural problematic areas such as stereotypes and values differences, further discussion focused on possible ways to enhance intercultural adjustment potential. It is suggested that both groups increased their ICAPS potential through training.

The Savicki et al. (2004) study presents the intercultural and international education fields with several relevant findings. First, the ICAPS instrument is a good measure of intercultural adjustment potential but not actual adjustment capacity. Second, the actual and potential intercultural adjustment capacity is amenable to change due to factors such as intercultural training or culture-specific knowledge gain. Third, the ICAPS instrument may be useful in predicting future success of those working or living overseas in addition to assessing concurrent relationships with psychological well-being. The authors call for replication of this study using larger samples to validate the findings (see chapter 7 of this volume for a follow-up study of this research project).

In a similar study related to variables that affect study abroad outcomes, Medina-Lopez-Portillo (2004) conducted a study that focuses on the effect of program duration on the development of intercultural sensitivity. The study examined the differences between students studying on a seven-week program in Mexico and those on a sixteen-week program, also in Mexico. The author referenced the Intergroup Contact Theory (Allport, 1979), suggesting that "the context in which study abroad programs are embedded— the way that programs are structured, in terms of duration, language of instruction . . . will impact the development of students' intercultural sensitivity and their understanding of the target culture" (Medina-Lopez-Portillo, 2004, p. 181).

The results demonstrated a difference in depth of culture learning between the two groups. The Intercultural Development Inventory (IDI) results showed a greater gain in intercultural sensitivity due to the longer duration of the program. Qualitative data supported the difference as well, with the longer-program participants stating that they developed a more critical stance toward the United States and more in-depth knowledge and understanding of the Mexican people.

The author concluded that further research must be undertaken focusing on other variables that affect learning outcomes. The author (Medina-Lopez-Portillo, 2004) notes, "where pre-program orientation is concerned, study abroad advisors would do well to help students make sense of the intercultural encounters, along with differences in cultural value orientations, socioeconomics, and politics that they were about to come into contact with while abroad" (p. 196).

Studies Focused on the Process of Learning

This section focuses on the process of learning in relation to study abroad outcomes in an effort to emphasize how the learning process may affect the outcomes. It is interesting to note that the authors of these studies claim that the process is as important as the outcomes themselves.

Unlike the previous studies mentioned that focus on outcomes only, Bacon (2002) examined the variables that have the ability to make the study abroad experience "successful." Bacon (2002) conducted a case study of one study abroad student studying in Mexico who was originally from the United Kingdom. The subject was fluent in Spanish and therefore had adequate language skills upon arrival.

Bacon (2002) found that, although the student had adequate language skills and an open personality, it was through difficult encounters with the host culture, in other words, encountering new values and behavior, that allowed the student to learn the rules of the culture and then perform in that culture. Bacon (2002) notes that mere competence (in language, for example) does not guarantee success. Bacon calls for study abroad sojourners to have mentors or informants that assist them in processing their adaptation. If mentors are not available, then sojourners should use journals that allow them to reflect on their experiences.

In a similar study focusing on the process of learning while abroad, Jurasek, Lamson, and O'Malley (1996) conducted a qualitative study on the addition of ethnographic field components into Earlham College's study abroad programs in order to enhance learning and to create components of the study abroad program that "provide avenues for students to gain insights into the complex societies in which they live and study" (p. 1). The main goal of the study was not to train students to become ethnographers *per se* but rather to "guide students to become autonomous, cross-cultural learners and explorers who can describe, understand, analyze, appreciate and enjoy cross-cultural differences" (p. 3). Mestenhauser's (1998) concept of meta-learning coincides with the idea of an autonomous cross-cultural learner.

The study examined three student ethnographic projects: the study of ecclesiastical base communities in Mexico, the study of discotheque culture in Vienna, and the study of a tortilla-making factory in Mexico. The students' journals reflected their success at obtaining the emic (insider) viewpoints of the cultures they were studying. Jurasek et al. (1996) emphasize the importance of reflection in testing and revising their perceptions. The authors call for further research to study the effect of adding ethnographic practices to study abroad programs.

Involving the addition of ethnographic components to assist in reflection, Laubscher (1994) conducted a qualitative study to look at students' perceptions of the learning they received from out-of-class experiences, which are common in the study abroad experience. The purpose of his study was to "lay the groundwork for developing a more systematic approach to helping students take maximum advantage of this feature [out-of-class experiences], which makes education abroad unique" (p. xiv). A secondary goal was to "determine how those categories of activity promote learning in terms of specific theoretical models" (p. 95). In his study Laubscher (1994) attempted to understand the process students go through to gain intercultural competence or intercultural understanding while studying abroad.

Laubscher (1994) referenced various learning and developmental models and frameworks for the learning process, including Bennett's (1993) Developmental Model of Intercultural Sensitivity. The main assumption of the study was that students already attempt to "engage in activities that will enhance their education" (p. xiv) but ultimately need the assistance of professional educators in order to avoid learning in a haphazard manner. In support of this argument, Citron (2002) claims in his study that some study abroad students form a "third culture" that does not actively promote integration or ethnographic discovery of the host culture, but rather fulfills the purpose of allowing study abroad students to function sufficiently in their host culture until their program ends.

Laubscher (1994) mentions the importance of predeparture orientation and training for students to gain the skills for ethnographic study before they depart for their sojourn abroad. He does not, however, discuss in detail how the aspects of study abroad programs such as the type of program, the nature of the personnel of the program, and the types of opportunities offered by the program affect the student's experience. The only reference as such is to the homestays of those students studying in Japan and how this relates to their out-of-class learning.

The data collected on participant observation, personal interaction, travel, and encounters with difference present the international education field a picture of what types of learning students engage in while abroad and the interpretations of their out-of-class experiences. Laubscher (1994) gives examples from the 30 students interviewed on each activity and how learning has occurred. For example, he cites a report by a study abroad student in Japan who is a member of a basketball team. The student observes that even though the president of the team is not the best player he is always given the ball. The student's observation allowed him to understand the importance of relationships and hierarchy in Japan.

Laubscher (1994) makes a concerted effort to address the need for further research on areas such as the personality of the student and its effect on out-of-classroom learning in order to understand other variables involved in the learning process. He also calls in a similar manner as other researchers (Bacon, 2002; Hanvey, 1979; Whalley, 1996) for more ways to invoke reflection on the part of the students and to prepare them with the skills to undertake ethnographic discovery. Laubscher (1994) concludes that efforts must be made to research other factors, in addition to successful predeparture and on-site training, that affect the study abroad experience. Laubscher's (1994) study is an important contribution to the study abroad field in that the study paves the way for further exploration of how students can learn through out-of-classroom experiences during their sojourn abroad.

Because of a perceived need for the development of a culture-learning theory in study abroad, Whalley (1996) attempted to develop a theory of culture learning in his dissertation entitled *Toward a Theory of Culture Learning: A Study Based on Journals Written by Japanese and Canadian Young Adults in Exchange Programs (Study Abroad)*. The theories described include Mezirow's (1991) Transformative Learning Theory as the main theory to be applied to the culture-learning process. In addition, the study reviews Ochs and Schieffelin's (Schieffelin & Ochs, 1986) theory on the relationship between learning language and learning culture. The focus of these theories is on the process of reflection as a way to transform or change one's perspective.

Whalley's (1996) focus on Mezirow's Transformative Learning Theory begins with a discussion of the influence on Mezirow's work by Freire.

Freire's (1990) concept of "conscientization" as evidence of using education to transform one's frame of reference is the basis for Mezirow's (1991) concept of "perspective transformation." Whalley (1996) focuses on emancipatory learning as pertinent to culture learning. Emancipatory learning involves perspective transformation through reflection. Whalley (1996) states that Transformative Learning Theory identifies "reflection as the central dynamic of learning" (p. 19).

Whalley (1996) cites Mezirow (1991) in using the following definition of perspective transformation:

> The process of becoming critically aware of how and why our assumptions have come to constrain the way we perceive, understand, and feel about our world: changing these structures of habitual expectation to make possible a more inclusive, discriminating, and integrative perspective; and finally, making choices or otherwise acting on these new understandings. (Whalley, 1996, p. 167)

To test Transformative Learning Theory as a culture-learning theory, Whalley (1996) conducted a qualitative study of 23 Canadian high school students and 24 Japanese university students studying abroad in each respective country. He utilized naturalistic inquiry and journals in order to collect data. After an extensive coding of the data, he then applied Mezirow's Transformative Learning Theory to the results.

Whalley (1996) concluded that learning did occur in line with Mezirow's (1991) Transformative Learning Theory except in two areas: second-language learning and the transformation of meaning schemes, or the meaning given to specific concepts or behaviors. Whalley (1996) found that, when learning a new culture, meaning schemes were not transformed in terms of being deleted, as in Mezirow's (1991) original theory; instead they were bifurcated—being appropriate to the culture in which one was participating. He concluded that more research on bilingualism and biculturalism was needed before further assessment was possible.

Whalley (1996) concluded that culture learning through perspective transformation is a form of emancipatory learning as per Mezirow's (1991) original theory. By understanding that culture is socially constructed, individuals are liberated from the idea of existing culture as "natural." As Whalley (1996) states, "another emancipatory feature of culture learning is that it presents people with concrete alternatives to possibly aspire to" (p. 254).

Thus, according to Whalley (1996), the process of culture learning can lead to perspective transformation that results in emancipatory learning as a study abroad outcome.

Paige, Cohen, and Shively (2004) attempted to examine one method of culture learning through the teaching of culture- and language-learning strategies. The main purpose of the study was to assess the impact of study abroad in general and also a curriculum intervention, the *Maximizing Study Abroad Students' Guide* (Paige, Cohen, et al., 2002), on the language and culture learning outcomes of study abroad students in the project. The goal of the guide is to teach culture- and language-learning strategies to study abroad students to maximize their learning while abroad. The study consisted of two groups: a control group that did not use the guide while abroad and an experimental group that did.

The quantitative results were derived from use of a variety of instruments, including the Intercultural Development Inventory (IDI) (Hammer & Bennett, 2001); the Strategies Inventory for Learning Culture (SILC) (Paige, Rong, Zheng, Kappler, Hoff, and Emert, 2002), the Language Strategy Survey (LSS) (Cohen & Chi, 2002), and the Speech Act Measure of Language Gain (Cohen & Shively, 2002). The results showed that there was an overall increase in intercultural sensitivity for both groups of students. Three of the five SILC factors developed in the study—Interpreting Culture, Nonverbal Communication Strategies, and Culture Shock/Coping Strategies—showed statistically significant shifts between the pre- and posttests for all students in terms of greater frequency of strategy use. The findings for the LSS pre- and posttests showed a higher frequency of strategy use for all students for two of the factors, Speaking and Listening, and a decline in strategy use for two factors, Learning Structure and Vocabulary and Reading. The authors explain the changes thus: "while abroad, students are likely to have more frequent opportunities than they would have at home to interact with native speakers. As such strategies for speaking and listening effectively may become more important" (p. 267). The results of the pre- and posttests using the Speech Act Measure of Language Gain showed gains on specific speech act measures by the experimental group students, but not all. Speech acts are speech functions such as requests or apologies representing the intersection between language and culture (Cohen, Paige, Shively, Emert, & Hoff, 2005).

In comparing the results for the experimental and control group students, there was no statistically significant difference in the overall results of the IDI. Likewise there was no statistically significant difference between the experimental and control groups in the overall results of the SILC and LSS based on the five factor models. On five individual items of the SILC and six individual items of the LSS there were statistically significant differences between the experimental and control groups showing both higher and lower mean differences for the two groups.

The qualitative results demonstrated in the e-journals required of the experimental students throughout their sojourn abroad provided extremely rich data demonstrating how the *Guide* provided students with the theoretical concepts of culture learning and perspectives. A student studying in Guatemala gave the following example of how the concepts in the *Guide* reinforced what the student was experiencing:

> I feel that after reading the section [on nonverbal communication], I will try to pay more attention to what people do in terms of eye contact but I have noticed that my tendency as a US American is to interject and almost interrupt much more than I have noticed my host family do. I am going to need to pay a bit more attention to this. (as quoted in Cohen et al., 2005, p. 167)

Another example shows how the concepts in the *Guide* gave the students tools for deciphering cultural differences:

> I have definitely used the [DIE Model 12 in the *Guide*] to evaluate cultural situations that seem "different" from what I'm used to. It seems that every-day I wonder about or question the French culture—Why do people I am meeting for the first time kiss me? Why do people yell at each other in the streets? I think that the suggestion to try to form these daily questions in a descriptive manner will help me out. I don't want to evaluate or criticize all of the cultural differences; I just want to get a better understanding of them. (Cohen et al., 2005, pp. 164–165)

The e-journal submissions also demonstrated how the *Guide* gave students new ideas on strategies for language learning.

The *Maximizing Study Abroad* research project (Paige, Cohen, et al., 2002) is the first study that attempts to examine the effect of a curricular intervention on the nonacademic outcomes of study abroad. Although further refinement of the instruments used must occur, and there was no noticeable change in overall intercultural sensitivity in the control and experimental groups, the initial qualitative results demonstrate that students in the experimental group who received the *Guide* were given the tools to reflect on their culture learning. Further, the students in the experimental group were given the tools to articulate their learning by gaining or revisiting intercultural communication concepts (new meaning schemes). The *Maximizing Study Abroad* research study sets the stage for future studies that examine the effect of curricular interventions on nonacademic outcomes.

Academic-Specific Focused Outcome and Other Outcomes Studies

There exists a growing research literature on nonacademic learning outcomes. Other outcomes studies examine such topics as academic-specific focused outcomes and the longitudinal impact of the study abroad experience. In addition, with the proliferation of short-term programs, there is a more concerted effort to look at outcomes related to study on short-term programs. For the purpose of inclusion, I discuss a few of these outcomes studies in the following text.

Currently, there is little research on the practicalities and advantages of learning a specific subject such as engineering overseas. Recent initiatives (Rubin & Sutton, 2001; Vande Berg, Balkcum, Scheid, & Whalen, 2004) will illuminate the international education field on the importance and benefit of studying a specific discipline overseas. Such studies are important for the international education field and the career aspirations of our students as the professional fields integrate study abroad into their curriculum. The results will hopefully allow international educators to effectively respond to the question, Why study [engineering] anywhere else but here?

Other outcomes studies include longitudinal studies such as that by the Institute for the International Education of Students (Dwyer, 2004). The longitudinal studies examine the effect of the study abroad experience on personal attitudes, intercultural development, educational attainment, and career development on study abroad alumni throughout their lifespan. The importance of such longitudinal studies is to examine the processing of the study abroad experience after the fact. With increased interest in this research area, the international education field may actually come to know the true "life-changing effect" of study abroad.

Conclusion

The historical and current research on study abroad outcomes documents that the experience of study abroad is a rich and complex experience that includes personal growth and the acquisition of new knowledge and skills. Studies throughout the years point to results in attitudinal change and a recognition by the students of the deep learning that occurs.

Recently, there has been a growing focus on the variables that affect the outcomes, including the process of learning. There is acknowledgment that, without reflection, students may not seek out the cultural differences that are not as visible as tangible items such as clothing or food.

As the study abroad outcomes research diversifies, other outcomes studies such as discipline-specific learning outcomes, longitudinal studies, and the effect of short-term study abroad on learning outcomes, are advancing to the forefront. The proliferation of study abroad research and its diversity are positive indicators that the international field as a whole is gaining a greater understanding of the personal and academic growth that results from the study abroad experience.

References

Allport, G. W. (1979). *The nature of prejudice.* Reading, MA: Addison-Wesley.

Bacon, S. M. (2002). Learning the rules: Language development and cultural adjustment during study abroad. *Foreign Language Annals, 35,* 637–646.

Bennett, M. J. (1993). Toward ethnorelativism: A developmental model of intercultural sensitivity. In R. M. Paige (Ed.), *Education for the intercultural experience* (2nd ed., pp. 21–71). Yarmouth, ME: Intercultural Press.

Carlson, J. S., Burn, B. B., Useem, J., & Yachimowicz, D. (1990). *Study abroad: The experience of American undergraduates.* New York: Greenwood.

Citron, J. L. (2002). U.S. students abroad: Host culture integration or third culture formation? In W. Grunzweig & N. Rinehart (Eds.), *Rockin' in Red Square* (pp. 41–56). Münster: Lit Verlag.

Cohen, A. D., & Chi, J. C. (2002). *Language strategy survey.* Unpublished survey instrument, University of Minnesota.

Cohen, A. D., & Shively, R. (2002). *Speech act measure of language gain.* Unpublished survey instrument, University of Minnesota.

Cohen, A. D., Paige, R. M., Shively, R. L., Emert, H., & Hoff, J. (2005). *Maximizing study abroad through language and culture strategies: Research on students, study abroad program professionals, and language instructors.* Retrieved February 26, 2007, from http://www.carla.umn.edu/maxsa/research.html

Dwyer, M. (2004). More is better: The impact of study abroad duration. *Frontiers: The Interdisciplinary Journal of Study Abroad, 10,* 151–163.

Engle, J., & Engle, L. (2003). Study abroad levels: Toward a classification of program types. *Frontiers: The Interdisciplinary Journal of Study Abroad, 9,* 1–20.

Erwin, T. D., & Coleman, P. K. (1998). The influence of intercultural experiences and second language proficiency on college students' cross-cultural adaptability. *International Education, 28,* 5–25.

Feather, N. T. (1967). An expectancy-value model of information-seeking behavior. *Psychological Review, 74,* 342–360.

Feather, N. T., & Newton, J. W. (1982). Values, expectations, and the prediction of social action: An expectancy-valence analysis. *Motivation and Emotion, 6,* 217–244.

Freire, P. (1990). *Pedagogy of the oppressed.* New York: Continuum.

Hammer, M. R., & Bennett, M. J. (2001). *Intercultural Development Inventory.* Portland, OR: Intercultural Communication Institute.

Hanvey, R. (1979). Cross-cultural awareness. In E. C. Smith & L. F. Luce (Eds.), *Toward internationalism: Readings in cross-cultural communication* (pp. 46–56). Rowley, MA: Newbury House.

Hoffa, W., & Pearson, J. (Eds.). (1997). Introduction. In W. Hoffa & J. Pearson (Eds.), *NAFSA's guide to education abroad for advisers and administrators* (2nd ed., pp. xi–xx). Washington, DC: NAFSA: Association of International Educators.

Ingraham, E., & Peterson, D. (2004). Assessing the impact of study abroad on student learning at Michigan State University. *Frontiers: The Interdisciplinary Journal of Study Abroad, 10,* 83–100.

Institute of International Education. (2006). *Open doors report.* Retrieved on February 24, 2006, from http://opendoors.iienetwork.org

Jurasek, R., Lamson, H., & O'Malley, P. (1996). Ethnographic learning while studying abroad. *Frontiers: The Interdisciplinary Journal of Study Abroad, 2.* Retrieved August 6, 2003, from *http://www.frontiersjournal.com/back/two/voltwo.htm*

Kelley, C., & Meyers, J. (2005). Cross-cultural adaptability inventory. Retrieved March 5, 2007 from http://www.pearsonreidlondonhouse.com/instruments/ccai.htm

La Brack, B. (1993). The missing linkage: The process of integrating orientation and re-entry. In R. M. Paige (Ed.), *Education for the intercultural experience* (2nd ed., pp. 241–280). Yarmouth, ME: Intercultural Press.

Laubscher, M. R. (1994). *Encounters with difference: Student perceptions of the role of out-of-class experiences in education abroad.* Westport, CT: Greenwood.

Lustig, M. W., & Koester, J. (1993). *Intercultural competence: Interpersonal communication across cultures.* New York: HarperCollins.

Martin, J. N. (1987). The relationship between student sojourner perceptions of intercultural competencies and previous sojourn experience. *International Journal of Intercultural Relations, 11*, 337–355.

Martin, J. N., Bradford, L., & Rohrlich, B. (1995). Comparing predeparture expectations and post-sojourn reports: A longitudinal study of U.S. students abroad. *International Journal of Intercultural Relations, 19*, 87–110.

Matsumoto, D., Leroux, J. A., Ratzlaff, C., Tatani, H., Uchida, H., Kim, C., & Araki, S. (2001). Development and validation of a measure of intercultural adjustment potential in Japanese sojourners: The Intercultural Adjustment Potential Scale (ICAPS). *International Journal of Intercultural Relations, 25*, 483–510.

Medina-Lopez-Portillo, A. (2004). Intercultural learning assessment: The link between program duration and the development of intercultural sensitivity. *Frontiers: The Interdisciplinary Journal of Study Abroad, 10*, 179–199.

Mestenhauser, J. (1998). International education on the verge: In search of a new paradigm. *International Educator, VII*, 2–3. Retrieved April 28, 2002, from http://www.oldsite.nafsa.org/publications/ie/spring98/verge.html

Mezirow, J. (1991). *Transformative dimensions of adult learning.* San Francisco: Jossey-Bass.

Milagros, R., & Reese, D. (1999). *Selecting culturally and linguistically appropriate materials: Suggestions for service providers.* Retrieved November 30, 2002, from http://ericeece.org/pubs/digests/1999/santos99.html

NASULGC. (2004). *A call to leadership: The presidential role in internationalizing the university.* New York: National Association of State Universities and Land-Grant Colleges.

Paige, R. M. (1993). *Education for the intercultural experience* (2nd ed.). Yarmouth, ME: Intercultural Press.

Paige, R. M., Cohen, A. D., Kappler, B., Chi, J. C., & Lassegard, J. P. (2002). *Maximizing study abroad: A students' guide to strategies for language and culture learning and use.* Minneapolis, MN: CARLA.

Paige, R. M., Cohen, A. D., & Shively, R. (2004). Assessing the impact of a strategies-based curriculum on language and culture learning abroad. *Frontiers: The Interdisciplinary Journal of Study Abroad, 10*, 253–276.

Paige, R. M., Rong, J., Zheng, W., Kappler, B., Hoff, J., & Emert, H. (2002). *Strategies inventory for learning culture (SILC)*. Unpublished survey instrument, University of Minnesota.

Rubin, D., & Sutton, R. (2001). Assessing student learning outcomes from study abroad. *International Educator, 10*(2), 30–31.

Savicki, V., Downing-Burnette, R., Heller, L., Binder, F., & Suntinger, W. (2004). Contrasts, changes, and correlates in actual and potential intercultural adjustment. *International Journal of Intercultural Relations, 28*, 311–329.

Schieffelin, B. B., & Ochs, E. (1986). *Language socialization across cultures*. New York: Cambridge University Press.

Sutton, R., & Rubin, D. (2004). The GLOSSARI project: Initial findings from a system-wide research initiative on study abroad learning outcomes. *Frontiers: The Interdisciplinary Journal of Study Abroad, 10*, 65–82.

Vande Berg, M. J., Balkcum, A., Scheid, M., & Whalen, B. (2004). The Georgetown university consortium project: A report at the halfway mark. *Frontiers: The Interdisciplinary Journal of Study Abroad, 10*, 101–116.

Whalley, T. R. (1996). Toward a theory of culture learning: A study based on journals written by Japanese and Canadian young adults in exchange programs (study abroad). (Doctoral dissertation, Simon Fraser University, 1995). *Dissertation Abstracts International, 57*(03), 988.

Woolf, H. B. (1977). *Webster's new collegiate dictionary*. Springfield, MA: G & C Merriam.

Yachimowicz, D. J. (1987). *The effects of study abroad during college on international understanding, and attitudes towards the homeland and other cultures* (Doctoral dissertation, University of California–Riverside, 1987). *Dissertation Abstracts International, 48*(10), 2561.

5

EXPERIENTIAL AND AFFECTIVE EDUCATION FOR INTERNATIONAL EDUCATORS

Victor Savicki

The study abroad experience for students is, in some ways, the epitome of experiential and affective education. Students studying abroad are immersed in real, not simulated, experiences in which they come face to face with a wide range of new, exciting, challenging, and sometimes scary and exasperating experiences. Experiences such as these call on students to exercise their emotional flexibility and resiliency. They find that their habitual ways of thinking, feeling, and behaving do not function as expected in the host culture. This experience, in the best of circumstances, generates moderate to intense affect, which helps mobilize students to step beyond their comfortable, automatic, unexamined reactions to think, feel, and behave in new ways. On the other hand, students may not be able to tolerate the type or intensity of felt emotions. They may retreat from the new experiences and reject alternate views as a means of protecting themselves. They may solidify a rigid rejection of the host culture when they are not prepared for the challenges that await them. Clearly, educating study abroad students to cope with and learn from their experiences and accompanying emotions will be of benefit. The current chapter discusses aspects of experiential and affective education as models through which international educators may conceptualize their work. Effective application of the experiential and affective learning approach can maximize the likelihood of positive outcomes for study abroad students. These approaches also provide a theoretical foundation for study abroad educators' endeavors. Experience and emotion are two undeniable parts of the study abroad experience. The goal is not to minimize them but rather to harness them in a planful way that benefits students.

This chapter will discuss experiential education and affective education in turn as well as their implications for the practice of international education. Each approach has its own literature and historical origins, yet they overlap to a certain degree. It is difficult to think of one without the other. We consider both in this chapter, since affective education in particular has been sorely neglected, and the emotional reactions to study abroad form a rich pool of experience to utilize. In the day-to-day life of a study abroad student, it is difficult to draw a hard boundary between the two approaches.

Experiential Education

For the purposes of this chapter, we will adopt the definition of experiential education endorsed by the Association for Experiential Education: experiential education is both "a philosophy and methodology in which educators purposefully engage with learners in direct experience and focused reflection in order to increase knowledge, develop skills, and clarify values" (Association for Experiential Education, n.d.). This definition attends to several important aspects.

Philosophy and Methodology

Experiential education is based on the premise that experience is the foundation of all learning. This philosophy is wary of "mediated learning" that simplifies or translates experience and thus insulates the learner from direct experience, such as lectures and text-only information (Moon, 1999). Putting the student in direct contact with experiences maximizes interaction between the student and learning opportunities. The methodology also flows from the goal of putting students into direct contact with the appropriate environment. Implicit in this goal is the assumption that such contact will evoke reactions on the cognitive, emotional, and behavioral level. Such reactions become a part of the learning experience as much as or more than the original environmental situations or events that elicited these reactions. That is, student perceptions and responses are central, not tangential, content for learning.

Direct Experience

Experiences that serve as the source of learning may range from structured classroom activities (e.g., role plays) to simulations (e.g., extended laboratory-like interactions with materials and/or people) to exposure to specific environment (e.g., service learning) to unstructured, dynamically changing environments (e.g., living in a foreign country). The key is holistic involvement of the learner at the cognitive, affective, and behavioral level. A complete exposure to the environment is required. Although a teacher/educator/trainer may focus the students' attention or even structure a learning environment, it is the encounter with the experience that provides the content for learning.

Focused Reflection

Not all experiences yield learning. Students can, for a variety of reasons, merely skate through the experience at the surface level with no deeper appreciation for what they may gain from the experience. As the joke has it, one can have ten years of experience or one year of experience ten times. The key to learning from experience is focused reflection. Learners are asked to examine in retrospect the environmental demands, their own thoughts, feelings, and actions and to step back from the intensity of involvement with the experience to draw more general conclusions about the processes involved (Moon, 2004). Often, learners will engage in reflection spontaneously as a reaction to the confusion and emotional arousal generated by the experience. However, effective reflection is a skill that can be learned, and focused reflection, as a pattern of thought, is more likely to yield positive gains than is unstructured rumination. Therefore, experiential educators emphasize this reflection process (e.g., Bennett, Bennett, & Stillings, 1977). As a side note, reflection does not mean simply repeatedly venting one's emotions or telling "war stories" about cross-cultural contacts. Sometimes excessive repetition of unexamined experiences can lock in prejudices and ethnocentric views. Rather, focused reflection entails, to some degree, disaggregating the experience to discover its underlying meanings.

Increase Knowledge, Develop Skills, and Clarify Values

Just as the learner's contact with the defined experience is holistic, so too is the learning outcome. Emphasis in the past has been on the cognitive component of learning since this may be the more easily measured result.

However, new skills and especially gains in the realm of attitudes and values are crucial, yet less quantifiable, results (Ward & Kennedy, 1999). In terms of the study abroad experience, it is often the affective level outcomes that learners appreciate and carry with them well beyond their sojourn in a foreign country. In the best of outcomes, the experiential learning process during a study abroad is a self-perpetuating cycle. As students learn new knowledge, skills, and value nuances, their openness to and awareness of new experiences alters. This alteration of awareness can help students become attracted to and actually seek out new experiences that "push the envelope" of their intercultural learning and adjustment. Another constructive outcome of the process is the ratification, over time, of a more sophisticated way of thinking. This is a transformational outcome based on a changed meaning perspective, which is discussed in the next chapter in this book.

Cycle of Experiential Learning

Although there are several conceptualizations of experiential education, we will follow the general approach proposed by Kolb (1984) and illustrated in Figure 1. According to this model, experiential learning occurs as a cycle starting with concrete experience, which is then processed by observation and reflection about that experience, leading to new understandings, skills, and affective reactions, which are, in turn, tested for effectiveness, thus generating a new concrete experience. This model has implications for the experiential learning process in that such learning is seen as not only a single cycle, as illustrated in Figure 1, but a repetition of cycles that move the learner along a trajectory of more complete and sophisticated thought, feeling, and behavior. Some have envisioned this figure as depicting a single slice of a spiral (Moon, 2004). The graphic, though simplistic, captures the key features of the experiential learning process. Study abroad educators can enter this cycle at any point to facilitate learning.

Educators can intervene at the *concrete experience* node in a number of ways. They can develop role plays that highlight aspects of intercultural learning, they can assign observations of everyday or special events, they can ask students to interview key informants, they can arrange field trips and excursions to new venues, and they can arrange for contact between students and host nationals, to name a few. At another level, harnessing concrete experience can happen not by active assignments from the educator but rather by students being asked to record critical incidents that arise spontaneously

FIGURE 1
Experiential Learning Cycle*

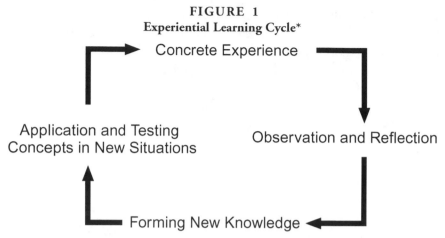

*Adapted from Kolb, 1984

while students engage the host culture. In some ways, these spontaneous incidents are more powerful for students because they are part of the fabric of the students' lives. The fact that specific events and specific values in the host culture evoke intense reactions for students marks these events and values as worthwhile to the intercultural learning process. They may define the boundaries of "teaching moments" during which students are more available for learning.

Educators can intervene at the *observation and reflection* node. A key goal of reflection is to slow down and disaggregate student reactions to concrete experience in whatever form it takes. Students may be of the opinion that their reactions are "hardwired" and can't be changed. When asked about their reactions, students may respond by saying something akin to, "The experience *made* me feel/think/behave the way I did. I didn't have any choice." From the point of view of reflection, such a reaction is unexamined. Students caught up in the action may find it difficult to stand to the side of the situation to examine it from a slightly detached position. In most cases there will be several different possibilities concerning (1) how the event can be described, (2) the emotions that may be appropriate to the event, and (3) the list of actions that might be taken. In the intercultural situation, a valuable shift in perspective comes from helping the student think through the situation from the point of view of the host culture. It is important in helping the student achieve alternate perspectives not to imply that his or her current feelings are wrong. Discounting or denying feelings typically elicits anger and resistance. Rather, the goal is to engage in "constructive alternativism" (Maher, 1969), that is, to help students acknowledge that the situation might be construed differently. Even if they do not want to abandon their initial reactions, just the recognition that there is an alternative way of thinking about the situation helps to release them from the notion that events have forced them to react in a specific way. The goal of the reflection process is not to arrive at a specific conclusion but rather to engage in the process of examination. There may be a desire on the part of the educator to tell the students how they should view the situation. This is an error. The key for the educator is to help students learn how to think through the experience, not to guide them to a specific result. The process, not the immediate outcome, is the focus. It may take several repetitions of similar experiences coupled with reflection to penetrate older ways of construing.

Educators can intervene at the *forming new knowledge* node. Often in the reflection process more questions arise concerning what happened during the experience. These questions provide an opportunity for students to learn new knowledge and skills concerning the host culture and about themselves. Here educators can give context concerning the values of the host culture. They can give specific information concerning routine expectations of the culture, such as standing in line, dealing with store clerks and waiters, when it is appropriate to say "good morning" versus "good afternoon," etc. It is also possible to practice new skills based on this information, such as standing closer or farther away from another person than the student feels comfortable based on home culture norms. Based on the realizations formed during the reflection process, students will be more motivated to learn and accept this new knowledge. The reflection process will make evident the connection between the knowledge and the experience. Information prior to experience may be helpful, but according to the experiential learning theory, it is the reflection process that makes the bond between experience and knowledge compelling. Many study abroad classes are heavy on content. While this content is useful, the experiential learning theory emphasizes the linkage between experience and content that is forged through the reflection process. The student reports of their study abroad experiences that appear in the chapters in section three of this book give substance to this process.

Educators can intervene at the *application and testing concepts in new situations* node. New knowledge in the abstract may be helpful, but especially in the intercultural context, if it is not applied, it is sterile. Study abroad students need to test their newly acquired insights and knowledge in order to ratify their validity. For the most part this "testing" is not of the paper-and-pencil kind, but rather it is played out in day-to-day exchanges with real people in the host culture. Again, educators may help students rehearse new ways of behaving; they may assign observations, interviews, or visits to venues in which the new knowledge is likely to be utilized. At this stage, it is important to help students enter into an "as if" mindset. That is, the new knowledge gained in the previous step may feel uncomfortable and "foreign." Students can resist behaving in new ways because those ways are "not me." Students can be reassured that trying on a new way of thinking, feeling, or behaving does not mean that they are not true to themselves. Rather, such "as if" action demonstrates the openness and flexibility necessary to wring the most benefit out of their time studying abroad. The students do not need to like or agree with the manner in which the host culture functions. All they have to do is to try to understand and operate within the culture.

In summary, the experiential learning cycle illustrates a manner of learning that offers many opportunities to the study abroad educator. In some ways, much of this cycle occurs as a natural part of the study abroad experience. In addition, educators can harness the experiential learning approach to attain their goals in a systematic manner if they understand and utilize this process. In some ways the experiential learning approach can feel very strange and uncomfortable for students who are more familiar with sitting passively and being fed mediated knowledge. There may be initial resistance to this approach, but after they learn the process, students feel empowered to address new situations and events independently in a flexible and creative way. They learn how to learn from experience.

Affective Education

From the point of view of experiential learning, and especially from the study abroad perspective, the affective domain has been underemphasized. Qualitative, anecdotal responses of students returning from their study abroad experiences seem to center on affective outcomes such as happiness, a sense of mastery, an appreciation for their own and others' values, etc. Yet these outcomes have not been as well considered both in teaching and assessment as have easier to specify and easier to measure cognitive competencies. The current section of this paper attempts to address this problem.

In an effort to clarify educational objectives, Bloom (1956) and his associates developed a taxonomy of cognitive outcomes and goals as a classification framework for writing educational objectives. Subsequently, educational taxonomies were compiled for affective competencies (Krathwohl, Bloom, & Bertram, 1973) and psychomotor competencies (Simpson, 1972).

Cognitive Domain

The taxonomies identified sequences of observable actions in each domain (cognitive, affective, psychomotor) moving from the most simple to the most complex. For example, in the cognitive domain the following sequence was specified: (1) *knowledge*—recalls data or information; (2) *comprehension*—understands the meaning, translation, interpolation, and interpretation of instructions and problems; (3) *application*—uses a concept in a new situation or unprompted use of an abstraction; (4) *analysis*—separates material or concepts into component parts so that their organizational structure may be understood, distinguishes between facts and inferences; (5) *synthesis*—builds a structure or pattern from diverse elements, puts parts together to form a whole, with emphasis on creating a new meaning or structure; (6) *evaluation* makes judgments about the value of ideas or materials (Clark, 1999). Each level of performance in the taxonomy presupposes attainment of competency at the previous level. All are stated as verbs whose action can be validated through observation and measurement.

The cognitive taxonomy has a respected place in the history of education. It has been used to develop curricula that recognize and utilize cognitive complexity in educational material. With the recognition of this complexity came the ability to organize student learning activities to maximize student movement toward higher levels of complexity, based on sequential mastery of levels of complexity. This taxonomy has allowed educators to reach their outcomes by design, not chance. Such systematic curriculum design has long been a goal of study abroad educators also. However, many of the desired outcomes in the study abroad field fall outside the realm of the cognitive domain. Thus, in order to attain the same goal of "outcomes by design not chance," study abroad educators need to attend to a taxonomy that addresses noncognitive domains. The affective learning taxonomy meets this need.

Affective Domain

For the affective domain, a unique set of descriptors were developed following the same general assumptions about objectivity and sequencing inherent in the cognitive taxonomy. The following are the components of the affective taxonomy (Clark, 1999):

> *Receiving phenomena:* Awareness, willingness to hear, selected attention.
>
> *Responding to phenomena:* Active participation on the part of the learner. Attends and reacts to a particular phenomenon. Learning outcomes may emphasize compliance in responding, willingness to respond, or satisfaction in responding (motivation).
>
> *Valuing:* The worth or value a person attaches to a particular object, phenomenon, or behavior. This ranges from simple acceptance to the more complex state of commitment. Valuing is based on the internalization of a set of specified values, while clues to these values are expressed in the learner's overt behavior and are often identifiable.
>
> *Organization:* Organizes values into priorities by contrasting different values, resolving conflicts between them, and creating a unique value system. The emphasis is on comparing, relating, and synthesizing values.
>
> *Internalizing values* (characterization): Has a value system that controls behavior. The behavior is pervasive, consistent, predictable, and most important, characteristic of the learner. Instructional objectives are concerned with the student's general patterns of adjustment (personal, social, emotional).

Affective Domain and Study Abroad Example

To follow is a proposed linkage between the experience of study abroad and affective domain outcomes focusing on interests, attitudes, opinions, appreciations, values, and emotional sets. This list is a first approximation of this linkage, and many additional examples might be generated to illustrate the levels of the affective domain. Clearly, it can and should be expanded to accommodate the broad variety of educational objectives that reflect positive study abroad outcomes.

> *Receiving:* Demonstrates a willingness to participate in the study abroad culture

Example: I notice the aspects of my host culture that may be similar or different from my home culture.

Responding: Shows interest in the objects, phenomena, or activities of another culture by seeking them out or pursuing them for pleasure

Example: I engage the host culture by contacting people and places in it (e.g., talking to store clerks, asking directions, looking for good places to eat, things to do).

Valuing: Internalizes an appreciation for (values) the objectives, phenomena, or activities in another culture

Example: I try to understand why the host culture is different or similar to my home culture. I read about it, talk to people about it, go out of my way to understand it. I appreciate the experience of living in a different culture even if I find it difficult at times.

Organization: Begins to compare different cultural values and resolves conflicts between them to form an internally consistent system of values

Example: I compare the values in the host culture to those in my home culture. I try to resolve, or at least accept, conflicts between the cultures. I try to absorb the new ideas and compare them to my existing value system. I can begin to examine some values I have taken for granted in the past.

Internalization of a value or value complex: Adopts a long-term value system that is pervasive, consistent, and predictable

Example: I examine and possibly adjust my ideas about what is important to me. I perceive the advantages and disadvantages of both my host culture and my home culture. I plan to return to my host culture or to travel to other cultures different from my home culture to expand my perspective. I find the study abroad experience challenging and growth enhancing.

Clearly, this linkage between the taxonomy of affective education and study abroad is not comprehensive. Each level of the taxonomy could be fleshed out with more examples. However, it does illustrate that emotion-based reactions are an inherent part of the study abroad experience and its desired outcomes.

Affective Emphasis in Learning and Transformation

Over the past decades several approaches have attempted to add an affective emphasis to broaden and maybe even to supplant the cognitive emphasis in learning and transformation. In the broader context, emotional intelligence (EQ) (Goleman, 1995) was seen as more influential for academic and job performance than cognitive intelligence (IQ). Goleman (1995) defines emotional intelligence as the ability to monitor one's own and others' feelings and emotions, to discriminate among them, and to use this information to guide thinking and action (Abraham, 2004). The appeal of such an affective emphasis is that it helps to explain why measured, cognitive intelligence does not predict academic and job performance as accurately as might be expected. Success in a variety of contexts not only relies on intellectual abilities but also includes noncognitive factors such as motivation, flexibility, and perception.

In the intercultural adjustment area, Earley and Ang (2003) have attempted to extend the notion of multiple intelligences (Gardner, 1983) to the concept of cultural intelligence, or CQ. Cultural intelligence is defined as "A person's capability for successful adaptation to new cultural settings, that is, for unfamiliar settings attributable to cultural context" (Earley & Ang, 2003, p. 9). The notion is that some individuals show an ability to adjust to new cultures easily and others do not, and that this ability is independent of cognitive intelligence and most other personality characteristics as well. Included in the CQ concept is a strong affective component focused on motivation and the self. For example, the self is seen as an interpreter of events; therefore, a rigid self-concept may make it difficult for individuals to accommodate cultural variation.

Matsumoto and his colleagues (Matsumoto, LeRoux, Ratzlaff, Tatani, Uchida, et al., 2001) have developed and explored the concept of intercultural adjustment potential (ICAP), which is defined as "the ability to adapt successfully to life in a cultural environment different than that which one is accustomed to" (Matsumoto, LeRoux, Bernhard, & Gray, 2004, p. 282). They identify four factors that contribute to potentially successful intercultural adjustment: emotional regulation, openness, flexibility, and critical thinking. These factors are heavily weighted toward affective abilities. Indeed, Matsumoto et al. (2001) propose that the factor of emotional regulation may be the "gatekeeper" for successful intercultural adjustment.

While these conceptions of affect have forced us to expand our conceptualizations about what contributes to successful performance, both generally and in the study abroad context, they all bear a significant limitation for practicing international educators. That is, they are based on the assumption that these affective concepts are inherent abilities or traits, and as such may be less amenable to change or training. For the most part, emotional intelligence, cultural intelligence, and intercultural adjustment potential can be useful concepts for screening and selection of candidates for study abroad placement. The measures of these concepts have shown some promise in this regard (Abraham, 2004; Dulewicz & Higgs, 2000; Savicki, Downing-Burnette, Heller, Binder, & Suntinger, 2004), though the current state of research must be expanded (Nettelbeck & Wilson, 2005). Recent research on this topic indicates that several affective-laden, behaviorally expressed skills do indeed relate to successful intercultural adjustment: e.g., recognition of emotions in self and others (Yoo, Masumoto, & LeRoux, 2006) and appraisal and coping skills (Savicki, Cooley, & Donnelly, chapter 10, this volume). An affective emphasis on teachable knowledge and skills would be more congenial to the tasks of the study abroad educator.

Psychoeducation and Social-Emotional Learning

A more pragmatic approach for international educators may be found in an educational mode that directly addresses affective learning. This approach has been dubbed "psychoeducation" or "social-emotional learning." Its goal is to enhance psychological and interactional processes not ordinarily included in the standard school curriculum. Early proponents of psychoeducation characterized it as "the direct teaching of specific skills for everyday living" (Authier, Gustafson, Fix, & Daughton, 1981, p. 438). It relied on training of specific social and cognitive skills. Content of psychoeducational approaches may include the following: learning communication and social skills, learning problem-solving and critical-thinking sequences, learning time management and personal organization patterns, and learning effective strategies for coping with stress. Social-emotional learning approaches may emphasize "constructive use of time, commitment to learning, positive values, social competence, and positive identity" (Elias, Zins, Graczyk, & Weissberg, 2003, p. 306). In both approaches the support and learning of affective outcomes is emphasized. In addition, these approaches are more easily used on a day-to-day basis in the classroom and experiential learning venues.

As a brief example, study abroad students have been found to benefit if they are able to perform specific coping strategies in the face of intercultural stressors (Savicki et al., 2004; Ward & Kennedy, 2001). Specifically, active coping, planning, and positive reinterpretation aided adjustment, while behavioral disengagement, venting emotion, and denial hindered adjustment. These coping strategies can be taught directly, rehearsed, and coached by international educators. Active coping and planning are simple problem-solving strategies. Positive reinterpretation is the perceptual skill of generating an interpretation of an event that was initially viewed negatively that captures a possible short- or long-term benefit of the event. Disengagement, denial, and venting can be identified and counteracted by an international educator curriculum that focuses on intercultural issues in a realistic way rather than allowing students to avoid processing them. The task of the educator, then, would be to teach some coping skills directly, and to offset the negative effects of other coping skills through the structure and support of classroom and coaching assignments.

In summary, affective education is important for study abroad students, and it has structure and a research background. Affect is not some amorphous content that constantly eludes educators' efforts to concretize it. Rather, it is a well-researched aspect of the human condition that has been insufficiently incorporated into learning and teaching until now. Since affect is an important feature of students' study abroad experience, it is only natural to harness such reactions in a systematic way to enhance intercultural learning and growth.

Implications for Study Abroad Education

In this section is a series of discussions of key issues relating both experiential learning and affective education to the study abroad experience.

Nature of the Study Abroad Experience

Students living abroad are confronted with a dynamic and complex set of events that span a wide spectrum. Going to class and coping with academic expectations may be the most predictable events for students. Beyond academics are the requirements of everyday living from buying food to riding public transportation to using the toilet. The very scope of these events is bound to put students in contact with expectations and understandings that are different from those comfortable habits that have functioned so effectively in their home culture: thus, culture clash. For the study abroad educator, the very unpredictability of such clashes presents a problem concerning experiential learning. It is not possible to control the environment to present specific culture clashes at specific times so that they may be worked into the curriculum. There are at least two solutions from the point of view of experiential education. First, on the basis of past student experience, it may be possible to predict in a somewhat general sequence topics that students will confront and to address issues as they have arisen in the past (see chapter 9 of this book). There will, no doubt, be some mismatch between general sequences and the clashes faced by specific groups of students, so some flexibility will be required. The adage "forewarned is forearmed" fits this occasion. Even though students may still react to the predicted clash, they will have a sense of normalization. That is, the clash will not stand in isolation as a bolt from the blue.

Second, and more generalizable, is the development of a structured approach for processing cultural clashes that encourages reflection and generation of new ways of thinking, feeling, and behaving in such situations. The DIE process (description, interpretation, evaluation) (Bennett, Bennett, & Stillings, 1977) is an illustration of such an approach. When a culture clash erupts, students are asked first to write a description of the event in objective language, thus separating their emotional response for later consideration. Next they are asked to evaluate possible reasons for the clash, particularly in terms of cultural differences. Finally they are asked to discuss their reaction on a cognitive, affective, and, potentially, behavioral level. What were they feeling and thinking at the time, what did they feel like doing? What do they think would be a more functional response in the future? This approach has the benefit of slowing down the rumination concerning the event, asking the students to step outside their initial reaction and to engage in creative, critical thinking to analyze the situation. The approach can be used "on the fly" so that teachable moments may be taken advantage of. The DIE approach supports the positive coping skills of active coping, planning, and positive reinterpretation.

Nature of Affective Reactions in Study Abroad

Often in academic situations emotions are considered unfavorably because they can cloud rational thought. While such a viewpoint may be useful in mediated learning situations, it is not necessarily productive in experiential learning situations, which tend to be more holistic. Cutting off a major portion of information about an experience can severely limit possible beneficial learning. Therefore, the affective side must be recognized and considered. Interests, attitudes, opinions, appreciations, values, and emotional sets become content for the reflective component of experiential learning. Students experiencing culture clashes may feel a variety of emotions: excitement, irritation, anxiety, surprise, anger, fear, joy, etc. It is useful for educators both to expand their vocabulary of feeling-toned words and to learn to relax and appreciate voiced emotions in the learning setting. It is the very level of arousal in culture clashes that makes them engaging from a learning point of view. While teachers in mediated academic settings often bemoan the lack of student motivation for learning, study abroad educators can find learning motivation in the dynamic disequilibrium spawned by cultural clashes (Joyce, 1984). Often the level of arousal generated stems from the degree of unawareness of the assumptions held by the students (Johnson & Johnson, 1997). That is, habitual, well-practiced modes of thought, feeling, and behavior, when disrupted, can evoke the belief that the persons in the host culture who have violated the deeply held patterns are bad, chaotic, untrustworthy individuals. For example, when a host culture person insists on standing too close to the sojourning student despite the student's efforts to reestablish a comfortable speaking distance, the student feels uncomfortable but, unaware of the information concerning proxemics (Hall, 1982), attributes his or her discomfort to the malicious intent of the host culture person. The emotional arousal can serve as the end of the thread to unravel the out-of-awareness process that the student is experiencing. Thus, emotional reactions are important indicators of dynamic disequilibrium that can set the stage for reflection and learning.

Nature of Reflection

Reflection, as a cognitive process, can have many objects. Thus far in this discussion we have focused on examining in retrospect the thoughts, feelings, and behaviors inherent in a recent study abroad culture clash. The currency of such clashes make them "hot" and readily amenable for processing. However, reflection in the study abroad setting can also focus on resorting past events and on anticipating future events. That is, a current culture clash in the study abroad setting may trigger a reconsideration of previously unexamined beliefs, attitudes, values, and behavior patterns whose context is the student's home culture. Students often exclaim that they have learned more about their own culture through their exposure to a foreign culture. Thus, this focus of reflection is also useful. Likewise, considering anticipated interactions, especially those likely to take place upon return to the home culture, may help to generate further understanding.

The process through which reflection takes place is also an important feature to consider. The experiential learning approach prefers that students are active in the reflection period. That is, they should actively engage in objective descriptions of events and clear recollections of their affective responses. These steps seem to belong wholly to the students. However, also necessary from the experiential learning process is the generation of alternate explanations, interpretations, and evaluations. Students need to press themselves to create different ways of thinking. Sometimes a single individual is so wedded to a particular point of view that he or she cannot think of alternatives. In this case, reflection in a group setting may be useful, as others in the group may not be as rigidly fixed in their opinions. In any event, it is important that the study abroad educator not give the student the "facts" about the incident at the outset. Providing answers, even correct answers, without students having to struggle with the process, is mediation. It detracts from the development of creative reflection as a skill. Once alternatives have been generated, the study abroad educator's input may be helpful for clarification. It is often difficult for educators to stand back and allow the students to struggle; most of us value providing knowledge and do not like to see students experiencing disequilibrium or moving toward erroneous conclusions. Yet stepping in too soon detracts from building the skill of reflection that can be applied in future situations.

Conclusions

Experiential and affective education principles form a helpful philosophy and methodology for considering study abroad education. These approaches provide guidance to study abroad educators concerning how to structure their efforts and where to focus their attention. Much of what students value and what the study abroad experience can teach is augmented through these approaches. The challenge is to become fluent in approaches that put much of the responsibility for learning on the shoulders of the students—and that focus on affect as well as cognition.

As more and more students elect to study abroad, and as some programs shorten the duration of student sojourns, international educators will need to become more efficient at teaching, training, and coaching the skills and knowledge that yield the greatest positive outcomes for students. Study abroad programs that harness experiential and affective approaches will move more deliberately toward the goal of attaining program outcomes by design instead of chance.

The long-lasting changes engendered by experiential and affective education will endure well past the culture-specific content students need in order to function on a day-to-day basis in the host culture. When students talk about study abroad as being a life-changing experience, it is the experiential and affective learning that they are talking about.

References

Abraham, R. (2004). Emotional competence as antecedent to performance: A contingency framework. *Genetic, Social, and General Psychology Monographs, 130,* 117–143.

Association for Experiential Education (n.d.). *What is experiential education?* Retrieved February 4, 2006, from http://www.aee.org/customer/pages.php? pageid = 47

Authier, J., Gustafson, A., Fix, J., & Daughton, D. (1981). Social skills training: An initial appraisal. *Professional Psychology, 12,* 438–445.

Bennett, J. M., Bennett, M. J., & Stillings, K. (1977). *Description, interpretation, and evaluation: Facilitators' guidelines.* Retrieved January 7, 2007 from www.intercul tural.org/resources.html

Bloom, B. S. (1956). *Taxonomy of educational objectives. Handbook I: The cognitive domain.* New York: David McKay.

Clark, D. (1999). *Learning domains or Bloom's Taxonomy.* Retrieved November 8, 2005, from http://www.nwlink.com/~donclark/hrd/bloom.html

Dulewicz, V., & Higgs, M. (2000). Emotional intelligence: A review and evaluation study. *Journal of Managerial Psychology, 15,* 341–372.

Earley, P. C., & Ang, S. (2003). *Cultural intelligence: Individual interactions across cultures.* Stanford, CA: Stanford Business Books.

Elias, M. J., Zins, J. E., Graczyk, P. A., & Weissberg, R. P. (2003). Implementation, sustainability, and scaling up of social-emotional and academic innovations in public schools. *School Psychology Review, 32,* 303–319.

Gardner, H. (1983). *Frames of mind: The theory of multiple intelligences.* New York: Harper and Row.

Goleman, D. (1995). *Emotional intelligence: Why it can matter more than IQ.* New York: Bantam.

Hall, E. T. (1982). *The hidden dimension.* Garden City, NY: Doubleday.

Johnson, D. W., & Johnson, F. P. (1997). *Joining together: Group theory and group skills* (6th ed.). Boston: Allyn and Bacon.

Joyce, B. R. (1984). Dynamic disequilibrium: The intelligence of growth. *Theory into Practice, 23,* 26–34.

Kolb, D. (1984). *Experiential learning as the science of learning and development.* Englewood Cliffs, NJ: Prentice Hall.

Krathwohl, D. R., Bloom, B. S., & Bertram, B. M. (1973). *Taxonomy of educational objectives, the classification of educational goals. Handbook II: Affective domain.* New York: David McKay.

Maher, B. (Ed.). (1969). *Clinical psychology and personality: The selected papers of George Kelly.* New York: Wiley.

Matsumoto, D., LeRoux, J. A., Bernhard, R., & Gray, H. (2004). Unraveling the psychological correlates of intercultural adjustment potential. *International Journal of Intercultural Relations, 28,* 281–309.

Matsumoto, D., LeRoux, J. A., Ratzlaff, C., Tatani, H., Uchida, H., Kim, C., & Araki, S. (2001). Development and validation of a measure of intercultural adjustment potential in Japanese sojourners: The Intercultural Adjustment Potential Scale (ICAPS). *International Journal of Intercultural Relations, 25,* 483–510.

Moon, J. (1999). *Reflection in learning and professional development.* London: Kogan Page.

Moon, J. (2004). *A handbook of reflective and experiential learning.* London: RoutledgeFalmer.

Nettelbeck, T., & Wilson, C. (2005). Intelligence and IQ: What teachers should know. *Educational Psychology, 25,* 609–630.

Savicki, V., Downing-Burnette, R., Heller, L., Binder, F., & Suntinger, W. (2004). Contrasts, changes, and correlates in actual and potential intercultural adjustment. *International Journal of Intercultural Relations, 28,* 311–329.

Simpson, E. J. (1972). *The classification of educational objectives in the psychomotor domain.* Washington, DC: Gryphon House.

Ward, C., & Kennedy, A. (1999). The measurement of sociocultural adaptation. *International Journal of Intercultural Relations, 23,* 659–677.

Ward, C., & Kennedy, A. (2001). Coping with cross-cultural transition. *Journal of Cross-Cultural Psychology, 32,* 636–642.

Yoo, S. H., Matsumoto, D., & LeRoux, J. A. (2006). The influence of emotion recognition and emotion regulation on intercultural adjustment. *International Journal of Intercultural Relations, 30,* 345–363.

6

TRANSFORMATIVE LEARNING IN INTERNATIONAL EDUCATION

Amy Hunter

Have you ever stopped to wonder what it is that drives us—as international educators—to work long, odd hours, keep pace in understaffed offices, and labor tirelessly through bureaucratic processes—only to confront audiences on campus who insist that study abroad is a "nice" opportunity but not really central to the core academic experience of students attending our institutions? Have you ever found yourself on the phone with a colleague in London on Christmas Eve, discussing, resolving, and following up on an urgent student issue? Did you hang up thinking to yourself, "This is the one day a year when work should be the very last thing on my mind"? Is it possible that you have ever actually said to yourself out loud, *"I don't get paid enough to care this much about my job"*?

If you are anything like me, the answer to all these musings is a resounding "yes." I often ponder questions of this nature, especially when I am exhausted and frustrated by the institutional hurdles our growing field faces in gaining support for international education. How on earth will we prepare students to be the next generation of global citizens if study abroad is yet to be seen as an essential component in a student's university career? How, as educators, will we help students meet the demands of the twenty-first century if we fail to engage them in learning that prepares them to think and behave in more culturally sensitive ways? How long will it take institutions of higher education to realize that international experience will be crucial to the cognitive, affective, and behavioral development of learners as they go forth into lives that will increasingly demand intercultural competence?

My professional frustrations embodied in such questions were the impetus for beginning a study of educational theory. Each and every student who returned home from a term overseas and proclaimed, "I'll never be the same as a result of this experience," became my obsession. My interactions with students fed an insatiable curiosity for understanding what aspects of the study abroad experience precipitate changes in the way students perceive and interact with the world around them. I wanted to know *why* study abroad was "transforming" lives, and more importantly, I wanted a language to articulate it.

The following chapter offers an overview of Transformative Learning Theory as it has been formulated by adult education theorists and provides examples of how the theory may be applied to our field in order to better inform our practice. It is my belief that a shared understanding of the word *transformation* in learning will not only provide practitioners a roadmap for more intentional programming efforts but also help supply substance and sound reasoning for doing what it is we do.

Defining Transformation

The word *transformation* can be an elusive term. When I first learned there was a theory dedicated to transformation in education, I cynically laughed. I probably even rolled my eyes. I had a very distinct image of what the process of transformation looked like in practice, and I was sure there was no place for it in the context of learning. It was the charismatic religious leader who, with a whole lot of hollering and a bead of sweat on his brow, would place a hand on the forehead of one of his followers and give him or her a firm, but inspired, shove. Individuals would fall over backward, limp and lifeless, into a frenzied, wide-eyed crowd, proclaiming they had been *transformed.*

While I would be lying if I said that I am not a woman on a mission to convert students to global citizenry, over the years I have come to realize that the act of transforming learners must be founded on something more than a little faith and the proverbial push. We cannot continue to believe that simply dropping students into a foreign country will result in the kind of learning we want them to take from a study abroad experience. This just does not always happen, and, as international programs become more inclusive and accessible to students from a variety of different backgrounds, we must do more as educators than rely on serendipity in meeting our objectives. We must be clear about our goals and intentional in our efforts to reach them, not only for the sake of our students but also for the fulfillment of the missions we serve. We have an obligation to inspire learners who are curious and engaged and thinking critically about the world around them, not limp and lifeless, toppling backward toward the floor in utter frustration.

In the course of the last decade, the idea that transformation could, in fact, be an intended outcome of adult education is a notion that has grown quite popular. Institutions are increasingly seeking ways to *transform* the lives of their learners, or at least this is what they purport. But, what exactly does that mean? How is transformation in education defined? Moreover, if a student's development is somehow transformative, how is that different from, or even more desirable than, normative development (that is, cognitive and affective change occurring naturally as the result of normal life-cycle growth)?

These are especially important questions for international educators to answer. We tell our colleagues that student learning abroad is different from learning that happens in classrooms on campus. We tout it as more meaningful, more valuable, more "transformative" than other opportunities for learning. But if someone asked us to identify the most salient characteristics of transformation in students, or to outline the ways in which certain experiences facilitate such growth, what, as educators, would we say?

This is the question that Columbia University professor Jack Mezirow (1978) sought to answer when he first articulated his theory of transformative learning. In the simplest terms, *transformation*, says Mezirow (1991), is a deep and structural shift in the basic premises of our thoughts, feelings, and actions; it represents a permanent evolution in the way we filter, engage in, and interpret the world around us. Learning is understood by Mezirow as a process of making meaning (1996), but he articulates a distinction between the development of *meaning schemes*, which are specific attitudes, beliefs, feelings, and value judgments, and *meaning perspectives*, more broad and overarching philosophical worldviews (Merriam & Caffarella, 1999). Life experience that causes a student to reorganize existing *schemes* in order to accommodate new information and negotiate new environments represents learning that leads to normative development. On the other hand, life experience that challenges students to reconsider the fundamental reasoning behind their most basic notions of the way the world works can precipitate an entire change in *perspective*. Learning of this nature is said to be transformative.

Figures 1 and 2 give contrasting views of how a student might deal with a challenge to their view of their world. In a schematic fashion, Figure 1 illustrates the normative process during which a disorienting dilemma (D), does not fit with preexisting meaning schemes (A, B, C). A disorienting dilemma may be based on an experience, an observation, a piece of new information, or any encounter with a foreign culture that raises emotional and/or intellectual confusion and bewilderment. In the normative development case, the student retains his or her frame of reference (rectangle) and incorporates the disruptive information or experience that did not mesh with previous ways of thinking by fitting it within the existing meaning perspective. Previous ideas and concepts are reorganized to allow room for the disparate information. This strategy results in learning but does not demonstrate a change in perspective.

Figure 2, however, shows transformative learning in which the struggle with the disorienting dilemma (D) leads to a change in the student's entire

FIGURE 1
Learning Through the Reorganization of Meaning Schemes (Normative Developmental Learning)*

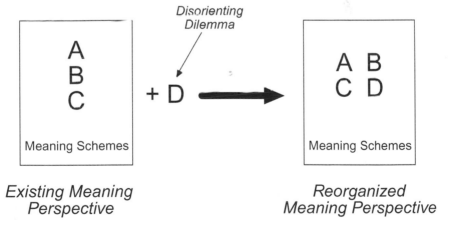

Existing Meaning Perspective

Reorganized Meaning Perspective

New experience (D) is integrated into an existing meaning perspective through the reorganization of previous meaning schemes (A, B, C). Change occurs in the learner's way of thinking; however, it is not considered transformative.

*Adapted from Mezirow, 1991

FIGURE 2
Learning Through Perspective Transformation (Transformative Learning)*

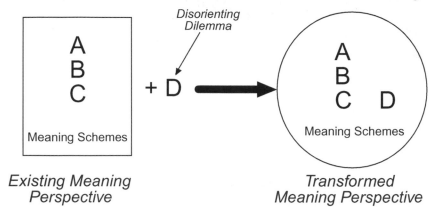

Existing Meaning Perspective   Transformed Meaning Perspective

New experience (D) cannot be integrated with existing meaning schemes (A, B, C) without the creation of a new meaning perspective. The framework of perceived meaning itself shifts.

*Adapted from Mezirow, 1991

frame of reference (circle). In this case, change in perspective, based on examination of the premises, assumptions, and presuppositions underlying the framework, results in a shift of paradigm. The new way of thinking, feeling, and valuing is based on a reinterpretation of not only *what* to consider but *how* to consider the meaning schemes. In Lewin's terms (as cited in Marrow, 1969), there is an "unfreezing" of the framework that the student uses to understand his or her world. This unfreezing sets the stage for "transition" to a new state of comprehension. Through this new lens, the same events or situations (A, B, C, D) take on different meanings. Things are not perceived in the same way. A transformation has occurred.

To further illustrate the differences between normative and transformative learning, consider the following examples. A very health-conscious vegetarian student chooses to study abroad in Spain. Her initial transition to Spanish life is marked with a euphoric sense of wonder, but by week three, part of the new experience has become a growing problem: she is increasingly anxious about her dietary practices abroad. She finds herself stifled by the lack of vegetarian-friendly choices in her homestay, concerned with the amount of oil being used in food preparation, and uncomfortable with the hours at which the family sits down to eat. Changes in her daily routine are testing her ability to integrate a new experience into her existing attitudes and beliefs around healthy eating practices. She eventually resolves this issue by finding ways to reconcile differences. She takes to buying her own food, preparing it on her own, and eating it at an hour that is comfortable for her, though she still enjoys the company of her hosts over a drink as the family sits down for their late-night meal. The student has effectively "fixed the problem" and, undoubtedly, learned a great deal in the process. She has confirmed her ability to problem-solve in the face of adversity and gained valuable new information about Spanish culture. This is normative developmental growth (see Figure 1). Her meaning schemes have been disrupted by new experience, while her overall meaning perspective (that is, her general philosophy toward dietary practices) has not changed. She has reorganized her attitudes and behaviors to accommodate difference within an existing worldview and will likely return home with the same perception of what "healthy eating" means as she had when she left: *"In Spain, they just don't eat healthy, and I can't understand why obesity and disease aren't more of an issue."*

By contrast, transformative development, in the very same context, would inevitably look quite different. The student's response to a disruption of meaning schemes would still result in movement toward resolving the issue at hand, but the way in which resolution is met would be completely different. The new experience would incite contemplation and reflection for the student. The nature of *what* "healthy eating" means, *why* she has come to hold these particular beliefs, and *how* she will reconcile the possibility that two equally valid truths may exist in the world will be called to question. Instead of working to integrate new experience through accommodation alone, she will be asking herself questions, talking with others about their experience, and practicing new routines. The result of this effort will be a deeper understanding of Spanish beliefs and values and also of her own. Her meaning schemes will reorganize in a way that elicits a change in her overall meaning perspective (see Figure 2). She will return home with a new way to think about dietary habits and a more discerning frame of reference when faced with similar challenges in the future: *"It's important to recognize that every culture has their own way of doing things and their own understanding of what it means to be healthy. I'm still a vegetarian and believe in its importance, but I also believe there are other ways to live that are equally valid."*

The Transformation Process

The transformative learning process begins with an experience that serves as a *disorienting dilemma* for students (such as a transition to life in a foreign country or the process of returning home from a semester abroad) (Mezirow, 1991). Disorienting dilemmas can be construed as the problems, challenges, and confusing hurdles a learner will encounter in the course of forging a new routine overseas, and they can arise as the result of a student's daily interactions with his or her host community or as the result of programmatic elements designed to stimulate ambiguity. From navigating an unfamiliar public transportation system to the more subtle challenge of negotiating unintentionally strained relationships with host family members, disorienting dilemmas provide students with an incentive to learn and grow. Whether the learning that ensues will be normative or transformative depends in large measure upon the student. Normal developmental growth tends to happen gradually over time, and often a student is not even conscious of the change transpiring. Transformative growth, on the other hand, requires an intentional act of learning on behalf of the learner (Tennant, 1991). Once students become aware that a disorienting dilemma has challenged the applicability of their existing worldview, it is their level of willingness to actively engage in learning as a result of that disruption that will, in large part, determine whether the experience will lead to transformation. Educators can encourage transformative learning by incorporating three essential processes into program design: critical reflection, discourse, and action.

Critical Reflection

Much has been written on the process of critical reflection, far more than I can capture here. Suffice it to say that international educators would be well-served in practice by exploring this topic in greater detail. The purpose of critical reflection is to increase learners' sense of self-awareness, while also engendering a desire to think dialectically about the world around them. Not all reflection, however, serves this function. *Content reflection* is reflecting on an experience itself: that is, recalling the details, the sequencing, and the particulars of a given experience or situation. *Process reflection* is thought given to fixing a problem and resolving the feelings of uncertainty within a new experience. For transformation to occur, however, the most essential type of reflection is *premise reflection*. Premise reflection requires learners to evaluate and explore their long-standing, culturally constructed attitudes, values, and beliefs in the face of new and unfamiliar experiences (Mezirow, 1991).

While it is not the purpose, nor intent, of every study abroad program to facilitate transformation in the lives of their learners, those who do wish to set the stage for a perspective change absolutely must find ways to systematically and structurally incorporate critical reflection into their pedagogy. Section three of this book offers examples of how this might be done.

Discourse

Inspired by the thinking of German philosopher Jurgen Habermas (1970), transformation theoreticians have articulated a particular type of critical dialogue, called "discourse," whereby learners engage to make and share meaning of the world around them in a nonjudgmental way. "Discourse involves an effort to set aside bias, prejudices, and personal concerns, and to do our best to be open and objective in presenting and assessing reasons and reviewing the evidence and arguments for and against the problematic assertion to arrive at a consensus" (Mezirow, 1995, p. 53). The primary purpose of discourse is, of course, to challenge learners to view difference as an opportunity for learning and to encourage students to make a mindful effort to find agreements surrounding reality, which leads to the development of new understandings of the world (Mezirow, 1996). Discourse is, in many senses, a time for creativity and curiosity, a time for exploration and discovery. And, again, programs that do not rely on the haphazard chance of students engaging in this process on their own, but instead very intentionally organize learning activities to encourage it, inevitably will be better poised to facilitate transformative outcomes.

Action

The third process involved in facilitating perspective change in students is action, and the matter of action is where many theoreticians diverge in their thinking. While all agree that action is a necessary component in facilitating transformation, some argue that action is a by-product of self-actualization and an expanding worldview, and others see action as the utmost objective of learning. For theorists maintaining the latter orientation, the aim of education (whether at home or abroad) is to liberate the lives of its learners so that they may bring about change for the greater good. Brazilian educator Paulo Freire believes that *conscientization*, or consciousness-raising, is borne of critical reflection, and he asserts that transformation occurs as learners participate in an ongoing cycle of reflecting, acting on one's insights from reflection, then critically reflecting again on that action, or *praxis* (Freire, 1970). For Freire, personal emancipation from previous patterns of thought is not the ultimate aim of education. It serves only as a necessary starting point for social change.

In the context of study abroad, this is an especially important distinction. If our goal as a profession is to create global citizens, capable of interacting with the world of others, we must encourage students to take action through their new learning, bringing insights full circle, either in the personal choices they make as individuals or in the activities they engage in for the greater good. Service learning programs and volunteering abroad are wonderful opportunities for students to develop and grow through action. They should be encouraged, however, only after learners have explored and achieved an in-depth understanding of the forces that shape their existing worldview. Students who march valiantly into the field with the best of intentions to do good, then return angry for not being well-received or embarrassed after inadvertently offending those they set forth to serve, offer an example of the consequences involved in engaging learners in action too soon. Not only will the experience breed student resistance to further learning and development, it can have disastrous effects on the communities that host our students—a precedent that international education should not be setting.

Timing and Transformation

We now know that transformative learning is a process that precipitates a deep and structural shift of perspective in students through new experience. When learners are challenged to reflect critically on disorienting dilemmas in light of personal biases, when they are encouraged to test and validate their new thinking in discourse with others, and when they are given the opportunity to integrate their learning into the fabric of their lives through action, the possibility of transformation exists.

Why Transformation and Study Abroad?

There is evidence to suggest that students studying abroad may, in fact, be a fairly self-selecting group, open to new experiences and inherently motivated to grow and expand in new directions (Savicki, Downing-Burnette, Heller, Binder, & Suntinger, 2004). But regardless of a student's individual predisposition toward learning, one could still make the argument that a study abroad experience holds greater potential for nurturing transformation in learners than would exist if they were to stay on campus for a term. More than ever before, students are plagued with commitments, obligations, and responsibilities that feed worries, insecurities, and anxiety over the nature of what their futures will hold. They over commit to extracurricular activities because it looks good on their resumés. They work two jobs because school is expensive. They obsessively fret over grades because they believe their fate depends on it. These distractions at home, while they may seemingly pale in comparison to the distractions presented by a term overseas, can in fact be roadblocks to learning. And, while staying out late and traveling extensively each weekend abroad can leave students fatigued and threaten their ability to learn effectively through organized program activities, this freedom of time abroad also affords students the space to explore who they are in an existential sense, and to cultivate a sense of self-efficacy that can actually enhance their learning potential (Bandura, 1989).

Student Readiness

As educators, of course we are focused on student learning. We want our learners to be inspired and engaged, and we would like to think we have an ability to help them grow and change in positive directions. But here is the forgotten little secret that we sometimes hate to admit: we can not always control their learning. Sometimes the question of whether a student's development will be normative or transformative doesn't matter at all—because that student is simply not yet ready to learn.

Being cognizant of student readiness for learning (and especially transformative learning) is essential to the ethical application of theory to practice. Learners should never be coerced into movement toward transformation, especially if they are downright unwilling. Each individual student's starting and ending point in the process will vary depending on a variety of factors, not the least of which is his or her desire and inherent motivation for growth and change. It is not our decision, as ethical educators, how far to push students toward transformation. If we choose to embrace the challenge of transformative learning practices, our task becomes mindfully creating educational opportunities in which transformation is made possible.

Teaching for Transformation: Theory to Practice

What is your personal philosophy on learning and teaching? Do you believe that students learn best through observation, group discussion, hands-on activities, or journaling? What role do you most frequently play in your interactions with students? Are you a mentor, coach, guide, or friend?

Every educator approaches his or her work with particular preferences and orientations toward teaching. Whether we are conscious of it or not, a great deal of the way we interact with learners is directly related to our fundamental beliefs about the way that students learn best. We tend to structure curriculum and arrange elements of programming around our own core values and learning assumptions, and we teach in ways that are generally more comfortable for us. But for educators with an interest in teaching for transformation, it is important to be mindful and aware of these tendencies derived from personal philosophy and teaching preference. The very nature of a study abroad learning environment quite likely demands that educators will play a variety of roles and employ a number of techniques in their pedagogy, and this is a good thing by all accounts. Versatile educators will find transformative teaching practices more familiar than those who rely heavily on one mode of teaching alone.

This section outlines four philosophical orientations toward pedagogy that present very different assumptions about the nature of student learning. Certainly, there are others, but these four form a basis for beginning to consider our own practices. Transformative learning theory has, in large measure, been inspired by the cognitivist and constructivist schools of thought, yet each of the different orientations offer something in the process of teaching for transformation. Each one articulates a particular bias, so reliance on one orientation alone can present a gap in teaching practice. It is important to be keenly aware of the tendencies we bring to teaching—not because any of them are fundamentally right or wrong—but because the process of transformative learning requires teachers, educators, and facilitators who are willing to expand their own beliefs about the way that students learn best, and to stretch their own levels of comfort in working with learners. Whether an educator chooses to cultivate a more well-rounded teaching style on his or her own or to partner with other educators in team-teaching arrangements to achieve a more balanced approach, the key is being mindful of the disparities that exists in our practice and finding ways to overcome them for the sake of increased student learning potential.

Humanism

Humanism is a school of thought that believes human beings are uniquely different from other animals and possess capacities not found in other species (Edwords, 1989). Humanists, therefore, give primacy to the study of human needs and interests. A central assumption is that human beings behave out of intentionality and values (Kurtz, 2000). Humanist educators believe it is necessary to study the person as a whole, especially as an individual grows and develops over a lifespan. The study of the self, motivation, and goal setting are areas of special interest (Huitt, 2001). Humanists argue that students will learn what they want and need to know best, that knowing *how* to learn is more important than acquiring a lot of knowledge, that self-evaluation is the only meaningful evaluation of a student's work, that feelings are as important as facts, and that students learn more in a nonthreatening environment (Gage & Berliner, 1991). Humanists are particularly adept at encouraging self-reflection and one-on-one dialogue. They are also exceptional at helping students process emotional responses to the world around them and aiding in the creation of individual plans for action. All these characteristics bode well for success in teaching for transformation. The challenge for humanists, however, is ensuring that self-reflection becomes *premise reflection* and that dialogue becomes *critical discourse*. Because maintaining a non-threatening learning environment is so central to humanists' ways of teaching, they must learn to move beyond asking *how* (e.g., how did that make you feel?) and toward the more critical question of *why* (e.g., why do you suppose that is?). In dialogue they must grow comfortable with the idea of challenging a student's self-created reality, despite a fear that it may compromise the student's motivation to continue learning.

Behaviorism

Behaviorists contend that learning is a process of acquiring new behaviors to meet the demands or expectations of a learner's environment. The impetus for learning is driven by external arrangements, and therefore, educational *environments* must be designed to elicit desired behavioral responses (Merriam & Caffarella, 1999). Conditioning, both classical (stimulus-reflex) and operant (stimulus-behavior-reinforcement), is revered as a universal learning process, while aspects of cognitive development (or whole-person development) are often unconsidered. The mind is seen as a processor of symbols that reflect a structure in the world around human beings. Thought is governed by external reality, and the structure of the real world is independent of understanding. Learning is shaped by repetition and reinforcement as the learner responds to specific environmental stimuli (Skinner, 1950). Behaviorists are exceptionally good at providing experiential, action-orientation activities that present opportunities for student learning. They tend to believe the most meaningful learning occurs through active trial and error (e.g., *"If you put a student on a bus toward home, and she gets lost enough times, she'll eventually learn to get it right"*). The challenge for behaviorists is facilitating critical reflection and dialogue in the classroom. The highly internalized process of making meaning is sometimes undervalued by behaviorists, so efforts to incorporate activities aimed at developing self-awareness or discourse may initially seem pointless. Behaviorists make excellent lecturers but would be well served by attempting to play the role of friend or facilitator as well.

Cognitivism

Cognitivists believe that learning occurs when connections are developed through the processes of assimilation and accommodation, and that it involves the formation of mental associations or representations. Learning does not always result in behavioral change but, rather, a change in the *way we think* about something. Learning is a sequential activity, as one bit of information is built systematically upon another. The emphasis is on understanding the way that learners *process* information. Cognitivists believe that learning represents a relatively permanent change in the mental networks, schemes, and associations that result from contradictory or expanding life experience. This philosophical orientation evolved from theorists concerned with the limitations of prevailing behaviorist thinking and behaviorists' failure to account for cognition (Ormrod, 2004). Cognitivists tend to focus on the development of scaffolding that helps learners develop increasingly more sophisticated ways of thinking about a certain subject. This can often involve premise reflection and even discourse within the classroom, not necessarily as a means of encouraging self-growth and discovery, but as a means of understanding a topic from a more critical, multifaceted point of view. The shared negotiation of meaning that arises from discourse can often be undervalued by cognitivists, though dialogue is in fact seen as instrumental in facilitating dialectical thought. Because a cognitivist's particular area of interest involves changes in the way a student thinks, action learning is the biggest challenge. Assignments that require community interviews, community observation, or increased host family interaction can be blended seamlessly into a cognitivist's learning program and complement that which they're already doing well in teaching for transformation.

Constructivism

The process of meaning making is a central concern for constructivist thinkers, who believe that learning transpires as we make and attribute meaning to the world around us. Learning is an active process that requires learners to construct knowledge in order to achieve understanding. Constructivists believe that the mind is an inner representation of an outer reality. Knowledge resides within, and therefore, learning becomes an individual or collective interpretation of the world. Meaning is internally engineered and developed on the basis of experience. Learning is the search for meaning. Communication between learners is encouraged. Meaning is negotiated from multiple perspectives (Habermas, 1970). Premise reflection and critical discourse are strongly emphasized and easily facilitated by constructivist educators, but it is sometimes assumed that action will naturally follow these processes. Constructivists can often forget to incorporate action planning into their learning modules, and when a conscious effort to include opportunities for active engagement is included in their teaching practice, educators with this orientation should expect that what they already do well will become even better.

Pitfalls to Transformation: A Word of Caution

Most international educators are drawn to the professional field in some way as a result of a positive, life-enriching experience that they themselves have had while overseas. This, of course, has its merits and lends itself to an entire industry of highly dedicated, motivated, and enthusiastic educators. Our deeply held belief in the benefits of study abroad, however, can also make us naive to the possibility that there is always a risk that the work we do—if not done well and with intention—will produce the exact opposite of the desired outcome. When we fail to remain committed to understanding the process of student learning, we teeter dangerously on the precipice of reinforcing old patterns of thought, behavior, and sentiment. Instead of promoting and encouraging an expanded worldview, the study abroad experience

may validate culturally insensitive and closed-minded perceptions of difference. We can inadvertently create "experts"—students who return home
from studying abroad with a "license" to perpetuate negative stereotypes and
biases they departed with in the first place. International educators must be
forever vigilant in remembering that everything we do results in specific outcomes. While we may often assume that these outcomes will be "positive,"
there is an equal potentiality that, at any moment, they could also work
against what we are trying to achieve. As such, once a program has resolved
to set the wheels of transformation in motion, educators must remain stead-
fastly committed to seeing the process through from start to finish in a very
intentional and well-designed way.

Conclusion

Perhaps that old cliche, "it's all a matter of perspective," is the very best way
to capture the essence of transformation. Transformative learning is learning
that permanently alters the way a student sees the world. It is fundamental,
it is deliberate, and it is, in fact, life changing. Our time with students is
short. But if our time is used wisely it can result in learning that lingers
positively throughout a lifetime. Our time with students can precipitate the
kind of change we hope to see within the world. It is my belief that this is
not only our job as international educators, but it is our responsibility. And
I hope our field will embrace this challenge. When we see transformative
changes in our learners, and when we know that we have given them the
skill sets they need to do great things with their lives and for the communities they serve, it somehow makes the phone calls on Christmas Eve, the
battles with bureaucracy, and even our meager wages, entirely worth the
while. Be vigilant in your practice, go forth confidently knowing that what
we do really matters, believe that we can make a difference . . . and teach.
Teach for transformation.

References

Bandura, A. (1989). Human agency in Social Cognitive Theory. *American Psycholo-
gist, 44*, 1175–1184.
Edwords, F. (1989). *What is humanism?* Amherst, NY: American Humanist
Association.

Freire, P. (1970). *Pedagogy of the oppressed.* New York: Seabury.

Gage, N., & Berliner, D. (1991). *Educational psychology* (5th ed.). Boston: Houghton Mifflin.

Habermas, J. (1970). *Knowledge and human interests.* Boston: Beacon.

Huitt, W. (2001). Humanism and open education. *Educational Psychology Interactive.* Valdosta, GA: Valdosta State University. Retrieved July 23, 2007, from http://chiron.valdosta.edu/whuitt/col/affsys/humed.html.

Kurtz, P. (2000). *Humanist manifesto 2000: A call for a new planetary humanism.* Amherst, NY: Prometheus.

Marrow, A. F. (1969). *The practical theorist: The life and work of Kurt Lewin.* New York: Basic Books.

Merriam, S., & Caffarella, R. (1999). *Learning in adulthood* (2nd ed.). San Francisco: Jossey-Bass.

Mezirow, J. (1978). *Education for perspective transformation: Women's re-entry programs in community colleges.* New York: Teachers College, Columbia University.

Mezirow, J. (1991). *Transformative dimensions of adult learning.* San Francisco: Jossey-Bass.

Mezirow, J. (1995). Transformation theory of adult learning. In M. R. Welton (Ed.), *In defense of the lifeworld* (pp. 39–70). New York: State University of New York Press.

Mezirow, J. (1996). Contemporary paradigms of learning. *Adult Education Quarterly, 46(3), 158–172.*

Ormrod, J. E. (2004). *Human learning* (4th ed.). Upper Saddle River, NJ: Pearson Education.

Savicki, V., Downing-Burnette, R., Heller, L., Binder, F., & Suntinger, W. (2004). Contrasts, changes, and correlates in actual and potential intercultural adjustment. *International Journal of Intercultural Relations, 28, 311–329.*

Skinner, B. F. (1950). Are theories of learning necessary? *Psychological Review, 57,* 193–216.

Tennant, M. C. (1991). The psychology of adult teaching and learning. In J. M. Peters, & P. Jarvis (Eds.), *Adult education: Evolution and achievements in a developing field of study* (pp. 191–216). San Francisco: Jossey-Bass.

SECTION TWO

RESEARCH ON THE PROCESSES OF INTERCULTURAL COMPETENCE AND TRANSFORMATION

It is always useful to view a situation from multiple perspectives. What one sees from one angle shifts or disappears while other features suddenly emerge. So too with research, several perspectives on the same general topic give a more complete, well-rounded picture. The research studies in section two are psychological and anthropological. They are longitudinal and cross-sectional. They are quantitative and qualitative. They are based on self-report questionnaires, open-ended archival essays, observations, and interviews. They all, however, focus on students studying abroad and the issues and concerns to which they are exposed. Much of what we know about learning and adjustment from other bodies of knowledge can be transferred to the study abroad setting. Yet, this setting is unique, and some of the variables of interest are not generally addressed elsewhere. Research specifically focused on the study abroad context is vital.

In general, the chapters in section two identify features of the study abroad experience that impact the positive outcomes that have been identified in section one. As international educators, we can apply the results of these studies immediately. Educators can help students clarify their study abroad goals; they can teach students the skill of positive reinterpretation; they can arrange the study abroad environment to "push" students into contact with host nationals while providing a secure atmosphere for retreat to lick one's wounds and receive social support. These and more are messages from the research studies in this section. An additional virtue to the studies reported here is that they all took place in study abroad sites whose international education approaches are elaborated in section three. That is, there is a consistency of approach between theory, research, and application.

7

CONTRASTS AND CHANGES IN POTENTIAL AND ACTUAL PSYCHOLOGICAL INTERCULTURAL ADJUSTMENT

Victor Savicki, Frauke Binder, and Lynne Heller

Study abroad educators and advisors hope that their students will experience positive outcomes during their sojourn in a foreign country. The predictable, structured environmental aspects of orientation to the sojourn, and components of the study abroad programs, of course, are important to set the stage for positive outcomes. However, exposure to a foreign culture cannot be completely structured. Part of the intrigue as well as the potential anxiety of study abroad is the unpredictability and uncertainty of day-to-day living in a foreign environment. Incidents emerge from the interplays between the student and the host culture as well as the unique people that the student encounters, and the contrasts between host culture values and the values brought by the students. The exact timing and form of these incidents are quite difficult to predict, though some foreknowledge of likely issues can be helpful. Given the unpredictability of the environment, investigators have also looked at the "person" side of the person-environment fit equation (Lewin, 1935). Is there something that the student carries into the study abroad environment that increases the likelihood of a positive outcome? Researchers have looked at many characteristics of individual students, such as personality factors (Bacon, 2002), past experiences with other cultures (Carlson, Burn, Useem, & Yachimowitz, 1990), and language competence (Erwin & Coleman, 1998), to name a few. In the current study, an individual characteristic will be examined that is oriented directly at aspects of positive study abroad outcome: intercultural adjustment potential.

Recently Matsumoto and his associates have conducted a series of studies developing a measure of intercultural adjustment potential (Matsumoto et al., 2001). Although these studies do a workmanlike job of demonstrating the psychometric properties of this measure, the Intercultural Adjustment Potential Scale (ICAPS), more needs to be done to evaluate the place of this concept of intercultural adjustment potential with regard to study abroad students. If this concept and the measurement of it apply in the study abroad context, then they may give direction to study abroad educators, advisors, and administrators concerning how to maximize the likelihood that their students will have a successful study abroad experience.

The current study attempts to consider potential and actual intercultural adjustment by addressing several relevant issues through the examination of (a) the contrasts between actual and potential intercultural adjustment in students who sojourn in another culture versus those who remain in their own culture and (b) the changes in potential and actual intercultural adjustment of sojourners over time. This chapter follows previous research done on this topic (Savicki, Downing-Burnette, Heller, Binder, & Suntinger, 2004).

Before delving into the specifics of the research study, a brief review of important concepts will be given, as well as the proposal and rationale for research hypotheses.

Intercultural Adjustment

Adjustment to a foreign culture is a complex, multilevel undertaking. Ward and Kennedy (1993) generally divide intercultural adjustment into two levels: psychological adjustment and sociocultural adjustment. "Psychological adjustment, then, is interwoven with stress and coping processes, whereas sociocultural adaptation is predicated on culture learning" (Ward & Kennedy, 1993, p. 222). While the emphasis in the current study is on psychological adjustment, it is clear that this type of adjustment was influenced by socio-cultural-level variables as well. Following this general suggestion of Ward and Kennedy (1993), the current study uses the general stress and coping model offered by Lazarus (1999) as a framework for conceptualizing the intercultural adjustment process.

Ward (2001) characterizes the stress and coping theory view of intercultural adjustment as emerging from "cross-cultural transitions entailing a series of stress provoking life changes that tax adjustive resources and require coping responses" (p. 427). In this model cognitive appraisal is an intermediate step between the stressors presented by the foreign culture and the psychological well-being of the individual. Too high a level of environmental stressors combined with too low a level of personal and environmental resources to deal with those stressors leads to the experience of threat with its attendant negative psychological and physiological outcomes. On the other hand, adequate resources and coping abilities lead to the experience of challenge and positive outcomes of self-efficacy, mastery, and other indicators of well-being. Much of the adjustment literature has been focused on problematic responses to intercultural stress in which the appraisal process resulted in a perception of threat: e.g., culture shock (Pedersen, 1995), emotional distress (Furukawa & Shibayama, 1994), and anxiety, depression, and difficult interpersonal relations (Matsumoto et al., 2001). On the other hand, intercultural adjustment can lead to more positive outcomes based on the appraisal of challenge: e.g., gains in self-esteem and personal awareness (Babiker, Cox, & Miller, 1980) and increases in self-confidence and positive mood (Matsumoto et al., 2001). The measurement of intercultural adjustment potential promises to help individuals faced with immersion in a foreign culture by alerting them to the need to bolster personal resources and coping strategies, thus preventing damage to their psychological well-being.

Intercultural Adjustment Potential

The potential to make a successful adjustment to a different culture calls upon personal resources and coping strategies (Ward, 2001) that may exist in different types and quantities in individuals prior to departure from their home culture. Clearly, one's specific experiences in a new culture will affect one's adjustment, but individuals also bring with them personal characteristics and codified prior learnings that may predispose them to appraise stressors differently and, thus, respond well or poorly to the stressors inherent in adjusting to a different culture. Matsumoto and his colleagues (Matsumoto, LeRoux, Bernhard, & Gray, 2004) define intercultural adjustment potential as "the ability to adapt successfully to life in a cultural environment different than that which one is accustomed to" (p. 282). They identify four factors that contribute to potentially successful intercultural adjustment: emotional regulation, openness, flexibility, and critical thinking. A person with a high potential to adjust well to a different culture will be able (1) to temper his or her emotional arousal (e.g., anxiety and anger) at unexpected events in the new culture so as not react impulsively, (2) to welcome and even seek out new experiences and situations, (3) to generate new responses and new ways of thinking about events and people in the new culture, and (4) to reflect on experiences in the new culture in order to create new understandings about the self and both host and home cultures. This combination of factors as the basis for the potential to adjust well to a different culture has high face validity as well as strong research support (Matsumoto et al., 2001).

Actual and Potential Intercultural Adjustment

Matsumoto and his colleagues (Matsumoto et al., 2001, 2003, 2004) have done substantial work in documenting the psychometric properties of the ICAPS scale as well as describing the relationship of the scale to psychological adjustment and other variables. The current study extends that work in several ways.

First, it would be useful to note differences in actual and potential adjustment between individuals who sojourned in a foreign culture in comparison to those who chose to remain in their own culture. For example, there is some suggestion that individuals voluntarily choosing to sojourn in a foreign culture may show higher levels of adjustment prior to their sojourn than do individuals not choosing such travel (Berry, 1997). This reaction may be based on enthusiasm and excitement concerning the "adventure" of experiencing a new culture. At the same time, the concept of culture shock (Pedersen, 1995) indicates that actual adjustment of sojourners may decrease during their stay in the foreign culture before returning to its original level. Thus, comparison of sojourners to those who stayed home suggests the following hypotheses:

Hypothesis 1a: At the beginning of their foreign sojourn, study abroad students will show higher intercultural adjustment potential and higher actual adjustment than students who stay at home.

Hypothesis 1b: This distinction will be maintained at the end of the study abroad semester.

Second, at the heart of the concept of intercultural adjustment potential is its ability to predict actual adjustment to a new culture. Matsumoto and his colleagues use this prediction as one of the bases for the development of the ICAPS (Matsumoto et al., 2001). Most of the studies reported by Matsumoto and his colleagues were concurrent; that is, they measured the relation of the ICAPS with other indicators of adjustment measured at the same point in time. In the few studies that related ICAPS to future adjustment, the time period between measures was either quite short or unspecified (Matsumoto et al., 2003). Therefore, from a longitudinal perspective the following hypothesis was tested:

Hypothesis 2: For study abroad students, intercultural adjustment potential at predeparture will predict actual adjustment at the end of the foreign culture sojourn.

Third, there has been no documentation of how the potential for intercultural adjustment may change during a foreign sojourn nor how potential and actual adjustment may be related to each other during a sojourn. The culture shock paradigm (Pedersen, 1995) would suggest that actual adjustment would dip and then recover during a sojourn. In contrast, it may be that potential for intercultural adjustment may increase over a sojourn, since individuals are being exposed to the broadening effects of exposure to a different culture. Matsumoto et al. (2001) reported that training on intercultural communication and adjustment resulted in increases in ICAPS scores, thus exposure to actual intercultural events might be expected to increase such scores also. The current study captures actual adjustment and intercultural adjustment potential at several points in time prior to departure, then at three points over a three-month period from the beginning to end of a sojourn in a foreign culture, and finally at three months after completion of the sojourn. Given these findings, two hypotheses are proposed:

Hypothesis 3a: For study abroad students, intercultural adjustment potential will increase over their stay in a foreign culture.

Hypothesis 3b: For study abroad students, actual adjustment will decrease then return to baseline during their stay in a foreign culture.

Methods

Participants

A group of 19 students from U.S. universities who studied abroad for three months (SA) were matched with 46 students who stayed in the United States during the same semester (Home). The Home students were enrolled in a social psychology class that dealt in a didactic manner with some of the same concepts that the SA students were actually experiencing by virtue of their study abroad placement, such as stereotyping, in-group–out-group labeling, individualism–collectivism, etc. The groups were matched for age (19 to 25, with 83% in the 20 to 22 range), gender (54% women), and class standing (all juniors and seniors).

Measures

Intercultural Adjustment Potential Scale (ICAPS)

The ICAPS consists of 55 items, with responses given on a scale ranging from 1 (Strongly Disagree) to 7 (Strongly Agree). A total score (ICAPS Total) was computed by summing all items (24 reverse coded) with higher scores indicating greater adjustment potential (Matsumoto et al., 2001). This scale has demonstrated predictive validity for adjustment to a new culture based on peer and expert interviewer ratings, as well as self and subjective ratings (Matsumoto et al., 2001, p. 492). Four factor scores were also derived: Emotion Regulation (ER), the ability to modulate one's emotional reactions to avoid employing psychological defenses; Openness (OP), the ability to engage in learning about the new culture; Flexibility (FL), being free of overattachment to previous ways of thinking and willingness to tolerate ambiguity; and Critical Thinking (CT), the ability to generate creative, new hypotheses about incidents in the new culture that go beyond one's home cultural framework. All five ICAPS scores were transformed to T-scores with a mean of 50 and standard deviation of 10 based on a normative sample. The authors of the scale reported alphas of .783 for the ICAPS Total, .638 for Emotional Regulation, .601 for Openness, .568 for Flexibility, and .433 for Critical Thinking (Matsumoto et al., 2001, p. 506).

Satisfaction With Life Scale (SWLS)

The SWLS is a five-item questionnaire using a 7-point Likert scale to rate overall satisfaction with life using statements such as "In most ways my life is close to my ideal" (Diener, Emmons, Larsen, & Griffin, 1985, pp. 72–73). The SWLS can be viewed as a measure of psychological adjustment, since the scale demonstrated moderately strong criterion validity with several measures of psychological well-being (Diener et al., 1985). Alpha for the current sample was .838.

Procedures

SA students' voluntary participation was requested at five points in time: within one month prior to departure for their study abroad experience, during the beginning, middle, and end of the academic term of the study abroad experience, and then three months following.

Home students' voluntary participation was solicited as one of several extra-credit activities in two sections of a social psychology course at a university in the United States at the beginning and at the end of the same term as the SA group's foreign stay.

Results and Discussion

Results will be presented in the order of the hypotheses proposed previously.

Hypotheses 1a and 1b: Contrasts Between Stay at Home and Study Abroad Groups

Repeated Measures ANOVA (analysis of variance) comparing groups (SA and Home) across two time periods (T_1 = beginning of the semester, T_2 = end of the semester) indicated that the SA group was significantly higher on Emotional Regulation (F (1, 61) − 3.96, p = .05), Critical Thinking (F (1, 61) = 5.19, $p <$ .05), and Satisfaction With Life (F (1, 61) − 11.53, $p <$ .001). There were no significant differences across time, and no significant interactions. Table 1 shows the means and standard deviations for SA and Home groups compared at the beginning and at the end of the academic term. Examination of univariate F's indicated that the SA group was significantly higher than the Home group on Emotional Regulation and Satisfaction With Life both at the beginning and at the end of the term. The SA group was higher on ICAPS Total at the beginning of the term, but not at the end; the SA group was higher on Critical Thinking at the end of the term, but not at the beginning.

In summary, hypothesis 1a, that the SA group would be higher on intercultural adjustment potential and personal adjustment at the beginning of the semester, was supported for ICAPS Total, Emotional Regulation, and Satisfaction With Life, but not for Openness, Flexibility, and Critical Thinking. Students higher on some of the intercultural adjustment potential and actual adjustment scales seem to have self-selected for a foreign study experience, but that difference did not extend to all intercultural adjustment factors. Hypothesis 1b, that SA students would be higher than Home students

TABLE 1
Comparisons of Study Abroad and Home Groups at the Beginning and at the End of the Semester on ICAPS Total, Factor Scores, and Satisfaction With Life

Variables		Start of Semester			End of Semester		
		Study Abroad	Home	F (1,63)	Study Abroad	Home	F (1,63)
ICAPS Total	M	65.368	58.370	4.364*	63.288	60.315	.967
	SD	14.566	11.243		12.911	9.723	
Emotional Regulation	M	54.290	49.342	4.485*	53.178	47.954	6.050*
	SD	9.283	8.263		7.686	7.407	
Openness	M	49.014	44.631	2.980	48.027	44.590	1.794
	SD	11.708	8.158		10.898	8.269	
Flexibility	M	48.078	47.353	.114	48.675	46.243	1.336
	SD	8.239	7.702		8.480	6.992	
Critical Thinking	M	54.813	50.587	2.737	56.944	50.860	5.898*
	SD	9.731	9.216		7.142	9.351	
Satisfaction With Life	M	28.157	23.608	5.160*	29.529	25.065	12.198***
	SD	3.862	8.338		4.445	4.523	

* $p < .05$, *** $p < .001$

on intercultural adjustment potential and personal adjustment at the end of the semester, was supported for Emotional Regulation, Critical Thinking, and Satisfaction With Life. ICAPS Total was not significantly different at the end of the semester. With the exception of ICAPS Total, the SA students either maintained or added to their levels of intercultural adjustment potential and personal adjustment over the course of their foreign sojourn.

Hypothesis 2: Predictive Validity for ICAPS

For the total sample, SA and Home groups combined ($n = 63$), two indices of intercultural adjustment potential measured at the beginning of the term were predictive of higher personal adjustment or Satisfaction With Life at the end of the term ten weeks later (ICAPS Total = .386, $p < .01$, Emotional Regulation = .424, $p < .001$), thus giving some credence to both the predictive validity of the ICAPS Total score, and to the notion that Emotional Regulation may be a "gatekeeper" for intercultural adjustment potential (Matsumoto et al., 2001).

In an even stronger test of the predictive validity, two indices of intercultural adjustment potential measured in the SA group alone ($n = 17$) prior to departure for their foreign culture sojourn were predictive of higher personal adjustment approximately six months after the initial measurement at follow-up, after their return to the United States (ICAPS Total = .768, $p < .001$; Emotional Regulation = .619, $p < .01$). Although not all factor scores showed significance, this result shows strong support for hypothesis 2 and seems to support the notion of ICAPS as a measure of *potential* for intercultural adjustment that demonstrates relatively high level of accuracy of prediction even over a long time period.

Hypotheses 3a and 3b: Changes in the Study Abroad Group

Figure 1 shows how the intercultural adjustment potential factor scores for the SA group, expressed as T-scores, changed over five time periods: predeparture, beginning of the term, middle of the term, end of the term, and follow-up. SA group averages for both Critical Thinking and Emotional Regulation were above the average for the ICAPS norm group (50) at predeparture. While Emotional Regulation dipped slightly during the middle of the term before returning to about the predeparture level, Critical Thinking increased steadily from the beginning to the end of the term, and on into follow-up. SA group averages for Flexibility and Openness started below the average for the norm group (50) and remained below that norm throughout the following time periods. Flexibility, however, did increase at a statistically significant level between predeparture and the end of the term (t-value = -2.63, $p < .05$). The largest increase in Flexibility occurred between predeparture and the middle of the term. Openness stayed virtually unchanged across the time periods. The pattern of changes illustrated in Figure 1 does not exclusively support one theory of intercultural adjustment over another. The dip in Emotional Regulation in the middle of the term might indicate a pattern of culture shock (Oberg, 1960), whereas the increases in Critical Thinking and Flexibility might indicate a continuous pattern of learning consistent with social learning (Ward, 2001) or anxiety/uncertainty management (Gudykunst, 1995) models of intercultural adjustment.

FIGURE 1

**Intercultural Adjustment Potential Factor Changes
for SA Group Across Four Time Periods**

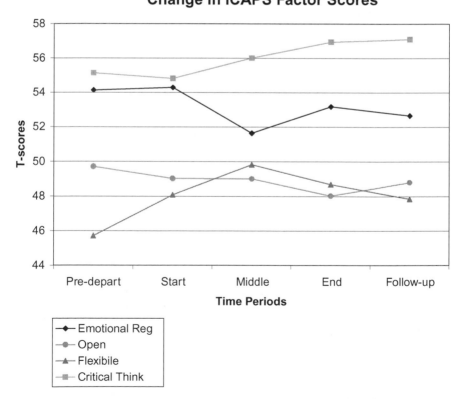

Change in ICAPS Factor Scores

Interestingly, for the SA group, the index of the *potential* for intercultural adjustment (ICAPS Total) changed in almost mirror-image fashion in relation to the index for *actual* personal psychological adjustment (SWLS) (see Figure 2). The decrease in ICAPS Total from predeparture to the end of the term was not statistically significant; however, the increase of Satisfaction With Life between predeparture and the end of the term did reach statistical significance (t-value $= -2.21$, $p < .05$). The decrease in ICAPS Total for the SA group over their stay in a foreign culture was unexpected. Clearly, the SA group did adjust well to the foreign culture in which they stayed. Not only did the Satisfaction With Life scores increase significantly, but self-report rating scales of adjustment and satisfaction also were quite high (4.24 and 4.62 respectively on a 5-point scale), as were ratings of intercultural adjustment by the foreign families with whom the students lived during the semester (3.92 on a 5-point scale). Looked at a different way, the relationship

FIGURE 2
ICAPS Total and Satisfaction With Life Changes
for SA Group Across Five Time Periods

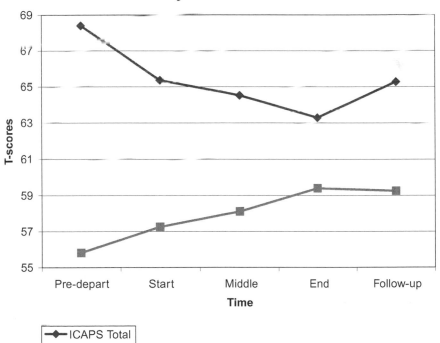

between ICAPS Total and SWLS in the SA group showed changes across time. At predeparture, the scales were significantly correlated ($r = .506$, $p < .04$). However, at the beginning of the semester they lost their significant correlation ($r = .348$) only to increase that relationship over the succeeding time periods (midsemester $r = .589$, $p < .02$; end-of-semester $r = .786$, $p < .001$; follow-up $r = .715$, $p < .001$). The contrast across time of measures of potential as opposed to actual adjustment and the variation in correlation of those measures raises questions about the relationship between these concepts as the actual intercultural adjustment process is underway. The rebound of intercultural adjustment potential at follow-up may indicate that such potential may be expended during the study abroad sojourn, but recouped when adjustment demands are lifted.

One other notable result illustrated in Figure 2 is that the SA group was appreciably above the norm ($M = 50$, $SD = 10$) for both ICAPS Total and SWLS (based on the normative groups used to validate the instruments) (Diener et al., 1985, Matsumoto et al., 2001). Despite the dip in the intercultural potential score, at its lowest point it was still more than one standard deviation above that of the norm group. Likewise, even though the SA group scored more than half a standard deviation above the norm on the SWLS in the beginning, they increased to nearly one standard deviation above the norm by the end of their sojourn. These findings indicate a strong self-selection phenomenon with study abroad students. The fact that these students voluntarily placed themselves in a situation that would put them in contact with significant stressors suggests their willingness to deal with such stress and, possibly, their resilience. Future research may be able to determine the impact of these strengths on intercultural adjustment.

Hypotheses 3a and 3b garnered mixed support. Actual psychological adjustment (SWLS) and two factor scales for adjustment potential (Flexibility and Critical Thinking) increased during the SA group's stay in a foreign culture. Although no intercultural potential score decreased to the level of statistical significance, the trend for ICAPS Total goes counter to hypothesis 3a. In addition, actual adjustment rose steadily, not showing the dip associated with culture shock, as predicted in hypothesis 3b. Clearly, the processes involved in relationships between actual versus potential intercultural adjustment need to be examined further.

There is some evidence that both psychological and sociocultural adjustment may contribute to both potential and actual intercultural adjustment

(Searle & Ward, 1990). With the SA sample in the current study, no systematic intercultural education was undertaken prior to departure, but an ongoing class on intercultural communication (ICC) was undertaken throughout the SA students' stay in the foreign culture. The ICC class focused on general themes concerning intercultural adjustment (e.g., communication, culture shock) as well as specifics regarding the local culture (e.g., customary greetings, navigating the local public transportation system) (see chapters 11 through 13 in this book for examples of the ICC class). In addition, a weekly assignment for each student—to find and analyze a stressful culture-clash incident—that then was subjected to group problem solving probably enhanced emotional regulation and coping. Even the Home group increased their ICAPS Total as a result of considering concepts related to successful intercultural adjustment (e.g., stereotypes, in-groups versus out-groups, prejudice). It seems that there may be systematic interventions that may enhance both potential and actual adjustment to a different culture.

Of particular interest was the steady growth of Critical Thinking throughout the sojourn and on into follow-up (see Figure 1). It is possible that the structured process carried out in the ICC class, of attending to and analyzing critical incidents of cultural clashes, first taught, then ratified, a constructive strategy of thinking. This strategy called for students first to describe objectively cross cultural incidents, then to interpret them from the point of view of the host culture, then to evaluate them in terms of their own feelings, attitudes, and values. Once learned, this strategy helped them think methodically about the incidents rather than react impulsively (Bennett, Bennett, & Stillings, 1977). Such a cognitive strategy encourages the student to consider the stressor he or she confronts in a manner that is more likely to lead to an appraisal (see Lazarus, 1999), which allows the situation to be evaluated as a challenge rather than a threat. This habitual cognitive strategy clearly can be taught, and is likely to serve students well in future encounters with unexpected incidents, whether culturally based or not.

Conclusions

The unexpected, mirror-image change of actual versus potential intercultural adjustment of SA students while they were in a foreign culture could be explained using Lazarus's (1999) formulations concerning stress, appraisal, and coping. Although students' primary appraisal (i.e., their perception of the level of difficulty in the situation) may have had to be revised upward based on actual exposure to the foreign culture, the students also received support and education in boosting their secondary appraisal (i.e., their knowledge and confidence that they could develop the resources necessary to resolve stressors effectively in the foreign culture). Thus, they could feel good about dealing with a difficult situation despite having to expend substantial effort.

On a more simplistic level, it may be that the SA students "used up" some of their potential for intercultural adjustment as they were called upon to actually adjust to the foreign culture. Consistent with the conservation of resources theory (Hobfoll, 1989), individuals would expend resources under conditions of threat. Hobfoll and Shirom (2001) state that strong resource pools lead to the greater likelihood that persons will seek opportunities to risk resources for increased resource gains. In other words, the more one has of a resource, the more likely that one would put him- or herself in a potentially threatening situation in order to gain other resources. Hobfoll and Shirom (2001) relate such resource-acquiring action to factors such as optimism, self-efficacy, and self-esteem. The SA group with a high level of initial intercultural adjustment potential could expend that psychological resource to accomplish actual adjustment under difficult conditions. The correlation of initial ICAPS scores with later actual adjustment gives substance to this idea. Also, this relationship between potential and actual intercultural adjustment supports the notion that the ICAPS measures intercultural adjustment *potential* rather than the moment-to-moment capacity for such adjustment (Matsumoto et al., 2004). The concepts of potential and realized adjustment are related but may function differently from one another. It will be necessary to see if the divergence of development in the concepts found in the current study can be replicated.

Actual and potential intercultural adjustment do seem amenable to change. The Home group in the current study increased their ICAPS Total score after taking a ten-week social psychology course that dealt, in part, with aspects of diversity and culture. The SA group increased actual adjustment and some aspects of intercultural adjustment potential, in part, due to a multifaceted class on culture and intercultural communication. It seems that three different levels of information can be helpful in increasing actual and potential intercultural adjustment: (1) general information about major concepts and reactions that are a predictable part of the intercultural experience, (2) culture specific information to increase a sense of personal efficacy in dealing with unique aspects of the culture that students have to negotiate, and (3) information and ongoing coaching concerning personality characteristics and coping strategies that might be harnessed during the inevitable clashes between home and foreign culture that sojourners may face. It may be that a modest investment in education and coaching may produce substantial gains in potential and actual adjustment. Such gains may help to overcome distressing, and expensive, consequences of poor intercultural adjustment (Kim & Gudykunst, 1988; Matsumoto et al., 2001; Shin & Abell, 1999).

The relationship between actual and potential intercultural adjustment at follow-up may be a sign of the "incubation" of study abroad effects. At follow-up the rebound of the ICAPS score while the SWLS remained high may be an indicator of continued cognitive and affective sorting of study abroad experiences. Reentry into U.S. culture did not depress but rather set the stage for a resurgence in potential intercultural adjustment. Just as exposure to the host culture challenged home culture assumptions, reentry challenged new learning and attitudes gained during the student sojourn. The effects of study abroad sometimes take weeks, months, if not years, to come to fruition. The rebound in potential intercultural adjustment may signal the beginning of that trend for this research sample.

The ICAPS scale (Matsumoto et al., 2001) shows promise not only for explaining concurrent relationships with actual psychological adjustment but also for predicting actual adjustment weeks and months into the future for sojourners who face the task of studying and working in a foreign culture. Prior knowledge of future sojourners' levels of potential for intercultural adjustment might be useful in identifying their risk for failure in a foreign culture, and in designing remedial steps to boost skills and abilities that may encourage better actual adjustment. A focus on aspects of emotional regulation and critical thinking seem to hold substantial promise for enhancing a student's readiness to overcome the unpredictable clashes that are a natural product of contact with a foreign culture.

Finally, the SA group in this study was quite small; therefore, caution is necessary in generalizing the findings of this study. Replication using larger samples is called for.

References

Babiker, I. E., Cox, J. L., & Miller, P. McC. (1980). The measurement of cultural distance and its relationship to medical consultations, symptomatology, and examination of performance of overseas students at Edinburgh University. *Social Psychiatry, 15,* 109–116.

Bacon, S. M. (2002). Learning the rules: Language development and cultural adjustment during study abroad. *Foreign Language Annals, 35,* 637–646.

Bennett, J. M., Bennett, M. J., & Stillings, K. (1977). *Description, interpretation, and evaluation: Facilitators' guidelines.* Retrieved January 7, 2007 from http://www.intercultural.org/resources.html

Berry, J. W. (1997). Immigration, acculturation and adaptation. *Applied Psychology: An International Review, 46,* 5–34.

Carlson, J. S., Burn, B. B., Useem, J., & Yachimowitz, D. (1990). *Study abroad: The experience of American undergraduates.* New York: Greenwood.

Diener, E., Emmons, R. A., Larsen, R. J., & Griffin, S. (1985). The satisfaction with life scale. *Journal of Personality Assessment, 49,* 71–75.

Erwin, T. D., & Coleman, P. K. (1998). The influence of intercultural experiences and second language proficiency on college students' cross-cultural adaptability. *International Education, 28*(1), 5–25.

Furukawa, T., & Shibayama, T. (1994). Factors influencing adjustment of high school students in an international exchange program. *Journal of Nervous and Mental Diseases, 182,* 709–714.

Gudykunst, W. B. (1995). Anxiety/uncertainty management (AUM) theory. In R. L. Wiseman (Ed.), *Intercultural communication theory* (pp. 8–58). Thousand Oaks, CA: Sage.

Hobfoll, S. E. (1989). Conservation of resources: A new attempt at conceptualizing stress. *American Psychologist, 44,* 513–544.

Hobfoll, S. E., & Shirom, A. (2001). Conservation of resources theory: Applications to stress and management in the workplace. In R. T. Golembiewski (Ed.), *Handbook of organizational behavior* (2nd ed., pp. 57–80). New York: Marcel Dekker.

Kim, Y. Y., & Gudykunst, W. (Eds.). (1988). *Cross-cultural adaptation: Current approaches.* Thousand Oaks, CA: Sage.

Lazarus, R. S. (1999). *Stress and emotion: A new synthesis.* New York: Springer.

Lewin, K. (1935). *A dynamic theory of personality.* New York: McGraw-Hill.

Matsumoto, D., LeRoux, J. A., Bernhard, R., & Gray, H. (2004). Unraveling the psychological correlates of intercultural adjustment potential. *International Journal of Intercultural Relations, 28,* 281–309.

Matsumoto, D., LeRoux, J. A., Iwamoto, M., Choi, J. W., Rogers, D., Tatani, H., & Uchida, H. (2003). The robustness of the Intercultural Adjustment Potential Scale (ICAPS): The search for a universal psychological engine of adjustment. *International Journal of Intercultural Relations, 27,* 543.

Matsumoto, D., LeRoux, J. A., Ratzlaff, C., Tatani, H., Uchida, H., Kim, C., & Araki, S. (2001). Development and validation of a measure of intercultural adjustment potential in Japanese sojourners: The Intercultural Adjustment Potential Scale (ICAPS). *International Journal of Intercultural Relations, 25,* 483–510.

Oberg, K. (1960). Culture shock: Adjustment to new culture environments. *Practical Anthropology, 7,* 197–182.

Pedersen, P. (1995). *The five stages of culture shock: Critical incidents around the world.* Westport, CT: Greenwood.

Savicki, V., Downing-Burnette, R., Heller, L., Binder, F., & Suntinger, W. (2004). Contrasts, changes, and correlates in actual and potential intercultural adjustment. *International Journal of Intercultural Relations, 28,* 311–329.

Searle, W., & Ward, C. (1990). The prediction of psychological and sociocultural adjustment during cross-cultural transitions. *International Journal of Intercultural Relations, 14,* 449–464.

Shin, H., & Abell, N. (1999). The homesickness and contentment scale: Developing a culturally sensitive measure of adjustment for Asians. *Research on Social Work Practice, 9,* 45–60.

Ward, C. (2001). The A, B, Cs of acculturation. In D. Matsumoto (Ed.), *Handbook of culture and psychology* (pp. 411–446). New York: Oxford University Press.

Ward, C., & Kennedy, A. (1993). Where's the "culture" in cross-cultural transition? Comparative studies of sojourner adjustment. *Journal of Cross-Cultural Psychology, 24,* 221–249.

8

TUSCAN DREAMS

Study Abroad Student Expectation and Experience in Siena

Anne Chambers and Keith Chambers

P romotion of the study abroad experience has long emphasized transformation, challenge, and growth. "Move on to global citizenship."
"Meet the world on its own terms." "Broaden your horizons." "Sur-
mount new challenges in new places." Urged on by such culturally salient
expectations and advisor support, U.S. students have increasingly come to
see study abroad as a key part of their undergraduate education and career
preparation. To make this vision a reality, they sift through program and site
descriptions to discover the "perfect" site, fill out application forms, submit
to being interviewed and hope for selection, arrange the thousand-and-one
details that make it possible to exchange the routines of daily life for an
almost-unknown life overseas for an academic term or longer.

Students are drawn to study abroad by powerful but ambiguous reso-
nances in which socially appropriate constructions meet (and intertwine

We acknowledge with gratitude the support we received for this sabbatical research project from Southern
Oregon University (International Programs, the School of Social Sciences and the Department of Sociol-
ogy/Anthropology, and the Carpenter Foundation). We are particularly indebted to AHA International,
both its Portland office (especially Bob Selby, then AHA's Executive Director and also Gail Lavin) and
its Siena site staff (including then Site Director Dott. Massimiliana Quartesan, Academic Coordinator
and Associate Site Director Dott. Silvia Minucci, and Housing Coordinator Ms. Claudia Todaro). We
enjoyed the collegiality of Northwest Faculty members in Siena, Lois Bronfman and Ann McClannan,
and benefited especially from Lois' generous sharing of experiences. Finally, we are indebted to the students of winter and spring terms 2004 in Siena, without whom there would have been no project—grazie
tante for sharing your hopes, fears, successes and for your enthusiastic good will!

with) their own personal desires. There are many ways to have an "overseas experience," of course, and studying abroad is just one of them. Electing to go overseas in an all-encompassing study program, together with a fairly similar group of peers, provides a particular kind of learning opportunity, one in which elements of structure and support coexist (sometimes uneasily) with possibilities for discovery and serendipity. The resulting experience is both something of an escorted Hero's Journey and an unpredictable Dance With Fate. Recognizing the complexity and ambiguity inherent in these contrasting orientations provides the essential starting point for our efforts to depict some of the educational outcomes created via study abroad. Hopefully, our assessment will be useful to program administrators and planners seeking ways to better align program content and structure with students' own motivations and goals.

This chapter is an ethnographic case study of student experience in a popular American study abroad program in Siena, Italy. Our focus here is on the goals and motivations that student participants themselves articulate and on assessments they themselves make. Students' commentary on their experiences provides unique insights into the explicit and tacit values that guide their choices, reactions to life in a new cultural setting, and the learning patterns that characterize an eleven-week program. The program side of the equation is a key component at every step of the study abroad process, providing the structure within which student experiences and assessments are framed. Thus, our case study begins with a brief description of the Siena program itself before moving on to analyze student goals and motivations. We conclude with some comments regarding optimal program structure, emphasis, and design, drawing from student reactions that we observed and documented.

Indeed, as students anticipate and discover, and just as advisors promise, immersion in another cultural world can provide a transformative undergraduate experience. As many other studies in this volume document, the "inner disturbance" (Barnett, 1997) of being abroad is likely to catalyze many aspects of personal development and self-realization. Language ability can blossom at a prodigious rate, as can cultural reflexivity and mastery of important life skills. Recent studies confirming improvements in fundamental cognitive abilities, especially critical-thinking and problem-solving skills, through study abroad have increased public awareness that international study experiences are developmentally valuable at the personal level (see

Mitchell, Johnston, Ford, Brumfit, & Myles, 2004; and the Criticality Project at the University of Southampton [Economic and Social Research Council, 2007]). In addition, educators, civic leaders, and government policy advisors have also recognized that study abroad typically increases specific knowledge of the world and develops transferable skills such as cross-cultural agility and language ability.

With increasing globalization, interdependence, and multiculturalism as the unquestioned order of the day (Gacel-Ávila, 2005), students with study abroad experience are increasingly seen as more globally competent employees and citizens, with unique ability to enhance national prosperity and strength. Indeed, the transformative potential of study abroad has itself become a valued commodity in the United States (and in other societies too). For example, according to Van Hoof and Verbeeten (2005) the widely recognized

> payoffs of international education as identified in the literature can be summarized as follows: a) exposure to different social and cultural environments; b) changing of stereotypes that might exist; and c) students become more mature because they live in other cultures and become well-rounded, culturally sensitive adults (p. 44).

However, such wide public enthusiasm for the value of study abroad also creates unique challenges. As Geller (2005, p. 3) notes, study abroad is now in danger of becoming an "instrumental and commodified" interlude, a "check-off item" in the college career of affluent students, "something to buy and consume without . . . savoring."

Within this context, it is not surprising that U.S. student participation rates in study abroad programs have been increasing annually for many years. The Institute of International Education (IIE) provides a comprehensive analysis of trends of dramatically rising participation in study abroad. Despite the shock dealt to the international mobility of students by the attacks of September 11, 2001, in 2002–2003 U.S. outbound study abroad numbers increased 8.5% from the prior year, to 174,629. In fact, outbound study abroad numbers have increased annually for nearly two decades, rising 144% in the 10 years from 1995/1996 to 2004/2005, and 8% from 2003/2004 to 2004/2005 alone (Institute of International Education, 2006, pp. 16–17). International work placements and curricular-related internships are developing apace as well. Clearly, many students are willing to invest dollars, time, and energy in study abroad. But why, exactly? What logic motivates participants? How does a study abroad experience fit with students' personal desires and wider life goals? To what extent do students' own motivations parallel the advantages recognized by educators and employers? What images, values, and assumptions persuade students to leave family and friends at home and submit themselves to the exotic but foreign demands of living and studying overseas? What *is* the student perspective on study abroad?

While a single case study cannot itself provide definitive answers to all these questions, it can suggest some initial possibilities. This report outlines our findings regarding the goals and motivations of 41 American undergraduate students, participants in the spring 2004 program of Northwest Council on Study Abroad (NCSA)/AHA-International (AHA) in Siena, Italy. Since Europe in general, and Italy in particular, is a highly popular study abroad destination for U.S. students, we see our findings as reasonably generalizable, though the effects of specific situations must always be considered. Europe hosted about 60% of U.S. students abroad in 2004/2005, with Italy being the second most popular destination after the United Kingdom. Half of all U.S. study abroad students currently select short-term programs such as this one in Siena (Institute of International Education, 2006, p. 18).

Ethnography in the Siena Study Abroad Program

The central principle in ethnographic work is experiential: the researcher enters into the social system and shares in the lifestyle of its members, as both participant and observer, systematically interpreting the sociocultural system as faithfully as possible. While ethnography (the word refers both to the methodology and to its products) has its roots in anthropological efforts to understand the lives of non-Western peoples, ethnographic methods are now used to elucidate corporate culture, school classrooms and bureaucratic hierarchies, political and monied elites alike—*any* complex social or cultural system where grasping the insider's point of view can yield useful insights. Ideally, ethnographers spend considerable time, ranging from months to years, living with hosts and interacting with them casually and in more structured ways. Systematic and often-quantifiable data is gathered by questionnaires, observations, and interviewing, and is used to augment the core data gathered through sharing the lives of one's informants and having them explain things. There is a lot of "hanging around" in ethnography, but it is *focused* hanging around, driven by the desire to get to the heart of the meanings that motivate "insiders."

In addition to participant-observation—in classes, in the AHA office suites, and on program excursions—data we have drawn on for this paper include the following: DIE ("describe, interpret, explain") papers written by all students for the cross-cultural class taught by a local staff member; application essays (two by each student) explaining background and goals; academic history backgrounds; questionnaires we administered eliciting student assessment of experiences at two midpoints in the program; structured, open-ended interviews conducted with each student toward the end of the program; and informal conversations on an ongoing basis throughout the term with students and with local program staff.

As might be expected, the ethnographic emphasis on the meanings important to (and created by) participants is methodologically very different from standard questionnaire-based research. Different types of information are also produced by each methodology. For example, a web-based questionnaire administered by Van Hoof and Verbeeten (2005) to undergraduate students who had studied abroad through Northern Arizona University in 2001–2003 queried students on their reasons for studying abroad, but responses had to be selected from a preestablished (albeit a "distinctly different") range of reasons. The three most important reasons identified in this study were "It is/was a good opportunity to live in another culture," "It is/ was a good opportunity to travel," and "I liked the country my exchange program was located in" (Van Hoof & Verbeeten, 2005, p. 47). These responses are much more general and less nuanced than responses derivable from an ethnographic study such as the one described here. Furthermore, simple, preselected questionnaire responses cannot be connected with the wider experiences of individual students.

The Siena program, run by AHA International as part of the NCSA study abroad consortium, provided the setting for our ethnographic efforts. With support from AHA we were resident ethnographers at the Siena program from mid-February to late June 2004, a period that spanned the second half of winter term and all of spring term. Subsequent to our 2004 research we team-taught at the Siena program for the spring 2007 term (late March to mid-June). While this experience deepened our connection with and knowledge of the program and brought us into close contact with a new group of 44 lively Northwest undergraduates, it did not substantially change our findings and is not reported here.

When we arrived in Siena in February, 2004, the weather in Tuscany was still cool and rainy, the 15 students in the winter program were well bonded, and their Italian language and other classes were at the midterm point. Accompanied by our 16-year-old son, we settled into the apartment AHA staff had arranged for us just outside Siena's ancient walls, not far from the apartment of the Northwest faculty member teaching during winter quarter. Fortunately, we already knew something of the Siena program and were familiar with its three staff members, since Keith had visited the Siena site several times previously.

We soon became a constant presence in the suite of offices and classrooms that form the focus of the Siena program. We sat in on elective classes, talked with students informally, went on program excursions (some of several days duration), and conducted individual interviews. We assisted the Siena staff where we could and sought insights from them about the program, the students, Italian culture, cultural differences, and students' learning processes. We also gleaned understandings from the Northwest faculty members assigned to teach in Siena those two terms. By the time we returned to the United States in July 2004, we had been active participant-observers at the Siena site for almost five months. We had come to know nearly 60 students, some quite well. We ourselves had studied Italian at the *Università per Stranieri* for 10 rigorous weeks alongside the students, shared many small cups of espresso with them, hosted some to dinner at our apartment, and provided supportive counsel to others. We developed an especially detailed understanding of the experiences of the 41 students in the spring group, having been engaged with that program from the first moments of students' arrival in Siena through their farewell dinner. Experiencing a complete "cycle" of social activity is an ethnographic goal, and we were fortunate to be able to accomplish this.

The Siena program in which we were immersed is one of 19 programs in 14 countries administered by AHA International in Portland (a unit of the University of Oregon) for NCSA, the Northwest Council on Study Abroad, a consortium of mainly public universities in the Pacific Northwest. In the NCSA model, each study abroad site operates from rented facilities that include classrooms, computer facilities, and common rooms, plus space for administrative functions. Local staff, usually natives of the country, include a site director and one or more assistants plus adjunct faculty who can be hired in differing combinations each term. A key feature at most sites is the "Northwest Professor," brought over from a U.S. member university for one quarter to teach one or two site-specific elective courses and to provide student support "from home." Course offerings by local instructors are selected to complement the Northwest faculty's course topics in any given quarter, and students themselves select which (and how many) elective courses to take. The one mandatory course is a cross-cultural communication class, usually taught by a local staff member, whose goal is to enhance students' cultural understanding and provide tools for processing their experience abroad. Programs in non-English-speaking countries also offer language instruction, with contact hours per week varying by site. Siena is the most language intensive of the NCSA programs, with (in 2004) 150 contact hours of Italian language instruction in the program's 11 weeks.

Siena is also one of the oldest NCSA programs and one of the consortium's most popular sites. Applications soar in fall and spring and are capped at about 45 students per term. Most students join the program for one quarter, though a few do continue on for two or three quarters. In study abroad jargon, Siena is an "island program," or perhaps more accurately, an enhanced island program. In a true island program, U.S. students live and learn as a group in classes designed for them, isolated from other local learners. Most of the Siena students live in program-provided apartments with their fellows, creating an English-speaking living environment. However, they enroll for their language classes at the *Università per Stranieri di Siena* (USS), classes that include students of many nationalities other than American. For example, Keith's USS class of 22 included six U.S. students from our program alongside individuals from Japan, Korea, Malaysia, Taiwan, Poland, Slovakia, Ecuador, and Canada. Thus, through their Italian language class, study abroad students gain access to a diverse group of fellow students from around the world. This exposure to USS international students forms a highly important component of our students' cross-cultural experience in Siena.

Students in the Siena program are drawn from the NCSA group of 13 northwestern universities including nearly all the region's public universities and, recently, one private university. In practice, somewhat over half of the students (56% in 2003/2004) tend to come from the two largest universities, the University of Oregon and the University of Washington. Nevertheless, the student groups at the Siena site are broadly regional: 9 of the 13 consortium universities were represented in spring 2004, and 8 in the fall of 2003. Even in the smaller winter cohort, its 15 students were drawn from 7 universities. (Information on AHA International, the NCSA member universities, and their abroad programs can be found on the AHA website, http://ahastudyabroad.org.)

Summary information on the spring 2004 cohort of students is presented in Table 1. In accord with gender distribution patterns typical of national study abroad, a group with more women than men is to be expected. For example, study abroad data compiled by the Institute of International Education shows that students participating in U.S. study abroad programs were 62–66% female over the past 10 years, with only minor variations by year (Institute of International Education, 2006, p. 62). Adkins's (2004) investigation of similar gender imbalances in School for International Training (Brattleboro, Vermont) abroad programs suggests that causal factors are complex, perhaps even including differences in psychological development. Regarding the appeal of Italy in particular, recent popular books and films such as Frances Mayes's (1997) *Under the Tuscan Sun* have exoticized Italy via domestic and romantic themes with which women seem to identify more easily. Stereotypes of Italian masculinity are also more likely (in our view, backed up by students comments) to attract women and repel men. The fact that Italy is a destination that seems to be particularly attractive to women makes gender imbalance even more likely. Nonetheless, the 2004 spring term included an even higher proportion of women (95%) than national data, trends in NCSA programs overall, and even Siena's normal patterns led us to expect.

In other qualities, however, the spring cohort was representative of typical Siena site patterns. Nearly three-quarters of the term's 41 students were juniors or seniors, and all but one were Caucasian. Eighty percent were 20 to 22 years of age, with only one older than 25. Most were from Oregon schools. While the Siena program is run for NCSA, it is open to students from other AHA-run consortia and to out-of-consortium students, and each term usually sees several such students. In our spring group one student was from an Ohio university that participates in the AHA affiliate MCSA, the Midwest Council on Study Abroad. While just over 2 out of 5 (41%) had no prior Italian language study, a significant minority (22%) had completed at least Italian 202 or 203. In terms of personal connection to Italy, 79% of the

TABLE 1
Student Characteristics, Siena Program—Spring 2004 (41 students in group)

Characteristic	Detail	Number	%
Gender	Male	2	5
	Female	39	95
Year at University	Sophomore	12	29
	Junior	21	51
	Senior	8	20
Race/Ethnicity	Caucasian	40	98
	Asian	1	2
Age	17–19	3	7
	20–22	33	80
	23–25	5	12
	26 or above	1	2
State of Sending	Oregon	29	71
University	Washington	10	24
	Alaska	1	2.5
	MCSA	1	2.5
Previous Italian Language	None	17	41
	only 101	6	15
	through 102 or 103	6	15
	only 201	2	5
	through 202 or 203	9	22
	also upper division courses	1	2
Connection to Italy	Family origin	8	20
	Marriage	1	2
	None	32	79
Catholic background	Yes	6	15
	No	35	85
Living Situation	Program students only	28	68
	Program students & others	6	15
	Program students & Italians	2	5
	Homestay	5	12

group reported no connection, but some 21% had Italian heritage or family relationship. Interestingly, almost all those with Italian heritage or connection (7 out of 9, 78%) had studied Italian prior to coming to Siena. Only a handful (15%) of the students were from a Catholic background. While on the program, 68% lived only with fellow program students (rather than sharing accommodation with other local students or with a family), a distribution largely reflective of students' own choices.

Spring quarter students knew our research interests from our first contact with them, and we followed a carefully planned institutional review board process in our interactions. Perhaps because we were part of the program from its start and because we tried to offer whatever encouragement and support we could to individuals, students appeared to genuinely welcome our interest and questions. Many were intrigued that study abroad experience could be the focus for anthropological study.

Student Goals and Perspectives

So, what brought these students to study abroad in Siena? What expectations did they themselves hold, and how were their goals modified as the program unfolded? What lessons does this information about student goals and motivations offer for program content and coordination?

In answering questions like these, it is important to remember that any person's motivations and goals compose a complex, intertwined web. Thus, identifying precise strands requires a somewhat artificial teasing-apart of aspects that naturally fuzz together. Some aspects lend themselves to more conscious specification, others less so. Student intention is also inherently dynamic, both a response to and a shaper of events, evolving and changing through time. For all these reasons, an interpretive approach that pays careful attention to the way students themselves construct meaning is methodologically essential. Student statements, oral or written, are best understood through the holistic and contextual lens that participant observation can provide.

These methodological complexities notwithstanding, clear patterns regarding students' motivations and goals for study abroad emerged from our data. For the spring 2004 students, seven components were most important. Let's look briefly at each of these in turn.

Learn Italian

Learning to speak Italian, that is, "having conversations with Italians in Italian," was stated by most students to be of primary importance. Individual reasons for this varied, as did the amount of effort students actually put toward language learning, but the centrality of this goal was unmistakable. Not only did virtually all students explicitly state that language learning was a prime motivation for coming on the program, but language learning remained an enduring goal through to the program's end. As one woman explained, "If I didn't learn any Italian, I'd just come back with a couple pairs of cool shoes!" In Siena, where 40% of students arrived with no previous language preparation, and where most students chose to live with each other rather than with a host family or in shared accommodation where Italian could be expected to be spoken, this stated commitment to language learning surprised us at first.

Perhaps we shouldn't have been surprised. The Siena program does have a language-intensive orientation that is highly publicized in promotional material, even though no Italian language background is required. Students spent all morning, five days a week, in Italian classes with strict attendance requirements that limited both program excursions and students' independent travel. While students with high language commitment may self-select for the Siena program, it seems likely to us that the hope of connecting with Italians through language is a strong factor motivating student emphasis on "learning Italian." Gradually, however, we began to realize that the stated goal of "learning Italian" was, for many, a cover term for broader relational goals, carrying symbolic meanings that went well beyond mere instrumentality. We will return to this aspect later.

Some students' expectations about language learning were unrealistic and inflated. "My first goal was to be able to speak semi-fluently and hold a conversation in Italian," explained a young woman who had never studied a foreign language before. Achieving this level of language competency would be nearly impossible in any 11-week program, of course, even for an experienced language learner. Most students with these inflated hopes seemed able to scale down their expectations to more realistic proportions fairly quickly. Not doing so could leave a student feeling disappointed, inadequate, or perhaps even traumatized by failure, especially if also hard hit by culture shock. However, for most students the program's own intensity, its frequent group excursions, the development of close roommate friendships, and constant within-program socializing all helped to buffer any disappointment about language learning. But as some students also recognized, deep engagement with program activities and fellow students also inevitably distanced and distracted them from focused language study, making language learning through immersion nearly impossible.

Students who had already studied some Italian had the advantage of being able to anticipate what the language learning process entailed. They could draw on previously developed learning skills and more realistically assess their progress in relation to past experience. For example, a student who had completed an Italian 202 course before arrival said that she had "expected more progress in speaking" than she achieved, but she also recognized that, if she were to take her present skills back to her old Italian class, what once had been hard would be easy for her. Students with previous Italian language background varied just as much in the energy and effort they devoted to "learning Italian" as did less experienced students.

Typically, however, when students spoke of "learning Italian," they seemed to mean more than language ability itself. This phrase appeared to function as a cover term for something deeper and broader: a language-based relationship. The image of "speaking Italian" seemed to involve not so much linguistic performance as meaningful personal connection with Italians. Students' emphasis on engaging with local culture (i.e., learning Italian, experiencing Italian life and culture, and meeting people and making new friends) resonates well with Williams's (2005) finding that *exposure* to other cultures rather than the study abroad experience *per se* was the strongest predictor of increased intercultural communication skills. Siena students showed a remarkably strong desire for the very sorts of personal, relational experiences that are widely recognized as producing "cultural agility" and other attributes valuable in cross-cultural interactions. They accepted that "learning Italian" would necessarily involve attending class, studying, and personal effort, but this work was not the full extent of the process they were envisioning. For example, in explaining how her language learning hopes had been "smashed," one student confided:

> I wasn't accepted into the community. People were not actually rude, they just didn't pull me in. I guess I expected this a little but I thought people would be more receptive when I tried to talk, would be wanting to interact. Everyone has their own life. They don't even notice us. I thought people [that we saw every day] might notice that we had been here for a few months. I do talk with people sometimes but it has not gone to the level I wanted, like to be invited home, be asked regularly to hang out.

While Siena is renowned as a tourist town, local life is largely inaccessible to visitors, focused instead on activities within centuries-old traditional districts (*contrade*) with exclusive, inherited membership. Many students were disappointed to realize that outsiders, whether transient tourist throngs or longer-term committed visitors like themselves, were essentially peripheral to local inhabitants.

When this became apparent, many students resolutely changed their expectations. One student described the logic behind her accommodation this way:

> I just wanted to have acquaintances, not make friends. I didn't really expect Italians to become friends in such a short time. Italian culture is closed that way. You have to be born in a place to be really accepted. So many students come here for three months and are gone again. A "new batch" is always arriving. We're just tourists who stay a little longer. Why should people bother?

Of course, some students *were* successful in finding people who would "bother" in their neighborhoods, in their USS language classes, in bars and other social settings. Italian language skills were often central in these efforts to engage and served to reinforce students' language learning goals.

Experience Italian Life and Culture

Most students also said they had chosen to study abroad specifically to experience a new way of life, "to be in Italy," "to become part of Siena." Highly romanticized stereotypes were often involved. One participant sketched for us the images that drew her to Italy: "Cobblestone streets, arches, green shutters on brick buildings. Everyone so friendly, kissing each other on both cheeks. Pasta every day. Everyone chic and beautiful. Get to see the Vatican, the Colosseum. . . ." Others said they had envisioned "buying clothes and hearing opera," sitting on the piazza eating gelato, hanging out drinking coffee with friends in a cafe, enjoying the parade of passersby on the street. People-watching was mentioned by many. So was eating new food, encountering new customs, being immersed in different life routines, shopping for new things in new places. Learning about Italian art and history was also greatly anticipated.

While students were attracted to Italy as "complicated and fun to look at," many students also expressed experiential hopes for their sojourn abroad. Some explicitly sought to "get beyond just feeling like a tourist" in their new surroundings. Other students saw themselves as engaged in building up a knowledge base that would have practical uses later on, often in relationships with friends and family: "I wanted to learn about Italian art, to really know what I was seeing and to be able to show things to my boyfriend when he comes." Still others envisioned themselves as making an investment, anticipating that their new experiences would make them more attractive in the future to others back home: "People in America want to be original, to stand out from the crowd. Doing this program was a way to do this."

Few students seemed to come to Italy intent on gaining new perspectives regarding American life itself, or explicitly hoping to deconstruct their own ethnocentrisms. However, many students did recognize and value the subtle changes in worldview that they saw occurring through immersion in Italian life. One woman exulted: "I've started living like an Italian in some ways. I saw that when my parents were here. I know the ropes and they didn't." Another student explained: "I was blind before—the way we do things is how they are done. Why don't Italians do it like we do? Now I accept that the Italian way is different."

Meet People and Make New Friends

The "American approach" to friendship typically involves the continual creation of a wide range of "friendly" relationships typically marked by informality and warm personal feeling rather than deep commitment, exclusivity, or significant mutual obligation (Stewart & Bennett, 1991, pp. 100–103). People expect to continuously add to their friendship circle as they go through life. From this perspective, the study abroad experience is expected to offer many opportunities for new relationships. Predictably, "meeting people and making new friends" constituted a clearly articulated goal for most students on the Siena program. There were significant differences, however, in individual students' ideas regarding the appropriate focus for these new friendships and who the "people" they hoped to meet were imagined to be. Three main configurations were apparent, dividing the spring term cohort into three fairly equal-sized groups.

Some students wanted specifically to get to know Italian people, an orientation that did not always yield fully positive results: "I really wanted to meet local people and I'm disappointed in myself that I didn't try harder."

> I wanted to meet Italian people and I assumed they would be local. I thought it would be really important to meet local people, but I haven't really. When you are fearful of speaking Italian, it's hard to meet people.

Many students holding the goal of Italian friendships found that opportunities to really get to know Italians (whether true Sienese or other Italians living in Siena) were limited. Even with an introduction, most relationships seldom moved beyond the level of acquaintanceship. The following comment was echoed by many:

> Meeting locals was important when I came. But then I've thought about it. The women don't want to have anything to do with you since you might steal their men. And the men want everything to do with you, but in the wrong way.

Few students had encountered any actual anti-American responses from the Italians they met, though many had worried in advance about this, given political events occurring at the time. Nor did many develop romantic relationships, though many wished to have them.

A second cluster of students can best be described as simply being open to new relationships, eager to enjoy and develop any friendships that became possible. The following perspective was common among this group:

> I just wanted to make good friends. I assumed these would be with people in our group, or maybe some Italians. Meeting local people wasn't overly important to me. I thought I might become friends with some Italian people who spoke English, but I didn't. It would have been fun to meet some guys and go out more, but I'm not sad that I didn't meet more Italian people.

A third cluster had always looked explicitly to fellow students within the Siena program as the most appropriate source for new relationships. Even with these expectations, the depth of friendship developed with fellow students as the weeks passed surprised many. One student explained: "The fact that you have such a big group that's going through all the same things that you are, it's a huge thing. So you reach out and grab on to them with both hands." Clearly, struggling to adapt to a new place, homesickness, and culture shock all reinforce the importance of within-program friendships. Many students turned to their roommates as a natural support circle:

> I enjoy the people I live with. You're put in a situation together and are expected to be friends. This has worked out well. We generally enjoy the same things, have similar amounts of money, like to travel together.

Key friendships sometimes developed outside roommate circles as well, creating bridges between roommate groups as well as links with local student networks.

Develop Independence Skills and Self-Confidence

Approaches to this goal ran the gamut from a focused process of self-testing to a simple, optimistic hopefulness along the lines of "I heard study abroad changes you as a person. I wanted to see if this is true, if it happens to me." Seeing study abroad as primarily an opportunity for personal transformation was typical, however. What sorts of transformation, exactly? How did students themselves describe the changes they anticipated and experienced? The following six qualities were most often mentioned:

- Ability to cope resiliently with stressful situations ("When I got lost in Milan, I found I could laugh, not have a melt-down")
- Greater maturity ("It would be the end of not being an adult")
- More patience
- Acceptance of what can't be changed, and productively moving on
- Greater self-confidence ("Becoming more sure of myself," "Standing on my own feet," "Defining things for myself")
- Ability to be cheerful in the face of adversity, to stifle complaints

Students appeared firmly to believe that challenges posed by travel and new cultural experiences could call forth character traits that were lying dormant or not yet fully developed. As one student put it, "I wanted to prove to myself that I was strong and that I could make it on my own." Once found and awakened, it was assumed, these traits would become enduring personal resources, widely applicable to other areas of life. Most students could appreciate the value of what this student felt she had achieved: "I've learned I can go to another city without knowing anybody and stand on my own two feet."

By the end of the 11-week program, most students felt that their personal development goals had been reasonably well met through study abroad experiences, sometimes to an extent or in areas they had never anticipated. However, there were dissenters at both ends of the spectrum. For a few, the personal challenges of being abroad had proven disheartening. One told us sadly,

I am a bigger wuss than I had anticipated. It's not me to cry when I'm home, but I cried a lot here and complained. The overall result is that I'm less confident in myself. I worry about what it will be like when I'm back home. I'm afraid I will need therapy after this trip.

And for some students, the group experience inherent in an organized study abroad program had taken the edge off the challenges they anticipated so eagerly. As one of these students explained, "I thought everything would be so hard, that I would become more sure of myself and capable. But it wasn't hard, since we are padded by being with forty American students and everyone speaks English."

Figure Out Who I Am

Students often frame study abroad as an individuating process of separation, especially from parents. As one student put it, "My goal is to become closer to my family by being far away. See how I'm different from them. Knowing this will help me maintain a good relationship with them in the future." The study abroad experience is also viewed as a way to learn about other people, and thus by contrast, to pinpoint one's own distinctive personal qualities. For example, one student said that she had specifically hoped to learn from other people about "how they work . . . what the personal differences are between us." But the most constant theme was the direct intention to better understand one's own character traits, life goals, and needs: "I want to realize who I am, who I want to be. What I want out of life." "I value being here in a more relaxing environment, so I can discover more things about myself than I knew at home."

There's no other way to get this much understanding and to come to know what I need. Now I know I need lots of sleep. Privacy. As life gets more complicated later, then you can be sure to make time for what you need. It will help me to learn my tendencies, like what I tend to do when I'm unhappy.

Do Something Different and Exciting

Because it is *study* abroad, overseas educational programs offer students an approved break from normal academic and work routines, one that family, friends, peers, and advisors generally find it easy to encourage and support. As one student explained, "Family, friends, peers all said you're going to have the best time! They were over-excited for me." In academic circles, as well as in many elite and middle-class families, study abroad is seen as an integral part of the undergraduate experience, a kind of "icing on the cake" of a liberal arts education. One student articulated this approach clearly:

> I didn't want later to regret never being abroad, where I never knew anyone. I'm here for the memories—anything that will make me smile later, instances I can use to make decisions from later on. I'll have a breathe-easy feeling afterwards: I've done this, I can graduate now.

Such emphasis on being in a novel, different setting encouraged students to draw specific contrasts to "normal life" back home. Many seemed to juxtapose the present excitements they so valued in study abroad against the rigors of the lifestyle they saw as looming after graduation. Student comments revealed a widely shared expectation that weighty, adult responsibilities of work and family would crash down once students left university. Thus, study abroad was portrayed as both a temporary respite from (or even a compensation for) future obligations and a last chance for a focused experience of personal autonomy and pleasure. Students said, for example: "I won't be afraid to have a job because I've seen a little of the world before life got too stressful." "I want to have some fun while I'm still young, before I have kids." For some, this sense of impending restriction made it hard to fully believe that the freedom, open-ended exploration, and serendipity hoped for in studying abroad might actually be an achievable reality. Two students admitted somewhat ruefully to managing-down their hopes: "I let myself make expectations but didn't let myself really believe in them." "I try not to think about a trip a lot before I go over. I don't like having expectations not met."

Have a Good Time

Given students' wariness about the future, it is not surprising that study abroad also holds a vacation-like allure. While learning opportunities, credits, and classes *are* genuinely important, students also explicitly value the nonacademic aspects of studying abroad. Sometimes pleasure is the dominant motivation. As these students put it: "I wanted to have a good time— enjoy sunny weather, lay out and relax. Go out a lot. Meet Italians." "I wanted to enjoy myself, not be even thinking of going home." For others, "having a good time" is simply the context within which other goals were expected to be achieved. Nonetheless, this emphasis can turn the *study* aspect of the program into an inconvenient, unpleasant necessity rather than a central purpose in coming to Siena. Course readings and assignments can feel like impediments to more experiential learning opportunities such as being "out on the town," visiting bars, partying with friends, shopping, or personal travel adventures.

A few students explained forthrightly that study abroad had provided them with an escape, an easy quarter: "Get to travel and get credits. That's how I saw it, too. I thought classes would be a breeze. Fridays off, so I can travel on three-day weekends. I didn't think Italian classes would be so intensive." "I had heard that study abroad classes were supposed to be a joke." While some students may see the elements of *study* and *being abroad* as fundamentally at cross-purposes, representing this as an intrinsic opposition oversimplifies the study abroad situation. While overseas, most students *do* engage in study with some degree of genuine interest and desire to learn, but they also have chosen (and paid considerable money) to *be abroad* while studying. Not surprisingly, informal social activities are explicitly valued as learning opportunities.

Learning From the Learners

Students' goals, motivations, and reactions offer useful information for those engaged in the design and implementation of study abroad programs. Here we offer some insights that relate directly to program design and administration.

The "narrative" that we heard students create around their study abroad experience was overwhelmingly personal. Events were typically presented as centrally connected to the student's own identity and were primarily experienced in relation to personally formulated needs, desires, hopes, fears, and objectives. Students appeared to be little interested in larger political and economic issues or much driven to try to understand the sociocultural contours of Italian life in the abstract. Students' highly personalized orientation to being overseas fits with the individualism known to characterize United States culture and the fact that young people must themselves assume responsibility for their own development, typically by investing energy in identity creation and display (Althen, 2003, pp. 5–13). Two implications for program organization, especially the academic structure of programs, follow from this.

First, since students' own approach to knowledge and skill development while abroad tends to be so experiential and relational (rather than abstract and academic), this type of learning situation deserves serious pedagogical attention and assessment. Siena students entered the program wanting to learn through direct interaction with local people and settings: by tasting, seeing, smelling, feeling. Most saw themselves as open to possibilities, willing to take some risks to fully engage. Of course, program structure itself is crucial in providing the security and support that make these explorations and risk taking possible. Second, students' emphasis on projects of personal development and expanded interpersonal connection can easily conflict with a program's own structure and goals. Students can find it difficult to accept, much less value, standardizing experiences when they themselves are so committed to building up identities that must be as unique as possible.

Given these two tendencies, what broader generalizations might be made about study abroad program structure and the needs and expectations of students? Following are six ways that programs can support and enhance the type of student experience that Siena students seemed to value.

Attention to Facilities

Physical facilities, including entry foyer, offices, classrooms, computer room, library, lighting, restrooms, common room, even paint colors—all these are probably more important to students abroad than they are at home. Students spend considerable time at the program site itself, and are in a sense "cooped up together" there. Many are also experiencing stresses that are unprecedented. Small inconveniences tend to be magnified, and students typically spend a lot of time comparing their situation abroad to their situation at home. As a result, even relatively minor inconveniences can become focal points for discontent. Students also appear to have a strong sense of entitlement regarding what they "deserve." Thus, attention to facilities, even to simple things like bright lighting, appealing paint colors, and interior decoration, is likely to pay dividends in student satisfaction.

Calculating Value for Money

In the Siena program, students compared program price versus value received constantly and talked with each other about their assessments. There is an infectious quality to this talk as it spreads within the group. Students compare their own apartment to others: does it have more or less space per person, more or nicer appliances, a more convenient location, and so on? Scarcity of computers or cell phones can become a point of critique representing the program's overall quality. Discontents about amenities, such as the quality or quantity of refreshments on excursions, loom large. A definite "consumer knows best," "customer's always right" orientation is obvious, reinforced by the consumer orientation pervading most aspects of higher education in the United States today.

Making a conscious effort to make program amenities appear generous, with particular attention to things that students themselves value, is a sensible first step. Helping students to understand the care and thought involved in program decisions is equally important, however, as is educating them about the monetary and cultural value of the amenities they receive. Were "strings pulled" to arrange admission to this site? Does this dinner feature a regional specialty? Are the paintings in this church hardly ever seen by the ordinary tourist? Sharing this contextual information with students allows them to be better informed (and more appreciative) consumers. Since students have no way to know the actual economic value of their study abroad experience, programs should be proactive in helping students appreciate the value of the amenities, knowledge, and help they receive.

Relationships Within the Program

As we've seen, students tend to arrive at a study abroad site nurturing hopes for developing relationships, both within the program and within the local setting. Inevitably, for participants in short-term programs, hopes for local relationships can be satisfied only partially at best due to the limited time available. As the original dreams of acceptance into local life fade, program activities continue on unabated. Relationships with staff and fellow students typically take on new allure and become more important. Especially for students at a site for only one term, the program itself typically provides the primary set of social relationships. As Talburt and Stewart (1999) have argued, study abroad "peer groups constitute important sources of identity and cross-cultural understanding for students abroad" (p. 163). In Siena, differences in social class, religion, and ethnicity clearly were an important ingredient in the social "glue" that made program relationships so satisfying.

Primed for cross-cultural encounters with Italians in particular (and Europeans and other "strangers" in general), students seemed able to appreciate any sociocultural differences they encountered. In fact, for students hoping to develop significant cross-cultural relationships, finding evidence of diversity within the program itself seemed to legitimize the important role that within-program friendships came to fill. In their ethnographic study of a 5-week study abroad program in Spain, Talburt and Stewart (1999) found students also grappling with interpersonal issues of privilege, racism, and identity in a deeper, more sensitive way than they probably could have done without the incentive of their shared "outsider status" vis-à-vis local people.

On the down side, however, clique development is an ever-present possibility in bounded programs too. Restrictive social groupings do form, often so quickly that students themselves have little sense of what is happening. As many Siena students realized in retrospect, the existence of cliques reduced the overall quality of their study abroad experiences. Some students told us that they became dissatisfied with the limitations of the group they were "in" but found it hard to break out. Others were self-critical because they had chosen "the easy way" by relating intensively to certain people from home, instead of pursuing their original goal of meeting "new friends," whether from the "world outside" or from within the program. While cliques provide an easy support group, they can be a trap, since once group boundaries are in place, crossing them can be seen as disloyalty rather than simple exploration. Program cliques also run counter to the strong value students *say* that they put on meeting local people. Many students struggled with knowing how reliant to be on relationships within the program itself, including those with faculty and local staff.

Thus, efforts to nurture relationships widely across a program are helpful. Local and Northwest staff might make clique identification a goal and actively subvert their development through program activities. Invitations to coffee, to a home dinner, or for a walk could purposely include students from the different social groupings that are known to exist, offering opportunity for new social combinations. Siena students who felt trapped by limiting relationships especially seemed to appreciate opportunities to mix and match in program activities. An overnight excursion in the third to fifth weeks of the program, for example, can facilitate new friendships if seat partners and roommates are drawn from a wider pool of acquaintances.

Experiential Learning Opportunities

Our conversations repeatedly showed how much students value actual experiences over academic or theoretical components. They want to utilize the site, the city, the surrounding countryside, even the whole of Europe itself, as the primary center for learning. They want to get out, see, sense, and feel the texture of things, though—for many—in a safe and mediated way. This hunger for entry into backstage areas of life can be hard to satisfy in heavily touristed sites like Siena. When local staff share personal experiences and offer examples drawn from their own lives and experiences, student understanding benefits immensely, and they often become more curious about local institutions. Finding ways to help students venture out and providing venues that encourage local staff to share personal anecdotes are both pedagogically sound in the study abroad context, resulting in more positive student experiences and program evaluations alike.

Personal Challenges Rather Than Risks

Students say that they want to be challenged but may nonetheless pull back from challenging experiences. This push-pull dynamic can sometimes be hard to manage effectively, especially when there is a sizable student group to look after. With responsibility for everyone's well-being to consider, program staff find it impractical (and also unwise) to allow students to simply go their own independent way. Some students have been abroad before and are expert travelers. Some are very self-sufficient, while others are timid and easily discomfited, requiring substantial support if their study abroad experience is to fulfill its potential. Distinguishing between these different types of students quickly, in the first weeks of the program, is almost impossible. Not only do individual needs reveal themselves gradually but they are also inherently situational responses to the events, relationships, and experiences that are unfolding day by day.

As a result, program efforts to balance students' needs for personal challenge with their needs for hand-holding must be ongoing, creating a drain on staff energy as well as a dilemma for program design and management. One possible strategy is to put this issue forward to students themselves for discussion, both at the outset and in end-of-term evaluations. Participants may be able to identify situations where challenge and/or support are most important as well as to suggest creative ways to balance these conflicting demands. Simply acknowledging the existence of a dilemma often makes it less a frustration and more of a challenge that everyone can work thoughtfully through. After all, "every challenge is an opportunity."

Support for Personal Growth

With students drawn to study abroad because it enhances independence and self-confidence, it is remarkable that support for these goals has typically been shunted to the margins of program planning. More explicit attention to opportunities for students' personal growth through experiences such as classes, excursions, activities, and staff interactions would be helpful for students. While individuals' overt commitment to personal development naturally varies, all can benefit from reflective exploration of the implicit assumptions and other forms of "cultural baggage" brought with them. In NCSA programs, the cross-cultural communication course provides the starting point for identifying and processing the values and assumptions that color student interpretations of local life. (See section three of this volume, Applications to Enhance Intercultural Growth and Transformation, which provides site-specific examples of how these courses are structured and what they achieve.) Every effort should be made to help students appreciate how "required" program components such as these support their own personal development goals.

Toward a More Experiential Focus in Study Abroad

Perhaps the most striking result of our research is the documentation it provides of a gap between student motivations and program goals. Significantly, this same gap is replicated in American educational institutions generally. Like study abroad programs, higher education emphasizes content-based learning in structured environments, paying only lip service to experiential learning for the personal development of learners themselves. Students themselves tend to do the reverse: they value and seek out learning opportunities directly connected with and relevant to their actual lives. As Rebekah Nathan (2005) documented in her recent ethnography of undergraduate life at a public university, students assess in-class learning as making a much smaller contribution (i.e., 35% on average) to their overall learning in college than do "elective social activities and interpersonal relationships" (p. 101). Similarly, while professors and administrators tend to overestimate the role of academics in student culture, students themselves are more likely to see classes as the "price one has to pay" to participate in the relational learning opportunities that college life provides (Nathan, 2005, pp. 101–103, 140). Parallel disjunctures were evident in Siena students' experience of study abroad.

While it may be tempting to see differences between student and program orientations as evidence of a problem in the way study abroad is envisioned and organized or, alternatively, in the priorities students bring to study abroad, this finger-pointing seems unproductive. Instead, we urge a creative response that could align study abroad with other pedagogical revisions on the cutting edge of contemporary education. For example, could the traditional priorities of study abroad be revised, and some of its traditional structures reinvented, to give more emphasis to experiential learning? Could ways be developed to better connect student and program goals? "Best practice" in liberal arts education increasingly demands the identification and assessment of specified learning outcomes. To what extent is this a part of study abroad programming? If outcome assessment were undertaken systematically, study abroad outcomes could be formulated to include goals that students themselves find relevant. More attention might also be devoted to linking students' drive for personal understanding with public needs for globally competent citizens.

Study abroad curricula are inherently flexible. Because explicit attention to students' personal needs already drives some aspects of program structure, study abroad seems well positioned to engage with the learner-centered educational model increasingly seen as central in the twenty-first century.

References

Adkins, M. K. (2004). *Why are more women studying abroad than men? Investigation of the gender imbalance at SIT study abroad.* Master's thesis in International and Intercultural Management (111 pp). Brattleboro, VT: School for International Training.

Althen, G. (2003). *American ways.* Yarmouth, ME: Intercultural Press.

Barnett, R. (1997). *Higher education: A critical business.* Buckingham, England: The Society for Research Into Higher Education and Open University Press.

Economic and Social Research Council. (2007). *Criticality project.* Retrieved February 27, 2007, from http://www.critical.soton.ac.uk

Gacel-Ávila, J. (2005). The internationalization of higher education: A paradigm for global citizenry. *Journal of Studies in International Education, 9,* 121–136.

Geller, J. (2005, July). *The ethnographic participant/observer in study abroad: Training the eye.* Paper presented at the Global Education Conference, Singapore.

Institute of International Education. (2006). *Open doors 2006: Report on international educational exchange.* New York, N.Y.

Mayes, F. (1997). *Under the Tuscan sun: At home in Italy.* New York: Broadway Books.

Mitchell, R., Johnston, B., Ford, P., Brumfit, C., & Myles, F. (2004, September). The contribution of residence abroad to student critical development. In B.H.M Johnston (Convenor), *The Development of Criticality Among Undergraduates.* Symposium conducted at the British Educational Research Association Conference, Manchester, England.

Nathan, R. (2005). *My freshman year: What a professor learned by becoming a student.* New York: Cornell University Press.

Stewart, E., & Bennett, M. (1991). *American cultural patterns: A cross-cultural perspective.* Yarmouth, ME: Intercultural Press.

Talburt, S., & Stewart, M. W. (1999). What's the subject of study abroad? Race, gender, and "living culture." *The Modern Language Journal, 83,* 163–175.

Van Hoof, H. B., & Verbeeten, M. (2005). Wine is for drinking, water is for washing: Student opinions about international exchange programs. *Journal of Studies in International Education, 9,* 44–61.

Williams, T. (2005). Exploring the impact of study abroad on students' intercultural communication skills: Adaptability and sensitivity. *Journal of Studies in International Education, 9,* 356–371.

9

INTERCULTURAL DEVELOPMENT

Topics and Sequences

Victor Savicki, Ingrid Adams, and Frauke Binder

When people travel from their own home culture to a different culture, they experience variations not only in terms of scenery and societal arrangements but also in terms of daily routines, interpersonal interactions, and expectations. Many differences are based on a divergence in the underlying values and concerns of the home versus the host culture. On a day-to-day basis, events that reveal such differences may pose threats and lead to anxiety, confusion, anger, and depression. Conversely, they may pose challenges whose resolution can lead to feelings of mastery, excitement, appreciation for aspects of the host culture, and a clearer understanding of one's home culture. The exposure and reactions to such events form the foundation of intercultural development. But what types of events are important to such development, and how do sojourners change their perspective about those events as they continue through the adjustment process? The current paper tracks reports of cultural events and topics deemed salient by university student sojourners over their semester of study abroad, in an attempt to discover not only which topics were identified but also the sequence in which the sojourners found those topics salient. Evidence for sequences of topic salience has implications for education and

This study is reproduced with permission as it first appeared in *Frontiers: The Interdisciplinary Journal of Study Abroad*, Volume XV, September 2007.

support of sojourners both prior to departure and during exposure to a new culture. The successful negotiation of the developmental processes in the study abroad experience can have long-lasting effects for students. It is hoped that this research will increase the understanding of how to facilitate such positive development. Before reporting results of the current study, we'll present a brief review of relevant issues.

Intercultural Adjustment

Adjustment to a different culture occurs at several different levels at the same time. Ward (2001) uses the ABC model to focus on the affective, behavioral, and cognitive aspects of acculturation. Affective aspects of intercultural development have been explained using features of the stress and coping literature (Lazarus, 1999). Behavioral aspects have been described using a socio-cultural learning approach based on social skills learning (Argyle, 1969, 1982). Cognitive aspects have been discussed using social identification theories (Phinney, 1990). Although it is difficult to tease these reactions apart as they are happening, the focus of the current study is on socio-cultural aspects, which Ward and Kennedy (1999) defined as "The ability to 'fit in,' to acquire culturally appropriate skills and to negotiate interactive aspects of the host environment" (p. 660).

Socio-Cultural Adjustment

In order to "fit in" and acquire culturally appropriate skills, sojourners must first recognize that much of their existing knowledge and abilities, based on learning in their home culture, will not completely suffice. These skill deficits are brought to light through encounters with the host culture. Some of the required changes are overt (e.g., driving on the "wrong" side of the road), and some are "'hidden' in the sense that the participants are not fully aware of their presence until something goes wrong" (Ward, Bochner, & Furnham, 2001, p. 51). It is the quality of the encounter that demonstrates the salience of underlying cultural assumptions.

What type of encounter is likely to reveal cultural assumptions? Most simply, any encounter may serve as a vehicle for such revelation (e.g., purchasing an item in the store, waiting in line, riding public transportation). However, the number and intensity of such encounters may depend on factors such as the cultural distance between the home and host cultures. If home and host cultures are similar, the differences will be less frequent and less intense than in very dissimilar cultures. Nevertheless, cross-cultural contact can be seen as a major stressful life event, and the buzzing confusion of shock upon entering a different culture is a predictable result (Ward, Bochner, & Furnham, 2001).

Ward and Kennedy (1999), building on the work of others (Furnham & Bochner, 1982; Trower, Bryant, & Argyle, 1978), have identified a list of encounters and issues that may be relevant to socio-cultural adjustment. A brief sample of their 29-item scale includes "Making friends," "Using the transport system," "Going shopping," "Dealing with unsatisfactory service," "Getting used to the local food/finding food you enjoy," "Dealing with people in authority," and "Understanding the locals' worldview" (Ward & Kennedy, 1999, p. 663). Longitudinally, socio-cultural adjustment is most difficult in the earliest stages of transition, but within 4 to 6 months it reaches a plateau. Thus it seems to follow a reasonably predictable learning curve (Ward, 2001; Ward, Bochner, & Furnham, 2001).

In the interests of developing a measurement instrument, Ward and Kennedy (1999) used the sum of responses to their list of topics relevant to intercultural adjustment rather than describing responses to individual topics. This method has merit, but it may conceal the possibility that different topics may gain salience at different points in the intercultural adjustment process. Reports of overall socio-cultural adjustment may obscure differences in underlying developmental processes. In addition, asking sojourners to react to a predetermined list of topics may limit the range of issues identified. Thus, Ward, Bochner, and Furnham comment, in relation to such a methodology in a similar study (Opper, Teichler & Carlson, 1990), "we have no way of knowing if the same types of problems would have been spontaneously generated" (Ward, Bochner, & Furnham, 2001, p. 155). The current study attempts to rectify both the averaging and topic-limiting methodological concerns.

Intercultural Adjustment Development Theories

One hypothesis concerning the development of intercultural adjustment is that adjustment proceeds via the challenges and resolutions of specific between-culture encounters, and that those encounters vary randomly based on the chance contacts that sojourners experience within a specific host culture. In this case, there would be no predictable sequence of topics, since the randomness of encounters would, over time, equalize specific adjustment topics. Given previous measures of topic salience, there is no way to disprove this particular hypothesis.

An alternative hypothesis is that the salience of intercultural adjustment topics may vary depending on the stage of adjustment that the sojourner is experiencing. That is, the perception of salience of topics may be related to a predictable process of adjustment, in that "readiness" to identify and label an event as a difficulty may be connected to the particular phase of development of the individual sojourner. It is this hypothesis to which the current study subscribes. Prior to hypothesis testing, however, we will examine three theories of intercultural adjustment that may be informative.

Several theories of intercultural adjustment have been proposed. For the purposes of the current research, we will discuss briefly the classic culture shock theory (Oberg, 1960), the anxiety/uncertainty management theory (Gudykunst, 1995), and the culture-learning approach (Ward, 2001).

Culture shock

The classic description of culture shock follows three phases (Oberg, 1960). In the first phase, sojourners experience "entry euphoria" during which their enthusiasm and fascination with the host culture overshadow the day-to-day difficulties they encounter. In the course of the second "crisis" phase, encounters that reveal clashing values between home and host cultures lead sojourners to experience feelings such as inadequacy, anxiety, frustration, and anger. This is when the "shock" in culture shock becomes predominant. In the third phase, "recovery," sojourners begin to resolve some of the cultural clashes and to learn skills and knowledge to help them navigate successfully in the host culture. Given the spike in the level of discomfort and distress during the second phase, it is likely that sojourners would report more troubling encounters during the second phase than during the first and third phases. During both the "entry euphoria" and the "recovery" stages various culture clashes would be less salient, since in the first phase the sojourner would ignore or shrug off the conflicts, and in the last phase he or she would find such conflicts less arousing. The question remains, Which topics would sojourners perceive as following the inverted-U form of the culture shock development sequence?

Anxiety/uncertainty management

The personal adjustment version of the anxiety/uncertainty management developmental theory focuses on the reactions of sojourners entering new cultures and interacting with host nationals (Gudykunst, 2002). In the initial stages of cross-cultural contact, sojourners are uncertain about host nationals' feelings, attitudes, and behaviors, thus attempts to predict how best to react are fraught with anxiety. If this anxiety does not diminish, sojourners are unable to communicate effectively and are more likely to process information in simplistic, ethnocentric ways, thus perpetuating the anxiety. Alternatively, if sojourners can be open to new information and creatively develop new ways of thinking that take into account the perspectives of host nationals, then the probability of successful communication increases and anxiety is reduced. Over repeated, successful encounters, sojourners continue to reduce their anxiety. Thus the salience of cultural clashes is driven by the level of uncertainty. More clashes would be reported early when uncertainty is high, and fewer clashes would be reported later when uncertainty is lower. The question remains, Which topics create the most uncertainty in sojourners, and which topics are likely to decrease in intensity of anxiety as experience with the host culture continues over time?

Cultural learning

The basic change dimension of the cultural learning developmental approach is the learning curve. Based on social and experimental psychology, the assumption is that sojourners have difficulties in intercultural adjustment because they lack "culture-specific skills that are required to negotiate the new cultural milieu" (Ward, 2001, p. 413). Early in their exposure, sojourners are likely to display skill deficits related to the host culture and to respond to discriminative stimuli in the host culture by overgeneralizing responses that would be appropriate in their culture of origin. As learning proceeds through exposure to the host culture, skills increase, and competence in the culture grows. From this developmental point of view, salience of topics increase over time as sojourners developed the knowledge and skills to notice and respond to cultural clashes. As their repertoire of skills and knowledge increases, so would the number of new situations into which they would place themselves. The question remains, Which topics would sojourners identify as increasing over time as their skill repertoire expands?

A comparison of the three developmental theories of intercultural adjustment suggests that, if topic salience does follow a sequence, the three theories predict different patterns. The culture shock pattern would show a peak of salience of topics during the middle of a sojourn, both preceded and followed by lower salience. The anxiety/uncertainty management theory would predict a pattern of high initial salience of topics followed by steady decrease as anxiety is resolved. The cultural learning approach would predict a pattern of low initial salience based on lack of culture specific skills, followed by a steady increase in salience as skills lead to greater exposure to various aspects of the culture. The mechanisms by which an event would become salient are different in the three theories. The literature does not indicate the dominance of one pattern over another. Our hypothesis remains that there will be a sequence of topic salience over the sojourn in the host culture.

Methods

Participants

Participants were 72 U.S. university students studying for 3 months to study in a major European city. They were of traditional student ages, between 19 and 25. Men composed 53% of the sample and women 47% . The students came primarily from the U.S. Midwest and Pacific Northwest. Most (60%) did not speak the language of the host culture upon first arriving. A class appropriate to their level of language proficiency in the language of the host culture was required for all students. All classes in which they enrolled were taught in English with only fellow U.S. students. Students lived with host culture nationals in a typical homestay arrangement. The sample included students from four different semesters spanning a 2-year period.

Materials

Students in a required intercultural communication class were assigned to write a report on a salient cultural issue 9 or 10 different times during their 3-month sojourn. The identification of such issues was entirely chosen by the student; no lists or categories of issues were proposed to choose from. The reports were to be spontaneous and contemporaneous rather than retrospective. The issues gained salience to the students only with regard to their own experiences and perceptions; thus, they conformed to the definition of "critical incident" as "an event that matters" (Ward, Bochner, & Furnham, 2001, p. 5). Students were to write about this issue following the description, interpretation, evaluation (DIE) format, in which their report first indicated the description of the event in objective terms, then an interpretation of the event that focused on identifying underlying aspects or values of the host culture that could be at play in causing the specific event, and finally an evaluation including why, from their own viewpoint, the event occurred and how they felt about it (Bennett, Bennett, & Stillings, 1977). In all, over the four different semesters 491 DIE reports were submitted. Subsequent analyses were conducted using the DIEs as the source of information.

Procedures

The construction of the topic coding system and subsequent coding of DIEs was a multistep process following principles of qualitative research (Liamputtong & Ezzy, 2005). First, an initial team of researchers read the DIEs for significant statements (Moustakas, 1994) that identified salient cultural issues. A total of 165 relevant meanings were identified. Second, these meanings were clustered into 23 different nominal categories on the basis of the nature and focus of the students' experience (Moustakas, 1994). These categories were designed to be comprehensive and mutually exclusive based on overlap of topic themes, discrimination between themes, and similarity of themes to those previously found in the literature (Creswell, 1998). Third, a three-person panel of judges then classified each DIE report into one of the 23 nominal categories. Inter-rater agreement for classification was 75%. Disagreements in coding were resolved through discussion. The categories identified are the following:

1. *Assertion:* The ability and ease with which participants were able to make their needs and desires known to people in the host culture.
2. *Cross-Cultural Comparisons:* A comparison of U.S. and host culture values and behaviors as compared with other European cultures that the participants encountered during their travels.
3. *Cultural Bias:* Bias of the host culture, usually against the U.S. culture; anti-Americanism.
4. *Cultural Rule:* General differences in overall values of the host culture with the home culture; especially with regard to overt public interactions with strangers.

5. *Communication:* Usually the lack of accurate understanding communicated between participants and members of the host culture, often based on differing communication styles.

6. *Food:* Differences in food preferences, presentation, and availability between the host culture and the home culture.

7. *General Environment:* Differences with regard to environmental concerns (e.g., recycling), features of architecture, and civic actions with regard to environmental issues.

8. *Homestay Environmental:* Concerns about the physical environmental conditions in the homestay setting.

9. *Homestay Social:* Concerns about the interpersonal interaction occurring while in the homestay setting.

10. *Hygiene:* Differences in levels of cleanliness and concern for habits of personal hygiene.

11. *Intrapersonal:* Reflection on personal affective, cognitive, and existential reactions with regard to the intercultural adjustment process.

12. *Transportation:* Issues concerning public transportation, differing requirements for walking, and differences in expectations concerning personal travel.

13. *Language:* Concerns with the use of the host culture language and feelings of inadequacy concerning use of a foreign language.

14. *Public Displays of Affection:* Differing expectations for romantic and sex-related behavior in public settings.

15. *Privacy:* Differing expectations concerning what types of behavior and events should be shared versus held private, and mechanisms by which privacy is maintained.

16. *Public Interactions:* Differing expectations about where specific social events were most likely to take place, and the frequency of unexpected public behaviors.

17. *Public Meeting Places:* Different expectations concerning the availability and use of public spaces.

18. *Smoking and Drinking (Health):* The prevalence of smoking and the differing expectations and laws regarding drinking of alcoholic beverages; health concerns.

19. *Social Contact:* Contact with others from the host culture, not related to the academic or homestay environments.

20. *Social Conversation Preference:* Differences in the intensity of conversations concerning politics and other "sensitive" subjects.

21. *Social Preferences:* Differences in acceptable general behavior of daily living such as shopping, advertising, expectations concerning appropriate dress, etc.

22. *Social Rules:* Differences in expectations of the "rules" of social interaction such as eye contact and personal space; especially differences in what was socially appropriate versus inappropriate.

23. *Social Value of Time:* Differences in the pace of events and in the value placed on informal, non-work-related activities.

The reports were then organized by the date upon which they were submitted. For the analyses described in this study, reports were deemed to fall into three different time periods: Early (participants' first three DIEs), Middle (participants' second three DIEs), and Late (the last three or four DIEs).

Results and Discussion

Overall Distribution of Intercultural Adjustment Categories

When looking simply at the percentage of each intercultural adjustment category reported (Figure 1), it is clear that, overall, some categories were much more salient to participants than others. For example, Social Preferences, Social Rules, and Public Interactions all were reported 8% or more times overall, while Assertion, Food, Intrapersonal, and Public Displays of Affection were all reported less than 2% of the time overall. These differences were significant (X^2 [550] = 655.28, $p < .001$). The most reported categories contain events that coincide quite closely with those reported by others (Spradley & Phillips, 1972; Ward & Kennedy, 1999). Sojourner attention to various categories related to intercultural adjustment was not randomly distributed. There were no significant differences in percentages reported by men versus women.

Distribution of Intercultural Adjustment Categories Over Time

In order to simplify discussion of the changes in intercultural adjustment categories over time, three different analyses will be presented depending on the manner in which the changes occurred. In each analysis the 3-month

FIGURE 1
Percentage of reports of intercultural adjustment categories.

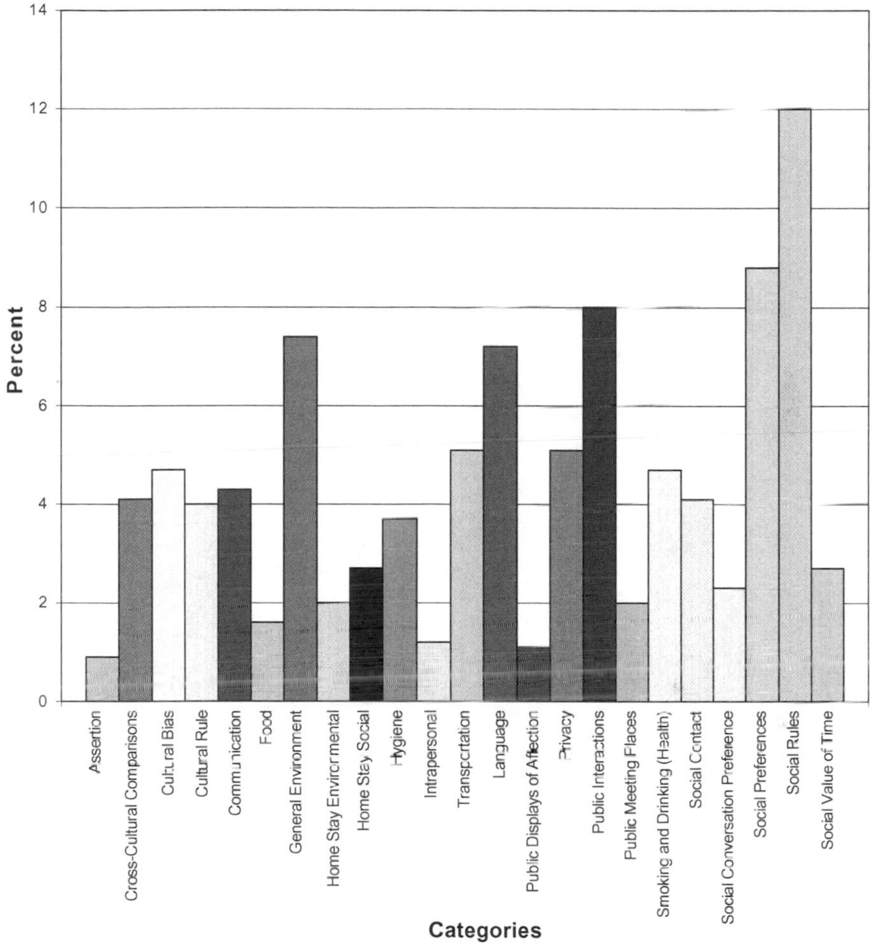

sojourn was broken into three time periods: Early, Middle, and Late. Discussion will be limited to those categories that showed substantial salience to the study abroad students (i.e., the number of reports equaled or exceeded 6% for at least one time period).

Categories that decreased over time

Figure 2 indicates those categories in which there was a decrease of reports from Early to Late in the sojourn. For Communication (X^2 [2] = 15.93, $p <$

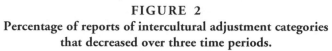

FIGURE 2

**Percentage of reports of intercultural adjustment categories
that decreased over three time periods.**

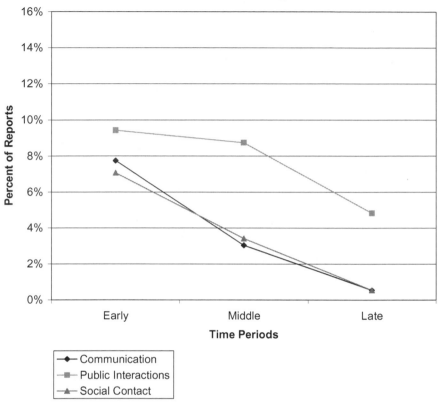

.001) and Social Contact (X^2 [2] = 12.74, $p < $ .01) the differences over the three time periods reached statistical significance, but not for Public Interactions. The trend with these categories was for the salience to be much higher early in the sojourn and lower late. For Communication many of the early experiences of students focused on understanding others in the host culture and making themselves understood. Independent of specifically mentioned language issues, the concern about communication and miscommunication focused both on interpersonal communication patterns and on expectations about how communication was to occur. Throughout their stay, the students continued to learn these patterns and expectations, so that by the end, not only were they communicating better but also misunderstandings were not so mysterious and shocking. For Social Contact the decrease from Early to Late probably reflects the newness and difference of the host culture at the beginning of the sojourn and the familiarity at the end. As cultural differences became more recognizable and as students developed an understanding of how to react, incidents of shocking contact with people in the culture most likely faded into the background.

For Public Interactions a similar familiarity most likely accounted for the drop in reports from Early to Late. Some of the Early concerns focused on urban phenomena such as dealing with panhandlers. Not only did the students become more adept at handling these incidents over time, but also their attitude and bearing probably changed enough so that they no longer stood out as foreigners and therefore became less of a target for such interactions. These three categories that decreased over the three time periods illustrate that the relevance of intercultural adjustment issues can decrease over time consistent with the anxiety/uncertainty management theory of development. That is, students who initially generated quite a bit of anxiety while dealing with the different/strange aspects of the host culture learned over time to manage the uncertainty inherent in living in a different culture. They were able to decrease the attendant anxiety through developing routines to cope with recurring cultural issues.

Categories that changed trajectory

Figure 3 indicates those categories in which there was a change in trajectory of reports across Early to Middle to Late in the sojourn. These four categories include Language, Privacy, Health, and Social Rules. No changes in these categories reached statistical significance. First, Language showed a dip in the middle time period preceded and followed by a higher percentage of reports. The most likely scenario for this pattern was that students were very concerned about their lack of fluency in the host culture language early in the sojourn, but then by the middle of their stay learned enough of the language to have satisfactory interchanges in public settings with strangers such as store clerks, bus drivers, etc. However, later they discovered that deeper conversations with acquaintances who were not facile with English left them again feeling challenged by their lack of fluency in the host culture language.

The other three categories that changed trajectory did so in a similar pattern, in which lower Early and Late reports bracketed a higher percentage of reports in the Middle time period. For both Privacy and Health (Smoking

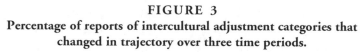

FIGURE 3
**Percentage of reports of intercultural adjustment categories that
changed in trajectory over three time periods.**

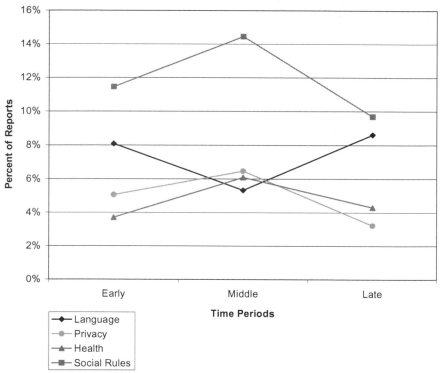

and Drinking) it is likely that initially students were not as aware of the
degree of difference between their home culture and the host culture on
these issues because they were preoccupied by other cultural differences.
When more pressing adjustment demands waned, these two concerns became more relevant. Then by the end of the sojourn students had adapted
to these cultural issues as well; therefore, the percentage of reports fell.

The Social Rules category was the most salient of all 23 categories during
the first two time periods. Early in their sojourn students noticed social *faux
pas* and were troubled by them. However, as they adjusted to other aspects of
the host culture, they began to put themselves into more new and different
situations for which they had not learned the rules of behavior for the host

culture. This increase in reports in the Middle time period probably represented the level of struggle they had concerning cultural differences surrounding simple, everyday interchanges that were habitual in their home culture but required focus and heightened awareness in the host culture. The drop in percentage of reports in the Late time period probably indicates some success at mastering the host culture rules of behavior, though the number of reports remained high in comparison to all other categories. With the exception of the Language category, the other categories that changed trajectory over the three time periods showed a pattern consistent with the developmental theory of culture shock. In this theory, as in the anxiety/uncertainty management theory, the driving force for salience is emotional arousal. Early enthusiasm and naiveté, were followed by some anxiety, irritation, and bewilderment at cultural differences, to be then followed by the resolution of many of those reactions as the cultural patterns became more familiar and understandable.

Categories that increased over time

Figure 4 indicates those categories in which there was an increase in percentage of reports from Early to Late in the sojourn. For Cross-Cultural Comparisons (X^2 [2] = 15.18, p < .001) and General Environment (X^2 [2] = 18.67, p < .001) the differences over the three time periods reached statistical significance, but not for Social Preferences. The general trend with these categories was for the salience for participants to be much higher later in their sojourn and lower early. For Cross-Cultural Comparisons, this difference probably stemmed from the individual travel activities of the students. Early in the semester they remained close to their host city, but later they traveled to other European countries so that they were faced with comparisons between their home culture, their main host culture, and the cultures to which they were exposed on their travels. Differences in General Environment may have become more salient as the students became more aware of features of their host culture that dealt with conservation and other environmental concerns. These may have become relevant only after some adjustment to the host culture had taken place. Social Preferences probably increased over time as students immersed themselves in the routines of daily living and exposed themselves to a broader range of situations and activities in which such preferences could be discovered. Once having mastered some of the simple

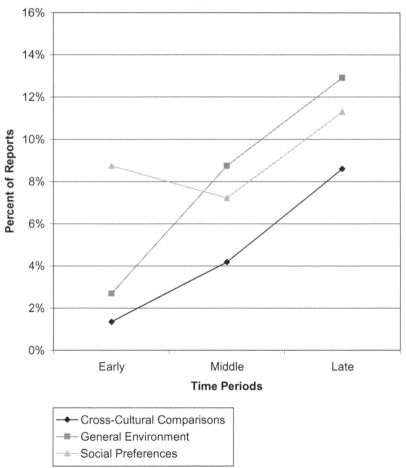

FIGURE 4

Percentage of reports of intercultural adjustment categories that increased over three time periods.

patterns of behavior, they could delve more deeply into those about which they were initially unaware.

These three categories that increased over the three time periods illustrate that the relevance of intercultural adjustment issues can increase over time consistent with the culture-learning theory of adjustment. That is, students continued to learn about various aspects of their host culture, and some of that learning was related to opportunities that unfolded during the sojourn. Topics that were not particularly salient at the beginning gained relevance as the students passed through stages of immersion into the host culture and were exposed to a wider range of issues.

Conclusions

In summary, the relevance of specific categories of intercultural adjustment issues was not randomly distributed, nor did the categories occur with equal frequency over the length of the sojourn. The patterns of change in reports of categories over time suggest that participants found some categories more relevant at different times. In addition, the fact that three different patterns of change appeared seems to indicate that several different phenomena might have caused the patterns.

One likely candidate as a causal factor underlying differing patterns of reports is the developmental stage or process involved in participants adjusting to a foreign culture. Results of the current study seem to support the notion that more than one theory of development may be operating at the same time. Three different theories might predict three different patterns of change in the relevance of topics. So, one possibility is that the theories of intercultural adjustment are not mutually exclusive, but rather, different categories of issues are more explainable using one theory than another.

For example, with regard to Social Rules, the culture shock hypothesis might have more influence, since early ignorance of issues was followed by heightened concern over those issues, followed by mastery and decrease in relevance. On the other hand, attention to issues in the General Environment might be more amenable to the social-learning theory, in which people undergoing intercultural adjustment might become more attentive over time to specific issues as they develop skills and knowledge making them more competent to navigate the host culture. What was hidden or difficult to understand in the beginning becomes more understandable and central to comprehending the host culture as time goes by. Finally, concerns about Communication might fit better with the anxiety/uncertainty management theory, in that the relevance of this issue decreased steadily over time as the difficulties were understood and mastered. Rather than postulate that one theory fits all intercultural adjustment issues, it might be more accurate to assign specific issues to specific theories of development. It may be more useful to begin to hone in on the possible relationships between types of concerns and types of developmental processes.

Averaging the three different patterns (increasing, decreasing, and inverted-U shaped) yielded results consistent with Ward and Kennedy's (1999) findings that early phases of exposure to a different culture placed intense demands on sojourners, who began to adjust so that later the level of stress diminished. High early and middle-sojourn demands were followed by late-in-the-sojourn expanded exploration and appreciation of the host culture. To be sure, sojourners would continue to encounter culture clashes as they exposed themselves with ever-increasing intensity to the host culture, but after the initial adjustment process, such misunderstandings might not be as shocking and mysterious and therefore would be perceived with less anxiety. Breaking apart the average response revealed the multiple patterns that had been masked by averaging. An area for further empirical study is the notion that successful reduction of stressors in the early stages set the stage for later freedom and motivation to explore the host culture in more depth.

Implications for student advisors, study abroad educators, and personnel in study abroad locations have several emphases. First, predeparture and early on-site orientations might emphasize some topics and touch lightly on others. For example, rules of social interaction and communication outweigh food preferences and discussions of perceptions of time. There is some predictability about when and how intensely various topics will arise. Given that such orientation activities are likely to suffer time constraints, some guidance concerning prioritizing topics may be useful. Second, just the notion that change in perception and level of arousal will occur in an approximate developmental sequence may be informative. Students who can anticipate such changes may be able to tolerate the negative emotions that may accompany early stages with the realization that they will move beyond such responses. Likewise, study abroad educators and coaches may be able to sequence their courses and assistance to anticipate the emergence of topics. Finally, all developmental theories of intercultural adjustment agree that early successes in adjustment are necessary to move students toward later, overall success of their study abroad placement. Anticipating when and where to intervene with individual students may increase the probability not only that early developmental movement occurs but also that later delays or plateaus can be addressed.

Although the current study addresses some of the methodological concerns raised in previous considerations of topics of intercultural adjustment for sojourners, these findings need replication. Clearly, the categories used in this research were culture specific, and linked to the stressors generated by academic demands and the structure of living arrangements. Different arrangements may yield a different set of categories. Yet, the finding that sojourners evaluated the salience of topics differently across time suggests that predeparture training and during-sojourn coaching and support can be more precisely focused to address concerns as they evolve, thus leading to a more efficient and effective transition of sojourners into their host culture.

References

Argyle, M. (1969). *Social interaction*. London: Methuen.

Argyle, M. (1982). Intercultural communication. In S. Bochner (Ed.), *Cultures in contact: Studies in cross-cultural interaction* (pp. 61–80). Oxford: Pergamon.

Bennett, J. M., Bennett, M. J., & Stillings, K. (1977). *Description, interpretation, and evaluation: Facilitators' guidelines*. Retrieved January 20, 2007 from http://www.intercultural.org/resources.html

Creswell, J. W. (1998). *Qualitative inquiry and research design*. Thousand Oaks, CA: Sage.

Furnham, A., & Bochner, S. (1982). Social difficulty in a foreign culture: An empirical analysis of cultural shock. In S. Bochner (Ed.), *Cultures in contact: Studies in cross-cultural interaction* (pp. 161–198). Oxford: Pergamon.

Gudykunst, W. B. (1995). Anxiety/uncertainty management (AUM) theory. In R. L. Wiseman (Ed.), *Intercultural communication theory* (pp. 8–58). Thousand Oaks CA: Sage.

Gudykunst, W. B. (2002). Intercultural communication theories. In W. B. Gudykunst & B. Mody (Eds.), *Handbook of international and intercultural communication* (2nd ed., pp. 183–205). Thousand Oaks, CA: Sage.

Lazarus, R. S. (1999). *Stress and emotion*. New York: Springer.

Liamputtong, P., & Ezzy, D. (2005). *Qualitative research methods* (2nd ed.). London: Oxford University Press.

Moustakas, C. (1994). *Phenomenological research methods*. Thousand Oaks, CA: Sage.

Oberg, K. (1960). Cultural shock: Adjustment to new cultural environments. *Practical Anthropology, 7*, 177–182.

Opper, S., Teichler, U., & Carlson, J. (1990). *Impacts of study abroad programmes on students and graduates*. London: Jessica Kingsley.

Phinney, J. S. (1990). Ethnic identity in adolescents and adults: Review of research. *Psychological Bulletin, 108*, 499–514.

Spradley, J. P., & Phillips, M. (1972). Culture and stress: A quantitative analysis. *American Anthropologist, 74*, 518–529.

Trower, P., Bryant, B., & Argyle, M. (1978). *Social skills and mental health.* London: Methuen.

Ward, C. (2001). The A, B, Cs of acculturation. In D. Matsumoto (Ed.), *The handbook of culture and psychology* (pp. 411–445). Oxford: Oxford University Press.

Ward, C., Bochner, S., & Furnham, A. (2001). *The psychology of culture shock* (2nd ed.). London: Routledge.

Ward, C., & Kennedy, A. (1999). The measurement of sociocultural adaptation. *International Journal of Intercultural Relations, 23*, 659–677.

10

ACCULTURATIVE STRESS, APPRAISAL, COPING, AND INTERCULTURAL ADJUSTMENT

Victor Savicki, Eric Cooley, and Rosemary Donnelly

Exposure to a foreign culture presses sojourners to adjust on many different levels to the strange, exciting, exasperating, and sometimes threatening encounters embedded in everyday living. Even short sojourns during a study abroad experience can expose students to "acculturative stress" (Berry, 2005) because of contact with a perplexing and multifaceted array of foreign values, attitudes, behaviors, and environmental conditions. Ward and Kennedy (1993b) generally divide intercultural adjustment to these stressors into two levels: psychological adjustment and socio-cultural adjustment: "Psychological adjustment, then, is interwoven with stress and coping processes, whereas sociocultural adaptation is predicated on culture learning" (Ward & Kennedy, 1993a, p. 222). The linkage between psychological adjustment and appraisal and coping has been well documented (Lazarus, 1999); however, the relationship of appraisal and coping to socio-cultural adjustment is less well researched (Ward & Kennedy, 2001). The current study examines both psychological and socio-cultural adjustment within the context of another conceptualization concerning intercultural adjustment: acculturation. Acculturation strategies (Berry, 2005) have implications for intercultural adjustment of study abroad students, especially within the context of the interaction between the students' home and host cultures. It may be that such strategies can more easily understood by using stress appraisal and coping concepts.

Psychological Intercultural Adjustment

Various authors have offered theories concerning intercultural adjustment. For example, Kim (2005) focuses on communication acculturation; Gudykunst (1998) focuses on anxiety and uncertainty management; McGuire and McDermott (1988) focus on assimilation, deviance, and alienation states; Tajfel (1978) focuses on social identity; and Trower, Bryant, and Argyle (1978) focus on cultural learning. Following the general suggestion of Ward and Kennedy (1993a), the current study uses the general stress and coping model offered by Lazarus (1999) as a framework for conceptualizing the psychological intercultural adjustment process.

Ward (2001) characterizes the stress and coping theory view of intercultural adjustment as emerging from "cross-cultural transitions entailing a series of stress provoking life changes that tax adjustive resources and require coping responses" (p. 427). In this model cognitive appraisal is an intermediate step between the stressors presented by the foreign culture and the psychological well-being of the individual. The presence of environmental stressors that are perceived as dangerous, accompanied by a perception of inadequate personal and environmental resources to deal with these stressors, leads to the experience of threat or loss with its attendant negative psychological and physiological outcomes. On the other hand, adequate resources and coping abilities lead to the experience of challenge and positive outcomes of self-efficacy, mastery, and other indicators of well-being. Much of the adjustment literature has been focused on problematic responses to intercultural stress in which the appraisal process resulted in a perception of threat: for example, culture shock (Pedersen, 1995); emotional distress (Furukawa & Shibayama, 1994); anxiety, depression, difficult interpersonal relations (Matsumoto et al., 2001); and depression (Ward & Kennedy, 2001). On the other hand, intercultural adjustment can lead to more positive outcomes based on the appraisal of challenge, such as gains in self-esteem and personal awareness (Babiker, Cox, & Miller, 1980) and increases in self-confidence and positive mood (Matsumoto et al., 2001). Psychological intercultural adjustment does not stand alone but rather is proposed to have relationships with both socio-cultural adjustment and acculturation (Berry, 2005).

Socio-Cultural Adjustment

The attainment of knowledge and skills to manage the tasks of daily life in a foreign culture mark adjustment at the socio-cultural level (Ward, 1996). The proposed theoretical basis for socio-cultural adjustment is learning theory (Ward & Kennedy, 1999). The decrease in difficulty in dealing with daily encounters with the host culture follows a learning curve, which changes slowly at first then accelerates as one new piece of knowledge or skill builds upon others until finally reaching a relatively asymptotic level. Factors influencing the course of socio-cultural adjustment may include "length of residence in the new culture, cultural knowledge, amount of interaction and identification with host nationals, cultural distance, language fluency, and acculturation strategies" (Ward & Kennedy, 1999, p. 661). Acculturation strategies may be related to appraisal and coping strategies, although little research speaks to this issue (Ward & Kennedy, 2001). In most situations, socio-cultural adjustment and psychological adjustment are modestly related and change most rapidly early on in a sojourn in a foreign culture.

Acculturation

Berry (2005) has developed a model for acculturation that subsumes both psychological and socio-cultural adjustment: "Acculturation is the process of cultural and psychological change that takes place as a result of contact between cultural groups and their individual members" (p. 291). Adjustment and coping with acculturation stress in this model depends on four acculturation strategies that are expressed both at the individual and at the cultural level. At the individual level the *Integration* strategy identifies strongly with both the home and host culture; in contrast, the *Marginalization* strategy shows weak identification with both cultures. The *Assimilation* strategy shows strong identification with the host culture and weak identification with the home culture, while the *Separation* strategy shows weak identification with the host culture and strong identification with the home culture. According to the theory, these four strategies yield differing results for intercultural adjustment. For example, Berry (2005) states that individuals following the Integration strategy are more likely to be better adapted and those following the Marginalization strategy to be least well adapted. Appraisal and coping concepts may be able to make more concrete and explicit the cognitive, affective, and behavioral responses of sojourners who employ the four strategies.

Appraisal and Coping

The concepts of cognitive appraisal (how one perceives stressors) and coping (what one does to deal with stressors) have strong research support in the psychological literature (Carver, Scheier, & Weintraub, 1989; Ferguson, Matthews, & Cox, 1999). Some literature addresses how functional and dysfunctional coping strategies specifically relate to psychological adjustment in the face of acculturative stress (Ward & Kennedy, 2001). However, the relation of appraisal and coping to socio-cultural stress remains unexamined. This study fills that void.

Previous research and theory suggests the following hypotheses (Berry, 1997, 2005; Ward, Bochner, & Furnham, 2001; Ward & Kennedy, 1993b, 1994, 2001; Ward & Rana-Deuba, 1999):

1. Students studying abroad will show lower psychological adjustment.
2. Students remaining at home will show greater home culture identification.
3. Higher identification with the home culture will be associated with better psychological adjustment.
4. Higher identification with the host culture will be associated with better socio-cultural adjustment.
5. Psychological and socio-cultural adjustment will be correlated.
6. Appraisal and coping strategies will be related to both psychological and socio-cultural adjustment.

Method

Participants

A group of 26 students from U.S. universities who studied abroad in Greece for 3 months (SA) were matched with 37 students who stayed in the U.S. during the same semester (Home). The Home students were enrolled in a social psychology class that dealt in a didactic manner with some of the same concepts that the SA students were actually experiencing by virtue of their study abroad placement, such as stereotyping, in-group/out-group labeling, individualism–collectivism, etc. The groups were matched for age (19 to 23), gender (75% women), and class standing (85% juniors and seniors).

Measures

Satisfaction With Life Scale (SWLS)

The SWLS is a five-item questionnaire using a 7-point Likert scale to rate overall satisfaction with life using questions such as, "In most ways my life is close to my ideal" (Diener, Emmons, Larsen, & Griffin, 1985). The SWLS can be viewed as a measure of psychological adjustment, since the scale demonstrated moderately strong criterion validity with several measures of psychological well-being (Diener et al., 1985, pp. 72–73). Alpha for the current sample was .877.

Psychological symptoms

Psychological strain was measured using an index based on the sum of four subscales from the *Brief Symptom Inventory* (BSI) (Derogatis & Melisaratos, 1983). The five- to six-item symptom cluster scales included Somatization, distress arising from perceptions of bodily dysfunction; Depression, dysphoria and lack of motivation and energy; Anxiety, nervousness, panic attacks, apprehension, dread; and Hostility, thoughts, feelings, or actions of anger. Coefficient alphas for the subscales were Somatization, .838; Depression, .869; Anxiety, .827; and Hostility, .714.

Socio-cultural adjustment

Ward and Kennedy (1999) have identified a list of encounters and issues that may be relevant to sociocultural adjustment. Respondents rate their difficulty in adjusting to cultural situations using a 5-point Likert scale with 1 representing No Difficulty and 5 indicating Extreme Difficulty. A brief sample of their 29-item scale includes "Making friends," "Using the transport system," "Going shopping," "Dealing with unsatisfactory service," "Getting used to the local food/finding food you enjoy," "Dealing with people in authority," "Understanding the locals' worldview" (Ward & Kennedy, 1999, p. 663). Alpha for this sample was .858.

Acculturation

Ward and Rana-Deuba (1999), using Berry's (1997) acculturation concept, developed a 21-item questionnaire that compares how much respondents identify with their culture of origin in comparison with the culture they are visiting or living in. Each item is rated on a 7-point Likert scale ranging from Not at All Similar to Extremely Similar for both the home and host cultures. Subsequent analysis develops scores for home and host culture, which can then be compared to determine the category of acculturation expressed by each respondent: Marginalized, Integrated, Assimilated, Separated. Alpha for identification with Home culture was .912 and for Host culture was .854.

Coping

The COPE scale by Carver, Scheier, and Weintraub (1989) is a 60-item, theory-based scale with fifteen 4-item subscales. Alphas reported are for the current sample.

1. *Active coping* is the process of taking active steps to try to remove or circumvent the stressor or to ameliorate its effects. Examples include initiating direct action, increasing ones efforts, and trying to execute a coping attempt in a stepwise fashion (α = .624).

2. *Planning* is thinking about how to cope with a stressor. Planning involves coming up with action strategies, thinking about what steps to take and how to best handle the problem (α = .851).

3. *Suppression of competing activities* means putting other projects aside, trying to avoid becoming too distracted by other events, even letting other things slide, if necessary, in order to deal with the stressor (α = .628).

4. *Positive reinterpretation and growth* is construing a stressful transaction in positive terms with the result of helping the person continue or resume problem-focused coping (α = .747).

5. *Restraint coping* is waiting until an appropriate opportunity to act presents itself, holding oneself back, and not acting prematurely (α = .685).

6. *Instrumental social support* is seeking advice, assistance, or information (α = .802).

7. *Emotional social support* is getting moral support, sympathy, or understanding (α = .893).

8. *Religion* is seeking comfort, consolation, and/or guidance from a higher power. This might be either within the framework of an organized religion or more informally through attention to the spiritual side of life (α = .960).

9. *Humor* is seeing the absurdities and potentially funny side of a stressful event. It may include jokes, sarcasm, irony, wit, and other ways of reevaluating the event through use of humor (α = .916).

10. *Focus on venting emotions* is the tendency to focus on whatever distress or upset one is experiencing and to ventilate, or express, those feelings (α = .753).

11. *Denial* is refusing to believe that the stressor exists or trying to act as if the stressor is not real (α = .639).

12. *Mental disengagement* is distracting oneself from thinking about the stressor. Tactics may include using alternative activities to take one's mind off the problem (α = .550).

13. *Behavioral disengagement* is reducing one's effort to deal with the stressor, even giving up the attempt to attain the goals with which the stressor is interfering (α = .687).

14. *Acceptance* is accepting that the stressor cannot be changed and getting on with accommodating to the situation as it is (α = .575).

15. *Alcohol and drugs* means using chemicals to blunt the feelings associated with exposure to the stressor (α = .923).

Appraisal of stress

The Appraisal of Life Events scale (Ferguson et al., 1999) assesses cognitive appraisal of stressful situations via three dimensions: Challenge (6 items), the degree to which the environment is perceived as one that allows for personal growth and development through potential mastery of stressors; Threat (6 items), the degree to which the environment is perceived as hostile, apt to generate anxiety, and potentially harmful; and Loss (4 items), the potential for suffering and sadness. Participants were asked to appraise "my study abroad experience" on 16 factors, all adjectives (e.g., Stimulating, Exciting, Fearful, Hostile, Depressing, Painful), using a 5-point Likert scale ranging from 1, Not at All, to 5, Very Much So. Alphas for the current sample were Challenge .805, Threat .879, and Loss .855.

Procedures

SA students' voluntary participation was requested at two points in time: within 1 month prior to departure for their study abroad experience and at the end of the academic term of the study abroad experience.

Home students' voluntary participation was solicited as one of several extra-credit activities in two sections of a social psychology course at a university in the United States; it occurred at the beginning and at the end of the same term as the SA group's foreign stay.

Appraisal and coping measures were taken prior to departure for SA students. Outcome measures were taken at the end of the term for both SA and Home groups. All responses were confidential.

Results and Discussion

Contrasts

Table 1 shows differences between Study Abroad and Home groups for out-come scales on which they were compared. Despite the SA group being ex-posed to acculturation stressors during their study abroad sojourn, they did not show lowered psychological adjustment. To the contrary, they showed no difference from the Home group in Total Symptoms, and significantly higher Satisfaction With Life. Figure 1 shows the relationship of symptoms and satisfaction for the two groups. The scale scores have been transformed to the z-scores with a mean of zero and a standard deviation of one. The norm group comparitor is derived from the scale manual in the case of the BSI (Derogatis, 1994) and the scale development group for the SWLS (Die-ner et al., 1985). Hypothesis 1 is rejected.

Table 1 also shows that at the end of their sojourn the SA group was significantly higher in Identification With the Home Culture. That is, de-spite exposure to their host culture and separation from their home culture, study abroad students viewed themselves as more similar to other people in the United States than did students who remained ensconced in U.S. cul-ture. Figure 2 shows comparisons between SA and Home groups on the indi-vidual items of the Home Culture Identification scale. Note the significant differences between the groups on items such as Worldview, Communica-tion Styles, and Political Ideology. Hypothesis 2 is also rejected.

These results suggest that the study abroad context has factors at work that moderate the impact of acculturative stress. Merely the accumulation of stressors is not sufficient to account for the psychological well-being of the study abroad students (Savicki, Downing-Burnette, Heller, Binder, & Sun-tinger, 2004). Likewise, perceptions of one's similarity to other co-nationals grew rather than diminished in this specific study abroad setting, suggesting an active evaluation of students' perceptions of their base cultural assump-tions. A favorable identification with one's own in-group has been termed "in-group bias" by social psychologists. This in-group bias is strengthened when the in-group is smaller and of lower status; thus the obvious minority status of study abroad students may have caused them to be more favorably identified with their home culture (Ellemers, van Rijswijk, Roefs, & Simons, 1997; Mullen, Brown, & Smith, 1992; Myers, 2005). Indeed, Berry (2004) suggests that one's cultural identity becomes more evident and important

TABLE 1

Means and Standard Deviations for Study Abroad and Home Groups on Outcome Variables

Groups: Outcome Variables	Home		Study Abroad		
	M	SD	M	SD	F
Satisfaction With Life	25.32	5.24	29.5	3.27	12.90**
Total Symptoms	19.3	9.04	15.75	9.38	2.28
Anxiety	5.19	2.63	5	3.08	.07
Somaticism	4.16	3.21	3.12	4.18	1.26
Hostility	4.81	3.82	3.06	2.22	4.41*
Depression	5.14	3.40	4.58	3.79	.37
Identification With Home Culture	93.76	16.47	104.58	17.37	6.30*
Identification With the Host Culture	a	a	67.27	15.30	
Socio-Cultural Adjustment (reversed)	a	a	112.79	10.85	

$* p < .05, ** p < .001; a$ scales not taken by Home participants

FIGURE 1
Group comparisons on psychological symptoms and satisfaction with life.

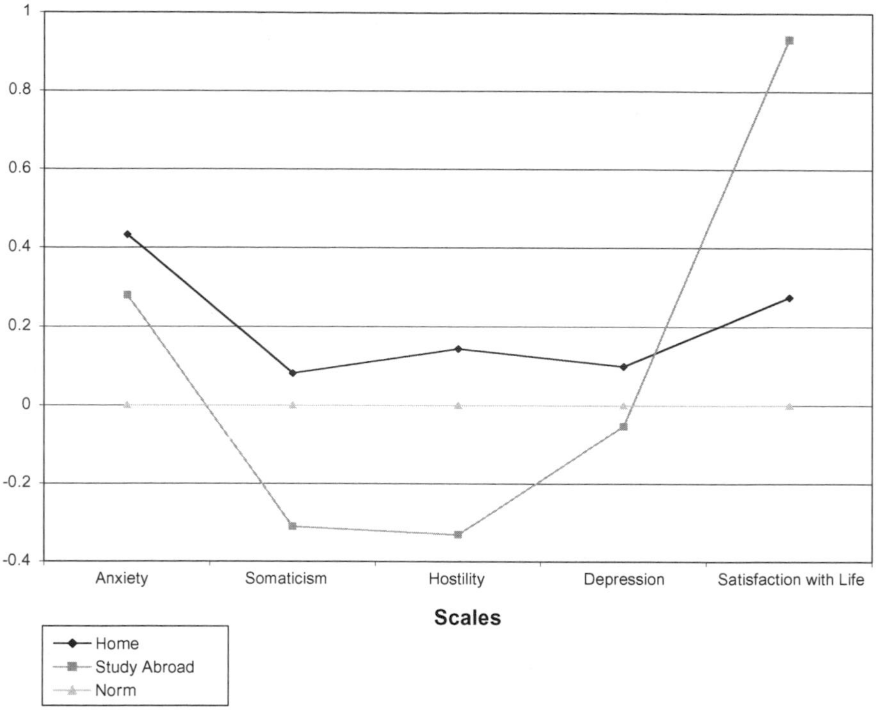

when one is in contact with a different culture rather than when one is living within one's home culture.

Acculturation Relationships

Figure 3 shows the frequencies of acculturation strategies present in the SA group. Categorization was based on a median split methodology suggested by Ward and Rana-Deuba (1999). Two strategies were employed significantly more frequently: Separation and Assimilation ($X^2 = 5.57$, $p < .05$). Low cell frequencies did not allow for direct analysis by acculturation strategies; therefore, a multiple regression using the continuous Home Culture Identification and Host Culture Identification variables was used (Ward & Rana-Deuba, 1999). In general, students indicated only slight difficulty in dealing with a wide range of host culture issues ($m = 1.97$ on a scale of 1 to 5). Table 2 shows that, as in previous research, strong Home Culture Identification

FIGURE 2
Study Abroad and Home group comparisons in home culture identification.

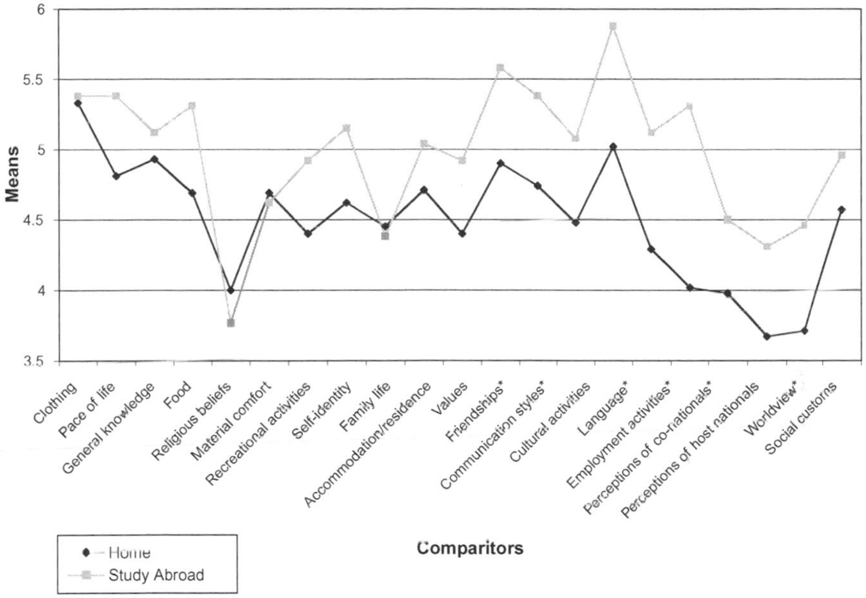

* $p < .10$

was significantly related to positive psychological adjustment (high satisfaction with life) ($r = .427$, $p < .05$), and strong Host Culture Identification was significantly related to positive socio-cultural adjustment ($r = .423$, $p < .05$) (Ward & Rana-Deuba, 1999). Multiple regression analyses showed only the relationships illustrated in Table 2, with no interactions (for Total Symptoms, Home Culture Identification $\beta = -.477$, $p < .05$; for SWLS, Home Culture Identification $\beta = .427$, $p < .05$; for SCAS, Host Culture Identification $\beta = .423$, $p < .05$). Hypotheses 3 and 4 are supported.

In addition, Table 2 indicates that, contrary to previous research, there was no significant relationship between psychological and socio-cultural adjustment (Berry, 2005). Hypothesis 5 is not supported.

Although discrete acculturation strategies were not able to be analyzed, the relationships of the underlying dimensions indicate that the levels of identification with home and host cultures are related to different modes of adjustment. The lack of relationship between psychological and socio-cultural adjustment in this sample is likely attributable to the high degree of

FIGURE 3
Frequencies of study abroad student acculturation strategies.

Identity With the Home Culture

		Low	High
Identity With the Host Culture	Low	Marginalization 4	Separation 10
	High	Assimilation 9	Integration 3

$X^2 = 5.57, p < .05$

cultural distance between U.S. and Greek cultures (Ward & Rana-Deuba, 1999).

Appraisal and Coping Contributions

In order to elaborate and explain the previous results, relationships between appraisal and coping with various study abroad outcomes are shown in Table 3. Although correlation is not causation, it may be useful to remember that both appraisal styles and coping strategies were assessed prior to students' study abroad. Students' measured tendencies to perceive and react to stressors were sampled approximately 3 months before measures based on their exposure to acculturative stress.

Appraisal and coping related to psychological adjustment

The appraisal style most beneficial for students' psychological adjustment was Challenge. It correlated significantly with Satisfaction With Life ($r = .324, p < .05$) and inversely with Total Psychological Symptoms ($r = -.354, p < .05$). Disaggregating psychological symptoms further shows that Challenge is significantly inversely related to both Hostility ($r = -.333, p < .05$), and Depression ($r = -.405, p < .05$). In contrast, the appraisal style of

TABLE 2
Correlation Matrix of Outcome Measures for Home and Study Abroad Groups

Outcome Variables by Group	Satisfaction With Life	Total Symptoms	Home Culture Identification	Host Culture Identification
Study Abroad				
Total Psychological Symptoms	−.366 −			
Home Culture Identification	.427*	−.336		
Host Culture Identification	−.315	.065	−.517**	
Socio-Cultural Adjustment (reversed)	−.131	−.015	−.014	.423*
Home				
Total Psychological Symptoms	−.430**			
Home Culture Identification	.338*	−.173		
Host Culture Identification	*a*			
Socio-Cultural Adjustment (reversed)	*a*			

a = scales not taken by Home participants; $+p < .07$, $*p < .05$, $**p < .01$

TABLE 3
Appraisal and Coping Related to Study Abroad Outcomes in the Study Abroad Group

	Psychological Symptoms	Socio-Cultural Adjustment	Home Culture Identification	Host Culture Identification	Satisfaction With Life
Outcome Measures					
Socio-Cultural Adjustment	-.015				
Home Culture Identification	-.336*	-.014			
Host Culture Identification	.065	.423*	-.517**		
Satisfaction With Life	-.366*	-.131	.427*	-.315	
Coping Strategies					
Active Coping	-.261	.173	-.072	.257	.211
Planning	-.185	.058	-.046	.237	.151
Suppression Coping	-.243	-.016	-.072	.589**	.159
Positive Reinterpretation	-.127	.164	-.330	.365*	-.059
Restraint Coping	-.233	.029	.001	.196	.147
Instrumental Social Support	-.192	.076	.080	.334	.181
Emotional Social	-.098	-.015	.119	.146	.291
Religion	-.435*	.096	.051	-.008	.236
Humor	.535**	-.316	-.238	-.043	-.082
Venting Emotions	.133	-.113	.058	.177	.024
Denial	.105	-.589**	.063	-.233	.132
Mental Disengagement	.185	-.395*	-.159	-.080	-.287
Behavioral Disengagement	.239	-.489*	.126	.001	-.160
Acceptance	-.039	-.308	.099	-.171	.258
Alcohol and Drugs	.525**	-.210	.059	.032	-.236
Appraisal Styles					
Challenge	-.354*	.066	.216	.195	.324*
Threat	.283	-.159	-.010	.104	-.058
Loss	.256	-.164	.017	-.218	-.122

*p < .05, **p < .01

Threat was positively correlated with Anxiety ($r = .406, p < .05$), while the appraisal style of Loss was related to Depression ($r = .353, p < .05$). When students were able to view acculturative stressors as opportunities for experiences that were within their capabilities, they fared better than when they viewed stressors as possibly overwhelming their abilities to cope.

No coping strategies were related to Satisfaction With Life; however, three strategies were related to Total Psychological Symptoms. Both Religion ($r = -.435, p < .05$) and Alcohol and Drugs ($r = .525, p < .01$) were related in the expected direction, with reliance on a higher power related to lower symptoms and reliance on chemical relief related to higher symptoms. Interestingly, Humor was related to psychological symptoms opposite from the expected direction ($r = .535, p < .01$). Disaggregating symptom scales seems to indicate that the humor used by students in this case was less self-enhancing or affiliative humor than aggressive or self-defeating humor (Martin, Puhlik-Doris, Larsen, Gray, & Weir, 2003), since it was correlated with Hostility ($r = .534, p < .01$) and Anxiety ($r = .474, p < .05$). It may not have functioned well as a protective mechanism. The lack of connection between coping and satisfaction may indicate that many coping mechanisms are employed in the service of positive self-evaluation, but only a few seem to interact with psychological symptoms related to acculturative stress.

Appraisal and coping related to socio-cultural adjustment

No appraisal styles related to either Socio-Cultural Adjustment or Host Culture Identification. However, several coping strategies may help to explain student adjustment and identity at the socio-cultural level.

For Socio-Cultural Adjustment a cluster of coping strategies were significantly inversely related: Denial ($r = -.589, p < .01$), Mental Disengagement ($r = -.395, p < .05$), and Behavioral Disengagement ($r = -.489, p < .05$). Staying engaged with the host culture and not trying to ignore cultural stressors seems to be related to higher levels of adjustment to the host culture. For Host Culture Identification, two coping strategies were significantly positively related: Positive Reinterpretation ($r = .365, p < .05$) and Suppression of Competing Activities ($r = .589, p < .01$). These coping strategies suggest that an intense focus on host culture issues and an ability to find positive meanings in acculturative-stress situations were related to higher identity with the host culture.

In general, it appears that the ability to stay engaged, to focus on the problematic situations rather than ignore them, and the ability to find the "silver lining" were related to socio-cultural adjustment.

Conclusions

The dramatic differences between the U.S. and Greek cultures set the stage for a disconnect between psychological and socio-cultural adjustment in this study. Greece and the United States are very different on two of the four dimensions used to calculate cultural distance (Kogut & Singh, 2001). On the cultural dimension of Individualism, the United States ranks 1st and Greece ranks 30th out of the 53 countries and regions included in Hofstede's most recent calculations (2001, p. 215). On the dimension of Uncertainty Avoidance, Greece ranks 1st and the United States ranks 43rd out of the 53 countries and regions (Hofstede, 2001, p. 151). These extensive differences combine to yield an index of cultural distance between the United States and Greece of 21, whereas comparing the United States to the United Kingdom produces an index value of .04; with Italy the index is 3, and with Germany it is 2.67. In addition to cultural distance, the Greek language, especially the alphabet, posed high hurdles for U.S. students who, with one exception, had no prior exposure to the Greek language. Cultural distance and language are two important factors listed as barriers to the relationship of psychological and socio-cultural adjustment (Ward & Rana-Deuba, 1999). This cultural distance calculation has implications for students placed in "distant" cultures, as well as for their advisors and educators. Other distance calculations give some perspective concerning the challenges faced by U.S. students: Japan, 14.6; Taiwan, 10; South Korea, 22; Mexico, 19; Brazil, 13; East Africa, 15. Clearly, there are many study abroad locations, particularly in Asia, Africa, and South America, that present difficult adjustments for American students.

At the same time, Berry (2005) lists voluntariness and cultural knowledge as aids to acculturation. Clearly, the U.S. students voluntarily elected to study abroad in Greece. Likewise, they all participated in a required intercultural communication class that dealt with cultural knowledge and skills throughout their sojourn. These factors helped the students adjust to acculturative stress.

Berry (2005) promotes the acculturation strategy of Integration as the most beneficial for individuals, in part because it allows sojourners to call upon resources from both home and host cultures. However, Integration may be too difficult a goal for study abroad students living only 3 months in a foreign culture, especially when that culture is vastly different from their home culture. Only 11.5% of students in the current sample fell into the Integration quadrant of the Berry model (Berry, 2005, p. 297). As a first priority, it seems ethical to support positive psychological adjustment. In that case, identification with one's home culture should not be restricted or undermined. Berry (2004) asserts the "multicultural assumption" that "only when people are secure in their own cultural identity will they be able to accept those who differ from themselves" (p. 180). At the same time, efforts need to be made to help students connect with and understand their host culture. Different students will be at different states of readiness for intense cross-cultural contact. The key may be maintaining both engagement with the culture and encouragement for adaptive appraisal and coping strategies at the same time.

In the current study, the reliance of U.S. students on their fellow, home culture classmates helped them avoid psychological problems. While the concept of cultural immersion can be beneficial, in the current study the touchstone of co-nationals was related to better psychological adjustment. In addition, in the face of difficulties and with effective on-site support, they met the challenge of acculturative stress and transformed it into a satisfying experience. More modest Host Culture Identification helped them with problems of daily living. The result was a very challenging but very satisfying study abroad. Berry (2005) suggests that researchers move beyond thinking about psychological adjustment through the frame of psychopathology. In the current study, it was not the absence of symptoms alone that defined psychological adjustment, but also the more positively framed life satisfaction.

The matrix of associations between appraisal and coping with psychological symptoms, socio-cultural adjustment, and acculturation fleshes out some of the processes that may be connected to these positive outcomes. The advantage of clarifying appraisal and coping linkages is that appraisal and coping strategies can be taught and coached. In fact, for the study abroad students such coaching and teaching did occur, at least in part, through the required intercultural communication course. This course insisted on engagement with the host culture through various assignments required throughout the semester, such as active journaling and analysis of intercultural clash incidents using the DIE format (Bennett, Bennett, & Stillings, 1977). Reflection and analysis that followed incidents emphasized positive reinterpretation, blocked denial, and framed events as challenges rather than threats or losses. With the specification of the appraisal and coping linkages identified in this study, class design can become even more focused. For example, educators both at home and on-site can anticipate stressors; acknowledge current and future feelings associated with the stressors; provide realistic, positive interpretations; and revisit incidents to encourage engagement and revised perception, attitude, and behavior. See the chapters in the section three of this volume for more detailed examples of educational strategies.

Clearly, this study suffers from a small sample size and the connection with only one host culture. Future research should expand the number of participants and the cultures in which they study abroad in order to clarify more general principles.

The significant difference between Home and Study Abroad groups on satisfaction and Home Culture Identification highlights the intensity of the study abroad experience, expressed thus by one of the students:

> Is it possible for something to be both the best and the worst experience at the same time? I thought that I was prepared to live in Greece for three months, but what I realized was that I had not even begun to prepare myself. Not only did I miss all of the people I had left back home, I also felt a lot of culture shock. Through this experience I have learned so much about both myself and my own culture, as well as a lot about Greek culture. A lot of that new information came to me through class, but a good portion of it I discovered just interacting with my environment on a daily basis.

Overcoming the "worst" led to the "best."

References

Babiker, I. E., Cox, J. L., & Miller, P. McC. (1980). The measurement of cultural distance and its relationship to medical consultations, symptomatology, and examination of performance of overseas students at Edinburgh University. *Social Psychiatry, 15*, 109–116.

Bennett, J. M., Bennett, M. J., & Stillings, K. (1977). *Description, interpretation, and evaluation: Facilitators' guidelines.* Retrieved April 2, 2007 from http://www.intercultural.org/resources.html

Berry, J. W. (1997). Immigration, acculturation and adaptation. *Applied Psychology: An International Review, 46*, 5–34.

Berry, J. W. (2004). Fundamental psychological processes in intercultural relations. In D. Landis, J. M. Bennett, & M. J. Bennett (Eds.), *Handbook of intercultural training* (3rd ed., pp. 166–184). Thousand Oaks, CA: Sage.

Berry, J. W. (2005). Acculturation. In W. Friedlmeier, P. Chakkarath, & B. Schwarz (Eds.), *Culture and human development* (pp. 291–302). New York: Psychology Press.

Carver, C. S., Scheier, M. F., & Weintraub, J. K. (1989). Assessing coping strategies: A theoretically based approach. *Journal of Personality and Social Psychology, 56,* 267–283.

Derogatis, L. R. (1994). *Symptom Checklist-90-R.* Minneapolis, MN: National Computer Systems.

Derogatis, L. R., & Melisaratos, N. (1983). The brief symptom inventory: An introductory report. *Psychological Medicine, 13,* 595–605.

Diener, E., Emmons, R. A., Larsen, R. J., & Griffin, S. (1985). The satisfaction with life scale. *Journal of Personality Assessment, 49,* 71–75.

Ellemers, N., van Rijswijk, W., Roefs, M., & Simons, C. (1997). Bias in intergroup perceptions: Balancing group identity with social reality. *Personality and Social Psychology Bulletin, 23,* 186–198.

Ferguson, E., Matthews, G., & Cox, T. (1999). The appraisal of life events (ALE) scale: Reliability and validity. *British Journal of Health Psychology, 4,* 97–116.

Furukawa, T., & Shibayama, T. (1994). Factors influencing adjustment of high school students in an international exchange program. *Journal of Nervous and Mental Diseases, 182,* 709–714.

Gudykunst, W. B. (1998). Applying anxiety/uncertainty management (AUM) theory to intercultural adjustment training. *International Journal of Intercultural Relations, 22,* 227–250.

Hofstede, G. (2001). *Culture's consequences: Comparing values, behaviors, institutions, and organizations across nations* (2nd ed.). Thousand Oaks, CA: Sage.

Kim, Y. Y. (2005). Adapting to a new culture: An integrative communication theory. In W. B. Gudykunst (Ed.), *Theorizing about intercultural communication* (pp. 375–400). Thousand Oaks, CA: Sage.

Kogut, B., & Singh, H. (2001). The effect of national culture on the choice of entry mode. *Journal of International Business Studies, 19,* 411–432.

Lazarus, R. S. (1999). *Stress and emotion: A new synthesis.* NY: Springer.

Martin, R. A., Puhlik-Doris, P., Larsen, G., Gray, J., & Weir, K. (2003). Individual differences in uses of humor and their relation to psychological well-being: Development of the Humor Styles Questionnaire. *Journal of Research in Personality, 37,* 48–75.

Matsumoto, D., LeRoux, J. A., Ratzlaff, C., Tatani, H., Uchida, H., Kim, C., & Araki, S. (2001). Development and validation of a measure of intercultural adjustment potential in Japanese sojourners: The Intercultural Adjustment Potential Scale (ICAPS). *International Journal of Intercultural Relations, 25,* 483–510.

McGuire, M., & McDermott, S. (1988). Communication in assimilation, deviance, and alienation states. In Y. Y. Kim & W. B. Gudykunst (Eds.), *Cross-cultural adaptation: Current approaches* (pp. 90–105). Newbury Park, CA: Sage.

Mullen, B., Brown, R., & Smith, C. (1992). Ingroup bias as a function of salience, relevance and status: An integration. *European Journal of Social Psychology, 22,* 103–122.

Myers, D. (2005). *Social psychology* (8th ed.). New York: McGraw-Hill.

Pedersen, P. (1995). *The five stages of culture shock: Critical incidents around the world.* Westport, CT: Greenwood.

Savicki, V., Downing-Burnette, R., Heller, L., Binder, F., & Suntinger, W. (2004). Contrasts, changes, and correlates in actual and potential intercultural adjustment. *International Journal of Intercultural Relations, 28,* 311–329.

Tajfel, H. (Ed.). (1978). *Differentiation between social groups: Studies in the psychology of inter-group relations.* London: Academic.

Trower, P., Bryant, B., & Argyle, M. (1978). *Social skills and mental health.* London: Methuen.

Ward, C. (1996). Acculturation. In D. Landis & R. S. Bhagat (Eds.), *Handbook of intercultural training* (2nd ed., pp. 124–147). Thousand Oaks, CA: Sage.

Ward, C. (2001). The A, B, Cs of acculturation. In D. Matsumoto (Ed.), *Handbook of culture and psychology* (pp. 411–446). New York: Oxford University Press.

Ward, C., Bochner, S., & Furnham, A. (2001). *The psychology of culture shock* (2nd ed.). London: Routledge.

Ward, C., & Kennedy, A. (1993a). Where's the "culture" in cross-cultural transition? Comparative studies of sojourner adjustment. *Journal of Cross-Cultural Psychology, 24,* 221–249.

Ward, C., & Kennedy, A. (1993b). Psychological and socio-cultural adjustment during cross-cultural transitions: A comparison of secondary students overseas and at home. *International Journal of Psychology, 28,* 129–147.

Ward, C., & Kennedy, A. (1994). Acculturation strategies, psychological adjustment, and socio-cultural competence during cross-cultural transition. *International Journal of Intercultural Relations, 18,* 329–343.

Ward, C., & Kennedy, A. (1999). The measurement of sociocultural adaptation. *International Journal of Intercultural Relations, 23,* 659–677.

Ward, C., & Kennedy, A. (2001). Coping with cross-cultural transition. *Journal of Cross-Cultural Psychology, 32,* 636–642.

Ward, C., & Rana-Deuba, A. (1999). Acculturation and adaptation revisited. *Journal of Cross-Cultural Psychology, 30,* 422–442.

SECTION THREE

APPLICATIONS TO ENHANCE
INTERCULTURAL GROWTH
AND TRANSFORMATION

Theory and research are all well and good, but how does one translate them into curricula and programs that reach real students facing real intercultural issues in real time? The chapters in the section three address these issues. They embody both the theory and research findings in the previous parts. It is challenging to incorporate such information in a planful, systematic way. The carryover from general concepts and specific studies takes imagination, creativity, and sweat.

Although the intercultural curricula illustrated here spans several types and locations of intercultural education, they have several features in common. These features may be helpful for international educators who are developing or revising their own curriculum. We hope that readers will be able to generalize the methods and ideas beyond the countries and orientations identified in these chapters. First, a strong characteristic running through all of the chapters is the notion of experiential, affective, and transformational learning. As you read the chapters, you will note that not only are specific activities described but also the manner in which these activities are organized is explained. Mere classroom elucidation and recitation are not sufficient to attain the growth and transformation outcomes we desire for our students in study abroad settings. Engaging the whole student becomes a goal along with imparting specific information. Learning and growth go hand in hand. Often, emerging student self-discovery is more important than the details of the assignment. Emotional reactions may be at the core rather than at the periphery of the lessons.

Second, we have tried to illustrate key points in these chapters using the thoughts and reflections of students. Everyone returns from their study abroad with stories to tell. These narratives capture student learning in a holistic way. Some of these stories are humorous, some reflective, some exasperating, some mundane. Nevertheless, they allow us to peek into student's intercultural adjustment and transformation process, and the meaning students make of their encounters. We encourage intercultural educators and administrators to use these stories to illustrate concepts and ideas for future study abroad students. What better sources of understanding for future students than past students. What better way to grasp the issues facing new students than through the challenges and perspectives of those who have already transitioned through those issues.

Finally, the chapters in this applications section are written by educators and administrators who are currently plying their trade. The ideas and approaches elaborated here have stood the tests of reality. Their application takes skill and persistence, and they actually do function to help students to move toward attaining intercultural competence and transformation. Of course, different cultures and circumstances will require creative alteration and refinement, but that is the challenge of intercultural education. Some of the chapters are crafted to speak to issues related to a specific culture; opportunities exist in any culture for such topics. It is both the learning of a culture and the growth of the student that are the dual focal points.

11

ACTION METHODS FOR INTEGRATION OF EXPERIENCE AND UNDERSTANDING

Frauke Binder

". . . learning with head, heart and hand"
—educational philosopher Pestalozzi (Green, 1912)

Action methods are an effective means to make daily encounters with a foreign culture more transparent and easy to comprehend. For better understanding it is often necessary to act out a situation again. Action methods like role plays, theater techniques, and rituals help students approach those situations not only through cognitive elements but also at a level of emotional intelligence.

For a real integration and understanding of another culture this emotional level is essential. Emails and reports after their return showed that students best remember situations in which they were emotionally involved. In a program where a group of people are brought together who did not know each other before, integrating aspects for the group are a must. Where excitement and concentration are requested, relaxation and processing time have to be offered.

The body is not simply an appendage of our head but holds its own kind of recollection. Movement is, therefore, a good way to help the students express and experience new things. Action methods help students process their experience in a foreign environment through more than one channel as they reflect, reexperience, and express their impressions with movement. This helps them to prepare for similar situations, such as reentry shock.

Modern learning techniques and innovative training methodologies deal with playful ways to convey knowledge, too. Unfortunately, in an academic setting experiential learning sometimes will be regarded as suspect. But indeed, a more holistic approach helps to integrate the wide array of new things experienced in a foreign culture with all senses. Usually, American students embrace experiential learning as a change from the ordinary program. According to their evaluations, the methods were met with enthusiasm. Some of the students would have liked even more of them, and for many of them a self-reflecting approach was relatively new.

The instructor can expect a very lively lesson and dedicated students who not only sit and consume but participate actively. An instructor's empathic connection to the class and a feeling for what is suitable are necessary. This requires flexibility and smoothness regarding the syllabus, sometimes taking advantage of spontaneous improvisation.

American students in Vienna are confronted with cultural differences in many ways. Being abroad in Austria or Germany seems to be an encounter with another "Western culture" (Nees, 2000), and initially the Austrian culture does not appear very different from that of the United States:

> I feel, there is nothing I can't handle. The Underground-system is very easy to understand, everybody speaks a little English, and it was easy to make my way from the airport to the city.

In fact, there are subtle differences that American students often do not expect:

> Closed doors have a different meaning, "public" and "private" space are different, you are insecure about what you may do without asking and what you may not, communication styles vary, body language (which you rely on far more than you realize) difficult to interpret (or rather easy to misinterpret). (Heller, 2002)

In order to give a broad picture of action methods, I wish to exemplify how the students live in Vienna and what kind of preparation they get through their first orientation of the program. Various extracts from their journals show frequent topics that appear almost every semester. A detailed discussion of role plays, theater techniques, simulation games, and other activities that I use for the intercultural communication (ICC) class in Vienna will round out the chapter. The goal is to give a sampling of action methods, along with student reactions, and suggestions for implementation.

First Orientation: Do's and Don'ts

Vienna Program students are hosted in Austrian families. Close contact is desired and, in most cases, established from both sides. However, sometimes the contact is a source of misunderstandings. In their first days of orientation, students are informed of the "do's and dont's" regarding privacy, curfew, telephone, laundry, breakfast, meals, kitchen use, bathroom, energy, and invitations. Some of the topics remain as issues in the cross-cultural course. The *Do's and Don'ts in Homestays* (Heller, 2002) for the Vienna students says:

> It is important to be aware that the tiny differences are often the most difficult ones to recognize and—hence—to deal with. All of you are expecting differences in the way a city functions, problems if you are not fluent in the language, a stronger emphasis on history and art, realize that you will need time to feel comfortable with public transportation, to find your way around, etc. What you often don't realize or are not expecting are the many small differences, above all those in your immediate surroundings, things you normally take for granted, that gestures have a different connotation. A certain adjustment is always necessary when living in someone else's household, but the differences are far larger and often more difficult to adjust to in a different culture. . . . In addition though all of your hosts speak English at least to some degree it is not their native language, in many cases their choice of words may seem blunt or insensitive to you though it is certainly not intended as such. (p. 1)

Frequent Topics of Adjustment in Student's DIEs

The student's weekly "describe, interpret, evaluate" (DIE) journals (Bennett, Bennett, & Stillings, 1977) are full of surprising, exciting, and sometimes unforeseen experiences with the new culture. A few examples will, however, show also that the students' reactions and reflections vary largely. Whereas some students adopt a rather aloof position, others use their chance and experiment with new behavior. This section addresses the most frequent topics students in Vienna deal with.

Differences at Their Host's Home—Communication Problems

One of the major source of close contact are the student's host families. The Vienna host "families" are different: Some have children ("host brothers/sisters"), some are single and live on their own. In some of the households the students have their own small apartment; in some the space is limited, and they have to share a room with their roommate. It depends on both the students and the hosts whether the contact established will be closer or more independent. Especially in the first few weeks cultural differences regarding time, table manners, and communication become apparent. Everything is carefully examined by the students, as extracts from their DIE journals show:

> I was sitting at the table with my host-family at dinner, but instead of concentrating on the meal they discussed and talked during the entire time. Even after everyone had finished eating the table remained covered with dishes and no one made any sign to move. But there were long pauses between the sentences and I thought this might be a sign that the conversation is over, but it wasn't.

Cleanliness/Hygiene

The fact that everything is reported in the journals—from different light switches to toilet flushes and washing procedures—shows how much flexibility the unexpected "otherness" in a foreign culture constantly requires. A satisfying adjustment may take weeks or may never really be accomplished. The conglomeration of changes can make the first adjustments especially strenuous and often contributes to culture shock.

But all this contributes to broadening the students' perspectives. A two-way reflection often is the result:

> The size of the washing machines is much smaller. Also it takes much longer for the load of clothes to finish, then the complete lack of any dryer at all. . . . This is only a good thing for the planet and economy. But it is an inconvenience for me if any at all to think ahead of time for a plan on when I need the clothes to be finished.

One could think that Western cultures have the same levels of hygiene. In fact, many students are surprised to encounter other conventions at every turn:

> The toilets here in Austria sometimes have a plateau where the leftovers stay suspended in the open air. The water when flushed will make a high speed river which sweeps everything down the drain.

Contradictory behavior within the same culture often troubles the students and hinders a realistic estimation of cultural values.

> I have read in our Germany-book about how order, cleanliness and respect are important tenants of German society. Yet people all over Vienna allow their dogs to poop on sidewalks and don't clean up after them. This seems to be a direct contradiction with the idea of order and reason that exists behind everything.

Children's Education/Upbringing

In order to get to the program classrooms, the students use the Viennese public transportation. The underground and buses are great places to watch people. Here is the report of two students regarding children's education. The observation helped the students to compare their own culture with the new one regarding safety:

> When travelling on the U-Bahn I saw a very young child riding alone. By American Schools, this boy would not have been able to read according to his apparent age. The boy got on the U-Bahn, rode for a few stops and got off alone on a crowded platform. I saw this in the morning at about 8:15. I think that Viennese parents must be more relaxed and/or trusting of fellow citizens and their child's ability than American parents. My host pointed out that while the child may not be able to read, he could still hear the stop announcements. She also pointed out that violent crimes are rare, and parents who might send children to school would probably not send them out at night. I can see, that the city is a great deal safer than American cities. But I would not feel comfortable sending my child out alone only because of the tons of chances to get lost.

Another observation in the underground deals not only with differences in children's education but also with another approach to love and affection, about which many of the American students are unacquainted:

I have seen many different displays but one in particular caught my attention. A boy of about 8 or 10 was sitting next to his mother on a subway car. He leaned over and kissed his mother on the cheeks. He then told her he loved her and held her hand. . . . I do not really know why people are more affectionate in Austria but I assume that it has something to do with the importance of family and friends. Other things in the European culture point to this, like long lunches at home with family and not as much dependency on computers and phones. These are things that I can find missing from American culture and may have something to do with the lack of expression of love and affection. . . . I look forward to seeing my boyfriend and being able to express in public how we feel, without feeling like people are staring or pointing us out. I will also definitely stress these ideals with my family and future family.

These are just two examples of how observation influences the students and gives them many other perspectives of how life can be lived somewhere else. The students' conclusions range from incomprehension to enthusiasm, but always contribute to an examination and forming of opinion.

Lack of Customer Service

One of the biggest problems and complaints is the missing customer-service value in Austria/the European Union (EU). In the United States, the "customer is the king"; in Austria it is different for many reasons. Some of the students consider the lack of customer service simply "anti-American." A closer examination through role plays in the ICC class can help them get to know the many possibilities hiding behind the missing service.

The waitress was very short and impatient with a group of us when ordering drinks one evening. She did not greet us in any way or thank us for coming before leaving. She stopped by the table only to drop off drinks and never returned to see if we needed or wanted anything else. . . . For all my life I have witnessed and been trained in jobs the importance of customer service it does come as quite a shock to be treated so poorly in a public place.

Nutrition

At the supermarkets, the students discover a whole host of products unknown to them. Some enjoy the new choice, but some miss their food from home and things they took for granted. A new understanding is necessary:

Often, the students criticize their own culture, and mixed feelings meet new intentions:

> The bread here is in such great variety—dark, heavy, nuts, carrots, seeds, raisins, so much stuff in it. It seems also the supermarkets offer organic eggs and milk products more so than in the US. . . . I don't understand why Americans eat so much processed flour.
>
> Austrian cuisine seems to lack the amount of beef that I am used to. . . . Austrian meat consists mainly of pork and chicken. Most likely this is historical. Beef was probably not traditionally something raised in the area and was therefore never really integrated into the diet in the amount that it is in America. Also, it might have to do with scares of bad beef, such as in England which has been plagued with mad cow disease. . . . I have mixed feelings on the lack of beef. I miss hamburgers and I definitely have had moments of steak cravings. However, at the same time I'm forced to try new ways of preparing meat and I find I enjoy these also.

Space and Time

For many of the students, Vienna is the first big city they have lived in. In the beginning it is hard to distinguish what is a big-city phenomenon and what is a cultural difference regarding space and time. Here is another example of how people-watching itself can become an informative object to be studied:

> Like most Americans, I value the space immediately around me. This is often referred to as one's "personal space bubble." I was surprised at how on the Underground people (Viennese) will sit next to anyone when a seat is available, arranged in 4-seat clusters I have seen 4 complete strangers sit together. They almost always avoid eye-contact and communication, but they are not hesitant to be extremely close, even touching. . . . I think with Vienna being a large city with many inhabitants there is no chance but to give up some privacy and personal space.
>
> I am surprised at how pushy and hurried some Viennese seem to be. When going up escalators, walking down crowded small corridors or getting on and off the U-Bahn it is not uncommon for a Viennese to cut ahead of you or push past if you are moving too slow for them. . . . Usually they got very close to you and look at you waiting/expecting you to move. Usually Americans are labelled as hurried and pushy, but it

seems the Viennese are as much, just more with body language than verbal communication.

Different Approaches to Sexuality

Young men and women are naturally interested to get to know members of the opposite sex. Often the different approach toward nakedness and sexuality in daily life is confusing and so are the rules about how men and women in a foreign culture approach and get to know each other.

A student's description shows how challenging a more open approach to nudity and sexuality is for many of our students:

> While riding the bus on Sunday, I saw a number of advertising flags hanging on the lamp posts that show the back side of a naked man on them. I thought: How in the world did anyone allow this shown a number of times in their town? Who approved a banner with the back side of a naked man flapping in the wind? Don't the little children look up and see this, too? What could possibly be so important to sell that they needed the back side of a naked man to be their spokes model? . . . I know that Europe has a number of nudist beaches and when you walk into most saunas, everyone is butt naked. So why should I be surprised to see the bare bottom of a naked man on public banner? . . . It might be my strict religious background or the beliefs that nurtured my homeland but I don't agree with nudity on public places.

Another student's report shows how humor can help in unexpected and unsettling encounters:

> I was in the swimming-pool, enjoying the pleasant experience of showering before swimming [*sic*] when a woman came in with an electric vacuum. First I was shocked because I was naked, normally I prefer to know a female very well before they see me naked. . . . The woman didn't even seem to care that naked men were everywhere also. . . . I believe nakedness here in Europe is a somewhat indifferent topic. . . . After coming to terms with the woman, I didn't mind really and thought it was funny.

Two of the students enjoyed their new "freedom" and started going to the sauna every week:

> After experiencing the sauna in person and talking with other Europeans it seems that nudity is far more natural and accepted than in America. . . .

Too much in American culture tends to be forbidden which causes people to get overly excited and think in terms of sexuality. . . . Nothing about the steam rooms was sexual to me. I did not feel that the older men were gawking or looking at me in an uncomfortable way. I wish more than anything that more Americans could be open to experiences like this. There is a very negative image of women's bodies that is far too sexual and unrealistic. . . . It is important for women to know the reality of what their body looks like and how to accept and love what you have. I think the situations that do not have to do with sensuality are the best for people to experience. I really enjoy the idea and feelings that Europeans have about the body. I look forward to many more relaxing trips to the sauna!

The number and variety of topics indicate how cognitively and emotionally challenging the student's life is in the new culture, requiring a high level of adjustment every moment of their stay in Vienna.

Travels and Excursions

Apart from the adjustment in their homestays and their academic life, the students also need to deal with cultural diversity during their travels and class excursions. The European Union with its many cultures differs greatly from the United States. Austria's close borders to the Czech Republic, Slovakia, Italy, Hungary, Yugoslavia, Germany, and Switzerland offer the chance to meet another different culture within less than an hour. Austria itself is split up into nine provinces, each with different traditions and dialects. Most of the Vienna students use their chance to get to know as many countries as possible and use their free weekends to travel all over Europe. They are confronted not only with other languages but also with different cultural habits. They must learn to distinguish individual from cultural behavior of people. In smaller groups or on their own, students lack the protective support of their class. Being on the road requires permanent adjustment, and indeed they often perceive returning to Vienna as "coming home": "Although the weekend in Rome was nice and exciting, I am glad to be back in Vienna, where I know everything and have my daily routine."

Experiences from the students' daily life, their travels, and excursions constitute the basis for role play, simulation games, individual and group exercises, and class discussions in the mandatory cross-cultural communication course in Vienna. The aim is to convert the frustrations and surprises many students are confronted with during their stay in a foreign culture into a useful learning experience, while at the same time allowing those students not so sensitive to cultural differences to reflect on their role and identity abroad (e.g., what it means to be an American in Austria/Europe/Central Europe; how to keep one's identity and still adapt; what defines the "foreignness" of the culture one encounters). The course activities should lead to a deeper understanding and appreciation of the interstitial spaces and negotiated identities produced by cross-cultural encounters. The students will acquire a general applicability of concepts and skills for any cross-cultural context, be it in the United States or in any other foreign situation.

Action Methods in the Classroom

The following action methods for integration of experience and understanding have been applied in the Vienna Program with considerable success.

Also, the reaction of the students shows that they don't regard it as strange to have action methods within an academic program. Instructors at a European site, however, might find it more difficult to think about including experiential learning in their classes, because it is still more typical in European education to have only lectures during a class session.

The results of action-directed methods show that it is worth the effort to accept the challenge and apply them little by little in the ICC course. If the instructor takes the risk, he or she will experience that the lessons have a more lively and more personal character, and that the students will actually ask for more: "Will we do something again that makes us move today, Frauke?"

Role Plays

Most of the American students are enthusiastic about any kind of class activity and like to present inventive ideas in role plays and other group activities: "I liked to get out of my seat and to do some movement. I loved the role-plays, we had so much fun." The intercultural communication course in Vienna uses these abilities to work on the students' integration of experience. Role plays, exaggeration, and humor usually release a lot of tension that was built up in the actual situation. The student learns to view the situation in another light and to approach the situation with a more playful attitude. Students are also able to experience how they themselves contributed to the experience of a certain situation through their personal assumptions and values.

Theater techniques enrich role plays and make them more exciting both for students and teachers. The following techniques have been applied in my class (all from *Structuring Drama Work: A Handbook of Available Forms in Theatre and Drama* by Neelands & Goode, 2000)

Collective character

Every student can speak as a character that is improvised by the whole group. Everybody can speak as that character. Also an individual can take on the role, and the group whispers advice and lines of dialogue. This way, a large group can be involved in the creation of a dialogue, and subgroups can take on responsibility for each of the characters. There need not be conformity in responses; different attitudes can be given expression so that there is also dialogue between members of the collective character.

For example, students can take on the role of the "typical Viennese shopkeeper." By contributing to the development of this "character," students can stand aside from their reactions to receiving "poor" service and begin to develop an understanding of, and even some empathy with, the "character" toward whom they had developed only animosity before. Different outcomes of a situation may be simulated and make possible a deeper understanding of the students' own behavioral patterns.

A day in the life

This method works backward from an important event in order to fill in the gaps in the history of how the characters have arrived at the event. A chronological sequence is built up from scenes prepared by groups, involving the central character at various different times in the preceding hours or days.

An encounter by one of the students with an unfriendly person in the underground could be the subject. By drawing attention to the influences and exposing the forces that drove the person in the U-bahn to the moment of conflict, they will learn how inner conflicts and tensions shaped the event and its circumstances. That will help the students not to regard every event as personal.

Alter ego

One of the students works as the character and one as that character's thoughts. The "double" provides a commentary of "inner speech," focusing thoughts and feelings of the character. The protagonist plays out the surface action and dialogue as though the alter ego is not there.

The alter ego might help students understand the thoughts and values behind a waiter who gives them bad service (and discover a couple of unexpected reasons). After the role play, the situation will be discussed in class. Students exchange their opinions, create solutions for problems, and develop another outcome or a different approach that can be re-played as well.

Simulation Games

Simulation games help students experience another "culture" within the classroom. The simulation of another culture will usually enrich the experience of homogeneous classes like the one in Vienna, consisting only of U.S. students. Self-reflection on the students' reactions, their assumptions, and the values and motivations that create their experience will be the object of the class talk. Possible solutions and techniques to cope with cultural differences are developed.

Simulation games can give more understanding about our own reaction with unexpected events in foreign cultures. Using those methods more in the beginning of the ICC classes can serve as a preparation for what is actually going to happen in daily life situations. The student's frustration at not knowing the rules of the games properly is similar to not knowing the rules of different cultures. The games explore the fundamental aspects of unexpected change and resulting communication breakdowns. They assist in understanding problems regarding communication, group awareness, and cultural awareness and help the students to think about flexibility and change.

Two simulation games used for the cross-cultural course in Vienna will be introduced here: *Bafá Bafá* (Shirts, 1977) and *Barnga* (Thiagarajan & Thiagarajan, 2006).

Bafá Bafá

The game divides participants into two cultures: Alphas and Betas. Each culture goes to a separate room and is given instructions simultaneously by two organizers. The Alphas and Betas have very different "cultures," with respective specific tasks and ways of behaving.

Once participants have had their new cultures explained, they each practice in their separate rooms to become comfortable with their new way of life. After this, a few members of each culture are allowed to exchange with a few members of the other culture for two minutes each. These exchanges continue until all members have had a chance to "experience" the other culture. At this point the "game" side of the simulation ends and the more enriching "discussion" side of the game begins. In the discussion, all participants are brought together into one room where they discuss what happened and consider other issues regarding the interpretation of the other cultures. The game usually leads to greater tolerance and understanding of other people in all spheres of life, and most of the students considered it to be useful. Although at the beginning the students thought the game was rather confusing, at the end they found it involving and very interesting: "At the beginning I didn't really like the game, because I didn't understand it quite well, but as soon as I realized its rules, I got very interested."

The activity may create a problem with the class time: It takes approximately 2½ hours to run it. About 1 hour is necessary for the debriefing session, which is the most important aspect of the activity, and a full hour enables participants to get the most learning from it. Questions and prompts like this can be useful:

- Do you remember real-life situations that you considered similar to your experience in Bafá Bafá?
- What do you think: Is it possible to work with people from another culture without understanding their language?
- How should the salesperson react when clients use acronyms, initials, and words that he or she doesn't understand?
- Mention some of the underlying causes of the problems that arose during the game.

Following are common student reactions to this simulation. Although everybody realized that they were playing a game, the final discussion looked more like a serious argument between the representatives of two cultures. Students didn't easily believe that if they were assigned to the second culture they would become its "fans"—so strongly did they believe in priority of "their" culture. Moreover, quite surprisingly, both sides stressed that the "other" culture was aggressive, primitive, and worse than their own. Their interest in the other culture was very high—they were proud to be able to go and visit it as observers—but in fact they did not try to understand it, but rather evaluated it in a critical way. Probably not all the students realized this equally well, but some of them did. After all, one student remarked: "This wasn't just a game for me, it gave me new understanding for tolerance and how deeply culture is ingrained into our behavior."

Making the students understand all this was another matter. All of them felt that the game was interesting and involving, and although they knew nothing about the cultures before the game, they became true patriots of their "own" cultures. By the end of the game, some of them claimed, "No one will ever make me change my culture." Others demonstrated more understanding regarding the aims of the exercise: "The aim of this game was to make us realize that it's not a good idea to make judgments in a hurry, before we learn more about this or that event or fact."

> After this game, I came to the conclusion that people tend to make judgments which are not based on knowledge or understanding, and are made in a rush. That's what happened to all of us during this game. And it was intended to happen, as the main goal of the game, as well as I understood it, was to make us think about the fact that before we get to know each other, to learn what's happening around us, we shouldn't make judgments.

Barnga

In this game of intercultural awareness, participants experience the shock of realizing that, despite many similarities, people of differing cultures perceive things differently, or play by different rules. Players learn that they must understand and reconcile these differences if they want to function effectively in a cross-cultural group.

Participants play a simple card game in small groups, and conflicts begin to occur as participants move from group to group. This simulates real cross-cultural encounters. People initially believe they share the same understanding of the basic rules. In discovering that the rules are different, players undergo a mini culture shock similar to one's actual experience when entering a different culture. They must struggle to understand and reconcile these differences to play the game effectively in their "cross-cultural" groups. Difficulties are magnified by the fact that players may not speak to each other but can communicate only through gestures or pictures. Participants are not forewarned that each is playing by different rules; in struggling to understand why other players don't seem to be playing correctly, they gain insight into the dynamics of cross-cultural encounters.

The game lasts about 50 to 60 minutes; the debriefing session should last about 30 minutes and begin with a reflection about what happened and what it all means.

> Here is the beauty of BARNGA—everything appears to be the same, and in fact almost everything is the same, yet great confusion, uncertainty, misunderstanding and misjudgments fill the room because of just a few differences. Even those who understand that the rules are different (and many do) are not necessarily clear about how they are different. And even those who understand how they are different have difficulty bridging the communication barriers to work out a solution. These concepts spark the energy generated by the game and provide the starting point for a group follow-up discussion rich in observations (Beyer, 2006).

The students will be asked about their changes of thought and feeling during the play, and about their greatest frustrations and successes. The following questions could be posed:

- What specific real-life situations exist in our educational system that Barnga simulates?
- Choose a couple of these situations. What are the underlying causes of the problems which they raise?
- What does the game experience suggest about what to do when you are in a situation in the real world? (Try to remember what you did during the game that "worked.")
- What is the single most important principle you learned from Barnga today?

A comment of one of the students shows the result of the simulation game:

> I was surprised at how ruthless and unforgiving I was to the people who entered my little community. I made them play my way and never took the time to understand their point of view or the rules that they knew. . . . I didn't think that I had any prejudices but I do and Barnga made me realize them.

Other areas Barnga covers are problem solving, communication, group awareness, cultural awareness, change and cross-functional team development.

Other Activities

There are a number of books that contain a variety of class activities for intercultural learning. They provide clear directions for participants and cover a broad spectrum for those who prefer experiential activities and who learn best if they can reflect on ideas (Seelye, 1996; Storti, 1994; Stringer & Cassidy, 2003). Other class activities help to highlight different important stages of the students' stay in Vienna. The last intercultural communication lesson for reentry to the home culture contains a ritual, a personal approach to the students' survey of their stay in Vienna.

Appreciation of your 12 weeks in Vienna

Every student works with a classmate, and the filled-out questionnaire belongs to the respective students. The activity lasts about 1 to 1½ hours, and—different from other activities—results are not shared with the class. The instructor is there only to answer additional questions regarding the instruction; otherwise the activity remains "strictly private."

Using the questionnaire, partner B helps partner A to set an "imaginary timeline" from the beginning of the stay in Vienna to this day. Different symbols stand for events, situations, and/or people. At the end, A is asked to turn around and reconsider his or her 12 weeks in Vienna again. While A creates the timeline, his or her answers and remarks are jotted down by B. When the questionnaire is filled out, the partners change. Now A guides B along his or her self-created timeline. Some questions from the questionnaire include the following:

- Remember the time when you arrived in Vienna. How did you feel then, physically, emotionally, and mentally?
- Which hindrances did you meet during your stay? Externally (e.g., relationships, cultural differences)? Internally (e.g., inactivity, disturbance, ambition)? Name them and mark them with symbols on your timeline.
- How did you deal with those hindrances? Which of your abilities were helpful? Did you get help from others? Mark your abilities and sources of help on the timeline.
- What has changed? What new abilities did you develop (e.g., more trust, better communication, establishing borders)? Name some situations in which you would react differently today than before your stay in Vienna.

- What do you want to take home with you? New abilities, new customs? What would you like to leave behind?
- Go to the point of "now," and look back and compliment yourself on the progress you have made.

Usually the students are fully engaged in the exercise and have a lot to tell to their partner. Student evaluations indicated that the students found this process very helpful to look back on their stay in Vienna and reflect on their personal change. It also helped them summarize their experience in Vienna and to contribute to a better departure.

Relaxation/Perception Exercises

Short relaxation exercises often help the students compose themselves at the beginning of a lesson, to relax more effectively, and to cope with their different life stages while abroad. Most of them are modified exercises from self-experience activities (see Chuen, 1991; Lazarus, 2000; Lewis, 2004).

Stretching and shaking for a while, focusing on the breath with eyes closed, and feeling where the tension in the body is and trying to loosen it up are short and small exercises but very effective. Many of the students adopted these techniques and used them during their breaks or on excursions (and had great fun being watched by people!).

In the beginning it can be hard for the students to stay silent, because they are busy and talkative thinkers. Nevertheless it is useful to show them what they are occupied with most of the time, and that it might be useful to pull the attention back from the outside in order to relax and to calm the mind.

The human mind resembles a vase. Most of the time we are busy with directing our attention to the outside of the "vase"—concentrating on something, focusing, judging, reacting. Rather seldom are we taught techniques that direct our mind inward, that "collect" instead of "scatter." One of the techniques for "collection" can be to focus on the inside, on our breath and body-feelings for a while.

Other techniques show how the mind "works" while perceiving new things (Braza, 1997). Perception is defined as being aware of in one's mind, or to achieve understanding of (Jewell & Abate, 2001). Perception can be influenced by our own cultural, ethnic, or racial filters. Our filters are colored by what we have been taught or have learned through experience. One's perceptions about people or groups that may be different from oneself inevitably lead to assumptions, interpretations, behaviors, and conclusions that are very often incorrect. Because we may filter out or filter in certain information, our conclusions about groups of people may not be based in fact or reality.

The following exercise helps students to become aware of their own fantasies and feelings and how they add these to experiences. The students are slowly guided through a half-hour process in which they get to know how their mind works and try out a new skill. They start with closed eyes, then focus on their breath and their body-feelings, becoming aware of their thoughts and feelings. After that, some music is played. Then they open their eyes and watch their hands; afterward, they turn around to one of their classmates and look into their eyes for a while. Then eyes are closed, and they focus on themselves again. With each of these steps (lasting about 3–5 minutes), the students are instructed to try to only listen, only watch, and only perceive, and then watch the fantasies and/or feelings they add on to this direct experience. This step-by-step exercise shows how we permanently add our own projections to things we experience and how our mind is skilled to form immediate judgments. To recognize what our own fantasies and thoughts are is very useful, not only in our own daily life at home, but also in dealing with perceptions of another culture.

During the class discussion that follows, the students have considered this exercise to be very useful. They said they never thought before about what their mind actually "does" when forming conclusions about a certain situation, and also that one could possibly decide to make use of one's fantasies/ thoughts or not, if only the skill to "switch on/off your thoughts" worked better.

Both relaxation and perception exercises help to slow down student reactions and thought processes so that they can be examined. Recognizing how one thinks and perceives presents an opportunity to insert choice into the stream of reactions. Often, students experience their reactions as fixed, rapid, and externally caused. Action methods help them understand the degree to which they may be able to alter and control the course of their reactions. Such skills fall within the realm of emotional regulation and emotional intelligence.

Conclusion

If we wish to engage students and help them develop methods of reflection, action methods are vital for integration purposes and a richer understanding of new cultures, as well as the students' own culture and themselves. Applying action methods in a foreign studies program may be a new challenge for the instructor's flexibility, but at the same time it offers a never-ending experimental field of creativity. It is worth taking the risk and trying out educational material offered on the Internet or in the respective literature mentioned in this chapter, as well as sharing a lively personal experience with the students.

Everything that helps the students to communicate in a more effective way, form a clearer understanding of personal assumptions and motivations, and improves their awareness of their cultural background contributes greatly to their personal development.

References

Bennett, J. M., Bennett, M. J., & Stillings, K. (1977). *Description, interpretation, and evaluation: Facilitators' guidelines.* Retrieved January 9, 2007 from http://www .intercultural.org/resources.html

Beyer, J. (2006). *Barnga Master—Game Guide and Instructions.* Retrieved December 29, 2007 from http://www.fourh.umn.edu/ydca/youthnu_handouts/06_hand outs/jbBarngaMaster.pdf

Braza, J. (1997). *Moment by moment: The art and practice of mindfulness.* North Clarendon, VT: Charles E. Tuttle.

Chuen, L. K. (1991). *The way of energy: Mastering the Chinese art of internal strength with* chi kung *exercise.* New York: Gaia Books Limited.

Green, J. A. (Ed.). (1912). *Pestalozzi's educational writings.* New York: Longmans, Green & Co.

Heller, L. (2002). *Do's and don'ts in homestays.* Vienna: AHA International, Vienna.

Jewell, E. J., & Abate, F. (Eds.). (2001). *The new Oxford American Dictionary.* New York: Oxford University Press.

Lazarus, J. (2000). *Stress relief and relaxation techniques.* Boston, MA: McGraw-Hill.

Lewis, D. (2004). *Free your breath, free your life.* Boston, MA: Shambhala.

Neelands, J., & Goode, T. (2000). *Structuring drama work: A handbook of available forms in theatre and drama.* New York: Cambridge University Press.

Nees, G. (2000). *Germany: Unraveling an enigma.* Yarmouth, ME: Intercultural Press.

Seelye, H. N. (1996). *Experiential activities for intercultural learning*. Yarmouth, ME: Intercultural Press.

Shirts, R. G. (1977). *BaFá BaFá: A cross culture simulation*. Del Mar, CA: Simile II.

Storti, C. (1994). *Cross-cultural dialogues: 74 brief encounters with cultural difference*. Yarmouth, ME: Intercultural Press.

Stringer, D., & Cassidy, P. (2003). *52 activities for exploring values differences*. Yarmouth, ME: Intercultural Press.

Thiagarajan, S., & Thiagarajan, R. (2006). *Barnga, 25th anniversary edition: A simulation game on cultural clashes*. Yarmouth, ME: Intercultural Press.

12

ITALY
Every Day Another Soulful Experience to Bring Back Home

Silvia Minucci

"Please describe in one sentence your experience here in Italy," I asked my students:

"Italy: every day another soulful experience to bring back home" was one of the phrases that a student wrote to describe her study abroad experience in Siena, Italy. This chapter voices my students' thoughts, emotions, and statements in their own words, showing their path to reach a level of integration and understanding of the host culture, their home culture, and of themselves. Cross-cultural adaptation is, in fact, a continuing process that involves the evolution of insights, knowledge, and emotional skills. In this chapter I first describe briefly aspects of the intercultural communication class that all students take, and then I present, in the students' own words, their reactions and thoughts concerning important aspects of their adaptation to study abroad in Siena, Italy.

Intercultural Communication Class Organization and Methods

The mandatory Cross-Cultural Communication/Cross-Cultural Perspectives course is held 10 times for 2 hours each during the term (in fall, winter, and spring terms), and it is a 1- or 2-credit course, according to each university's policy. Many of the techniques I use to help students adjust to Italian culture are based on active, experiential learning methods. To follow are a few of these techniques with some description of how to use them.

DIE

One of the common techniques in my intercultural communications (ICC) class is Janet Bennett's description/interpretation/evaluation format (DIE) (Bennett, Bennett, & Stillings, 1977), which I have used since I started this course. I ask the students to write weekly papers about the topics we discuss in class. In this way they are forced to observe the reality that surrounds them more carefully and reflect on the experience they are having, thus becoming more able to face and learn about a new culture.

Each paper consists of three related but distinct parts (Description, Interpretation, Evaluation). I insist on the importance of keeping these parts separated from one another. It does happen, in fact, that the students, especially at the beginning of their experience, mix their interpretation and evaluation statements, reporting their evaluation reactions in the interpretation part. Since at the end of the lesson there is a conversation with Italians (cross-cultural conversation), I request that my students reflect on what they have written and add a short summary (New Evaluation) of what they learned about the Italian interpretation based on this conversation; this is followed by a discussion in class.

Meeting local people (university students) gives our students the opportunity not only to learn how the locals behave in different situations but also to be able to understand why. In order to give a new evaluation, the students should suspend their evaluation until they can find out what is the real meaning of any behavior in the host culture by interviewing Italian students. In fact, "quick judgmental reactions can lead to misunderstandings, misjudgments, and negative opinions" of what they observe (Althen, 2003). This doesn't mean that the students should "uncritically embrace all local behavior no matter how strange or offensive, but only that you should not reject behaviors *before* you have understood them" (Storti, 2001). This is why students should avoid making definitive, prejudicial judgments that may stem from their own cultural responses, but rather stay open-minded and receptive to different ideas, concepts, and behaviors.

After meeting face to face with the Italian students in the second part of the class, they may reach a possible, reasonable evaluation, which may be the same as or completely different from the one they had originally given. Both the American and the Italian students enjoy these encounters because both of them deepen their understanding of different cultures, realizing that everything can be perceived from different perspectives.

Other Techniques of Cross-Cultural Training

Cross-cultural conversations. These conversations take place with Italian students after American students deal with each different topic in the ICC class. The conversations are in class, but they may be extended to other places such as a cafeteria, a pub, or simply a street, once the American students have made friends with the locals.

Short cultural skits. Often these skits take place during the first week of the course. Topics may include "Greet some friends you have unexpectedly encountered in the street and stop to chat"; "Enter a coffee shop, order and drink your coffee, and leave"; or "Introduce your friends to your landlady/landlord." In preparing these skits the students are encouraged to include cultural actions that people naturally do without much conscious thought (e.g., facial expressions, gestures, distance between people, eye contact, and other features of interpersonal style).

Final performance. The final performance usually takes place in the last day of the course. Since the students themselves are starring actors in their study abroad drama, the course ends with *a final performance*, in which all students collaborate and act in their own cultural sketches, revealing the real story of life in Siena. This is a good chance for them to display their understanding of Italian culture and to use the Italian language they have learned during their stay. They are asked to assemble in groups of five students, and each group has to write the script for a sketch. Working in groups, they create skits that are lively and entertaining but also culturally accurate, including aspects of general Italian style, body language, hand gestures, idiomatic expressions. They are told to act as Italians would. Given a list of suggested scenarios, students decide which scenarios they would prefer to perform (e.g., "Late at night on the streets of Siena"; "Meeting friends on a stroll around town"; "Friends having food and drinks in a bar"; "Buying perfect fruit/vegetables in a small greengrocer's"; "Getting lost"; "Trying on and then buying something stylish with input from your friends and the shop

assistant"; "Meeting guys/girls in a bar/disco"; "Family dinner table discussing recent problems and events that are important to the family"; "Italian
problems in coping with American tourists"; "A mother supervising kids").
Depending on the students' Italian language level, they may decide to perform in English or in Italian, pretending to be locals or foreigners. We usually organize the final performance not in class but in a "theatrical" setting
where guests, sometimes their Italian language teachers, are able to watch the
performance.

Journal. Keeping a notebook or a journal to record everyday observations
and reflections.

Memorable incident. "Write about what you consider the most interesting
cultural experience you have had during your stay in Siena. It can be something you have noticed in people's behavior, it can be something that has
really happened to you, it can be something extremely funny that you will
never forget, the first thing that you will tell your friends when back home."

Observations of everyday events. Everyday observations are exemplified in the
"Grocery Store Ethnography Exercise" (Bennett, 2000): "The exercise forces
the students to engage in thick description of a culture attempting to discover the hidden symbolic webs of which it is composed," and "students
should particularly be encouraged to think of the grocery store as not merely
a store, but rather as a repository of cultural values, attitudes, and beliefs"
(p. 17). The students are given explanations about some important concepts
such as the use of space, nonverbal communication resources, and so on.
Then they have a set of 11 questions to help them "look around" the store
and then 5 more questions that focus on the differences between that store
and the ones they have at home, thus underlining the differences between
the two cultures.

Guest speakers. Several guest speakers have addressed culturally relevant topics
over the years. For example, Padre Alfred, an American who moved to Italy
as a young man and became a Dominican friar—I have always thought he is
perfect to talk about such a delicate topic as religion, being a man of the
church, American and Italian at the same time. There is also the guide at the
Castle of Brolio, who explains how wine is made and kept in the castle's

century old cellars, and the guide to the "bottini," the underground tunnels in Siena.

Films. Several films provide both history and stimulation for discussion. *One Hundred Steps* (Giordana, 2001) deals with the true story of Giuseppe Impastato who, in the 1970s, was the first person who openly criticized the Mafia and its bosses on his radio program *Radio Out.*

Cold Water (Ogami, 1988) is a video that stimulates students to talk about their difficulties in cultural adjustment. This is usually shown in the third or fourth week, when the students begin to open up and feel free to share with the others their tensions, their worries, and their expectations.

Siena—The Days of the Palio (Biliorsi & Domenichini, 2001) gives historical information about the *Palio* horse race and helps the students understand the Sienese people's attachment to their traditions and roots.

Field trips. Of course, visits to special places in Italy provide a window on the culture. Visiting a *Contrada* museum follows the watching of the video about the *Palio.* This visit is to show the students the deep sense of community, of belonging to their birthplace, that the Sienese people have. A *contrada* is, in fact, not simply one of the 17 districts into which the town is divided, but a tiny city within a city, with its leaders, its geographical borders, church, museum, and social club.

The *Castello di Brolio* (Castle of Brolio) is where the "Iron" Baron Bettino Ricasoli, a key figure in the unification of Italy, lived. Around the castle, the vineyards give one of the best Chianti wines of the region.

Readings. Written information supplements other class activities. Readings may include handouts (chapters and articles taken from the recommended readings) and newspaper and magazine articles. See the following references for issues relating to Italian culture: Aust and Zollo (2004), Costantino and Gambella (1996), Krause (2005), Mautner (2003), Flower & Falassi (2005), and Zanobini (2000).

Intercultural Class Topics

Most of the topics used in the ICC class are briefly introduced with some historical background that explains cultural transformations from generation to generation. For example, in presenting the "Gender and Sexuality" topic, I deal with three generations' interpretations of gender roles: my grandparents', my parents', and my own generation. A fourth generation's ideas are provided by the Italian students who participate in the class. Reporting personal stories and showing photographs, we discuss gender role changes in Italy, comparing them to those in American culture. From my experience, it's important to share real stories, even personal stories, since they catch students' attention and curiosity more.

My students are the main characters in this chapter, since they are the leading actors in the class. Creating a friendly and familiar atmosphere is extremely important in this course, so that all students feel free to share their opinions, their expectations, their worries, their hopes, and their difficulties in reaching a successful adjustment to another culture.

This section will report statements from some of the students' papers—focusing on the topics of gender and sexuality; family and discipline; religion; social status, values, and display; and relationships—and then a complete paper that I think is particularly meaningful. The students' statements, taken from their papers describing, interpreting, and evaluating the incidents occurred, are reported here word for word.

Gender and Sexuality

At first greeting, women will kiss their women friends on each cheek to say hello. Men greet their male friend in the same fashion. This occurs in all ages, from young schoolchildren, to older Italians. Couples in the park will passionately show their love for one another, kissing for a long duration of time, often cuddling in the open. In clubs, bars, or other loud atmospheres, men will get very close to their male friends and even whisper by cupping the other male's ears so that they can hear better. Men will get the attention of women who are strangers to them in loud atmospheres by placing their hands on their face or neck and whispering very close into their ear. Men coming up behind male companions of theirs will put their arm around their shoulder as a greeting to walk alongside with them, and often place their arm around a female companion's waist.

Two men are walking down the street candidly joking with each other. The space between them is very slight and they seem to have complete ease with their proximity to each other. As they approach the corner one leans in to embrace the other and they exchange two kisses, one for each cheek. I also observe two teenage boys behaving similarly except their actions are a bit more aggressive towards each other. In the same piazza I notice two young girls embracing each other while standing amongst their friends. With what looks like complete ease they grab each other's hands and share a laugh with their faces pressed against each other's foreheads. My eye is also caught by a middle aged man and woman that approach a bench and sit down. As they look directly into one another's eyes there is a very close proximity between their bodies and faces. Without noticing anyone around them they share a very intense kiss that lasts several minutes.

I have mentioned just two short descriptions but I might have added many more, almost one per student through the years. This is definitely one of the most noticeable differences between the American and Italian culture: showing affection in public. The reaction the American students have and the interpretation is similar. They think that "seeing Italians, both men and women, greet each other in such a way seems as if they have greater appreciation and excitement to see their friends," and "there is freedom of expression of emotion that justifies why couples will openly kiss and exchange their love in front of many onlookers." Even though "as an American it is very startling to observe a couple that is so open with their display of affection," and "all this kissing in public is the most shocking interaction to see because in America kisses are taboo," in the end the students agree that "the levels of comfort in one's own skin seems to be much higher in Italy than in America," and that "it is very refreshing to see people act in a way that is uninhibited by outside pressures to act in a certain way."

The experience that many girls have with Italian men is not very nice. One of them writes:

A gender role that I have noticed is how flirty Italian men are. They just stare at women as they walk by or they try to talk to them without hesitation. As I walked down the grocery the other day, I had about ten men honk at me as they drove by.

When I walked with just girls, we usually received whistles, some car honking and various comments, but once, while walking through a group of Italian men in their late 20s or early 30s one of them got very close to my face and said, "You are so beautiful!"

It may happen while the girl is waiting for a train to arrive, a man approaches her and tries to have a conversation. If the girl is kind, answers his questions and asks questions herself, the man may get closer and even try to kiss the girl on the mouth. He may leave definitely only when an old woman sits down next to the girl.

In relation to nightlife in Italy, "As soon as you, the woman, walk into the local pubs, you suddenly feel all eyes set on you as if you are on display behind a glass case."

The girls, then, even though they realize that Italian men like to flirt with young foreign girls, especially when on their own, often feel uncomfortable because "Italian men's aggressive nature is too much" for them and admit that "American men are flirty like Italian men, but not as often with women they do not know. Americans have more a fear of rejection, so they usually will not go after a woman unless they know she is interested." Another common remark is that "In the United States we have a strong value for personal space. We imagine a bubble around ourselves that should not be crossed unless someone is given permission and definitely not by people we don't know." Therefore when the bubble is crossed shock and embarrassment follow. Sometimes the girls may be in difficulty, "I understand that I am in a different culture and I don't know what kind of actions between genders are accepted or not accepted here," but after talking with other Italian girls report, "I felt a little better. It sounded like we have similar feelings toward this behavior of men."

Student paper on gender and sexuality.

The paper I have selected, however, deals with another aspect of the topic of gender and sexuality, role differences between genders, which are another frequent observation my students make, since the roles are quite different in the two cultures.

Description: An interaction that displays gender roles is the interaction between one of the students I live with, Miriam, and her brother. Miriam has her brother over for dinner very often. The interaction between Miriam and her brother at dinner caught my attention, in her preparation of dinner and the way dinner is carried out. She set the table with a fork, knife, plate, and glass filled with water. She prepared the meal, which included pasta with pesto sauce, steamed zucchini salad, and bread.

Before she sat down to eat, she served him his meal in courses. He sat there, blankly staring into space. She asked him if he would like some bread and his response was "yes." She went around the table to get the bread, which was sitting in a bag hanging on the chair next to him, and then placed it on his plate. She made sure that he had everything that he needed and sat down to eat her meal. After dinner she cleared the dishes, washed them, and cleaned up the kitchen. While she was doing this, he sat at the table and watched a game show that was on television. When Miriam's parents came to visit, I was able to observe the same type of interaction with them as well. When her mother cooked the meal, her father sat at the table reading a newspaper. When he wanted something to drink, he asked his wife and she got up to serve him.

Interpretation: I interpret this event to be a typical female/male interaction in an Italian household. Miriam is older than her brother and therefore has an obligation to care for him. She's also a woman, and stereotypically a woman's place is in the kitchen, she does the cooking and the cleaning. It was interesting to me how Miriam served her brother his dinner courses. I interpret this to be a cultural act because traditionally Italian dinners are very long affairs. The other scene that interested me was the scene where Miriam brought her brother the bread. This further endorses the idea that women are supposed to serve men.

It was interesting for me to see this same interaction occurring between her parents. This makes me think that it is a traditional act that is culturally ingrained into Italian families. Her parents demonstrated the same type of male/female gender stereotype that Miriam demonstrated with her brother. While Miriam's mother did all of the housework, her father sat there.

Evaluation: In my family, on the rare occasions that we eat together at home, my brother usually will cook the dinner which is set up in a buffet style, where we all serve ourselves. My brothers or dad usually do the dishes at the end of the dinner. However, my sister, mother, and I pitch in and help clean up.

This is the kind of family life I am accustomed to. Everyone does his or her part to achieve a certain goal, in this case dinner. I was shocked to see similar events take place between Miriam and her brother and I was surprised to see similar events occur every night. It seems like a very male dominated interaction, where the woman has to do everything and the man just sits there, expecting to be served. I was wondering if this is typical of an Italian household or it is specific to this particular family.

(New Evaluation:) The Italian students I talked to thought this was not common in households, but that it depends on the family and how the children were raised.

Family and Discipline

"I haven't had any interaction with families while being in Siena and I only know a little information about their customs from what my teachers have said in class." This is quite a frequent statement I find when reading the papers about this topic. In fact, most of the students share their apartments with either other American roommates or Italian ones. Rarely do they choose accommodation with a family. As a consequence, apart from a few, their observations come mainly from watching people in public situations such as walking in the streets, relaxing in squares, visiting museums, and eating in restaurants. However, the conversations they have with Italian students help them to confront their opinions. In spite of all this, the students do notice things, and usually the picture of daily family life that comes from their papers is correct and portrays what is really distinctive of Italian families.

One of the things they have written about and is very true is the fact that "Italian families consists of only a husband and a wife. If couples do have children, most seem to have only one." "Many couples don't have kids because they want time to have fun together and travel and they also like to have steady incomes and careers. By the time they have enough money to buy a house, they may be in their mid-30's and not care to have children any more." Although this attitude can be criticized, "in America I feel people get married too young and start a family before growing together as a couple and enjoying time being in love."

And, if children do come, a frequent situation is to see young children being cared for by their grandparents, while "in the United States it is very uncommon to see older people walking all over the town, and it is even rarer to see them caring of young children alone." "Family is a very strong bond in Italy and it seems that while a married couple must work to support their family, the grandparents are always there to support and help them." The conclusion is that "I think it is so refreshing to see these children with their beloved *Nonni* . . . a second set of parents when theirs are away." "These kids will probably grow up to care for their grandchildren some day. They will also be able to learn so much about their heritage. I think that this is a very neat aspect of Italian culture that I hope to incorporate into my life." The Italian students confirmed that this situation is quite common also because families often have enough room for multiple generations to live together.

Of course, it was not difficult for the American students to notice that "the mothers in Italy are very protective of their children and want to make sure they are safe at all times." "It seems that they keep constantly in touch thanks to the use of mobile phones everywhere they are." "I have overheard an Italian speak on the phone to their mother. One was on a train, one in the classroom and one in a pizzeria." But apparently this is what they had expected when coming to Italy, since the conclusion is, "This mother–child relationship isn't too surprising to me. This is part of Italian culture." As to discipline, the attitude Italian parents have seems to be very different, in some situations contradictory. If, on one hand, children running around in churches or urinating in the streets are not scolded, not even frowned upon by their parents, it seems that, on the other hand, "parents and grandparents do not seem to have a problem with disciplining their children in public, even spanking them hard. Something that in the States would be surprising if not considered an abuse, in Italy wasn't so shocking because I knew I was in another culture and that things are different."

This sort of relationship may lead to another phenomenon that is absolutely "politically correct" for Italians but may look a bit out of the ordinary to American young people. To one student's question, "How often do you see your parents?" came the shocking reply, "Well, a lot. Every day, in fact. I live with them." Of course the interviewer was surprised, since she, 7 years younger, had moved out of home 3 years before. The evaluation reflects what is absolutely evident to anyone.:

> I think that this practice (of leaving home only when they get married) can breed *mammoni* or "mama's boys" who can't take care of themselves, i.e. can't cook, wash their clothes, clean up for themselves, etc. Then when they are married, their wife becomes their "mother," doing these jobs for them, which deepens the schism between men and women in terms of being treated equally.

To follow is an example, even though it does not include manual work, of a possible result of such an education: As a family of four was observing the artwork shown at an exhibition,

> The father was pushing a carriage with a baby in it, and the mother was walking hand-in-hand with the four- or five-year-old daughter. When the baby started crying the father threw up his arms in disgust and marched away from the stroller, leaving his wife to deal with the crying baby. I think that this means that Italian men are not as patient or understanding of the young ones. In America, it is not unusual for men to stay at home with the children and be very patient with upset children, even though it was

visibly bothersome to them. I felt sorry for the woman because I feel that in all countries responsibility for children should be shared equally among both parents because it takes a well balanced family to raise a well rounded child. My friend told me that this type of behavior is very normal because a lot of men feel that the discipline of children is a woman's responsibility."

Student paper on family and discipline.

The experience I have chosen this time reflects the peculiar social structure in Siena called a *contrada*, which is not only a part of the city, like a simple quarter, but is much more, as this student discovered.

Description: It was Friday afternoon, I was walking towards the cafeteria located near by *Il Campo*, when I noticed the sound of drums, as I approached the top of the hill the sound increased. In front of the mentioned building a group of children of about 9 years old were playing the drums while another of the same age was throwing a banner. The latter was directed by a man of about 40 years old who was also throwing a banner; however, it was of a bigger dimension than that utilized by the apprentice. Not far from such peculiar actors were a group of women, and old people carefully observing the performance. However, such harmony did not last longer; one of the children took one of the banners and started chasing another, soon after all the children were playing among themselves while the grown ups were laughing.

Interpretation: Far from writing about a *contrada*, this paper looks beyond a mere competition to inquire into the meaning of extended families. All these people: the old, the women, and the children, as well as the instructors were not mere actors but rather actual characters representing reality. This interaction between them forms a bond of friendship and unity sealed by the exchange of common experiences. This in turn is what constitutes a family, it is perhaps for these reasons that Italians are well known for having a strong concept for what is a family.

Evaluation: Sometimes we complain about the lack of piety in modern society, but we neglect to look for the cause of such indifference. Perhaps, such a cause is to be found in the lack of interaction between human beings, or if such interaction is present in a deficiency of the quality of the such.

(New Evaluation:) A *contrada* is more than a competition, it is a reason for unity, which is the actual bond of a family—blood is not sufficient.

Religion

It has not been easy at all to make a selection of statements or extracts from papers about this topic. Many students write a lot, and the aspects they write about are so different and all equally interesting. This is to invite you to be aware of the fact that the following excerpts are only a minor part of what I have learned from my students.

I will start with a curiosity. Quite a few of the students on the spring program were "excited to spend Easter in Italy since it is one of the most important Catholic holidays and it is celebrated heavily in Italy, since Italy is predominantly Catholic." Consequently, they went to church on Easter Sunday expecting to find something similar to what they have in the States. They were quite surprised to see "people wearing t-shirts and jeans, few bouquets of flowers on the altar, simple at that!" and to find "a very simple environment: no choir, no entrance of the priest, no altar boys and elaborate decorations." The interpretation is that "religion is so important and in everyday life, that they do not have to have an elaborate celebration," and the evaluation is that "people in America choose to attend mass around two times a year, this being somewhat hypocritical and annoying. Thus the reason these holidays are so elaborate. Italians celebrate their religion and their faith all year round."

The fact that religion is part of people's lives in Italy is also shown by small practices (done also by young people) such as bowing their heads and making the sign of the cross when passing a church or (this is curious!) while, as one student observed, "staring at a point about 10 feet above a door," which the student later understood to be one of the "many Virgin Mary's (*tabernacolo*)" that "are seen on the buildings of Siena" and that "are a nice thing to have on the houses." The interpretation is that "while small, these practices reflect a great deal about the way Italians express themselves religiously," and in the evaluation the students appreciate them, since in the States "nobody ever does public display of their faith past wearing a cross" and since younger generations, although they do not go to church every week, "are still very religious and this is a small way of showing it."

Of course, the religious life of the Italians is also shown by "a plethora of beautiful churches" that "seem more like museums," with "great importance placed on the physical bodies of saints being within a church, usually visible." When visiting these churches, some of the students have been shocked by the lack of respect shown by tourists, their American fellows included; however, they felt better when reassured by Italian friends that the worshippers are used to such behavior and are capable of going on following a service without paying much attention to what is going on around them.

A shock for others has been the visit of a priest come to bless their apartment a week before Easter Sunday:

> It's assumed that all the residents of our building are practicing Catholics and will certainly want a priest to bless their apartment during Easter. In the United States, on the other hand, practicing religion is always your own initiative. It's almost unheard of for a landlord to organize a benediction of his apartments, or any other type of religious event concerning his tenants. Religion is seen as something very personal.

Student paper on religions

To finish this section I would like to include the experience a student had in Padua, while visiting the Cathedral of Saint Anthony. It is an interesting paper, with detailed descriptions that, I think, give a real sense of what happened.

Description: This cathedral is an important site for pilgrims, as people travel from all over the world to touch the grave of Saint Anthony. I observed men and women of all ages as they walked up to Saint Anthony's grave.

There was a long line leading up to the tomb. Everyone stood quietly and reverently holding their hands in a prayerful way in front of themselves. The only sound was that of sniffles, as tears ran down grieving family members' faces. In the tomb, people had placed pictures of loved ones and messages to Saint Anthony asking for his help and guidance. One particular woman who I observed was around the age of 60. She had a picture of a young man in her hand. Clutching it tightly, she walked slowly up to the tomb and placed her hand, which was holding the picture, on the tomb ever so softly. She began to quietly speak something. Tears were running down her face. After a few seconds, she withdrew her hand, kissed the picture, and placed it on the tomb along with hundreds of other pictures of loved ones. She took out a handkerchief and patted her eyes to wipe away her tears, She resumed her prayerful stance and slowly proceeded onward.

Interpretation: Witnessing this event gives me insight into the importance Catholicism, and believing in a higher power in general, has in the daily lives of Italians. On most occasions when I have been in a large group of Italians, they are constantly pushing and shoving their way to the front. The fact that everyone stood in a quiet line really surprised me. It shows how teachings of the Bible play out in church life. In addition people of all ages were present. I interpret this to be because Italians are taught from a very young age the importance of believing in a higher power that can help him or her through hard times. The woman came to the grave of Saint Anthony because she truly believes that the Saint has the power to do miracles and can help her. This event shows me how important Catholicism is to Italians and that they honestly believe that there is a God they can rely upon. It also tells me that they have enough faith in God to open themselves up freely and unconditionally and put the lives or memories of loved ones in His hands.

Evaluation: This was a very touching scene for me to witness. I come from a very Catholic family and so it was nice to see other Catholics practicing their beliefs. At my church at home, people do not become as emotional as they were in this cathedral, and so that surprised me. The fact that people of all ages were there and the emotions that they showed also surprised me. At my church, it is mostly the parents who attend church, so to see younger generations willingly going to church and praying to God was a beautiful sight. I love to see Catholicism in practice.

(New Evaluation:) After speaking to my Italian roommate I have come, once more, to the conclusion that Catholicism plays a large part in the lives of many Italians. My roommate described it as a way to live.

Social Status, Values, and Display

The students have made many really interesting observations about social status, values, and display, most of which are correct. A remark that is common to many students is that social status is very often displayed by what people wear:

> Italians dress really well. Most women wear suits with heels and most businessmen wear suits with ties. Even on the weekend, men wear nice shirts and sweaters. Both men and women seem to wear nice accessories, such as watches, rings, earrings and necklaces. Italians dress more conservative and more formal than do Americans.

When giving an interpretation, some of the students "had a hard time telling social status. Whether people really have the money or not, they seem to carry themselves as if they do. It is somewhat unacceptable to dress really casual like wearing jeans and a sweatshirt." The interpretation was absolutely agreed to by Italian students who, however, added that "Siena being a small wealthy city, it is more evident to be dressing more classy." The evaluation is that

> Everyone seems to take pride in their appearance and I like that. Americans are too casual. After being here and seeing the general dress code, I almost find Americans to be sloppy and rude. Almost a lack of respect as if they didn't care to dress to impress one another.

Other students have been able to notice that "many people wear things like jeans, sunglasses and belts from very prominent brands like Gucci. These brand labels are usually very visible and many, many people appear to be wearing them." They have also seen "many Italian women looking in a very judging manner at other Italian women as well as America women." The interpretation in this case is that "Italians want other people to think highly of them. Italian culture is very focused on how other people view you and that this aspect is seen through the use of such famous brand labels." In their evaluation they think "it is a little disconcerting that so much emphasis is placed on how other people view you and making sure that you fit in." The evaluation was almost all correct because it was confirmed by Italian students. However, sometimes American students had to admit that they "had only seen the shallow part of it" because, after a confrontation with Italians of their age, it had come out that "Italians enjoy high quality things in general, from wine to clothes, and that to buy famous brand name things is just an extension of that desire for high quality things."

Student paper on social status, values, and display.

This experience is a little different. It underlines the difference between men and women in Italy. The student has been able to make really interesting remarks from a simple conversation he had with an Italian male.

Description: The most accurate portrayal of social classes between men and women, I think, can be described through interaction (a conversation) I had with an Italian male. We had been talking about his future plans and his family. When I asked him what he wanted to do with his life he said he really didn't need or want to think about it, because he would be taking over his father's company. I was surprised to hear that he didn't think he needed to work hard to get ahead in life, but he figured the company was working really well now, so later when it was his, he just needed to know how to write the checks. Earlier in the conversation he was describing his two younger siblings, one who was in the US studying and the other in Rome going to university. He said that they (his sisters) were both extremely hard workers, while he, on the other hand, never worked hard in school because he didn't want to and because of his father's business. I asked him if he thought this was fair, that his sisters were working so hard in school and having to work to have a good career, when he isn't and gets to slide through life. He said this was fair because like in many Italian families the son inherits the business.

Interpretation: Although this social class differentiation doesn't have anything to do with the clothes people wear or where they shop, I think it shows a significant difference of the social status between males and females in Italy. The two sisters had been working hard their whole lives in school but still may never reach the same social status that their brother will reach by not working. In America everyone is told to work their hardest and good things will come to them, and usually this is true, and for a majority of people that have good work ethic and do find their way up the social ladder. Here, in this situation, it would seem opposite. The brother hasn't and isn't really expected to work hard in his life. Although maybe he has other responsibilities which I am unaware of in his life, it also could be that neither of his sisters wanted the company, although he was insinuating that it was because he was the male that the inheritance would be going towards him. This to me seems like it would make the possibility for women to advance their place in society, economically, difficult. They are combating people who still believe their place doesn't lie in business. On the other hand, this could be motivating women to excel, work harder and become more powerful. This cycle also gives women the psyche that they won't be able to change their place in social hierarchy since they have many things working against them. Families, it seems, are constructed to focus on the patriarch. This is a patriarchal based society which limits a women's participation.

Evaluation: The sad thing about this conversation was that, this isn't the first time I've heard this from a male (or son) in Siena. It seems there is almost an expectation of the oldest son to have the parents' or father's company. In general, I think men hold a much higher place in society. When I look at men here, because of how they are dressed and their mannerism, I see that they think of themselves as powerful which is probably true since this country does seem to cater to the males.

Relationships

The papers the students write about this topic are, I must admit, the least interesting. It seems as if most of them lead the same lives when staying here in Italy. They spend their time mostly with fellow American students. Sometimes they stay with foreign students from Europe and also South America, that is, the students they meet at the *Università per Stranieri* (University for Foreigners), where they have their Italian lessons.

> I see the same people every day. I mainly spend my time with other American students. . . . I tend to eat at the same place. I also purchase gelato from the same *gelateria* and the routine goes on with lessons, break, other lessons, night out with friend until 2 a.m. when they finally go to sleep because otherwise they would not be able to get up in time for school next morning.

They explain this because "with all the excursions (and trying to fit in personal excursions in between) and classes and homework," they "don't get to interact with the other foreign students unless it is a bar, which isn't very good for forming relationships."

Another explanation the students give for being with American students most of the time is "that unless you live with some (foreign friends) it's very difficult to break from the American group to form these ties."

However, none of them says that the experience is not positive. Having to share a room with other Americans also can be a challenge because it may be the first time students have to cohabit with strangers, and "you have to adapt yourself to their customs, understand certain things that you perhaps judged inadequate." Often they become very good friends with their roommates, and many of them say it will be a lifelong bond.

Another positive aspect is described by a student in these words:

> What makes studying abroad so amazing is that you really have to find your true identity without the people who usually define you. Although I do spend a lot of time with people from America, I am experiencing a sense

of community that I have never had. I see people I know when I walk down the street, everyone I know knows one another as well, and I know the names of everyone in my class for the first time since elementary school. I think that this sense of community is very important to many Italians, especially those that come from small places as small as Siena, so I am glad that I have been able to experience that for myself."

More attentive students say that

daily interactions often prove to be both surprising and at times pressing. Daily interactions occur with a plethora of diverse individuals, such as the local grocer, bartender, classmate or teacher. These interactions provide a window into the lifestyle of both Sienese and American individuals.

Student paper on relationships.

The paper that follows differs a little from the others, especially as far as relationships with Italians are concerned.

Description: Typically, I wake up to both my alarm and Brett's alarm going off at the same time, around 8:30 AM. I get out of bed and eat breakfast with Brad and then we walk to class together. We are always sleep deprived and groggy, but we manage to joke and talk about things. We enter class and take seats away from one another. We both like interacting with the foreign students. I like sitting near the Asian students while Brad tends to sit next to Norwegians. I talk and work with students from around the world such as Japan, Russia, and Norway. We are taught by an Italian professor. During the break, Brad and I walk back to our apartment and eat. When we are finished we go back to class. After class we join up with the other students (American and international students) and chat a bit. After making plans for possible reunion at night, my roommates and I walk back to our apartment. This is a big opportunity to hang out, eat, play chess; typically we individually take naps. At three I have my literature class with a group of girls and an American female professor. After the two hour literature class I have an Art History class with more American students and an Italian professor. After class I run to my boxing class. I have boxing class with all Italians including an Italian instructor. Afterwards I go to my apartment and make dinner and then have an opportunity to rest or hang out with my roommates. We tend to stay up late on weeknights talking, playing chess, reading, and studying. I am typically the latest one to go to bed and it's usually around 2 AM.

Interpretation: The main factors that dictate the way I interact with other people are my classes. Fortunately, I am involved in many things and with a diverse group of intelligent teachers and students. The majority of my time is spent with my roommates and because we have no TV I feel that we have been able to learn a lot about each other. Brad and I have developed a close and friendly relationship walking to and from class. I am sure our relationship will continue to our home University. My relationship with the Italian professors and foreign students is also friendly. Everybody appreciates learning from one another and respects one another. My other relationships with the American students are friendly but peculiar. We are somewhat distanced and I feel that the main reason is that many students are in long distance relationships with others back home. It seems that the guys and girls are in their respective groups rather than mingling. My boxing class is my biggest opportunity to meet Italians. Unfortunately, it takes least priority and I have missed many classes and thus opportunities to build stronger relationships. Nevertheless, I have built great relationships with a 15-year-old boxer, an old veteran, and my personal instructor, Philip. I believe they are fond of me because boxing is a small group of people and they appreciate that a foreigner such as me is willing to be part of their classes as a student learning from them. I not only am being taught knowledge of boxing, but language, and friendship.

Evaluation: I have thoroughly enjoyed making the relationships that I have made throughout this term. My time with my American roommates has been great and nobody is ever left out from any group activities. The Italian professors give intellectual insight and are surprisingly eager to learn from us as well. The mutual bond of learning from one another brings us closer and enhances our relationships. The foreign students we interact with allow us to make more and interesting relationships where we are constantly learning from one another.

Conclusion

American students *arrive* in Italy carrying invisible "cultural baggage," full of their patterns of behavior, values, beliefs, and norms that will influence their adaptation abroad. After their study abroad experience, American students are ready to go *back home* with new "cultural baggage" full of new skills, having learned how to interpret events from different perspectives.

Being good observers, witnesses of everyday life, talking to local people, writing DIE papers, keeping a notebook or a journal, taking pictures of "nonartistic" buildings like their grocery stores, their favorite restaurants, and their streets, and not using the computer as much as they would use at home (since each minute spent in front of the screen is time stolen from their experience abroad), students will leave Italy enriched by a thoughtful and *soulful* experience: "Italy: everyday another soulful experience to bring back home."

Does international education change lives? As I tell my students at the end of the course, *Close your eyes, think back to your first days in Siena, and realize that you will never be the same.*

References

Althen, G. (2003). *American ways: A guide for foreigners in the United States.* Yarmouth, ME: Intercultural Press.

Aust, D., & Zollo, M. (2004). *Teach yourself world cultures: Italy.* New York: McGraw-Hill.

Bennett, J. M. (2000). *Intercultural training for study abroad.* Portland, OR: The Intercultural Communication Institute.

Bennett, J. M., Bennett, M. J., & Stillings, K. (1977). *Description, interpretation, and evaluation: Facilitators' guidelines.* Retrieved April 17, 2007 from http://www.intercultural.org/resources.html

Biliorsi, M. (Screen Writer), & Domenichini, R. (Director). (2001). *Siena—the days of the Palio.* [Motion picture]. Siena, Italy: Video Professional Studio.

Costantino, M., & Gambella, L. (1996). *The Italian way—Aspects of behavior, attitudes, and customs of the Italians.* Lincolnwood, IL: Passport Books.

Flower, R., Falassi, A. (2005). *Culture Shock! Italy—A Survival Guide to Customs and Etiquette.* Singapore: Marshall Cavendish Editions.

Giordana, M. T. (Director). (2001). *I Cento Passi* [One hundred steps]. [Motion picture]. Milano, Italy: Medusa Video S.R.L.

Krause, E. L. (2005). *A crisis of births: Population politics and family-making in Italy.* Belmont, CA: Wadsworth/Thomson

Mautner, R. D'A. (2003). *Living la dolce vita: Bring the passion, laughter and serenity of Italy into your daily life.* Naperville, IL: Sourcebooks.

Ogami, N. (Producer). (1988). *Cold water* [Motion picture]. Yarmouth, ME: Intercultural Press.

Storti, C. (2001). *The art of crossing cultures* (2nd ed.). Yarmouth, ME: Intercultural Press.

Zanobini, F. (2000). *What do you think of Italy? Guide for getting to know Italians, not for tourists but for humans.* Lincoln, NE: iUniverse.

13

THE EYE OF THE BEHOLDER

Study Abroad in Spain Viewed Through Multi-Cultural Lenses

Carmen Arrúe

S tudy abroad offers many rewards as well as multiple challenges to students. Proper training in intercultural awareness and communication skills provides students with the tools that enable them to have more rewarding experiences abroad. Moreover, the knowledge gained in the practice of these skills should lead students to make better and more informed choices while they are away from their comfort zones. Additionally, students who possess a higher degree of intercultural awareness are more likely to portray a positive image to their host culture.

The premise for the on-site intercultural communication (ICC) course is a simple but powerful one:

> If one directs students into certain experiences, guides them to observe carefully, reflect on their reactions and then make analytical comparisons, it is possible to move students from being mere tourists or passive observers toward examining in self-conscious ways why they behave and react the

I would like to acknowledge AHA International, former executive director Robert Selby, and the universities that compose the Northwest Council on Study Abroad consortium for their vision in implementing and crediting an intercultural awareness training on-site. I am also very much indebted to my colleagues Frauke Binder and Silvia Minucci for generously sharing their experiences in developing and teaching their respective ICC courses and for the ensuing cross-fertilization that occurred. Finally, thanks are also due to Silvia Perez Sevilla and Isabel Alvarez Inguanzo, who have co-taught the Oviedo ICC class with me these past 3 years.

way they do. . . . Once they realize that they possess a culture that is different from others, they can begin to analyze apparently distinctive elements in their host culture, and from there on are better prepared to explore other new cultures in positive, analytical ways. (Selby, 2005)

This chapter focuses on an ICC as it is presently taught in Oviedo, Spain. The syllabus has been designed to accommodate the types of students that normally attend this particular program: a group of (45) American students from several university campuses, who vary regarding their Spanish language skills, cross-cultural experience, and previous knowledge about the country and the locality.

Course Design

Designed as a mandatory one-credit course consisting of 15 contact hours of instruction/discussion, the ICC course seeks to provide both an academic and a practical background to the study of culture as well as a framework within which students can analyze and process their own personal intercultural experiences. Beyond creating another cross-cultural or comparative culture class, our objective is twofold. First of all, the course strives to make students become more aware of the cultural baggage they have brought with them and the role it plays in their understanding and reactions to their present intercultural situation. Second, through various instructional methods and experiential techniques, students are taught first to develop and then to practice the intercultural skills necessary to view these experiences from multiple perspectives.

Methodology

Beyond receiving an introduction to the main concepts of intercultural communication, students apply the culture-general concepts they have learned to explore and understand elements of specific cultures, chiefly their own and that of the host culture. Selected readings on both Spanish and American culture (Althen, 2003; Richardson, 2001; Wattley-Ames, 1999) serve to complement experiential knowledge gained by the students through observation, self-reflection, and consultation with members of the host culture. In this sense, the students themselves act as informants (about their own culture and experiences with the host culture) and are asked to refer to host nationals, mainly members of their host families and conversation partners, as a base from which to explore different perspectives.

Weekly topics illustrate culture-general aspects and contrast differences between American and Spanish value orientations in areas where the students usually experience challenges. The cultural topics/themes are carefully selected and sequenced. These topics can be adjusted to suit student interest and are used to help students become more aware of current events and issues that are important to host nationals.

The instructors have found it convenient to have a varied array of exercises and materials ready for each class, because what works well in one session may not pique sufficient interest in another. Class lecturettes, handouts, film excerpts, group work on critical incident analysis (developed from student experiences), role plays, cross-cultural dialogues, and other techniques are used to introduce cultural-general concepts and the cultural topics. These are complemented with optional readings and homework assignments. The latter are used to involve students in the learning experience, and are presented in a sequenced manner from lower to higher challenge. Several tasks (reaction paper on American values, directed observation, attitude survey and questionnaire) are used early on to engage the students in cross-cultural exploration and in interaction with host nationals. Later in the course, a series of reflection papers serve to first develop and then put to practice specific intercultural dexterities.

These reflection papers are considered to be the "backbone" of the homework assignments and consist of five short papers based on an adaptation of the description, interpretation, and evaluation (DIE) exercise (Bennett, Bennett, & Stillings, 1977) in which students reflect on a particular incident they have either experienced or observed and that is, preferably although not necessarily, related to the cultural theme being discussed that week. Each paper consists of three clearly differentiated parts: The first part is an *objective description* without the use of any judgmental language (*What happened?*). The second part includes the students' *interpretation* of what they described (*Why?*), first of all from their own perspective, followed by a second interpretation from the point of view of the host culture. Students are encouraged to consult one or more representatives of the host culture (host family, conversation partner) as well as the culture-specific readings for further clues on this second perspective. The paper ends with the student's reaction/evaluation of the incident (*How do you feel?*). The students have to write a total of five DIEs, beginning about halfway through the course. The papers can be submitted in English or in Spanish, but students find it easier to use their native language.

At present, the course is organized in 10 sessions that meet for $1^{1/2}$ hours per week. With the exception of the first class, the classes consist of two parts. The first and most extensive (approximately 1 hour) is dedicated to class discussion based on the topic introduced the previous week. Students are expected to participate actively and are called on if they do not volunteer. The instructors act as facilitators for this discussion, taking special care not to interfere too much in order to allow students to come to their own conclusions. The second part (approximately 20 to 30 minutes) serves to introduce the topic for the following week, on which the homework assignment for the next class discussion will be based.

Intercultural Themes and Methods

The rationale and content of the 10 classes are described in this section. Following a brief introduction to each class theme, we discuss instructional methods and put the theme and methods into the context of the host culture: the city of Oviedo in the province of Asturias in Spain. An actual DIE submitted by one of our students, illustrating student reactions, follows. An evaluation of our experience with the DIE methodology as it is described here will be discussed at the end of the chapter.

The Intercultural Toolkit

Because the Oviedo students come from diverse university campuses, which vary in the extent and content of predeparture orientation, and may have no prior intercultural exposure, part one of the first class introduces the main concepts of intercultural communication (Bennett, 1998). The material covered in this class corresponds to an abbreviated version of that included under the section titled "Understanding Culture" from the training manual *Culture Matters*, developed for Peace Corps volunteers (Storti & Bennhold-Samaan, 1998). In the second part of the class we focus on cultural generalizations and compare these with stereotypes by introducing the next topic or theme.

Bullfighters and Cowboys: Stereotypes vs. Generalizations

During part two, the object of our discussion is to teach students to discern the difference between cultural generalizations and stereotypes. Americans tend to feel very uncomfortable about using generalizations, so this class helps the students to overcome this aversion by teaching them the value of carefully used generalizations. Class discussion explores the sources and impact of stereotypes, and students are prompted to reveal their own stereotypes of Spanish culture. The instructors also discuss regional stereotypes within Spain as well as common stereotypes of other European nations. For homework, the students conduct a short survey regarding which characteristics/traits Spaniards consider to be most/least associated with Americans. We tally the results in the following class, and the ensuing class discussion serves as an introduction to dominant American values.

Know Thyself: Dominant American Values

The objective of this class is to make students aware of their own culture. We begin with a short exploration of the sources of American culture. The handout *The Values Americans Live By*, Kohls's (1984) classic description of dominant American values, follows. The students choose one or more dominant American values from the list and write a short reaction paper for homework addressing the following questions: *Do you think it/they hold true for your own variant of American culture? Why do you think this is/isn't so? What about the majority of Americans that you know?*

We have found this to be a very effective exercise for the students. For a great many of them, it represents the first time they have given any thought to the fact that they have a culture or even that they share some common values, given their concept of America as a very diverse nation and especially due to the American notion of the uniqueness of the individual. Students are usually quite surprised to find just how much some of these values apply to themselves. Among the values that the students most strongly identify with are Time and Its Control, Individualism/Independence/Privacy, Self-Help/Initiative, Materialism/Acquisitiveness, Personal Control Over the Environment, Future Orientation, and Competition. A good many students recognize how these values are interconnected. They also write about how their particular variant of American culture (ethnic, gender, age group, college student) has moderated some of these core values or how change in American society is "tempering" some of them as well.

In Other "Words": Nonverbal Communication and Communication Styles

The class begins with an introduction to different communication styles. The students are introduced to this topic through the use of handouts based on the work of Edward T. Hall (1969, 1973, 1977) on the characteristics of low- versus high-context cultures.

One of the major causes of misunderstanding between students and their home stays is the result of differences in communication style. Spaniards, and Asturians in particular, have a tendency to speak loudly and with emotion, and this is often interpreted by the students as "scolding" even when what is being said (e.g., telling them to wear a scarf for the cold weather) is merely a recommendation and not a command. Indirect messages sent by the families regarding some sensitive topic are not always understood, and this in turn is misinterpreted by the family as insensitivity and carelessness on the part of the student.

American friendliness and informality also contrasts greatly with Spaniard's public seriousness. As Wattley-Ames (1999) points out, Spaniards behave differently with strangers than with people they know. However, as anyone who has lived for an extended period of time in Spain can ascertain, becoming a known person is often a question of contact and having created an impression of courtesy and patience during your first contact rather than a result of a formal introduction. Students often consider persons in the service sector to be unfriendly until they understand these differences.

The second objective of this class is to make students aware of the importance of the nonverbal aspects of communication. One of the main points to drive home is the fact that about 90% of what is communicated in any given culture is conveyed in the form of nonverbal messages (Hall & Hall, 1987). When one considers that these nonverbal messages are culture specific, it is easy for the students to become aware of the types of misunderstanding that can occur in intercultural situations. At this point, students have been on-site for a little over a month and are already beginning to notice and react to the challenge that differences in nonverbal communication present. In some cases, their responses can be quite adverse as they react to invasions of their personal space or find themselves unable to keep up their usual level of activity and fill their time as they are accustomed at home. Students find Spanish eye behavior, particularly staring, to be intrusive.

Often, it is the result of curiosity or an expression of Spaniards' favorite pastime while strolling, "seeing and being seen." American informality in dress, especially that of young college students, is often out of sync with the value Spaniards place on appearance and dress, particularly in the city center, where more formal attire is the norm. The students often express surprise when they repeatedly see their host mother change from comfortable "home" clothes to, say, a suit, just to go to the corner store for some bread.

For homework, groups of students observe and report on the following: time (monochronic/polychronic, daily cycle) and space (public, private, personal), haptics, kinesics, and other aspects of nonverbal communication. Reflection questions are provided to help the students tie in their observation of Spanish patterns and to analyze their own reactions to the differences they observe and experience. This task is considered to be a low-challenge observation activity.

Sample report on public and private space submitted by a 20-year-old female student.

It seems that public space in Spain is set up with an emphasis on socializing. There are many plazas and parks filled with benches (some of which face each other to facilitate interaction) which seem to often serve as meeting points or just hangout spots. During business hours, these areas are full of older people or people with children. Even in the evening and at night, these areas will be completely full of people just socializing. In the U.S. (in my experience at least) you never see the public areas full of people unless there is a special event or it's New Years Eve. When you do see people walking down commercial streets, they are usually rushing somewhere whereas here they seem to be enjoying a stroll. In Oviedo there are several "promenade" areas where people can just walk. The places are usually very pleasant and maybe even lined with fountains and trees to beautify them. I think that the public areas are designed the way they are because everyone goes "out" to socialize here.

Private space in Spain is also very different from ours. As far as I've seen, the places where people live (mainly apartments) tend to be much smaller than ours. The city is much more built up (i.e. lots of tall buildings which have stores at street level and residences on the upper floors) and concentrated in city center. Americans love to build huge sprawling spacious residences, usually in the suburbs. . . . The reason for this is probably that Americans do much of their entertaining inside their homes. Since Spanish people don't do much entertaining at home, their living space is much tighter and closer and is considered to be private to the family.

Society and the Individual: Community and Mobility

In this class we explore the relationship between society and the individual and how mobility affects the individual and the society. To introduce the topic, we pose the questions to the students, "What factors make individuals more or less prone to relocation? What effect does frequent relocation have on the community?" asking them to brainstorm about the characteristics one would find in each kind of society (more mobile/less mobile). Students also comment on their own mobility history.

In order to help them gain a deeper understanding of this issue, the instructors introduce the concepts of individualism/collectivism and low/high uncertainty avoidance (Hofstede, 2001). The ensuing discussion is usually lively, and with some help from the instructors and the readings, students begin to gain an understanding of the complex socioeconomic factors that are involved.

The students explore the subject further in their homework assignment by interviewing their host family or conversation partner regarding migration history, ties to the locality or home town, household composition, proximity and ties to the extended family, and sources of material and moral support. In the following class discussion, the results of the questionnaire are tallied, and we examine if the findings of the interview conform to the Spanish patterns described in the readings. Time and time again, the students find that, as representatives of Oviedo, their host families are deeply rooted in the locality/region and have an extensive network of kin and friends in the area with whom they maintain close contact and upon whom they count on for material and moral support to a much greater degree than they rely on institutions.

As a fringe benefit, the interview schedule has proven to be a good way to "break the ice" with the host families during the first few weeks of their stay. The class discussion also provides some important clues about the forces at work in Spanish society, relational styles, and lifestyles that they will further explore in subsequent weeks.

Commentary on host family interview submitted by a 21-year-old female Japanese student.

I interviewed my host mother, Asun, who is 70 years old with 6 children and 6 grandchildren. Different from the information about Spaniards staying in the same place, Asun has lived in four different cities for her husband's job. She favors Zaragoza (where she was born) and Oviedo because these are the places where she has lived for a very long time of her life. Family rather than place is essentially what Asun identifies with primarily. In fact, four out of her six children live in Oviedo. They are all married and have kids. Almost every day Asun's children come over to her place and bring the grandchildren. Her son in Oviedo cannot see her very often because he is busy, but for instance, Asun hugs him very tightly and gives kisses all over his face as if they have not seen each other in ages, even though it was only two weeks. Asun says she would respect her children if they wanted to move to another city as long as they are happy. I believe my host mother expresses a very strong connectedness with her family and not as much with the region. I feel that her children have naturally been settled down in Oviedo to live close to their mother because they are truly dependent on each other. In the US from my point of view as a foreigner, people are always moving to one place or another, depending on their job. Being independent from parents economically is considered to be the first thing to do among young people. Although Americans put great values on independence and mobility, in Japan we are more dependent on each other and we do not like to change our living style as much as Americans do.

Becoming Spanish or American: A Look at Formal and Informal Education

To introduce the important subject of socialization, we begin with a discussion of the formal education system. Whenever possible, this is done through a panel discussion where Spanish and American students give brief presentations on the formal education system (university level) in their respective countries. With the help of handouts on American and contrasting cognitive and learning styles, educational systems, and academic expectations, the students begin to understand how the Spanish formal education system mirrors other aspects of the culture. They are also asked to think about the U.S. formal education system in the same way. They do make these connections and recognize American values such as competition, informality, equality, fairness, individualism, and self-help/initiative in their own college experience at home. The Spanish students are both eager to share the details of their own experience and curious to learn about the differences.

After this introduction to the formal aspects of socialization in each culture, students focus on the informal aspects for homework. Because Spaniards tend to socialize outside of the home, it is not difficult to observe the interaction between adults and children in public places. Students are assigned their first DIE essay, for which they are asked to observe examples of child rearing and discipline and reflect upon how these provide clues to how different cultural identities are formed, both here and in the United States.

DIE on informal education submitted by a 20-year-old female student.

Description: I was walking to school one day. I stood at a crosswalk with a mother pushing her daughter in a stroller. There were two elderly women at the crosswalk as well, not in direct association with the mother and daughter. It was around 2 pm and the sun was hot and powerful. The child was in the stroller dressed for cold weather and had managed to unbutton her coat. One of the old women saw this and immediately reached down and buttoned the child's coat, talking and cooing to her. The mother was completely at ease during this whole interaction and just smiled at the old women and said thanks. The little girl was no more than 18 months old and was dressed like a little doll. Her hair was tightly pulled into a half ponytail with a big bow almost as big as her head. She wore a perfectly matching outfit with tights that matched the little flowers in her shoes. The little girl was fussy and fidgety in her stroller, clearly uncomfortable in the layers of clothing she had on. Almost every child I have seen here is often times dressed better than the parents . . . not a hair is out of place or shoelace untied. Playgrounds and courtyards are filled with kids until what in the U.S. is considered very late at night. Children accompany parents or what seem to be grandparents, to cafeterias and bars.

Interpretation: I think that my crosswalk example is without a doubt telling of how children are included and regarded in Spanish society. It is obvious that children here are the gems of the lives of adults. They are pampered and indulged here a lot more than in the States in the sense that independence and growing up are things parents don't seem to place much emphasis on at least in the same way as American do. I also got the impression that even if a child isn't yours by relation; the fact that they are a child gives you a right to look after them. In the U.S. people view raising and caring for their child as their responsibility or that of those that they specifically designate to care for their child. Not just anyone can adjust your child's coat in the U.S. We view strangers as possible predators to children. Here I feel as though children are the only group in the society that, universally, people don't dare harm; it's as though everyone here is on the same page about kids. Also I think that the lack of freedom parents give their children here at a young age is indicative by how they dress them. In the U.S. kids are expected to be capable and autonomous thinkers by age four. Children and are given the freedom to express themselves, especially through clothing. At four, I wore a tutu and tap shoes to Church and it was totally accepted. Here I don't get the sense that this would be ok. All personal growth for kids here is semi-stunted and one can see the implications of this later in adolescence and young adulthood as children stay in the home way longer than in the States.

Evaluation: I don't really know how I feel about the way children are here in Spain. By American standards they're all super spoiled and babied but maybe my country should do a little more of this. So much pressure is put on American kids to be successful, focused and driven. Parents in the U.S. are way less forgiving of their children and want them to grow up right away. The age threshold for parenting in the States is way lower. By the time I was 14 I had a part-time job and split the housework with my mother along with going to school and being active in extracurricular activities like sports. Here less is expected of kids and that's weird to me. Parents here are held way more accountable for the lives of their children than in America. What baffles me is that the parents and adults here seem to enjoy the responsibility; that they are willing and enthusiastic about it.

Relationships and Lifestyle

Oviedo students are required to live with a host family, and this comes coupled with the opportunity to gain firsthand experience in what constitutes *the* most important social group in Spain (Hooper, 2006; Wattley-Ames, 1999). Host families provide a natural opportunity to integrate into the community and learn about the daily life in Spain. It also is the setting where students experience the most challenges. For one, they suddenly find themselves being forced into intimacy with people that are, at least initially, strangers. Living with a host family is different from living with roommates or on one's own. There are new implicit and explicit rules and social conventions regarding mealtimes, comings and goings, and other day-to-day experiences that did not apply to the students in the independent lives they had enjoyed in the past. Vastly different concepts of privacy are also responsible for a great many misunderstandings. For Spaniards, the home is a very private domain reserved for members of the immediate family and household. It is difficult for students to assimilate that as temporary family members, they now do not enjoy the freedom of receiving friends or entertaining in their new home. For American students, on the other hand, privacy is valued chiefly with regard to the self and, second, one's room and one's possessions. Closed doors can be a very negative sign from the point of view of the host family. Intrusions in the student's room to clean, change the sheets, or even, as one student pointed out, "fold up dirty underwear" can create a lot of discomfort. Breaches of privacy on both sides are common, at least at the beginning. Unfortunately, some students and families are never able to fully understand or respect each other in this regard.

Another area that is a source of conflict has to do with the students' feelings of independence and self-reliance. Oviedo host mothers treat their host son or daughter as they would their own children. In other words, they clean, cook, wash the dishes, and do the laundry. In most cases they do not seek or welcome help from the students regarding household chores. Some students are delighted in being relieved of these tasks, but others find it trying not to be able to take care of these somewhat personal matters on their own or when and where they want to. Finally, Asturian "mothering," often imbued with lots of unsolicited and generally well-meant advice regarding food, proper clothing for the weather conditions, studying, or practicing the language, also tends to clash with the students' ideas of independence and privacy.

Oviedo students are also matched with one or more Spanish conversation partners in order to facilitate language practice and socialization with Spanish peers. The Asturian people are generally friendly and hospitable, and as there are few English-speaking visitors in the region, they tend to be curious and welcoming with foreign guests. Thus, it is not hard for the students to experience full linguistic and cultural immersion if they so desire. Of course, there is a limit to what a student can accomplish in this regard in just a few months' stay.

This class theme provides an excellent opportunity to deal hands on with some of the major challenges students face in their social relationships with host nationals, and permits us to coach students on strategies for establishing and maintaining relationships with the locals during the term while at the same time keeping their expectations at a realistic level.

One of the most important lessons a student can learn here has to do with the fundamental differences between friendship patterns in the United States and Spain and the important role that obligation and reciprocity play in relationships for Spaniards. For many students, it has proven to be a most difficult lesson to learn.

DIE on relationships and lifestyle submitted by a 20-year-old female student.

Description: One of the things I was most looking forward to in coming to Spain was meeting Spaniards and making Spanish friends. When I arrived I tried diligently to meet Spaniards at school and when I went out at night. I would spend time with my host mom and meet the people she knows and my host sister would introduce me to her friends. When meeting friends of my host family I would receive cordial greetings and if we met again they would greet me warmly but nothing more. At school and when I went out at night I found groups of friends together who did not seem interested in meeting new people.

Interpretation: In the U.S., university is considered a prime place to meet new people and make new friends. In fact, college and university students are expected to make new friends throughout their entire time and even meet a possible future spouse. Naturally, when I arrived, I expected students in Spain to have the same outlook. I expected to meet other students and gradually spend more time and get to know them, eventually becoming friends. Unfortunately I have found that for Spaniards, friendships are not something made in 3 months or by being introduced by mutual acquaintances. Just like my host family's friends did nothing more than greet me after we had been introduced. Spaniards do not normally consider an introduction sufficient to start a separate relationship. As for the Spanish student and groups that I have met at night, I soon found that these people grew up together. They had known each other since they were in school together as children and now are still friends at the University. They spend time together in and out of school. I have found that what makes a friendship in Spain is not necessarily knowing things about a person (meaning their personal life, likes and dislikes, etc.) but knowing them a long time like the students who have grown up together or the people who have gone to the same gym with my host mother for years.

Evaluation: It is now nearing the end of my exchange and I will go home having made few Spanish friends and with a bit of disappointment. However, in exchange for Spanish friends I have made many friends with other exchange students. I feel that because we are away from our friends, families and support groups at home and we are all going through similar experiences we were able to relate and bond quickly. Though I may have wanted Spanish friends I am not upset with the situation I encountered. First I have met many Spaniards and have been able to experience Spanish people and their culture. Also I have made many good friends regardless of the fact they are not Spanish.

Gender and Sexuality

This is a topic that is of great interest to the students. As young single people who are in the midst of the great adventure of living and studying abroad, the students often become involved in romantic relationships during the term. As foreigners, they enjoy special status and attention from the locals and tend to go out to the clubs more frequently than they do at home. In class, we analyze the way students go about showing romantic interest or disinterest and explore how this is done by host nationals. The students are quite perceptive and are quick to pick up on fundamental differences. For example, one student observed how his host brother courted his girlfriend. He referred to it as characterized by intensive contact on all fronts: email, phone, and spending time together. The rest of the class was in agreement with him that it was the opposite for Americans, where, in fact, there seemed to be what they called an unwritten "3 day rule," in which one is supposed to "play it cool" in order not to scare off the other person. The instructors took the opportunity to point out how these "formulas" were consistent with other aspects of each culture. American friendship patterns and values such as independence and privacy were at play here, whereas Spanish rituals of friendships and obligation also governed their behavior in romantic relationships. This discussion led to the types of misunderstanding that could arise when the American strategy was used on a Spaniard or vice versa, with results being contrary to what was intended.

Female students tend to receive quite a bit of attention in Spain. Cat calling and more intrusive behavior from male courters often produce feelings of sexual harassment, anger, and even fright. The instructors take the opportunity to coach students in dealing with some of the most common types of misunderstanding that can arise between an American and a host national of the opposite sex.

The class discussion often leads us to point out "hot" topics such as gender abuse, unfortunately on the rise, and the recently legalized gay marriages, which helps increase students' awareness and prepare them to take part in conversations and discussions over these controversial and often-talked-about issues.

DIE on gender and sexuality submitted by a 21-year-old female student.

Description: It seems like just about every day I get a comment from men. It is common for men to yell *"rubia!"* or *"guapa!"* from cars, across the street or right in my face. There was even one time when a group of about six guys saw me, walked up to me, put their arms over my shoulders and started walking with me and trying to convince me to go to a bar with them. Another time I was walking home one night and a guy yelled *"¿cuánto cuestas?"* (How much do you charge?) from down the street and then his friends all started laughing.

Interpretation: From my perspective this seems rude, offensive and sexist. In the United States when men do this type of thing, it's viewed as degrading and kind of a gross thing to do. Equal rights struggles have always been a big deal in recent U.S. history, so degrading women can, in a way, seem uneducated. From a Spanish perspective, these types of comments are seen as normal. It seems like Spaniards don't make as big of a deal about being politically correct. This type of thing is probably not seen as offensive. Spaniards seem to be a lot more communicative than Americans.

Evaluation: Honestly, in the beginning I found it kind of annoying, although flattering. But now I realize it happens all of the time to people who appear American or different from most Spaniards. I barely even notice it now and pretty much try to ignore it. I think if a man were to yell something at me in the U.S. I might be annoyed or alarmed just because it doesn't happen often. But here, I realize it's harmless and I'm used to it now. I don't feel threatened or offended at all, it seems completely normal now.

Us and Them: Identity, Diversity, and Social Status

This topic particularly interests the students, as they are indeed short-term sojourners and can easily identify with the "them" in this equation. We introduce the topic with a brief lecturette on the sources of Spanish diversity and how these contrast with those in the United States. Regional identity is very important to Spaniards, to the point that national unity is being compromised by the growing demands for regional nationalism, and separatist-inspired ETA terrorism. Not a day passes without reference to these matters in the news, be it the local press or the television newscast. Regionalism in the United States is experienced in a vastly different way, as is the incomprehensible idea of nationalism at the state level.

Immigration is another much-talked-about topic. Until recently, Spain was one of the most homogeneous societies in Europe and had a low level of racial diversity. About a decade ago, low Spanish birthrates prompted Spanish authorities to promote immigration, causing the population to become increasingly multiethnic in the span of just a few years. In fact, Spain's immigrant population has quadrupled since the year 2000 and is higher than the European Union average (Hooper, 2006). Coming from Latin America, Africa, and Eastern Europe, today Spain's immigrant population is particularly visible in large cities such as Madrid and Barcelona and is becoming more common in provincial capitals, like Oviedo, as well. The benefits afforded by the new immigrants have come hand in hand with an increase in social problems (illegal immigration, a rise in crime rate, and racism). These social changes have posed great challenges to a native population that has had very little time to adjust. One area where this is particularly evident is the lack of political correctness and racial sensitivity present in Spanish linguistic expressions and advertisement. In this sense, America's long experience with immigration contrasts greatly with Spain's recent one.

Another great contrast that students quickly notice is that between the American egalitarian mentality and the importance of status, social class, and authority in Spain. Here the instructors introduce the concepts of ascribed versus achieved status as a conceptual framework from which the students can comprehend better the inequalities and deference that they observe in the course of their daily lives in Oviedo.

For homework, the students write about an incident they have experienced or observed that points out the way society in Spain either includes or excludes people or makes some persons prevail over others. By making connections with what they have learned in previous classes the students can also reflect upon how Spanish patterns of forming relationships help or hinder the acceptance of a foreigner/outsider in the community.

DIE on "Us and Them" submitted by a 20-year-old female student.

Description: One way that I constantly note how Spaniards either include or exclude people is personally. Obviously, as I am not Spanish and am an American, I am seen as separate from Spanish people from the Spanish culture. Upon entering a café, I often end up waiting several minutes without service while several other groups of Spanish people ("regulars" to the café) receive help before me when they arrived after me. These people are most always more formally dressed than I (fur coats and all) as well as older. Both of these other factors are significant for their prompt service I am sure.

Interpretation: It may be that, as I am a new face to the waiters in the bar, they exclude me from service and elect to help a more well-known face first. It may also be a sign of respect to the elders whom they are serving before me. By now I am aware of the cultural respect for elders within Spanish culture; this certainly may contribute to my exclusion as I am younger. It may also be a matter of class. As wealth and/or prestige can often be expressed by dress, the fur coats and blazers may call attention (and service) to those with more money while I (in my tennis shoes and windbreaker) am left to wait until the waiter has already helped those who are bound to leave a bigger tip.

Evaluation: Of course I don't like being excluded or overlooked because of reasons of class, ethnicity or age. On the other hand, I am sure that I am not the only one waiting my turn. I realize that the Spanish culture is quite distinct from the American culture, including the idea that all should be treated equally. Accordingly I have adjusted and patiently wait my turn.

Ethics, Morality, and Religion

We begin this class by introducing the concepts of universalism versus particularism (Trompenaars & Hampden-Turner, 1998) as a framework from which the students can begin to explain the differences and contradictions that exist in regard to these issues both within Spain and also in contrast to American patterns. For one, many students come with a stereotypical view of Spaniards as profoundly Catholic and expect religion to be the driving engine in Spanish life. On first impression, this stereotypical view seems to hold true given how religion, namely Roman Catholicism, marks public holidays, the architecture, festivities, and the language, far more than is usual or even legal in the United States. However, it is not long before the students become aware that in present day Spain Catholicism is very much a cultural identity, and many Spaniards who call themselves Catholics and partake in some of the rites of passage (baptism, first communion, ecclesiastical marriage) may not attend church services on a regular basis. This unconventional religious practice can be interpreted by some of the students as "superficial" or "hypocritical," stemming from the consideration of "religious" in "either/ or," "black-and-white" terms.

Another thing that students often observe with surprise and a certain degree of vehemence is how readily Spaniards are willing to break the rules. Cars double parked, butting in line, and particularly, their conversation partners bragging about cheating on their exams—these things surprise, even shock, the students until they begin to understand the underlying reasons for these behaviors. In Spain, compliance is dictated by circumstance. Those circumstances, in the examples mentioned, have a great deal to do with what has been described as the Spanish "picaresque" mentality, that is, an attempt to gain advantage for oneself or one's group in what is considered, chiefly, an unfair world (Wattley-Ames, 1999). Coming from a different orientation, American students often brand this type of expedient behavior as "unethical" or, at best, "morally lax."

For homework, students choose between writing about how religion appears to influence the individual and society or about a moral or ethical dilemma that they have experienced during their stay.

DIE on ethics, morality, and religion submitted by a 20-year-old male student.

Description: When I arrived in Spain, I was informed that a surprisingly high percentage of the population considered themselves Catholic. After living here for a time and talking to a large variety of people, I found myself quite surprised by this statistic. Almost nothing of that which I considered Catholic was demonstrated by their way of life. One night I decided to ask my host mom what she thought about religion. She provided me with a very interesting and illuminating answer. To my surprise, she told me she was Catholic even though she mostly never went to church, observed nearly none of the traditional ritual of the church and that was pretty much the same for the majority in Spain. She continued to tell me that her daughter was technically "Catholic" although she had refused confirmation and would probably never attend a church service.

Interpretation: Although contrary to what I had previously considered a self-proclaimed "Catholic," I quickly understood that for Spain, at large, the Catholic religion embodies the cultural aspect of their society more than a deeply spiritual belief. My host mom and I fleshed out the idea that it is a way for them to remember their history and to keep it alive by re-membering it through names and labels. In Spain, Catholicism isn't thought of as a dogmatic system nor any similar set of rules by which to live, but simply as a means through which to describe themselves: *Somos católicos.* We appreciate our architecture, we acknowledge our past and we keep alive those attitudes that were birthed within the tradition of Catholicism. Spain is undoubtedly a country that takes great pride in its way of life and this sentiment is echoed even in the atheist who calls himself Catholic without thinking twice.

Evaluation: I did not have a strong emotional reaction to this entire topic when I first began learning about it. So Spain is Catholic, so Spain doesn't act how I would expect a religious country to act—they don't really embody much of what the "Religion" extols. I was a bit confused, maybe a little surprised, but in matters of religion, I usually try to suspend judge-ment, assuming that it takes time to reach clarity in matters so deep and integral. I suppose, however, that there may have been moments when what I perceived as the superficiality of their so-called "religion" annoyed me. To listen to my host mom call herself a Catholic and wondering how she could believe such words or if she even understood what it meant to be religious. But after waiting and listening and considering their history and way of life, I realized how the general idea of a "religion" can mean something quite different than I had experienced before.

Cross-Cultural Shocks and Stages

In the last class, we "revisit" the concepts of culture shock and return culture shock. Although most students have been introduced to these concepts in both the predeparture and on-site orientation, it is our impression that few tend to take them seriously. The Oviedo program offers both a fall quarter and a spring semester each academic year. During the fall quarter, the last ICC class coincides with the end of the program, and we ask the students to commemorate past/present culture shock experience and their individual reactions to it. We devote discussion time to the repercussions of return cul-ture shock and take the opportunity to make some recommendations. Dur-ing the spring semester, the ICC class end coincides with the midway point in the semester when many students are undergoing the second "dip" in the cultural adjustment cycle. They are usually quite tired both physically and mentally by this time. For this reason, the last ICC during spring term cen-ters on the phenomenon of culture shock and offers only an introduction to reentry shock. We later send the students a written reminder of the latter as part of the program wrap-up at the end of their stay.

We also try to have the students assess their individual adaptation to Spain during the term. We do this by introducing them to Bennett's Developmental Model of Intercultural Sensitivity (Bennett, 1998). We also distribute a diagram of cultural adjustment that correlates levels of cultural awareness and attitudes toward cultural difference with the adjustment cycle (Storti & Bennhold-Samaan, 1998), which the students find very useful in tracking their intercultural maturation during the term. Finally, we ask the students to complete a series of debriefing questions regarding their adjustment to Oviedo. The following are what some students have to say:

I think I am more reflective and stop to analyze the big picture more.

I am now a very good compromiser and I want to stay that way.

I have developed a greater appreciation for cross-culture blending. Once you become a minority on someone else's turf you find yourself analyzing the situation differently and even depending on inclusion. This will hopefully broaden my patience and acceptance in America for those filling the same role I've had.

I feel more confident in myself and my personality. When I encounter another culture either directly or indirectly and there is friction, I feel more prepared to handle it. I'll ask questions to myself about why perhaps this is happening, its significance, etc. I'll be aware of my own culture as well and how that affects the intercultural interaction.

As a final "fun" project, students work in groups to develop a skit that captures some of the cultural differences between Spaniards and Americans in a humorous yet respectful way. The groups perform their skits during the final class dinner. The dinner and skits bring closure to the class and provide us with an informal opportunity to laugh and make light of difficult and trying moments that are now past.

Challenges and Rewards of the DIE Method

The DIE method has proven to be a very effective technique for exploring different perspectives. Dissecting an experience by describing it aseptically and withholding judgment until having considered several possible explanations allows students to get a clearer picture of what has occurred and to learn from this experience. Repeated practice leads students to develop an important intercultural communication skill and takes them from self-awareness to awareness of the other. Students begin to question their own ethnocentric interpretations and become cognizant of the importance of cultural and personal relativity.

The instructors explain the method, but it is through self-practice and feedback from the instructors that the students begin to master the technique. We read *all* DIEs and return them with detailed comments in the following class. Students discuss their DIEs during class and often find comfort in the knowledge that their peers also share some of these challenges. Equally important, during the discussion students provide important insights to each other that help clarify a situation or problem more effectively than possible by the instructors or the readings. The instructors are careful not to interfere too much and allow the students time to reach conclusions on their own.

At first, it is difficult for students to master the mechanics of the exercise, that is, to separate the various parts of the DIE, or they omit some of them (e.g., their evaluation) altogether. Others fail to include one of the cultural perspectives. Curiously, this is often the American perspective, but it does come through implicitly. The contrary also occurs when students turn in DIEs that are excessively "academic or theoretical" and not grounded on a particular experience, which lessens the heuristic value of the exercise. Some students resort to deductive stereotypes about Spanish culture, often based on the behavior of a unique individual. Another thing the instructors have noted is that at first students are reluctant to evaluate an incident negatively. We think this may express a desire to be politically correct. Our task here is to encourage them to express themselves freely, if not openly, in class, at least in the privacy of their reflection papers.

A few students do not make an effort to write their DIEs conscientiously and turn in essays that are too short or carelessly written. We have witnessed students actually writing their DIEs in class, right under our very noses. In these cases, we have later asked them to refrain from doing this because we would rather accept a late essay and have them pay attention to the discussion. When the course was first introduced, students who were unhappy about the mandatory nature of the class or with what they perceived as an excessive workload for one credit confessed to "making up" the DIEs on their program evaluation. This is something that we find incomprehensible, much more difficult, and infinitely less productive with regard to skill development than actually basing the exercise on a real experience. Our philosophy in all these cases is that students learn best by doing and "one reaps as one has sown."

In spite of these difficulties, an increasing number of students recognize the benefits derived from the DIEs in helping them make sense of the cultural bumps that they experience. It is evident from reading the sample DIEs included in this chapter that students went beyond the mere observation of cultural difference to a deeper reflection by having to analyze it from various perspectives. The fruits of this exercise were new insights and understanding regarding the intercultural experience. Specifically, students say that the DIEs helped them get a sense of their own culture and of themselves, to question and/or to reaffirm values, enhance their communication and understanding abilities, and for many, to learn to be patient and to defer frustration in light of challenging situations. Students repeat these comments time and time again on the evaluation part of their papers.

Without a doubt this methodology, if carried out conscientiously, offers students a chance to explore other perspectives, which can and often does come hand in hand with an increase in their tolerance for difference. The skills gained are of immediate importance and have direct applicability during their study abroad sojourn.

Conclusions

In the ten years that I have been directing this program and assessing the hundreds of students who have studied abroad in Oviedo, it is my general impression that a great deal of personal growth and learning transcends the mere academic experience. The results are often uneven and vary from individual to individual. In 3 years of experience teaching the on-site ICC course, it is evident to me that students are thinking more and learning more than they would if left to their own devices. So far, I can offer only anecdotal impressions and look forward to the day when these can be verified and quantified through objective research endeavors such as the ones that have been included in this book. As international educators we have a responsibility to both the students we send abroad and to the host culture that receives them. We can accomplish this best by doing the most we can to provide students with the necessary tools to enrich their intercultural experience and by creating sensitivities that will have a positive impact on the host culture. The new abilities gained, coupled with other intercultural and personal competencies that are often enhanced by the study abroad experience, will surely prepare students to be better citizens in this globalized world.

References

Althen, G. (2003). *American ways: A guide for foreigners in the United States* (2nd ed.). Yarmouth, ME: Intercultural Press.

Bennett, J. M., Bennett, M. J., & Stillings, K. (1977). *Description, interpretation, and evaluation: Facilitators' guidelines.* Retrieved April 13, 2007 from http://www.intercultural.org/resources.html

Bennett, M. (Ed.). (1998). *Basic concepts of intercultural communication.* Yarmouth, ME: Intercultural Press.

Hall, E. T. (1969). *The hidden dimension.* Garden City, NY: Doubleday.

Hall, E. T. (1973). *The silent language.* Garden City, NY: Doubleday.

Hall, E. T. (1977). *Beyond culture.* Garden City, NY: Doubleday.

Hall, E. T., & Hall, M. R. (1987). *Understanding cultural differences.* Yarmouth, ME: Intercultural Press.

Hofstede, G. (2001). *Culture's consequences: Comparing values, behaviors, institutions, and organizations across nations* (2nd ed.). Thousand Oaks, CA: Sage.

Hooper, J. (2006). *The new Spaniards* (2nd ed.). London: Penguin.

Kohls, L. R. (1984). *The values Americans live by.* Retrieved December 20, 2007 from http://www.uri.edu/mind/VALUES2.pdf

Richardson, B. (2001). *Spanish studies: An introduction.* New York: Oxford University Press.

Selby, R. (2005). *AHA values statement.* Available from AHA International, 221 NW 2nd Ave, Ste 200, Portland, OR 97209.

Storti, C., & Bennhold-Samaan, L. (1998). *Culture matters: The Peace Corps cross-cultural workbook.* Washington, DC: Peace Corps Information Collection and Exchange.

Trompenaars, F., & Hampden-Turner, C. (1998). *Riding the waves of culture: Understanding cultural diversity in global business* (2nd ed.). New York: McGraw-Hill.

Wattley-Ames, H. (1999). *Spain is different* (2nd ed.). Yarmouth, ME: Intercultural Press.

14

CASE STUDIES FOR INTEGRATION OF EXPERIENCE AND UNDERSTANDING WHILE STUDYING IN VIENNA

Frauke Binder

Lack of time is a high hurdle to overcome in the process of helping students learn about and adjust to a foreign culture. One term of the Vienna program lasts for 10 to 12 weeks. This gives the students only a short time to learn more about specific aspects of the host culture. The Vienna program has set up a number of projects and case studies to enable the students to get to know Austrian culture from an insider's perspective.

These projects contribute to a richer understanding of the Austrian culture, support the students' process of adjustment, and help integrate aspects of both the host culture and home culture. They are not just an accumulation of factual knowledge but have a number of different functions that operate on several levels at the same time: for example, contact with people of the host culture, personal involvement, encouragement of intercultural adjustment, and flexibility. It is not only the content but the manner of completion of the projects that contribute to the overall results.

Overview of Approaches to Projects and Case Studies

In general, projects and case studies are arranged with some common requirements. The structure of the projects has the effect of encouraging experiential learning within a seemingly purely academic assignment.

Contact With the Host Culture

The students often complain that they do not have the chance to get to know Austrians during their 12 weeks in Vienna. Working on the case studies can act as a springboard for interacting with Austrians. Within the guidelines to the projects, a list of questions is provided that can be used as a basis for discussion.

Talking to host families and friends, the students get to know different reactions and the ways people are personally involved in the topic. During their interviews they will not only "study" body language but also different communication styles. Some students reported that they felt on an equal footing with the hosts in discussing a "serious" matter. These experiences enhance their flexibility within the cultural frame and help them understand the meaning of generalization (instead of stereotyping), when approaching another culture's values. Individual variation in responses of informants dramatically demonstrates that the culture is not monolithic.

Integration and Adjustment to Culture

Dealing with the projects as "specialists" helps students to examine how cultural values are expressed within a specific topic area. When many perspectives are offered on a wide range of topics, it is not easy for young people to form their own opinion. But by being involved with a special topic, the students can identify more with the host culture and at the same time compare their host's approach with their own. The smaller chunks of information make understanding the larger host culture more manageable. This encourages students to develop their own personal view. Overall, the experience will relativize the students' view regarding their own culture: every culture is different, and their own cultural values are only one way of living, among many others.

Multitasking Level of Information

There are a variety of information sources to be used by the students. Finding their way through the Internet and choosing from many different approaches, visiting the public libraries of the city, and probably participating in events is a multitasking challenge. The students of different projects will probably pay attention to many things in a closer way (for example, the labels on election billboards). One student reported how interesting it was when he accidentally got into a presentation of an election party and observed how people reacted when different representatives spoke. The projects promote a selective vigilance for information sources not previously within the awareness of the students.

Presentation of the Project

Another requirement of the project will be the presentation of the topic to fellow students. American students usually like to present their topics with enthusiasm and fantasy. In the Vienna class there is a suitcase for all "actors," containing false beards and noses, wigs, etc. These props make it easier and more fun for all the students to illustrate their topic.

Former students chose many possibilities to act out their experience with their projects. There was a scene where a "pregnant young Mutter" dropped in at the social services department to ask for maternity benefit, a balloon as the "baby" under her pullover. Of course, the serious aspect of the presentation was lost when the balloon burst. A special role play that achieved a very high level of attention from the rest of the class took place when five male students pulled down their trousers to sit, in colorful boxer shorts, on imaginary "toilets" to read and comment on the latest newspaper articles on recent political developments.

These examples show that the presentations can be held in an expressive and funny way and touch serious topics at the same time. The extra effort at crafting and acting out the presentations takes more involvement with the topic, and thus makes the content more memorable.

The Projects

The content of the projects is designed to broaden the student's understanding of life in Austria and to highlight key cultural differences. Projects include topics such as social politics, environmental policy, Austrian election politics, and Vienna and the Cold War. Minorities and Foreigners—the Expansion of the EU (European Union) is a larger project concerning the rising number of refugees around the globe and Austria's role in the European Union. The Holocaust project also serves as preparation for the excursion to a former concentration camp. These projects enrich the students' global perspective and highlight the role of both Austrian and U.S. culture. Most projects are linked to other courses and excursions in the program, such as Human Rights/International Law, The European Union, and 19th Century Habsburg Monarchy.

Minorities and Foreigners—The Expansion of the EU

In this project, students explore the views of citizens of the present EU member states regarding their role and function within the EU, particularly in view of the latest and upcoming expansion of EU member countries. What is the intention of the EU? How do member countries feel about having had to surrender sovereignty in many questions directly affecting their countries? What concerns are felt regarding the economic differences between the present member countries and new member states?

Austria's entry into the EU has also altered the legal situation of immigrants and asylum seekers. Students discover what the rights of minorities and foreigners in Austria are today and how Austrians feel about minorities, foreigners, immigrants, and asylum seekers. Has Austria's entry into the EU altered the emotional situation?

A student shows that it was not only a gathering of knowledge that shaped her impression, but also an emotional awareness. Relating back to a personal reference can contribute greatly to identifying with the host culture:

> Imagine moving to a new country where the customs, landscape, people, culture, smells, sights and sounds were all different and foreign. When I think of an immigrant, I imagine back to the 1500s and a person dressed like a pilgrim, travelling on either the Niña, Pinta or Santa Maria to a new land to start a fresh life. The truth is today, here and now, there are immigrants living in our towns and cities. They are coexisting with us in our world, riding the U-Bahn, walking on the streets, shopping and working with us. They look like us, live "normal" lives like us, and have loving families. They endure the hurt and fear caused by discrimination. Fear and uncertainty are consistently present when discussing the topic of immigration and integration. Many people still hold on to their prejudice and discrimination, rather than trying to accept and integrate immigrants into the culture. It is important for each of us to expand our minds and learn acceptance and understanding.

At an excursion to the *Integrationshaus* (Integrationshaus, 2007), a home for refugees and asylum seekers, students are informed how people live after successfully crossing the Austrian border, and under which conditions the legal status of a recognized refugee in Austria may be obtained. A student reports that, through the excursion to the Integrationshaus, his

> eyes were opened to that which I had previously had much ignorance. When I thought of immigrants previously I had thought of people traveling from their homelands with hope, dreams and plans to create happiness and success in a new land. . . . Hearing the stories of where these people came from and how they got to Austria gave me chills and nearly brought a tear to my eye. . . . The Integration House seemed almost uninhabitable to our standard living conditions that all of us students have had the luxury to come from. After I analyzed the situation I realized how lucky I really am.

Another student considered the trip to the Integration House as

> very educational, it gave me a peek into the life of an immigrant, their struggles, the support and help they receive, and what integrating into a new culture involves. The woman in the Integration house explained that many people look down on immigrants as uneducated, but many have previous vocational training, and work experience. It is important to realize that inviting immigrants to become an active part of a community can add color and culture to a city.

Additional excursions to the European Union Agency for Fundamental Rights (FRA) (FRA, 2007) and the United Nations High Commissioner for Refugees (UNHCR) (UNHCR, 2007) enhance the student's knowledge of discrimination of foreigners in employment, housing, and education, as well as racist crime data. Both excursions are linked with the program's Human Rights/International Law course.

Seeking reasons, explanations, and possible solutions, a student who grew up in Romania worked on her paper *Discrimination of Roma in Austria and Romania*:

> To my surprise I have even encountered begging gypsies on the streets of Vienna speaking the Romanian language. I asked about this topic during our excursion to the FRA, and the answer which I received inspired me to view the situation of the Roma people from a more accepting perspective. . . . I asked about the cause of Roma discrimination at the FRA, [and] the ideas which were introduced served to inspire me to further

research. . . . I have come to realize that it in fact does not matter "what came first," or in this case how the Roma came to such a low level of living and poverty. Rather, I think that the focus should be on working to better the situation by efforts on both the Roma people and on the governments of the countries in which they live.

One student reflected on his own temporary status as a foreigner in Austria:

> Coming to Austria I knew that I was going to be a minority as an American studying in Vienna. I had a bit of anxiety thinking more of how I was going to handle the vast communication, cultural and political differences, but was also very excited to experience all of it. As my semester progressed and I grasped a better idea of the Austrian culture I realized that . . . my citizenship of being an American granted me certain, if not more privileges that are unfortunately not granted to the minorities that live, work, and try to survive on a daily basis in Vienna. . . . I have learned much in my semester of being a minority in a foreign culture. My experience in Vienna has opened my eyes to discrimination issues throughout Europe while providing me greater insight on why and how it happens, along with possible solutions. As the world becomes increasingly globalized I believe it is only a matter of time before Europe makes a transition towards equal legislation and representation. . . . I look forward to going back to the States where I can keep a watchful eye on the news and media to see progressions of integration.

Common reactions

Most of the students are personally very concerned when visiting the *Integrationshaus*. Often they compare the destiny of the immigrants to their own family members who immigrated from Europe to the United States. Analyzing Austria's immigration policy gives them the opportunity to look into the subject in their own country more carefully and to find a personal position. Values of justice, inclusiveness, safety, and so on are made overt in the Austrian situation and compared and contrasted with students' perceptions of those values in their home culture.

Some of the students state that they had resentments or were prejudiced against immigrants in the United States. They can highlight the whole matter now from various perspectives and develop a deeper understanding. Through the project they had the chance to better understand the whole situation of immigrants who left their own country and the reasons why people left; they gained a more personal and individual insight. The students who already dealt with immigration policies in the United States may develop further criticism regarding improvements in Austria and the United States.

Holocaust

The Vienna program offers an excursion to one of the former concentration camps in Mauthausen, Austria, or Auschwitz, Poland. Although these excursions are voluntary, most students participate. Each semester some students trace their roots to Europe, for example, their Jewish grandparents having fled Europe. Students reflect on the special role of the United States as "liberator" in World War II and have the chance to gain a closer perspective of the historical events from the European side.

Many questions arise with the project. Some of them were asked in a presentation at the former concentration camp Mauthausen:

> Our project was to find out how the Austrian people feel about the existence of Mauthausen. However, when searching for this answer, there are a lot more issues that come up that cannot be avoided. Are the feelings of the Austrian people similar? Does it change with generations? If there is an attempt at justification, what could it be? What was happening in the minds of the soldiers, the SS-officers, the Nazis? Could something like this happen again?

Visiting places like Auschwitz is not an easy task, thus good preparation is crucial for the students and consists of two parts: information about the historical background and a reflection on Holocaust memorials in different countries such as Germany, Austria, Poland, and the United States. What precisely does the sight of Holocaust memorials awaken in visitors? Historical knowledge? A sense of incontrovertible evidence? Revulsion, grief, pity, fear? Visitors clearly respond more directly to objects than to verbalized concepts. But beyond emotion, what does our knowledge of these objects—a bent spoon; children's shoes; crusty, old striped uniforms—have to do with our knowledge of historical events? More specifically, what do we understand of the killers and victims through their remains? One student wrote:

> Being at Mauthausen was a chilling and terrifying experience for me. I felt that our presentation couldn't compare with the feeling that everyone has

when entering Mauthausen. Mauthausen can be better understood through study of history and sociology, but unless one has been there while it was running one cannot comprehend all of the emotions one feels about such a horrible place. But study and knowledge can bring us closer to never having something like Mauthausen ever happening again.

My experience at Mauthausen was one that I will never forget. It was very moving and terrifying to stand on the same ground where such horrible things took place, but it is an experience that I would never take back.

Facts, figures, and reflections help the students cope emotionally:

I think hearing everyone's different response to the questions really gave me more insight to the Holocaust. I had heard about Mauthausen before, but now I was getting real information that I could process. So many people feel so much emotion about the Holocaust that it is almost mesmerizing to hear them talk about it. It is a major part of history and will be remembered in hearts and history books forever.

The students are given pictures of the exhibition, but also reflect on questions like, How can "normal people" become mass murderers or contribute to the extermination of a whole population? Could we have been victims as well, for any reason such as skin color or our personal beliefs? Auschwitz stands for a monstrous crime against humanity, and as such it belongs to everybody, whether one lives in Europe, the United States or anywhere else.

After analyzing several reasons why the Holocaust could happen, a student related the events to other incidents:

While none of this can serve as an excuse for something so horrible as the holocaust, it can at least help to explain. While we can hope and pray that genocide of this magnitude will never reoccur, there are cases of thoughtless killing all of the time. For instance, the U.S. soldiers killing the innocent women and children of My Lai because they were ordered to do so. The genocide in Bosnia is another example.

The Holocaust is closely linked to the Minorities and Foreigners project. Sadly, the same mechanisms of discrimination and racial hatred that lead to atrocities still exist in many parts of the world.

Common reactions

A thorough preparation helps the students to process the impressions of their visit in former concentration camps. The students are confronted with many aspects of the atrocities. Because it is such an emotionally charged experience, it is hard to find a personal attitude to such a monstrous topic. To see the Holocaust in connection with atrocities that take place nowadays and also in their own countries is a hard task for the students. Where are the beginnings of such an act of violence? In discrimination or ostracism? Where can the students begin to relate the topic to themselves?

The examination of the Holocaust has a far deeper dimension: *How can people get that far? Am I able to hate people so much that I would accept an extermination? Would I protest if something similar happened in my country?* It is especially hard for American students to criticize atrocities and torture in the United States: a comparison with Guantanamo or the eradication of the Native Americans is rather seldom. Actual references to human rights questions are very limited. Personal references show up there where relatives were killed or hunted for racial reasons: Jewish family members, for example.

Although the thoughts or experience with the Holocaust project may only slowly sink in, the visit in Mauthausen or Auschwitz can remain a pivotal experience and broaden the student's awareness concerning human rights questions or behavior toward minorities.

Social Politics

The students find out about different aspects of social politics in Austria. Unlike in the United States, insurance for unemployment, retirement, and health services is compulsory in Austria. What rates are paid for medical insurance and how does it function? Is there more than one system available? What kinds of health services exist? What is covered? The students ask their hosts or other Austrian friends about medical insurance, maternity leave and child support, unemployment issues and retirement, and contrast these facts with the social politics and insurance practices in the United States. This helps the student form an opinion of the advantages and disadvantages of what both the Austrian and U.S. governmental systems offer. It provides an opportunity to consider and discuss aspects of their home culture that often are deemed irrelevant by college-age students. The topic exposes several value differences between host and home culture.

Some students could clearly identify the cultural reasons for the different social politics in Austria and the United States:

> In America people are more expected to bear costs of such things themselves. This probably stems from the American ideal of "the self made man" and the ideas of the American Dream, in which anyone can achieve success if they work for it and try. In Europe the idea of a "self made man" is not really valued. Another important factor contributing to this key cultural difference is the level of government involvement expected and valued. Such social programs rely on a large amount of government involvement, which seems expected and normal in Austria.

Many students desire a better health system for the United States, too:

> The ideas of providing universal health care and maternity leave and *Kindergeld* are interesting and American society might benefit from these programs, however I do not think that there is any chance, particularly with the current economic system, of people being willing to pay the amount of taxes that would be necessary to fund such endeavors. Nonetheless, this has been an interesting topic to explore, as it is a very important factor in everyday Austrian life.

Common reactions

Most of the students favor Austria's healthcare system to the social system of the United States. Of course they see advantages if the Austrian state pays for health insurance, pensions, and unemployment. But through the taxes that have to be paid by the employees a certain constraint is set. This project shows one cultural difference very clearly: Austrians, who belong to a more "group-related" society, are willing to sacrifice some personal freedom to support the social system; the Americans in a more "individual-related" society prefer to choose the insurance themselves.

Both ways of thinking have their worth in the respective societies. By getting to know another approach to how social care is handled in a different culture the student's perspective and cultural flexibility will be enriched: there is not only one way of thinking and arranging one's life.

Environmental Policy

At their host families, students soon discover different attitudes toward environmental protection. They see separated garbage, a lack of tumble driers, and smaller cars, among other things.

In Austria, many homes do not have clothes dryers or dish washers. This is seen as a frivolous waste of energy. Many Europeans even turn off the water when washing hair during a shower. Clothes are dried naturally, and fresh air is highly valued, as exemplified in the fact that the Viennese almost always have the windows open. Waste is not tolerated. Even food is sold in smaller portions so as not to create excess waste. Everyone uses public transportation at some point.

In their project, the students' task is to find out about the major source of electrical energy in Austrian households, what options Austria has regarding additional or alternative energy, how Austrians view these energies, and whether or not they are state supported.

Where are nuclear power plants located in countries bordering on Austria, and how far are they from Vienna? Are they considered safe by Austrian standards? How has the GAU (*größter anzunehmender unfall*, "worst-case scenario") in Chernobyl affected Europe's (and particularly Austria's) view of nuclear energy? What kinds of garbage can be disposed of separately? What is the Kyoto Protocol and what are Austria's plans for 2008 according to the protocol? What was the stance of the U.S. before November 2000 regarding the Protocol? After November 2001? How much does energy cost, how much does your host pay per month? How is the market for organic food in Austria?

Examination of such topics will induce students to reflect on their role as citizens of the world and to a different approach toward resources:

At my home in Vienna my roommate and I try to be as environmentally aware as possible. We only turn on the heat when we are home. Lights are only turned on when necessary. Showers are limited to 10 minutes, even if I really want to stay in longer. There are no opportunities for recycling in our apartment house, but often we walk to a recycling can to discard what we can.

Often, they are more aware of differences in their own country:

Americans feel that they have a right to resources when they are able to pay for them. Austrians seem to understand that those same resources are very limited and should be preserved through the efforts of everyone. . . . In the U.S., energy and water are barely limited. Watering of lawns is restricted in times of drought. In general, Americans don't have a sense of responsibility for things that do not affect daily life. For example, we all want to stop animal testing and save the whales, but we are unwilling to turn off the tap when we brush our teeth.

Common reactions

This criticism often builds the conclusion the students draw from the examination of environmental consciousness in Austria. After their return, some regret that they do not have a public transportation system any more. Other students would like to go on with garbage separation. Other students understand that the relation to environmental consciousness in Austria is somewhat more responsible, but that it is not possible to transfer one system into another culture. Mostly, the students reflect on and criticize their own smugness, the way they were brought up in the United States, and how this contributed to treating environmental consciousness differently.

Being conscious about the environment gives the students a wider perspective about cultural rules and the meaning of environmental care for the Earth. Getting to know another way of living enables the students to adjust to the culture more adeptly; they will know how to deal with garbage when they come back to Europe. The topic prepares them to expect other rules of behavior and ways of thinking in other foreign countries they will visit in the future.

Vienna and the Cold War

Most of the students were born in the 1980s. For them the history around the Iron Curtain exists only in books. This project enables them to get in touch with people who experienced this very special part of history. By hearing their hosts and friends tell personal impressions, the students will be involved on a personal level. Participating in this project, students gain additional insight into the history of the city of Vienna, which from the end of World War II until the fall of the Berlin Wall was located along the Iron Curtain.

How was Austria affected by being "between the borders" and by the changes since 1989, and did these events change the image Austrians have of their eastern neighbors? How strongly have the systems of communism and capitalism affected Western and Central Europe since 1945? What changed after the implosion of communism? What do younger and elder people think about the past? Why was Vienna a special meeting point for people from both sides of the Iron Curtain? How did people live in former Eastern-bloc countries? What were the advantages of the communist system, what were the disadvantages? Students choose special issues linked to communism that are personally significant.

The feeling of freedom in the former Eastern-bloc countries was obvious in 1989 when the Iron Curtain fell. One student reflects about the impression that her host mom's reports made on her:

> As a young American woman of the 21st century, living in a country that has housed such brutal wars and been on the border of incredibly oppressed countries in their recent past has allowed me to understand more of the emotional and social impacts of the last hundred years. I will always remember my host-mom's face as she stated how she would always remember the day the Berlin Wall fell.

After almost two decades, how do people from former Eastern bloc countries view the situation, especially the advantages and disadvantages of the communist and capitalist systems before 1989 and now?

Additional impressions and data can be gathered on one of our 3-day excursions to cities in former Eastern-bloc countries, such as Prague, Czech Republic, or Krakow, Poland. Especially the architecture and the cities' changes during the last few years can add to the impression and link the students back to history. The excursions are part of the 19th Century Habsburg Monarchy course.

The project provides a deeper understanding of the systems of communism and capitalism, reflecting back on the home culture's values:

> To me, it seems that Austria has for one become so small that war seems absolutely unfathomable from a practical perspective. Secondly, it appears that Austria has had to learn exactly how horrible war can be, . . . that the idea of war is completely exorcised from their thoughts. America could learn much from the countries that have housed wars, especially the World Wars.

Common reactions

Through this project and especially the interviews, the students understand automatically how the history of a country affects the perspective and the attitude of life in the present. Dealing with history has an impact on the consciousness in the future. Therefore it is necessary in any foreign culture to learn and understand more about the important incidents of history.

Not only facts and knowledge are important. The interviews with the host family or friends broaden the student's awareness of the emotional impact of historical events through gathering an oral history. This awareness can further be applied to the United States: How did the absence of world wars on their soil and their aftermaths reflect on the American lifestyle?

Austrian Election Politics

Often, Americans are astounded about the openness and directness of the Austrian communication style toward political issues. Politics are widely discussed, and students are frequently asked, "Who did you vote for for President?" A student reports:

> When I go out everyday, there are always people handing out flyers . . . about politicians and political parties. I see many Austrians having discussions over these flyers. . . . Here in Austria, talking about politics seems as natural as breathing.

The comparative paper required contains different views on political systems and election politics of both Austria and the United States. Billboards, advertisements, and signs that the students see on the streets or the mass media are utilized.

Discussions with locals and personal research helps students examine questions regarding politics in Austria, the ways in which they might differ, and how they compare to other countries in Europe and the United States:

> My primary source for this paper was my Austrian host, and political party posters and pamphlets. While much of what I've learned is fact, my sources obviously introduced a level of bias to the issues and party candidates themselves. Because an Austrian citizen votes not on issues directly as in the U.S., but solely for a party and the candidates therein, the party situation is central to an understanding of the upcoming election. . . . it is likely that the election will produce high voter turnout. The U.S. only reaches 50 percent for a presidential election. . . . My host predicts FPÖ will drop due to its wishy-washy past few months, and The Greens will gain. While much of the U.S. doesn't even care about its own elections, I'm quite excited how the Austrian elections will proceed.

The students analyze the following questions: What is Austria's military role as a member of the EU? What is its responsibility to protect itself militarily? How does the population feel about purchasing new jets to protect its airspace? What is Austria's position as a neutral country in the EU? How do the Austrians feel about the role of neutrality in their self-understanding? How did neutrality come to be? How does it differ from the German role?

An excursion to the United Nations Office in Vienna (UNOV) (UNOV, 2007) is linked to the subject Human Rights/International Laws. When participating in this project, the students come to understand more about the role of the United States in world politics. Many other questions are running aside the main topic: How does the two-party system affect the personal freedom of the voters? Why is talking politics in the United States rather taboo, and what is the role of the media? Many students enjoyed understanding more of the Austrian politics and comparing them to U.S. politics. They even started to discuss more with friends and hosts. Some of the students also brought their experience with other cultures and their election politics into play.

Common reactions

Neither culture has the "ideal political situation." The topic enhances more tolerance for other cultures and offers the great chance to develop political interest, insight, and criticism.

Research and Final Presentation in Class

Students are (should be) occupied with the various projects throughout their time in Vienna. The final paper (five to seven pages) contains interviews with the students' hosts and Austrian friends, instructors, and their own impressions and conclusions drawn from the excursions and their experiences in Vienna. The Internet also provides facts and figures about Austria and the European Union for such projects. Additional readings are given to the students in class, and two daily newspapers are available.

One excursion is mandatory and depends on the project chosen by the student. A presentation in groups of four to six includes one 10- to 15-minute role play and a class discussion.

A better knowledge of the host culture enables the students to take part in everyday conversation and contributes to contact with locals during their stay.

Projects and case studies help students to weigh cultural advantages and disadvantages, and enable them to "function in two cultures" (Kohls, 1984, p. 65). The impression of how things function and how life feels in a different culture as well as the comparison with the home culture broaden the students' perspective, their cognitive and emotional understanding. They experience how the cultures are affected and shaped by common topics, how different the opinions of people in the same culture toward one topic may be. The more energy the students give to their projects the more they will become insiders of another culture and the broader their perspective will become toward other lifestyles. There is not only one way to live our lives, there are multiple—and the way we live in our culture is just one of them.

Conclusions

To set up a project like the ones mentioned in this chapter, any topic can be chosen: from history to the present, topics that are widely discussed, important upcoming events such as elections, environmental matters, architecture and city structure, or a topic from the first pages of a newspaper. Social topics also offer a good basis for a project: for example, role models of men/women, teachers/students, newspapers, universities—nearly everything that people of the host culture are willing to discuss.

An exact outline for the students should explain the topic definition, further details, and also a few questions that the students can use as a reference to interview people and gather facts. The guideline should also hold information about which sources the students could use to get to know more about their project, such as websites, excursions, places, people, offices in the city, etc.

Approaching their project from different points of view, the students will get to know the foreign culture better—by talking to people and getting to know their communication styles, body language, and ways of expressing their different opinions about one and the same topic. Students' observations and impressions can be part of their role plays at their presentation. If necessary, there can be different role plays for the same topic.

Close examination of one topic helps students to distinguish cultural values from individual values. A variety of opinion helps to develop generalizations instead of stereotypes and will enhance a student's flexibility within and outside of the host culture's frame. Experiencing different communication styles while exchanging with hosts, friends, or instructors can help enhance intercultural awareness and adjustment.

Some of the students may feel that topics like social policies or the environment don't really have much to do with them. The projects are designed to awaken a fascination with cultural differences and to prepare students for those differences so that they can embrace them. The aim is to be pleasantly surprised when encountering cultural similarities rather than expecting only similarities and being shocked by unanticipated differences.

Young Americans especially do well to prepare for cultural differences, particularly in a world of globalization where contact with international business partners is required.

References

European Union Agency for Fundamental Rights (FRA). (2007). *About us.* Retrieved May 25, 2007, from http://www.eumc.cu.int/eumc

Integrationshaus. (2007). *The Integrationshaus "project."* Retrieved May 25, 2007, from http://www.integrationshaus.at/en/ih/

Kohls, R. (1984). *Survival kit for overseas living.* Yarmouth, ME: Intercultural Press.

United Nations Commission of Human Rights (UNHCR). (2007). *Basic facts.* Retrieved May 25, 2007, from http://www.unhcr.org/basics.html

United Nations Office at Vienna (UNOV). (2007). *Welcome to the United Nations Office at Vienna.* Retrieved May 25, 2007, from http://www.unvienna.org/unov/

15

DYNAMICS OF CULTURAL CONTEXTS

Meta-Level Intervention in the Study Abroad Experience

Kris H. Lou and Gabriele W. Bosley

How does one harness the transformative power of cultural immersion? Prevailing wisdom advises the more complete the immersion, the greater the intercultural learning. Efforts are typically focused on single student homestays, language "contracts," and coursework and co-curricular programming that intensify the connection and interaction with the host culture while minimizing the contact with home culture peers. Anecdotal evidence continues to support the experience of study abroad as our students, in general, appear to benefit and undergo some form of transformation. Yet, at the same time, these transformed students have difficulty articulating specific knowledge acquisition and behavioral changes resulting from that experience. More on faith than empirical evidence, international educators have gone forth confident that the payoff is there, however elusive it may be to isolate and articulate.

Most international educators would likely expect empirical evidence to support the premise that intensified cultural immersion leads to improved intercultural learning. What many might not have expected, however, is the need to strike a balance between effective, multifaceted immersion and providing the space and time for reflection and guided discussion *with one's home culture peers and/or instructors*. As Michael Woolf (2007) asserts, "Immersion as an objective needs to be modified by some element of reasoned distance, creating a distinct intellectual space" (p. 1). This recognition illuminates the drawbacks of full immersion and, more importantly, points to the need for intentional intervention in all types of study abroad programming. As Woolf points out, "full integration precludes curriculum innovation" (p. 2), and therefore efforts to work with our students toward specific intercultural learning outcomes run contrary to the model. Fortunately, the mounting evidence—anecdotal and empirical—is revealing that intervention invigorates the experiential learning that underlies the purpose and richness of study abroad. There are many possible approaches for intervention depending on a variety of factors including program types, durations, and learning outcomes. This chapter provides a look at one specific method that has met with promising success: a course that connects, via the computer-networked Blackboard software (2007), the students to home culture peers who are themselves situated in cultural immersion programs in other countries around the world, as well as to home university instructors *and* international students attending the home university.

We will first discuss the purpose of the course in the context of "value added" study abroad outcomes and intercultural learning. Next, we will discuss the course structure along with various assignments, including actual student writing excerpts demonstrating student growth resulting from intentional intervention. We will conclude the chapter with some closing observations regarding the limitations, challenges, and opportunities of teaching and administering this type of a course, along with the use of the Intercultural Development Inventory (IDI) (Hammer & Bennett, 2001) as one of the many instruments and inventories designed to measure specific traits, qualities, and developmental outcomes.

Course Purpose

The overall intent of this writing-centered course is for students to develop intercultural skills while immersed in another culture and thereby capitalize on the transformative experiential learning potential of study abroad. Accordingly, the course is organized to facilitate and intensify the experiential learning process in a cultural immersion context with two major goals: (1) to introduce students to the value of understanding, accepting, and adapting to cultural difference and (2) to improve the overall cultural immersion experience by providing essential predeparture, during-semester, and reentry instruction designed to help students develop intercultural skills.

Learning outcomes derived from the course goals are (1) to understand the advantages and disadvantages of culture study, including the contrast of internal versus external perspectives, and the concept of critical self-consciousness; (2) to encourage critical thinking about culture and to develop perspective-taking abilities; (3) to examine similarities and dissimilarities between and within cultures; and (4) to explore forces that contribute to the development and changes of cultures, including social, economic, political, geographic, environmental, agricultural, and religious factors.

The need for a course of this nature arose from the experience and recognition that, without explicit and intentional intervention into the study abroad experience, students, in general, will limit themselves to surface-level experiences. That is to say, we are providing tremendous (and expensive) experiential opportunities without guidance or facilitation of any intercultural learning from these experiences. The result is a strong sense, based initially on anecdotal evidence, that for the majority of students the semester abroad constitutes little more than exposure to cultural difference. Although we have continually sought to improve the nature of the exposure by providing access to and enhancing curricular, co- and extracurricular dimensions, the net effect for the majority is a "missed opportunity" for significant intercultural learning. Accordingly, this course is an example of, as Savicki notes in the preface of this book, "the combination of understanding the rationale, seeing the research connections between theory and outcomes, and utilizing the rationale and connections in program design that develops the most potent results." (p. xx)

In much the same way that service-learning distinguishes itself from volunteering, the intercultural learning process requires a framework within which students reflect on their experiences, analyze behaviors and values, suggest tentative conclusions or generalizations, and apply such to the next set of experiences. Repetition of this experiential learning cycle throughout the immersion experience is critical for the development of intercultural skills, not the least of which is an emergent understanding of how the student's own cultural identity is socially constructed. With both theoretical work and related research underscoring the importance of facilitating the development of intercultural competence in order to optimize the transformative nature of study abroad, we developed a response that combined both research and application. Additionally, we integrated an assessment tool that serves to measure intercultural development and to establish both general course goals and individualized learning objectives (more on this to follow).

It is important to note that individual students might autonomously capitalize on their immersion opportunity, depending on the level of maturity, cognitive tools, and previous experience they bring to the table. The duration of the immersion experience also plays a role. It is clear, however, that the vast majority of young adults studying abroad for a mere 4 to 5 months are incapable of extracting the lessons we value without purposeful intervention in the process. The scenario is akin to placing our students on our own campuses, showing them the library, and hoping they walk away 4 years later with the necessary tools and skills for success at the next level. Importantly, we recognize that valuable intercultural learning can and does occur without intervention. We also conclude, however, that such unguided learning is actually rather minimal and that the potential for transformative experiential learning is easily wasted.

Thus, in addition to the new and ongoing research and mounting anecdotal evidence, our best instincts led to the development of an intercultural course that would accompany and guide the student through the immersion process with the intention of capitalizing on the *laboratory of the other culture* to develop intercultural competence. Subsequently, our own empirical data, derived from the IDI, substantiated our earlier conclusions: namely, students left to their own devices will tend to gain very little in the way of intercultural development. Although our own data are still inconclusive due to small samples, they mirror those of broad-based studies such as the Georgetown University Consortium Project with 1,300 student participants (Vande Berg, Balkcum, Scheid, & Whalen, 2004), which found that study abroad without intervention results in consistent, but rather modest, intercultural development. More important, the Georgetown data also reinforce the argument for intervention by demonstrating that the greatest gains occur when students receive mentoring and that "own culture group" support results in greater intercultural development.

General Course Structure: A Meta-Level Approach

Our approach in designing this course is a blend of ethnographic and interculturalist-constructivist methods, focusing on a progression of critical analysis: moving from the examination of the *self* to the *other* and then to the synthesis or integration of the two. Specifically, students are provided with a series of ethnographic assignments designed to stimulate engagement with the host culture in a basic participant-observer mode. Notably, many assignments are not activities that students would normally do on their own, which at the very least has the effect of expanding the reach of experience. Each week students are asked to reflect on and write about their experiences by posting them on the home university's Blackboard site. The students' work is then accessible to the instructor at the home campus *and* to the other students in the course. The students are then required to review their peers' postings on the same assignment and provide feedback. The key here is that the students' peers are located in many different cultures around the world, not at the same program site or even in the same host culture. Advancing discussion of intercultural concepts with peers in other cultures as opposed to discussion with peers in the same host culture avoids the common pitfall of soothing one another's discomforts with judgmental references. It forces each student to focus on the essence of each situation because they cannot fall back on supposed common understandings. The students' peers will not know what is meant by "You know, that typical Japanese subway persona . . ." or "Spaniards in their typical way will . . ." The next step—the interculturalist-constructivist approach—raises the intercultural learning to a meta-level, that is, above the specific host culture and its idiosyncrasies. This feature enables the students and instructor to examine how similar cultural processes are at work in different settings with dissimilar outcomes. Within this framework the door is now open, first to recognizing how institutional processes (e.g., family, education, etc.) operate and, more important, to investigating how and why outcomes are different. Students are not limited to the particular cultural expression of their host culture and at the same time are pushed by the assignments to be active participant-observers in that culture alongside their peers living in various cultures around the world. In the process, the students begin to develop intercultural skills by raising the level of discussion from mere description to cross-cultural comparative analysis.

Intercultural Encounters

During their first week in the host culture, students are asked to simply reflect on and summarize their thoughts and experiences in just a few sentences, remembering that the onset of "culture shock" is to be viewed, not as a malady that afflicts all international travelers, but most of all as an opportunity to *re-discover* or *re-imagine* oneself. The guided discovery process begins during week two when students are asked to write about a particular experience that is reflective of the culture shock that most students are experiencing by that time. Although most students have studied the host culture prior to going abroad (especially language students), this is the time when students are beginning to realize the complexity of their host society, with corresponding variations in culture, class, ethnic and religious groups, geographical regions, rural and urban settings, each with its own distinctive characteristics. Moreover, the differences in language, institutions, systems, customs, and values all come together to form a host culture that can suddenly take on aspects that not only seem foreign but can alienate and cause dysfunction. At this stage, few students will go beyond mere description of what they are experiencing. Thus, the first assignment in the course is to simply describe an experience that constituted culture shock for the student. Students are asked to select and visit a particular location in their new town/community that seems particularly "foreign" to them. In this location, students should assume the "participant-observer" role, taking in the experience through all their senses. Observations, thoughts, and feelings of this experience are recorded and discussed with others at the host country site (natives and non-natives). Upon conclusion of the participant-observer exercise, a final report is submitted to the course instructor, including the results of shared discussions. In the following excerpt Beth offers her observations during week two as she struggles with the cultural differences she encountered:

> The past two weeks have been one continuous adventure. At times thrilling and at times frightening, living in Mexico is far beyond anything I could have imagined. Culture shock is something that has become part of everyday life. It is impossible to avoid it. Even the seemingly "all American" trip to Wal-Mart is filled with new colors, tastes, smells, sights, and sounds. Every aspect of every day is different. Whether that is a good thing or not I have yet to decide. Some days I am perfectly fine with where I am and what I am doing. Other days I just want to go home to my nice warm bed, and my extremely organized university.
>
> The assignment for week two was to visit a place that seems foreign. I had a difficult time deciding exactly what to do because everything here seems very foreign to me. I attended a church service with my host family my first Sunday here. It was very interesting to visit a different church full

of people that I did not know. All of the songs were sung obviously in Spanish, and the sermon was on the tower of Babel and how God created different languages, which was very appropriate considering my situation. I was amazed at the differences and similarities that I saw in the service when compared to the church I attend back home. . . . I discussed this with my roommates after the service, and they said they too had similar difficulties with all the differences that they saw each day.

Lindsey found that the more she compared her Mexican lifestyle to her life at home the more unhappy she grew with the place. She had found that taking every experience for what it was and not trying to over analyze it made her time here more enjoyable. I agreed that comparing was the perfect way to become homesick and disgusted with where I was. So far, I have found that it is better to just absorb what I see, and not to try and categorize everything as good or bad. I need to just relax and let the time here flow over me without trying to control everything. What happens will happen, my deciding whether or not it is like what I am used to is not going to change anything. What I am used to is not always best, it is just familiar.

The instructor can now engage the student—in *near* real time—with purposeful intervention and offer guidance: for example, assuring the student that it is appropriate to analyze and compare. Simply "letting the time flow over me" or "judging" the host culture are not productive ways of dealing with these experiences and emotions. While this first writing exercise during week two offers an initial gateway to self-reflection and cultural self-awareness, few students are able to offer more meaningful insights into the experience without guidance, in spite of having been introduced to the concept of the experiential learning cycle during the home campus predeparture workshop. In David Kolb's (1984) words, "immediate personal experience is the focal point for learning, giving life, texture, and subjective meaning to abstract concepts and at the same time providing a concrete, publicly shared reference point for testing the implications and validity of ideas created during the learning process" (p. 21).

Thus, guided intervention becomes more deliberate during week three. At this point, students are asked to analyze an experience, keeping in mind the stages of the experiential learning cycle based on experience, reflection, generalization, and application. It is gratifying to observe that the guided intervention helps to bring about not only shifts in attitudes but behavioral adjustments to the culture. The students begin to apply gained knowledge to their behavior, which positively impacts the student's experience, as Christy's comments demonstrate:

Experience: Salamanca is a town that completely revolves around students and thus housing for students. There are constantly ads for housing for rent, and constantly students moving in and out of the city. With this the good housing options will often be taken within one day. . . . When searching, I found a few that were not so good, and this one was completely renovated. It was perfect. However when I went there to view the apartment, I spoke enough Spanish to say what I wanted to say, but it was difficult to present myself effectively with my limited language. I was invited back for a second interview, but when speaking with them I did not know the slang and I did not pick up on their invitations to sit and converse (They invited me to take a *cana*, or beer). . . . I did not pick up on the invitation and I turned it down.

Reflection: When I left, I realized that I had turned down the invitation and the chance to present myself and thus the chance to obtain the apartment. And finally, I became aware of the Spanish culture and protocol. . . . Specifically, it is common to invite any potential relationships to a tea, beer, or wine, and if you make the invitations, you always pay first. This was later a key for me in obtaining successful Spanish friendships.

Generalization: I realized the importance of first impression. Especially with communication barriers, it forced me to evaluate how I am nonverbally presenting myself. With this I have become more aware of my nonverbal cues and have improved them to be more effective. In addition, I realized the importance of being assertive in my decisions.

Application: After not getting the apartment that I wanted, I started my search again. After much searching, I decided that the most important thing was to live with at least 2 or 3 Spanish people who were open to speaking with me and teaching me their culture. I also wanted a very comfortable living room for chatting. . . . With that said I found one apartment with 3 Spanish people and one German that had a very comfortable living room. . . . I consciously, assertively, and rapidly chose to stick to what was important to me and I immediately tried to take the apartment. When I went there, I was very conscious of my nonverbal cues and tried to fully present myself. I also made sure that I told them my hobbies and asked them about theirs. This was a great conversation starter and it allowed me to have an effective first impression and thus obtain the apartment. I also invited them for a coffee and I paid. Afterwards they accepted me and I immediately gave them money to lock the deal.

Cultural Bump

The next assignment, Cultural Bump, introduces the student to the next level of analysis. The following sample illustrates the benefit of elevating the examination of the issue to a cross-cultural level. The task is to select an event or experience that produced ambivalent, uncomfortable thoughts or feelings. Students then describe the perspectives they might take on the issue as well as their own feelings of ambivalence and discomfort. It is important to note that students are prepped for this activity (as they are for most) during the predeparture workshop. At that time we read and discuss typical "cultural bumps" in the abstract and discuss strategies to manage and learn from such situations. Naturally, at that stage students are not emotionally charged by such issues and can only imagine themselves into the situation. This is important, however, in that they are able to first consider the value of practicing a nonjudgmental approach that seeks to consider alternative perspectives or explanations. The following is an actual assignment in the students' syllabus, derived from Elijah Lovejoy's "Negative Red Flags" (1996):

> *Cultural Bump*: Cultural bumps (sometimes referred to as "critical incidents") are prompts that get us thinking about cultural differences, about the possible differences in the meaning of similar behaviors in the home and host cultures. Often there are parallels between the home and host cultures when a cultural bump occurs. Select an event or experience, which produced ambivalent, uncomfortable thoughts or feelings. For example, you might dislike a particular person from the host culture or dislike a certain common behavior of the host culture. Recall our activity in the predeparture workshop regarding "negative red flags" to help you identify an appropriate event or experience. 1) Describe in writing the two sides (more than two sides?) of the issue and your feelings of ambivalence/discomfort. 2) Post your written work on this experience to your peers. Include in your final report to me the additional conclusions or observations from your peers as well as your own resulting from reviewing your peer's work.

Once the students are in the country, and actually stumbling over real cultural bumps, they have at least the initial efforts to fall back on to work their way through uncomfortable challenges. When a student then addresses the assignment, the writing tends not to devolve into, for example, an expression of the student's disgust for the prevalence of smokers in the host country. Rather, the topic is more likely to be approached from a more detached vantage point. The student is more open to consider the values underlying the apparent greater tolerance for smoking in public and can also be pushed more easily to speculate on the implications of such a difference, especially if he or she is in conversation with peers in other cultures experiencing their own unique versions of the same phenomenon. For example, from her study site in Japan Shannon posted the following as her initial entry on the cultural bump assignment:

> One of the things that has been particularly difficult to ignore has been the widespread availability of pornography. I can be on the train here and see a guy just casually flipping through a pornography magazine, or see a flier of a naked anime woman as an advertisement. . . . Despite the seeming acceptability of pornography I am under the impression that if I, or another woman, were casually flipping through a magazine objectifying men, it would NOT be okay. It is also frowned upon for a couple to show affection in public beyond holding hands. . . . I have asked some people about it and the answer I tend to get is about how affection with another person is your private life, but for some reason viewing pornography is a public friendly activity. I don't really know why this is, I have found . . . the overt acceptance of objectifying women in Japan somewhat distressing.

Then, before the instructor had the opportunity to respond, Melinda provided the following from her study site in Spain:

> This is very interesting! Seems a little bit ironic, how come that is possible that it is ok to look at naked bodies while one can't be affectionate to a person he/she likes? It might be a sense of respect though. Personal relations are something that is very private and should not be done in public. But magazines and all that is just a game. . . . Here in Spain, I constantly see people making out. They could be just waiting to cross a street and in the period of 1 min they will kiss. . . . Parks are also the places where you can meet a couple doing something that you rather wouldn't like to see. . . .

Here the instructor's role is crucial. Although the observations the two students offer are interesting in their own right, they are only skimming the surface of analysis. At this point students typically need to be pushed to dig deeper. The instructor might then intervene:

> Your observations are excellent! Now try to think of some parallels within the U.S. culture. Consider the differences and the implications these have in each culture.
>
> Read through your own comments and ask yourselves how your own values are affecting the way you interpret the cultural bump you experienced. Isolate what you see from what you interpret.
>
> Consider, for example, what constitutes public space. Are you imposing your own definitions?

There are of course many more productive prompts and a host of issues at play in the scenarios the two have raised. It is important, however, to keep the process manageable and focused on just a few items at a time. Moreover, the students move on to a new assignment each week so the point is not to resolve issues but to train their mind to be open to recognizing the values underlying the behaviors they observe and the way in which they are interpreting what they observe. For example, Beth in Mexico nicely moves to the next stage. She observes a cultural phenomenon that underlies a particular behavior on the part of the males in Mexico. And while initially being disturbed by it, she chooses to adjust her behavior in order to avoid further conflict with the cultural difference that constituted a cultural bump for her personally (but might not for other American students).

> I am so glad for this assignment. I have wanted to just sit and think about this situation for some time now, but hadn't found the opportunity to just hash out my thoughts till now. My cultural bump has occurred every weekend that I have been in Mexico. I have tried every possible way that I can think of how to handle the situation without becoming angry, and have come to no solution that I like. I have just resigned to ignore it, but I know that will not last long.
>
> My cultural bump involves alcohol consumption, and how I do not drink. Now, back at home no one seems to have a problem with the fact that I don't drink, smoke, or take drugs. People seem to allow me to make my own decisions, kind of a "you don't judge me and I won't judge you" attitude. My American and Canadian roommates have the same attitude as my friends back home, but these Mexicans just can not seem to grasp the concept. First I am asked what I want to drink. When I decline saying

that I do not drink I am laughed at. Then I am asked if I am some sort of a Christian or a Mormon. The general consensus then is that I am a Mormon. After that I am asked if I live on a farm and if I am a nun. . . . By this time I am usually ready to make some sort of rude comment about how we need to build that wall around Texas a little faster. However, I refrain, and try to come up with some sort of story about how I am trying to quit drinking because my boyfriend does not like it. It seems that the only thing people respect here is what a man has to say. What I want to do with my life holds no weight, but what my imaginary boyfriend thinks does.

I believe that this incident shows the changes that the Mexican culture is experiencing. The youth of Mexico seems to be in a very unique place. Women's rights are not something that have been around for a very long time. Also, partying, drinking, and smoking is something that has only been acceptable in the past few generations. Many of the girls my age still have curfews, and are not given the option to move out of their parent's house until they are married. So where there is any freedom to be "young and frivolous" they seem to jump at the opportunity and soak it up like it may never happen again. It reminds me of the 1960's and 1970's in the U.S.

I have to keep this in mind every time I go out with my friends, and just remember that my ideas of who I am and what I do have been influenced by the generations that have come before me. My sense of self has come about because I have had the opportunity to experience what I want to, and can make informed decisions to do as I please. Most of the youth here seem to be fighting for that right, and that is what makes them seem judgmental to me. In their eyes I am turning down a privilege, when I see it as having the power to choose not to be privileged. Very different ideas on freedom cause a cultural bump.

This entry sparked responses from other students in the course around the globe focusing on other issues pertaining to the role of women in Latin societies in general. For Mary in Spain, Beth's assignment posted in Mexico contributed to her choice of topic for her final research paper for this course: "Gender Violence in Spain."

As the students' ability to analyze grows over the course of the semester, so does their understanding of cultural difference and with it their gradual adjustment to these differences via a variety of assignments and approaches examining their host culture's systems, institutions, values, beliefs, and cultural constructs (Sutton & Rubin, 2004). By the end of the course, the students' orientation toward cultural difference has generally undergone considerable development. A careful reading of the entirety of the semester's assignments reveals distinct patterns of growth that can be fairly characterized as increased sensitivity toward and openness to the cultural differences they experienced. One can observe in the initial writings judgmental tendencies, which over time develop into more considered analysis with an eye toward the cultural values underlying phenomena and the implications of these values in social, economic, and political realms. Perhaps more important, at least with regard to ease of communicating the effectiveness of intercultural learning intervention, the postprogram IDI data indicate the potential for significant developmental growth, in contrast to the postprogram IDI data of their study abroad peers who did not have the benefit of intervention. While the data sets are still too small to be conclusive, the initial results range from a few points of development to more than a full standard deviation of 14 points on the developmental scale. In addition to the promise of more conclusive data regarding assessment on the horizon, the more intriguing feature of the IDI is its usefulness as a teaching tool.

The Intercultural Development Inventory as a Teaching Tool

The benefit of an assessment tool such as the Intercultural Development Inventory is that it can be utilized to target specific types of issues that individual students are struggling with in their specific stages of intercultural development. The preassessment might indicate, for example, that student A has placed himself in the *Defense* stage of intercultural development. Defense against difference is described by Bennett and Bennett (2004) as the "recognition of cultural difference coupled with negative evaluation of most variations from native culture—the greater the difference, the more negative the evaluation. [It is] characterized by dualistic us/them thinking and frequently accompanied by overt negative stereotyping. [It is an] evolutionary view of cultural development with native culture at the acme" (p. DEF 1). Accordingly, the student attempts to protect his or her worldview structure with steadfast categorical thinking. Experience is polarized into judgmental alignments, and the student's behavior retrenches into same-culture segregation.

With this preprogram knowledge the instructor can look for manifestations of this developmental stage in the student's writings and attempt to mitigate the polarization tendencies by pointing and directing the student to examples of similarity or "common humanity."

A crucial point here is that the emphasis on common humanity is intended to help the student move along the developmental scale to the *Minimization* stage (Bennett & Bennett, 2004). Minimization, briefly stated, is the belief in the basic similarity of all people, the disavowal of deep cultural differences, and/or the avowal of essential humanity in terms of all people's embodiment of a similar principle (Hammer & Bennett, 2001). The tendency is for the student to subsume cultural difference into familiar categories. Moving in this direction is appropriate for student A, who is dealing primarily with Defense issues, but not for student B, who might have entered the study abroad program already at the Minimization stage. For a student in Minimization, the instructor will want to push cultural self-awareness and prompt the student to investigate difference while developing knowledge about his or her own culture.

The preassessment provides the starting point and signals to the instructor what to watch for in the students' writings. Our experience with this intercultural course is that the preassessment is generally quite accurate in predicting the manner in which the students will report their experiences. Moreover, we discover the importance of pairing each student with a primary interactive peer who is near to him or her in the developmental scale; typically, this would mean pairing students at various levels of Minimization, possibly even a "high Defense" student with a "low Minimization." It is not advisable, however, to pair two students if one is operating at an ethnorelative level of Acceptance while the other is in an ethnocentric, defensive mode. The pedagogical methodology of peer mentoring is a vital dimension to our course, but we must be mindful that the difference in developmental stages can be too large for effective peer mentoring. Whereas a student in the Acceptance–Adaptation range can certainly benefit from reading and responding to the writings of a fellow student in the Defense stage, the latter is not likely to process the former student's writings as effectively. The student coming from the ethnocentric perspective of Defense is simply not likely to appreciate, on a cognitive level, the nuances that characterize an ethnorelative, Acceptance perspective.

In addition to this targeted pairing, the course provides the broad forum for all course participants to interact. In fact, the multiplicity of experiences and perspectives surrounding common themes supplies enough material for relevant and effective feedback to each of the students. This broad forum is important and effective because the group of students has already had the opportunity to work together in the predeparture workshop. Moreover, the group will reconvene in the postprogram workshop at a point where each is coming to terms with his or her reentry into the once-comfortable home culture. The interaction throughout the semester tends to create a basis of trust and camaraderie among the course participants that can be tapped into in the postworkshop setting.

The Role of the Pre- and Postprogram Workshops

The blend in ethnographic and interculturalist-constructivist approaches is also found in the predeparture and postimmersion workshops. These two required components of the course accomplish two important objectives for any study abroad program. First, the predeparture workshop represents 10–15% of the student's final grade, creating both the space and the motivation to begin working with cultural concepts. The common lament that preprogram sessions are awash with discussion of logistical issues—ranging from the availability of toiletries to which gate the plane departs from—is resolved because this separate and additional session is devoted solely to preparation for the intercultural learning experience.

A word on tying the course to academic credit is in order. For better or worse this ultimate motivator—the almighty course credit—must be turned into an ally. On the "for worse" end of the spectrum one might argue that framing the immersion experience in terms of earning credit toward a degree and graduation back home already constructs a distorting lens around the project. Transporting the "consumer of credits" framework abroad necessarily defines the student *while abroad* according to imperatives that infect the student's approach to difference. The problem of students paying high tuition rates at home for "less expensive" credit abroad is one obvious lens that we must deconstruct daily. It is useful to imagine how we might reconstruct a study abroad program if instead of students needing to piece together a semester's worth of credit, we simply waive the requisite number of credits the participant needs toward graduation. Assuming the myriad problems associated with such an approach can be resolved, what would this tell us about how we could improve the immersion experience? How might we better utilize the "cultural laboratory" if we could cut loose the classroom, not to mention the concept of "contact hours"? In any case, we would argue, under current conditions, the effectiveness of an intercultural learning intervention into a study abroad program must carry with it course credit; all else communicates to the student—rightly or wrongly—a lack of importance and institutional commitment. The "pre and post" workshops carry slightly different weight at the two institutions involved (Willamette University, 15%; Bellarmine University, 10%) due to the added research paper at Bellarmine. Students in the Bellarmine version of the course are required to complete a research project worth 20% of their grade. This project must be an original, critical analysis of a concept, theme, or topic that emerges from the cultural immersion experience. While the focus of the project will emerge during the students' time abroad, students are strongly encouraged to develop some possible directions for their project prior to leaving Bellarmine. The project format may be written and/or multimedia. Students give a brief presentation of their projects during the postimmersion session. They are also invited to present a poster session on their research during Bellarmine's Undergraduate Research Week.

Predeparture Workshop

Specifically, the students begin working with cultural concepts such as the relationship between perception and interpretation. They engage in group activities that lay the groundwork for some of the ethnographic assignments to follow. For example, students will fill out a basic values questionnaire by providing their individual rankings of the listed values. They then work in a group and are asked to reach consensus on a group ranking. Discussion often becomes quite animated at this point. The exercise is a good entry point into how instructive it might be to discuss such questions with their future host peers, thereby establishing the framework for pursuing the assignment in the host culture. Finally, in the "post" workshop students are asked to re-rank their values list and compare it with the list they produced in the "pre" workshop. This activity has the effect of illuminating the transformation that the students sense but often have difficulty articulating.

The predeparture workshop alerts students to the fact that the transformative cultural immersion experience also encompasses the time and space before departure and after return. By engaging in cultural learning activities (many of which are focused on examining how one's own identity is socially constructed) the students begin to see the inherent potential of studying abroad. We must understand that the majority of students approach their semester abroad with little or no cognitive grasp of the process and potential of experiential learning, let alone the complexity and intensity of experiential learning within a cultural immersion context. Most students are in fact motivated to study abroad by the promise of *living in a different culture*. But they cannot be expected to comprehend the depth of the opportunity and will tend to fashion it as a series of fascinating experiences. Our survey of students, after approval but before departure, revealed the following when prompted, "I want to study abroad so I can . . .": *Live in a Different Culture* represented 85% of the total responses ranking number one (58%) or number two (27%) priority. The other options receiving top priority were *Improve Language Skills* (34%); *Take Courses in My Major or Minor* (6%); *Take It Easy/Have Fun* (20%); and *Other* (3%), among which the most often cited reason was *Meet New People and Travel*.

The "pre" workshop begins to frame the overall project even with something as straightforward as administering the preprogram IDI. The discussion of the Developmental Model of Intercultural Sensitivity is for most of the students the first encounter with the concept that one's orientation to cultural difference might be something one could intentionally develop. This discussion also engenders the notion that there is something valuable to work for and that it will be measured in the "post" workshop, thereby creating a sense of wholeness to the preprogram, in-country program, and postprogram dimensions of the entire experience.

Postimmersion Workshop

A common lament among international educators is the apparent lack of student interest in reentry programming. This component of the course also constitutes a percentage of the overall grade and signals to the student that there is significant work to be done upon return to the home culture. The importance of the postimmersion workshop cannot be overstated. This phase fulfills three significant objectives: (1) to capitalize on the learning opportunity embedded in the common realization that one feels like a stranger in one's home culture, that is, to be uncomfortable in the once-familiar, (2) to stimulate/facilitate a positive and productive reintegration into the home community, and (3) to assess and discuss how well course objectives were met.

For the instructor this dimension of the course is a delight. The energy and enthusiasm, infused by the common bond forged by a semester of inter-mittent yet regular sharing of struggles, insights, and growth, finds its culmi-nation in this forum. And yet this very same bond of adventuresome heroes returned to share their treasures with the wider community stands also as a framework to be deconstructed, at least cognitively. Like the mythical hero who slays the dragon and captures the gold only to have it turn to ashes upon return home, the students' transformation (their golden growth) be-comes the central focus of the postimmersion workshop.

One of the most promising results of our course is the observation that, due to its ongoing reflective and analytical focus, the students return with the predisposition and skills to meet the challenge of *bringing home the gold*. The discomfort or disorientation of reentry, while still applicable, is neither a surprise nor a frustration. They have been trained to identify and analyze dispassionately, or at least they will recognize that our regular lecturing and urging throughout the semester also applies here. This challenge—understanding and communicating the developmental growth one has achieved—is often not met by the typical study abroad student. Certainly, a student will have better results addressing this issue if he or she attends a typical reentry event. But such events, with study abroad returnees who have not had the benefit of explicit intercultural learning, often devolve into judg-mental sessions about the home culture, mirroring the many impromptu "bitch sessions" abroad in which they sought comfort from the trials of cul-tural immersion. As a result, not only does one typically achieve an atten-dance rate of 10–15% (no credit equals no interest), but the hoped-for results of reentry events often remain as elusive as the intercultural development itself during the semester abroad.

In contrast, primarily because of the meta-level cultural analysis resulting from working all semester with their peers around the world, the course par-ticipants easily recognize the *transferability* of the lessons to the reentry co-nundrums. The group reentry workshop is followed by a one-on-one student–instructor session to address aspects of the cross-cultural experience for which a group session might not have been the appropriate venue due to confidentiality issues and personal sensitivities.

Conclusions and Challenges

It is fair to say this course successfully addresses the five primary reasons for assessing education abroad outcomes: tracking student learning, personal growth, participant satisfaction/attitudes, program development, and the need for institutional data (Sutton & Rubin, 2004). The combination of using a syllabus designed to foster intercultural development along with an instrument like the IDI, both as a teaching tool and an assessment instrument, has proven to provide maximum learning outcomes, one student at a time.

Assessment (the evaluation of the students' written work and the IDI data) substantiates conclusions that the course meets its goals and the associated specific learning outcomes. We are confident the course can significantly improve the study abroad learning experience for the vast majority of students. This includes the programming associated with preparation, in-country, and reentry.

As noted in the beginning, the effort to intervene in the study abroad experience with intentional intercultural learning necessitates striking a balance between the cultural immersion itself and the connection to home in the form of contact with home culture peers and instructors. Accordingly, certain drawbacks are inevitable. Among them are English-language usage; the course must be taught in a language accessible to all of the participants around the world. Experiments with teaching the course in the target language of the student's host country have proven to be too labor intensive, attempting to develop both intercultural learning and foreign language proficiency through the online assignments. Another compromise is the ongoing connection to home. While some might dismiss the notion as simple nostalgia, the old days of *truly* being separated from home (letters that would take weeks and just one or two phone calls per year, since a mere semester abroad was considered short-term) produced certain lessons of personal growth and independence that are extremely difficult to capture in today's context. The course does perpetuate that ongoing connection to home; however, one might argue it exists in any case given the present state of instant connectivity.

Certain challenges remain as well. Ideally, the number of participants equals the number of different programs they are attending. This means 8 to 10 different semester schedules to coordinate, since the student pairings must be in sync with their course assignments. The question of whether to require the course is a significant issue. In the Bellarmine case, students can satisfy a university core requirement by taking this course. This has translated into a larger number of participants, and a certain percentage seems to be primarily motivated by this fact. The Willamette students who take the course are fewer in number but tend to self-select based on their interest in the subject matter, rather than to satisfy any particular requirement, because it is not tied to the core curriculum.

The pedagogical, administrative, and logistical issues involved in teaching this course are fairly manageable if class size is kept to no more than 8 to 10 students per instructor. The instructor can easily be a member of the international office staff (assuming a qualified teaching background), since the online format allows for maximum flexibility, even while traveling. It should be noted, however, that the IDI is restricted in use to qualified administrators. Although this component could conceivably be administered by someone else on campus, it would remove one of the more effective elements in the teaching of the course. One must learn to interpret the IDI to make full use of it as a teaching tool. Alternatively, there are many other assessment tools available, so one is, of course, not limited to this instrument.

There are many possible approaches for intervention depending on the dynamics of the cultural contexts. We argue in favor of a form of meta-level intervention to harness the transformative power of cultural immersion. Study abroad as a vehicle for intercultural learning will become even more effective if we continue to develop and implement different ways of enhancing the intercultural experience.

References

Bennett, J. M., & Bennett, M. J. (2004). *Developing intercultural competence: A reader.* Portland, OR: Intercultural Communication Institute.

Blackboard Academic Site [Computer Software]. (2007). Washington, DC: Blackboard.

Hammer, M. R., & Bennett, M. J. (2001). *The Intercultural Development Inventory (IDI) manual.* Portland, OR: Intercultural Communication Institute.

Kolb, D. (1984). *Experiential learning as the science of learning and development.* Englewood Cliffs, NJ: Prentice Hall.

Lovejoy, E. (1996). Negative red flags. In H. N. Seelye (Ed.), *Experiential activities for intercultural learning* (pp. 191–197). Yarmouth, ME: Intercultural Press.

Sutton, R. C., & Rubin, D. L. (2004). The GLOSSARI project: Initial findings from a system-wide research initiative on study abroad learning outcomes. *Frontiers: The Interdisciplinary Journal of Study Abroad, X,* 65–82.

Vande Berg, M., Balkcum, A., Scheid, M., & Whalen, B. J. (2004). The Georgetown University consortium project: A report from the halfway mark. *Frontiers: The Interdisciplinary Journal of Study Abroad, X,* 101–116.

Woolf, M. (2007, February). *It's not all about the numbers: Maximizing student learning abroad.* Paper presented at the Association for International Education Administrators annual conference, Washington, DC.

16

REFLECTION, RECIPROCITY, RESPONSIBILITY, AND COMMITTED RELATIVISM

Intercultural Development Through
International Service-Learning

Margaret D. Pusch and Martha Merrill

Intercultural growth and transformation through education abroad, the focus of this book, take on added dimensions when that education abroad involves service-learning. In service-learning abroad, the intercultural learning and growth of the student is of course a concern, but it is not the only concern. In ethically done service-learning, both abroad and at home, *reciprocity* is essential: all parties involved should learn and all should benefit. The service must be real and needed, and if students are to provide real and needed service in an intercultural context, they must be interculturally competent. Their intercultural mistakes are not simply a learning tool but can have a real impact on real people.

Definitions of service-learning are many, but most observers are likely to agree with the essential aspects of the definition and elaborations found on the "Declaration of Principles" webpage of the International Partnership for Service-Learning and Leadership (IPSL, 2007):

> Service-learning unites academic study and volunteer community service in mutually reinforcing ways. The service makes the study immediate, applicable, and relevant; the study, through knowledge, analysis, and reflection, informs the service. . . . Service-learning addresses simultaneously two

important needs of our societies: the education and development of people and the provision of increased resources to serve individuals and communities.

When academic credit is awarded, it is not for the service performed, but for the learning, which the student demonstrates through written papers, classroom discussion, examinations, and/or other means of formal evaluation. In service-learning programs that are not offered for credit, the learning should be intentional, structured, and evaluated.

Service-learning is different from community service unconnected to formal study in two important ways. First, it demands that the student understand the service agency—its mission, philosophy, assumptions, structures, activities, and governance—and the conditions of the lives of those who are served. Second, it is characterized by a relationship of partnership: the student learns from the service agency and from the community and, in return, gives energy, intelligence, commitment, time, and skills to address human and community needs. In addition, the service agency learns from the students. College and university faculty and service agency personnel both teach and learn from one another. Service-learning is different from field study, internships, and practica, although it may have elements of all of these. Unlike field study, service-learning makes the student not only an observer but an active participant. While the student may gain from service-learning many of the benefits of an internship or practicum, service-learning has two goals: student learning *and* service to the community. The success of a program is measured not only by what the student learns but also by the usefulness of the student's work to those served.

As this discussion makes clear, in international or intercultural service-learning, the intercultural learning and growth of the student is not only a desired learning outcome but also a necessary requisite: students who are not interculturally observant and sensitive cannot be of real service to others who are culturally different from themselves.

Reaching Intercultural Competence: Three Kinds of Learning

As already indicated, to be of real service, the student must understand the society in which he or she is serving. To do so, the student needs three kinds of learning: first, knowledge of the history, politics, social institutions, artistic heritage, etc., of the host country or culture, as well as its language; second, knowledge of experiential learning theory—how to not simply have an experience but to *learn from* experience; and third, knowledge of intercultural theories and issues.

The Need for Academic Work That Contextualizes the Service

Language competence is a necessary but not sufficient element for understanding the host society. In addition to knowing the language, with the specific vocabulary and nuances required by the service situation, a student also needs to understand the social, political, economic, and other conditions that have made the institution where the service occurs necessary and that affect its operation and continued development. For further discussion of language learning in education abroad, the reader is referred to Sharon Wilkinson (2007) as well as the 1998 special issue of *Frontiers: The Interdisciplinary Journal of Study Abroad* (Freed, 1998) dedicated to the subject and the first three articles in the 2004 special issue of *Frontiers* (VandeBerg, 2004) that focused on assessment.

Knowing the historical and social context in which institutions and practices developed and that influence them currently is important for students; without this knowledge, they are likely to misinterpret host behavior. For example, recent U.S. visitors to Moscow and St. Petersburg remarked upon the "unfriendliness" of the Russians. Later, they were reminded of the heritage of Stalin's repression, when, as Mikhail Bulgakov entitled the opening chapter of his novel *The Master and Margarita* (1967/1995) one should "Never Talk to Strangers" (in the novel, the stranger turns out to be, quite literally, the devil) and when, according to some estimates, 8 to 15 million died in labor camps, in prison, during the collectivization of the farms, and from disease, in addition to the estimated 26 to 27 million killed in the "Great Patriotic War," as World War II is called there (Moss, 1998; see Haynes, 2003, for a discussion of all the nuances involved in such estimates). Given that history, the U.S. visitors were able to contextualize their observations that Russian citizens did not smile at strangers or eagerly engage them in conversation, and to understand that such behavior was not "unfriendliness" but a very reasonable wariness of strangers that derived from specific historical conditions. In intercultural terms, "unfriendly" was an ethnocentric attribution of the cause of the behavior the U.S. visitors received. Similarly, if a student studying in Central Asia knows that the Kyrgyz and Kazakh people traditionally were nomads, spending summers high in the Tien Shen mountains, then that student, eager to have her host mother provide fruits, vegetables, and salads, might understand why the foods of sedentary agricultural peoples living in water-rich valleys—plants that require a caretaker staying in one place—are not part of the traditional Kyrgyz and Kazakh diet. The nomadic tradition also can explain why oral epics rather than long novels, and embroidery and leatherwork rather than landscape painting, are among the traditional art forms. Thus, academic learning in fields such as history can provide insight into culture.

Learning about history, politics, economics, and other academic subjects can help a student to better understand the context of the service placement: knowledge of a country's economic situation, for example, can help a student understand why certain services that at home might be funded by the state, such as education for the disabled, in the host country are provided by religious or private organizations. Understanding economic conditions also can prevent a student from inappropriately criticizing teaching styles in the school where he or she might work: a classroom style in which the teacher reads from a text and writes dates on the board for students to copy may say more about pupils' inability to pay for their own books and the school's financial inability to equip a library than it does about a teacher's preferred teaching style. A student's dropping out of school in the host country may arise from the need to contribute to the family income rather than from a lack of academic ability or from adolescent rebellion, as it might in the study abroad student's home country. Understanding the economic realities of the host country can help a visiting student to avoid misjudgments in these and other situations.

Students who study abroad but do not engage in service may read about societal conditions, but learning is often intensified when the impact of historical, economic, or political conditions are encountered on a daily, and personal, basis in the service situation. On the other hand, students who serve abroad but who do not combine that service with academic study are likely to make inappropriate attributions about the causes of everything from why services are provided by private organizations to the reasons for "top down" teaching styles. The interaction of formal learning and extensive service—IPSL recommends 12 or 15 hours a week for a full semester—permits the student's learning to be more profound and considered and the service he or she performs to be more useful to the host agency and its clients. The formal learning and the service work in synergy with each other.

Planners of international and intercultural service-learning programs should consider not only *what* is taught about a society but also *who* does the teaching. If teaching about the host country is done by home country professors, the underlying message students take away may be that the host country has no intellectuals or academics. Edward Said, in his classic study *Orientalism* (1978), quotes what Marx said in another context: "They can not represent themselves; they must be represented" (p. 293). A student whose academic learning about the host society does not come from host country academics may not only be deprived of local knowledge about the country but may also assume that analysis and policy choices for the host country most appropriately come from the World Bank or other multinational organizations. In reality, such organizations have their own perspective on problems, the etic perspective of an outsider, and may be oblivious to elements and issues that are important in the local context, important in the emic perspective of an insider. In a good example of how this may occur, Martha Brill Olcott (2002) points out that some Western analysts, in reviewing the degree of openness to different groups in the administration of President Nursultan Nazarbayev of Kazakhstan, missed the fact that most members of his administration came from his own clan. (For a discussion of the complexities of clan politics in Kazakhstan, as well as for a bibliography listing scholars, east and west, who did consider clan issues in their analyses, see Schatz [2004].) "Clan" was not a category of analysis they knew from their own societies, and so they were unable to recognize it when it was manifested in Kazakhstan. Thus, students who learn only from home country professors risk not encountering the very "difference" in intellectual categories that, one assumes, may have led them to study outside their home countries to begin with.

When service is part of the educational process students may need more time to process their learning than is often the case in classroom learning. The evaluation of students' learning should take this into account. Not only is reentry needed to complete the learning cycle (see the section on reentry, to follow), as with any "significant other-culture-living experience" (commonly referred to as "SOLE"), but also, in intercultural experiential learning and particularly in intercultural service-learning, the reflection and hypothesis-generation elements of Kolb's experiential learning cycle (1984) and the DIE (describe, interpret, evaluate) model come into play. These elements may mean that the kind of learning done through experience becomes evident or changes form even years after the encounters have taken place (see Pusch, 2004).

Experiential Learning Theory

David Kolb, drawing on the work of Kurt Lewin, John Dewey, and Jean Piaget, created a model of how learning may be drawn out of and tested through experience (Kolb, 1984, pp. 17, 41–42; see also chapter 5 of this book). The cycle begins with an experience that causes a person to reflect and then begin to generate some hypotheses about the meaning of the experience. These hypotheses are tested out through "active experimentation." Learning is taking place throughout the process. Kolb calls taking in information through the use of symbols and concepts "comprehension," and taking in information through feelings and intuition "apprehension." The information gathered may be transformed through internal reflection and hypothesis generation (what he calls "intention") or through interaction with the external world (what he calls "extension") (Kolb, 1984, p. 41).

When this process takes place in an intercultural context, it becomes particularly important that the reflection phase does not become a judgment phase. Immediate *evaluation* of an experience or a behavior, rather than consideration of a variety of interpretations of it, precludes *learning*, which requires openness to growth, development, and change. A student who is in a culture other than his or her own should be seeking multiple interpretations of experience, interpretations informed by both academic learning about the host society and the counsel and input of local academics and other informants. The goal is to have students aim for what Triandis (1990) calls *isomorphic attribution*. Making an attribution is the providing of a cause or reason for a behavior; making an isomorphic attribution is giving the same attribution that someone in the host culture would. For example, many people in Russia and Central Asia believe that sitting in a draft, even sitting in front of a fan on a hot day, will make a person ill. Thus, if a host mother in Samarkand moves a fan away from a student on a steamy summer day, the student should interpret that as the mother caring about her welfare, not as the mother being inconsiderate and not caring about her comfort.

A useful tool in helping students to generate multiple interpretations of an experience, rather than to assume that an experience in the host society has the same meaning it might in the home society, is the DIE (Bennett,

Bennett, & Stillings, 1977), which stands for "describe, interpret, evaluate." The first step is for a student to describe the experience using nonevaluative words: not "the man in the train was standing too close to me" but rather "the man in the train was standing less than a foot away from me"; not "she was dressed really sloppily" but "her clothes were wrinkled, her shirt was torn under the arm, and her shirt and pants had different patterns." "Too close" and "sloppy" are judgments, which immediately attribute motives to the actor; "less than a foot away" and "wrinkled, torn, different patterns" open up options: maybe standing less than a foot away means something different here than it does at home. Maybe her wrinkled, torn, mismatched clothes mean poverty or that she does not have the skills to take care of herself, not the *choice* that "sloppiness" implies.

In the DIE process, after *describing*, a student should attempt to generate multiple interpretations of the experience. Three is a good minimum number. One interpretation is the same as an evaluation. When students offer two interpretations, they often have in mind that one is more reasonable or "normal" than the other, and thus they are close to making a judgment. If students force themselves to come up with three interpretations, they have to get away from yes/no, either/or dualisms. Through further reflection and repeated interactions in the host society, students can begin to generate some hypotheses about what the behavior might mean. Those hypotheses can be tested out via "active experimentation," to use Kolb's term, in the host society. In addition, if a student is learning *and* serving in the host society, particularly when the professors and service supervisor and colleagues are host country nationals, then the student is likely to have "native informants" to ask for advice.

After considered generation of hypotheses, based on academic learning and on input from local hosts as well as the student's own reflection and interaction in the society, a student *may* need to *evaluate* an experience. However, it is also worth remembering that not every experience needs to be labeled as "good" or "bad." Some encounters are simply *different* from what they would be at home and do not need to be evaluated and categorized. Continued openness to gathering new data, new experiences, and new learning is essential for development and growth in an intercultural situation, particularly in an intercultural education situation involving service-learning. As Kolb (1984) notes, Dewey's model of experiential learning involves a spiral: one does not simply move around and around the learning circle, but instead brings to the next experience the learning of the previous cycle, so the new experience is perceived through changed lenses and a more sophisticated un-understanding. Experiences from which a student learns build upon each other, and the student is able to encounter subsequent experience from a higher starting plateau (Kolb, 1984, pp. 22–23).

Young Yun Kim's "Stress-Adaptation-Growth Dynamic" (2001) is based on a similar upward-spiraling pattern. Kim (2001) writes:

> Stress, adaptation, and growth . . . constitute a three-pronged . . . dynamic of psychic movement in the forward and upward direction of increased chances of success in meeting the demands of the host environment. None of the three occurs without the others, and each occurs because of the others. . . . The . . . dynamic plays out not in a smooth, linear progression, but in a cyclic and continual "draw-back-to-leap" representation. . . . [Students] respond to each stressful experience by "drawing back," which in turn activates adaptive energy to help them reorganize themselves and "leap forward." . . . The process continues as long as there are new environmental challenges. (pp. 56–57)

In addition to working through the stages of Kolb's experiential learning cycle, supplemented by challenging themselves to consider the elements of the DIE process and to see stress as a precursor to adaptation and growth, students can learn through experience by comparing and contrasting their own experience with that of other intercultural sojourners. This is the underlying concept in Linda Chisholm's book *Charting a Hero's Journey* (2000), which is based on Joseph Campbell's idea of "the hero with a thousand faces." Campbell (1968) maintained that the story of a young person who leaves home, goes off into the world, perseveres through trials and overcomes tribulations, attaches meaning to his or her journey, and returns home transformed is a nearly universal story: almost all cultures have such a myth or epic. Moses, Siddhartha, and Odysseus are examples of such sojourners. Chisholm updates those traditional stories with reflections from writers as diverse as Jane Addams, Langston Hughes, and Octavio Paz, asking students to think about 12 possible stages in a journey, based on Campbell's categories, from "hearing the call" to leave home, to departing and separating from what is familiar, to finding "guardian spirits" during the trials of the journey. Using the journals and essays of writers who have experienced journeys and transitions, Chisholm (2000) asks students to think about similar situations in their own sojourns. For example, paraphrased from Chisholm (2000) questions may include: *What did your friends say to you when you told them you were going away? How did you respond to them? What does that tell you about the ways in which you are thinking about this journey and the hopes and expectations you have?* (pp. 45–60) *What values are guiding you on this journey? How did you learn them?* (pp. 101–132) *Who is looked up to in your host society as "a good example"?* (p. 190) *Does that person have values that are different from yours?* (p. 197). In other words, other sojourners have gone before. Their experiences can help a student think about new ways to interpret experiences. But the cultural context is always an essential piece. A service-learning student, in order to learn deeply and to serve effectively, must engage in intercultural learning as well as academic learning and must develop the skills to learn from experiences, as well as simply to go through them.

A link between academic learning, experiential learning, and intercultural learning is William Perry's Scheme of Ethical and Cognitive Development (1999). Although many other models of student growth and development exist (see Evans, Forney, & Guido-DiBrito, 1998, for a summary of many of these models), the Perry Scheme not only influenced Kolb in the development of his theory (Knefelkamp, 1999) but also underlies the most commonly used developmental model of intercultural learning, Milton Bennett's Developmental Model of Intercultural Sensitivity (1993), and thus is an appropriate model of student development to use with regard to learning that is both experiential and intercultural as well as academic.

Perry's theory, developed by a group of faculty at Harvard over a number of years of longitudinal interviews with students, and since found to be valid in other contexts by Knefelkamp, Widdick, and Parker (1978) and by Moore (1989) in their research, posits that students move through four primary stages in their attitude toward knowledge. First, students just entering college, Perry and his colleagues found, often see the world in dualistic terms: yes/no, right/wrong. Authorities have The Answer, and the good student is the one who listens to the professor and learns what The Answer is. However, as the student moves through his or her courses and discovers that for some questions The Answer has not yet been found, or worse yet (from the point of view of the student in dualism), authorities disagree on some questions, then a student may move into Multiplicity—the idea that people have opinions, all opinions are valid, and the professor who critiques a student's interpretation isn't being open-minded: "That's just her opinion, and she should respect other people's opinions." Later, the student develops Contextual Relativism: he or she begins to understand that some answers *are* better than others, and a "correct answer" depends on context: historical, situational, and cultural. At the same time, students and young adults are finding that they need to make choices and commitments: to a college major, to a career, to a life partner. When they make such choices while understanding that other choices are possible and that in different contexts different choices may be necessary, they are said to have made a "commitment in relativism"—understanding, as the Dualist does not, that more than one "right" choice is possible and understanding, as the student in Multiplicity does not, that choices are not simply "opinions" but rather are judgments, based on analysis, comparisons, and criteria (Perry, 1999; see also Knefelkamp's quotation of Perry in Knefelkamp, 1999, pp. xix–xx).

What will happen to this progression in the early twenty-first century remains an open question. As Andrew Keen points out in *The Cult of the Amateur* (2007), Wikipedia and blogs have become authoritative to many readers, and search engines bring up the most popular sites first, rather than the most scholarly or considered. People listen to music they already know they like on their iPods. One wonders, if Perry and his colleagues were doing their research in 2007, would they find students staying longer and longer in Multiplicity, unable to compare, contrast, apply criteria, and to recognize quality and the standards for it?

Students learning in classrooms may move through these stages, but the student doing service almost undoubtedly will have his or her dualisms challenged as the necessity of responding to specific situations that do not fit neat, preordained paradigms arises. The student serving in an intercultural situation is even more likely to have his or her assumptions challenged, as the assumptions involved in a service such as providing healthcare in Thailand or in the Lakota Nation in South Dakota or in the national health care system in Britain are likely to be quite fundamentally different from the assumptions about healthcare that a student may make at home. The important element here is for the student not to fall into Multiplicity—"that's all right for *them;* that's how *they* do things"—but rather to see that the difference is part of a system, a pattern, and a logic, to see the reasons underlying behavior. The behavior, rather than being simply a choice or an opinion, grows from a context: from history, economics, and values. Figuring out what that pattern or logic is parallels the "hypothesis generation" stage of Kolb's experiential learning cycle (1984). It is not enough for the student simply to reflect and to decide what a behavior meant in one particular instance; in order to become interculturally competent in a particular society, the student must be able to fit specifics into patterns—not patterns cast in concrete, from which there is no variation, that is, not through dualism and stereotyping. But hypothesizing about a pattern and analyzing the context in which a behavior occurs is essential to intercultural competence.

Intercultural Learning

Intercultural communication, as a field of study, is relatively young. The two world wars in the twentieth century, combined with technology, made encountering "the other," either through travel or through the media and communications devices, a characteristic of the last century (see Pusch, 2004). Therefore, the theoretical perspectives of intercultural communication are still developing. Early theory often grew out of descriptions of individual societies as discreet entities. With the model devised by Kluckhohn and Strodtbeck (1961) generalizations began to be drawn. This early theoretical construction, along with the work by Edward T. Hall (1984), attempted to create "culture-general" categories, within which comparisons could be made. Categories such as individualism and collectivism or monochronic and polychronic conceptions of time (Hall, 1984), allowed for comparisons of experiences in one or more cultures outside the observer's home culture. Such categories attempted to *describe* cultures rather than to theorize how individuals *adjusted* to cultures different from their own. This was essential groundwork for a new and developing field of study.

When writers first began to describe adjustment, often they again extrapolated from their own experience, supplemented by their observations of others like themselves, rather than doing quantitative or qualitative research on a variety of populations to generate theory; such research would come later in the field's development. Thus one finds reference to the "U-curve": the idea that a sojourner's time abroad starts with an "initial euphoria," followed by a decline in well-being as the sojourner has to cope with more and more daily realities in which he or she encounters difference, followed by a regrouping and upward motion as the sojourner gains the skills that allow him or her to cope with the new environment (Oberg, 1954). The U-curve later was expanded to the "W-curve" (Gullahorn & Gullahorn, 1963), as observers began to notice the importance of reentry into the home society and hypothesized that it followed a similar pattern: initial euphoria at being home; depression upon realizing, based upon the time and experiences away, both that people at home have changed and the sojourner's perceptions of home have changed; then an upward swing as the sojourner readjusts. When research was done, and when groups other than voluntary, temporary sojourners were considered (refugees, for example), a much greater variety of patterns of adjustment became apparent (see, for example, Ward, Bochner, & Furnham, 2001, on the ABCs of adjustment—the affective, behavioral, and cognitive elements).

Five essential theories that students doing service-learning abroad ought to be aware of are the following:

1. Contact theory (Allport, 1954) and the many analyses of the situations in which contact with "others" does and does not alleviate prejudice, plus more recent critiques of contact theory and the research designs used to analyze it (Dixon, Durrheim, & Tredoux, 2005).
2. The ABCs of acculturation (Ward, Bochner, & Furnham, 2001)—the affective, behavioral, and cognitive paradigms of adapting, more specifically described as "stress, coping, and adjustment" (the affective piece); "culture learning" (the behavioral piece); and "social identification theories" (the cognitive piece).
3. The Developmental Model of Intercultural Sensitivity (DMIS) (M. Bennett, 1993).
4. "Intensity Factors" (Paige, 1993)—the factors in the interaction between the individual and the environment that make the intercultural encounter more or less intense for specific individuals.
5. Reentry theory and the factors that affect it in practice (Martin & Harrell, 2004), including reentry styles (Pusch, 1998).

These theories in no way "cover the waterfront" of theories about intercultural adjustment. However, considering a few of these ideas may open the student's mind to new ways of interpreting experiences that take place in intercultural contexts.

The Theories

Contact Theory

Sometimes it is assumed that, simply by going to a new culture, students will become more interculturally sensitive and will develop a more relativistic perspective in their beliefs (see Perry, 1999, as noted, for a definition of and discussion of the concept of relativism). John Engle and Lilli Engle (2002), in a chapter critical of the assumption that what they call "The Magic" will work its wiles when a student is abroad, state:

> The implicit assumption, again: life abroad will simply work its magic. . . . we assume that our students will progress linguistically in ways impossible on the home campus; they will develop intercultural skills and new sensitivity to the other; they will see links between in-class learning and their first-hand exposure in the field; they will grow personally because they are challenged to adapt as never before, and, in a startlingly new cultural context, required to call into mature question much of what they have previously simply assumed to be true. (pp. 26–27)

It is rarely this simple.

Gordon Allport, in his classic work *The Nature of Prejudice* (1954), made it clear that "magic" has little to do with increased sensitivity to "the other." As Thomas Pettigrew summarizes in his 1998 article,

> Allport (1954) held that positive effects of inter-group contact occur only in situations marked by four key conditions: equal group status within the situation; common goals; inter-group cooperation; and the support of authorities, law, or custom. (p. 66)

Pettigrew notes that "equal status" may be difficult to define, but a reader can appreciate that study abroad students working together with host culture students in a classroom might be more likely to change their opinions of their hosts than would a group from a wealthy country that travels to a less wealthy country to put a roof on a school for "them." With regard to "common goals," Pettigrew cites researchers who use the example of an athletic team; its members have the common goal of winning, and need each other to do so, so they come to appreciate each other's strengths. Additionally, Allport hypothesized, the attainment of the common goal must require intergroup cooperation. If subgroups compete, then the prejudice between the groups will not be reduced. Finally, authorities, law, or custom must sanction the cooperation (Allport, 1954).

Since 1954, hundreds of studies have tested Allport's hypotheses in various contexts. Pettigrew and Tropp (2000) summarize what they call "recent meta-analytic findings." There is a small but significant reduction of prejudice for a great variety of contact situations that do not meet the standard conditions previously held essential. However, when the theory's key conditions are met, there are typically far larger decreases in prejudice. Increased prejudice will occur when negative factors such as anxiety and threat are involved. Paige's "Intensity Factors" (1993, see following discussion) are important in this regard.

Dixon and his colleagues (2005), while supporting the general veracity of contact theory, have questioned the wisdom of current research designs that focus on trying to create those conditions under which prejudice should be mitigated, rather than on studying contact between different groups as it actually occurs and what then results. They also express concern about the focus on changing the individual's mindset through contact and wonder if a focus on the societal structures that cause contact to occur in the way it does might be a more productive line of research.

ABC—Affect, Behavior, and Cognitions

Colleen Ward, Stephen Bochner, and Adrian Furnham, in a comprehensive survey of "the major theoretical approaches to understanding and explaining intercultural contact" entitled *The Psychology of Culture Shock* (2001), categorize those approaches as *affect, behaviour* (spelled with the British "u"), and *cognitions*. (1) By "affect" they mean "the stress and coping perspective, . . . making particular reference to those factors that facilitate and impede psychological adjustment . . . such as self-efficacy, emotional resilience, and social support, as well as culture-specific variables" (p. 2). (2) "Behaviour" presupposes culture learning; the authors state, "effective intercultural interactions are often hampered by the fact that participants are unaware of the subtle, culturally-defined rules and regulations that govern social encounters. These include verbal and nonverbal forms of communication, as well as etiquette, the use of time, and strategies for resolving conflict" (p. 2). (3) "Cognitions" includes "both inward-looking Cognitions, i.e. how one views oneself in terms of social and cultural identity, as well as outward-looking perceptions, i.e. how an individual perceives and makes judgments about members of other ethnic, cultural, or national groups" (pp. 2–3). These latter perceptions, of course, could be influenced by the conditions that Allport hypothesized.

The Developmental Model of Intercultural Sensitivity

Most educators, and perhaps particularly service-learning educators, hope that students will change, grow, and develop as a result of their learning and their experiences. In this regard, the Developmental Model of Intercultural Sensitivity (DMIS) is particularly important, precisely because it is a model of *development*, a model of change.

The stages in the DMIS are divided into two segments: ethnocentrism, which includes Denial, Defense, and Minimization, and ethnorelativism, which includes Acceptance, Adaptation, and Integration (M. Bennett, 1993).

Ethnocentric states

Denial indicates an inability to construe cultural differences, which may be due to living in isolation in a homogeneous group or due to intentional separation from different others. Any recognition of difference is reduced to broad categories such as "foreigner," "Asian," or "black."

Those in *Defense* recognize cultural differences but tend either to denigrate them and engage in defending their own culture or to see their own culture as superior to all others. There is the possibility of Defense reversal that can occur when someone becomes deeply involved in another culture and begins to see that culture as superior to his or her own. It is important to note that, in both these states, extreme dualistic thinking is common.

Minimization is a state in which there is recognition and acceptance of superficial cultural differences (clothing, food, quaint practices) in the context of seeing all human beings as essentially the same and having common values. The measure for sameness is being like "us." This sameness can be expressed in terms of physiological similarity (basic needs and the like) or transcendent universalism (for example, all people are children of God, whether they know it or not). While Minimization is a somewhat more benign form of ethnocentrism, the tendency is still to judge other groups from one's own cultural perspective. It can be seen as a stage of transition, however, to becoming ethnorelative.

Ethnorelative states

Acceptance is a state in which people recognize and appreciate differences in behavior and values and see those differences as viable alternative solutions to achieving satisfaction in human existence. It is characterized by an ability to interpret various phenomena within the context in which they occurred and develop categories within which they can be compared. (Kolb's [1984] reflection and hypothesis-generation categories are relevant here.) Values, beliefs, and other ways of indicating that one is "good" or "bad" are seen within the cultural contexts in which they arose; behavior is analyzed within the cultural context as well. In other words, attributions begin to become isomorphic.

Adaptation to difference requires the development of communication skills, the use of empathy, or frame-of-reference shifting that allows one to be understood and to function effectively across cultures. A more sophisticated step is what Milton Bennett (1993) terms "pluralism," the internalization of more than one complete worldview and the ability to both interpret and respond within that frame with little conscious effort (behavioral adaptation). There is an intentionality to adaptation; it is an expansion of one's capabilities and options for behavior and valuing, not a substitution of one set of cultural behaviors with another (assimilation).

Integration is not only the internalization of bicultural or multicultural frames of reference but seeing oneself as "in process" or "self-creating," and accepting that identity is not based in any one culture. People in this state may see themselves as marginal. "Constructive marginality" was a term devised by Janet M. Bennett (1993) to indicate that this is not a pathological state but a way of being that allows one to have rich experiences in any culture rather than having one's reference point always based in a particular culture. These are people who are "at home" anywhere. They can function in ways that are consistent in any culture while maintaining a position "at the edge."

The Intensity Factors

Michael Paige (1993) proposed that there are a number of factors that make an intercultural experience more or less intense for a specific student. Those factors include the following:

Cultural difference: The degree of actual difference between two cultures and how negatively the students evaluate those differences influence their attitudes and ability to adapt.

Ethnocentrism: The more ethnocentric the student is, the more difficulty he or she will have in accepting the other culture. Conversely, the less accepting of difference the host culture is, the more difficult it will be for the student to become engaged with members of the host culture.

Language: The less language ability the student has, and the more essential language is to functioning well in the host culture, the more difficult it will be for the student to function in the culture, and, as a result, the experience will be more stressful.

Cultural immersion: Students who are deeply immersed in the culture will have a higher level of anxiety, since they are repeatedly confronted with difference, ambiguous situations, questions about how to behave, and the need to learn. Clearly this is what students who are doing service-learning abroad, particularly when they are taught by local professors and are living in homestays, are going through.

Cultural isolation: If the student has little or no access to fellow students from home, there will be a higher level of anxiety.

Prior intercultural experience: If this is the first time the student has been out of his or her own culture, the intensity of the experience will be higher than it will be for the student who has been abroad before and has developed coping strategies, an understanding of the adjustment process, and other intercultural skills.

Expectations: If the student's expectations of the host culture and of his or her own ability to function in it are unrealistically positive, disappointment can be a serious factor and intercultural adaptation can be adversely affected.

Visibility and invisibility: Being physically different from the host nationals and thus being very visible can make the intercultural experience more intense. Conversely, having to keep parts of one's identity hidden, such as being homosexual, can also increase the intensity of the experience.

Status: Feeling that one is not getting appropriate respect can raise the intensity of the experience. Conversely, receiving attention that, to the student-sojourner, does not seem warranted can be equally distressing.

Power and control: When sojourners feel they have no power and control in intercultural situations, especially over their own circumstances, the intensity of the experience increases. This factor consistently emerges as a major problem. The behaviors that allow one to control a situation in the home culture—language, relationships, academic and other roles—all are likely to be missing or changed in the new society.

Reentry

Martin and Harrell (2004) write, "Intercultural reentry has been defined as the process of reintegration into primary home contexts after an intercultural sojourn (an intensive and extended visit into cultural contexts different from those in which one was socialized)" (p. 310). Although, as Martin and Harrell point out, the definition has subsequently been modified (more individuals now have multiple experiences in different cultures, and reentry for voluntary sojourners can differ from reentry for those for whom leaving was forced, such as political exiles or labor migrants), this definition is useful for examining the reentry experiences of college students. They are often on their first extended sojourn out of the country (but not always!) and have gone abroad by choice (although with a growing number of institutions requiring study abroad of all students, this may not always be the case).

Pusch (2004) maintains that, "reentry is the hardest and, for learning, the most productive time of study or, indeed, any stay abroad. It takes the complete cycle of departure/sojourn/return to solidify the learning" (p. 121). Part of the issue here is that for many sojourners the difficulties of reentry are unexpected: it is going home, so everything should be the same. In actuality, however, friends and family and the home society have changed while the sojourner was gone, and also the sojourner has changed—how profoundly the sojourner has changed is often not obvious until "familiar" ideas and situations are encountered and they are seen through the new lenses of experiences in another culture.

In summary, a student engaging in intercultural service-learning needs to be aware of, at a minimum, the following concepts: Allport's contact theory and its critiques (1954); Ward, Bochner, and Furnham's ABCs of acculturation (affective, behavioral, and cognitive dimensions) (2001); Bennett's Developmental Model of Intercultural Sensitivity (M. Bennett, 1993); Paige's "Intensity Factors" (1993); and intercultural reentry. A student who is lacking the understanding of such concepts is likely to make inappropriate attributions about the behavior of host country nationals.

Reciprocity

Service-learning abroad differs from other forms of education abroad with regard to issues of growth and development in that it is not simply the student's growth and development that is under consideration. The growth and development of clients, agencies, and communities also is essential. If that does not take place, then the service-learning encounter cannot be deemed a success, regardless of how much growth and development has taken place in the student.

The effect of service-learning on communities, and particularly on communities where the service-learning partners are of different cultures, remains little studied (see Deelcy, 2004, for an exceptional look at the intercultural context). Harkavy and others have written fairly extensively on the work of the University of Pennsylvania with a neighboring community in Philadelphia (Harkavy & Puckett, 1991). Cruz and Giles (2000) enumerate some of the reasons for this lack of research: that faculty have needed to prove to dubious administrators that service-learning is indeed an effective means of producing learning, so they have focused on research on students and on learning; the difficulty in defining "community"; and the problems in determining variables, such as how one knows if "improvement" has taken place, what caused it, and how it can be shown that student service had anything to do with it. Additionally, Cruz and Giles (2000) note the lack of a constituency demanding such research and the difficulty of finding funding for it. The list of references in the Cruz and Giles article (2000), plus the section of their article headed "What Do We Know? The State of Inquiry Related to the Value of Service-Learning for the Community," suggest some additional readings on the topic of community benefits in a U.S. context.

Despite the lack of research, it is possible to suggest that for reciprocal growth and development to take place certain conditions must be met. First, service placements must be chosen by, or at least in collaboration with, local hosts. Outsiders generally do not have the cultural knowledge or the "on-the-ground" knowledge to understand where foreign students can actually make a difference. If real community needs are to be met, those living in the community must have a hand in defining the needs to be addressed. Perhaps the physical labor of young people building a school is the most important need, as happens with many short-term, one-time-only projects. However, it may be that the labor for this project could be provided by others indigenous to the community while a foreign student volunteer, by playing basketball, can bring street kids to a community shelter and engage them in a way that suggests alternatives to living on the streets, or a volunteer patiently coaxing a "failure to thrive" baby to eat may make a more important contribution to the growth and development of a community than building a school. Local partners are needed to provide clarity about the best choices for effective service.

Second, the presence of the foreigners who come to give service has to be long-term. While this does not mean that an individual volunteer must always stay a year or more in order to make a difference, it does mean that the sending organization must have a long-term commitment to the host community. The value of the service given must outweigh the disruption to the host agency caused by orientation, supervision, rescheduling activities, etc., in order to accommodate volunteers. The value outweighing the disruption is possible if the host agency knows that semester after semester a student will be there, and thus the tasks that relatively inexperienced young people with imperfect language skills can do are built into the agency's work. Short-term, intense projects by a group of foreigners who have no continuing connection to the community bear the potential of being more disruptive than useful.

A current debate about reciprocity in service-learning circles provokes new questions when the student and community come from different cultural traditions. Drawing upon John Dewey's distinction between *doing for* and *doing with* (Westbrook, 1991), writers such as Morton (1995), Kahne and Westheimer (1996), and Kahne, Westheimer, and Rogers (2000) have asked readers to rethink the purposes of service-learning. Their models suggest that social change rather than charity is an appropriate goal. This model, while potentially useful in getting students to do the learning involved in determining root causes of social problems, such as seeing the connections between the de-institutionalization of psychiatric patients and the growth in homelessness in the United States, also has the potential to minimize learning, if students are taught that a social problem has one distinct cause and that their role should be political action rather than direct service to those in need. The model, in other words, contains the possibility of suggesting that students leap to the "E" in the DIE model, rather than consider multiple interpretations of a situation, and it opens the door for students to define both problems and solutions in dualistic terms, thus obviating some of the complexities that experiential education can introduce into the learning process.

The social change model of service-learning is a more dangerous one to employ when the service is being done in an intercultural context and when the definition of what kind of social change is created by outsiders. Students need to do culture learning and academic learning; with their limited experience in the culture and often limited language skills, they are not in a position to determine what kind of social action is needed to "solve" the problem the agency they are working in is addressing. Their ideas about social action will be derivative; they will be following someone else's agenda. In this situation, learning will be minimized rather than maximized, and community growth and development are unlikely to occur as a result of a foreign undergraduate's one-semester attempts at social change. Social change is much more likely to result when there are long-term reciprocal *institutional* collaborations, with college–community partnerships in the host culture involved in the definition of problems and in the decisions about constructive action (see, for example, Harkavy & Puckett, 1991).

Additional insight into this issue is provided by Ward and Wolf-Wendel (2000), who write about the differences between service-learning at colleges and universities designed to serve a broad range of constituencies and the institutions they call "SFCUs"—special-focus colleges and universities, such as historically black colleges and universities, tribal colleges, and colleges serving a predominantly Hispanic student body. Such colleges, they maintain, are much less likely than the colleges and universities that serve a broad student body to be engaged in "doing for" service; since the student body and the community are coterminous, service in the community, for students at SFCUs, naturally is "doing with." They urge those involved in service-learning at non-SFCU institutions to try to find connections between the individual student and the community into which he or she is placed: a Catholic student for whom Catholicism is an important identity might work at a Catholic agency, for example.

Applying Ward and Wolf-Wendel's (2000) ideas to intercultural service-learning underscores the degree of difficulty of moving to "doing with" in such contexts, and the necessity for intentional curricular and practice designs to achieve reciprocity. If the community is seen by students (and often faculty as well) as "other" at non-SFCU institutions *within* the United

States, how much more likely is it that the community will be seen as "other" when a student is learning and serving *outside* of the United States? In this context, culture learning is essential; the student cannot feel connected enough to the host community to do service *with* if he or she does not understand that community. However, determining what each student needs in order to create that degree of connection with the community brings us back to Bennett's Developmental Model of Intercultural Sensitivity. What student A, who is in Minimization, needs in order to be connected with the community is different from what student B, who is in Acceptance, needs to form such connections.

Conclusion

Growth and development are important themes in all forms of education abroad, but in service-learning abroad, the student's growth and development are not the only forms of development that need to be considered. In service-learning, the element of reciprocity is essential: the host must benefit, as well as the student. If clients in an agency in the host society are to benefit, then the sending university or agency and the host university must be committed to a long-term partnership, and the host university must have long-term links to the agencies in which students serve. In addition, the student needs to do three kinds of learning: academic learning, learning about the processes of experiential education, and learning about some of the theories surrounding the process of intercultural adaptation. Service-learning in a culture other than one's own makes many demands on all of the parties involved, but it also provides opportunities for richly rewarding growth and development for both students and hosts.

References

Allport, G. W. (1954). *The nature of prejudice*. Reading, MA: Addison-Wesley

Bennett, J. M. (1993). Cultural marginality: Identity issues in intercultural training. In M. Paige (Ed.), *Education for the intercultural experience* (pp. 109–136). Yarmouth, ME: Intercultural Press.

Bennett, J. M., Bennett, M. J., & Stillings, K. (1977). *Description, interpretation, and evaluation: Facilitators' guidelines*. Retrieved August 16, 2007 from http://www.intercultural.org/resources.html

Bennett, M. J. (1993). Towards Ethnorelativism: A developmental model of intercultural sensitivity. In M. Paige (Ed.), *Education for the intercultural experience* (pp. 21–71). Yarmouth, ME: Intercultural Press.

Bulgakov, M. (1995). *The master and Margarita* (D. Burgin & K. T. O'Connor, Trans.). New York: Random House. (Original work published 1967)

Campbell, J. (1968). *The hero with a thousand faces*. Princeton, NJ: Princeton University Press.

Chisholm, L. (2000). *Charting a hero's journey*. New York: International Partnership for Service-Learning.

Cruz, N. I., & Giles, D. E. (2000, Fall). Where's the community in service learning research? [Special Issue]. *Michigan Journal of Community Service-Learning, 28–34*.

Deeley, S. J. (2004). Service-learning students within welfare agencies in Scotland and Jamaica. In H. Tonkin (Ed.), *Service-learning across cultures: Promise and achievement—A report to the Ford Foundation* (pp. 197–237). New York: The International Partnership for Service-Learning and Leadership.

Dixon, J., Durrheim, K., & Tredoux, C. (2005). Beyond the optimal contact strategy: A reality check for the contact hypothesis. *American Psychologist, 60*, 697–711.

Engle, J., & Engle, L. (2002). Neither international nor educative: Study abroad in the time of globalization. In W. Grunzweig & N. Rinehart (Eds.), *Rockin' in Red Square: Critical approaches to international education in the age of cyberculture* (pp. 25–40). Hamburg: Lit Verlag.

Evans, D. W., Forney, D. S., & Guido-DiBrito, F. (1998). *Student development in college: Theory, research and practice*. San Francisco: Jossey-Bass.

Freed, B. F. (1998). Introduction: Language learning in a study abroad context [Special Issue]. *Frontiers: The Interdisciplinary Journal of Study Abroad, IV, i–v*.

Gullahorn, J. T., & Gullahorn, J. E. (1963). An extension of the U-curve hypothesis. *Journal of Social Issues, 14*, 33–47.

Hall, E. T. (1984). *The dance of life: The other dimension of time*. New York: Anchor/Random House.

Harkavy, I., & Puckett, J. L. (1991). Toward effective university-public school partnerships: An analysis of a contemporary model. *Teachers College Record, 92*, 556–581.

Haynes, M. (2003, December). *Joseph Stalin and the harvest of death*. Paper presented to the New Socialist Approaches to History Seminar. Institute of Historical Research. Retrieved August 16, 2007 from http://www.londonsocialisthistorians.org/papers/nsa031206b.html

International Partnership for Service-Learning and Leadership (IPSL). (2007). *Declaration of Principles*. Retrieved August, 16 2007, from http://www.ipsl.org/programs/servicelearning.html

Kahne, J., & Westheimer, J. (1996). In the service of what? *Phi Delta Kappan, 77*, 592–600.

Kahne, J., Westheimer, J., & Rogers, B. (2000, Fall). Service learning and citizenship: Directions for research. *Michigan Journal of Community Service Learning, Special Issue,* 42–51.

Keen, A. (2007). *The cult of the amateur: How today's Internet is killing our culture.* New York: Doubleday/Currency.

Kim, Y. Y. (2001). *Becoming intercultural: An integrative theory of communication and cross-cultural adaptation.* London: Sage.

Kluckhohn, F. R., & Strodtbeck, F. L. (1961). *Variations in value orientations.* Evanston, IL: Row, Peterson.

Knefelkamp, L. L. (1999). Introduction and theory update. In W. G. Perry (Ed.), *Forms of intellectual and ethical development in the college years* (pp. xi–xxxviii). San Francisco: Jossey-Bass.

Knefelkamp, L., Widdick, C., & Parker, C. A. (1978). *Applying new developmental findings.* San Francisco: Jossey-Bass.

Kolb, D. (1984). *Experiential learning: Experience as the source of learning and development.* Englewood, NJ: Prentice Hall.

Martin, J. N., & Harrell, T. (2004). Intercultural reentry of students and professionals: Theory and practice. In D. Landis, J. M. Bennett, & M. J. Bennett (Eds.), *Handbook of intercultural training* (3rd ed., pp. 309–336). Thousand Oaks, CA: Sage.

Moore, W. S. (1989). The learning environment preference: Exploring the construct validity of an objective measure of the Perry Scheme of Intellectual Development. *Journal of College Student Development, 30,* 504–515.

Morton, K. (1995). The irony of service: Charity, project, and social change in service learning. *Michigan Journal of Community Service Learning, 2,* 19–32.

Moss, K. (c. 1998). *Stalinist terror.* In a website devoted to Bulgakov's novel *The Master and Margarita.* Retrieved August 30, 2007, http://cr.middlebury.edu/pub lic/russian/Bulgakov/public_html/terror.html

Oberg, K. (1954, August). *Culture shock.* Presented to the Women's Club of Rio de Janeiro. Retrieved August 30, 2007 from http://www.smcm.edu/academics/internationaled/Pdf/cultureshockarticle.pdf

Olcott, M. B. (2002). *Kazakhstan: Unfulfilled promise.* Washington, DC: Carnegie Endowment for International Peace.

Paige, R. M. (1993). On the nature of intercultural experience and intercultural education. In R. M. Paige (Ed.), *Education for the intercultural experience* (pp. 1–20). Yarmouth, ME: Intercultural Press.

Perry, W. G. (1999). *Forms of ethical and intellectual development in the college years: A scheme.* San Francisco: Jossey-Bass.

Pettigrew, T. F. (1998). Intergroup contact theory. *Annual Review of Psychology, 49,* 65–85.

Pettigrew, T. F., & Tropp, L. R. (2000). Does intergroup contact reduce prejudice? Recent meta-analytic findings. In S. Oskamp (Ed.), *Reducing prejudice and discrimination* (pp. 93–114). Mahwah, NJ: Lawrence Erlbaum.

Pusch, M. D. (1998). Going home: Styles of reentry. In D. Lynch, A. Pilbeam, & P. O'Connor (Eds.), *Heritage and progress* (pp. 248–255). Bath, England: SIETAR Europa.

Pusch, M. D. (2003, November). *International service-learning and intercultural competence development.* Paper presented at the 3rd Annual International Conference on Service-Learning, Salt Lake City, UT.

Pusch, M. D. (2004). A cross-cultural perspective. In H. Tonkin (Ed.), *Service-learning across cultures: Promise and achievement—A report to the Ford Foundation* (pp. 103–130). New York: The International Partnership for Service-Learning and Leadership.

Said, E. (1978). *Orientalism.* New York: Vintage Books.

Schatz, E. (2004). *Modern clan politics: The power of "blood" in Kazakhstan and beyond.* Seattle: University of Washington.

Triandis, H. C. (1990). Theoretical concepts of use to practitioners. In R. Brislin (Ed.), *Cross-cultural applied psychology* (pp. 34–55). Newbury Park, CA: Sage.

VandeBerg, M. J. (2004). Introduction: Assessment of student learning abroad [Special Issue]. *Frontiers: The Interdisciplinary Journal of Study Abroad, X,* i-xxii.

Ward, C., Bochner, S., & Furnham, A. (2001). *The psychology of culture shock* (2nd ed.). Philadelphia: Taylor and Francis.

Ward, K., & Wolf-Wendel, L. (2000). Community-centered service learning: Moving from doing for to doing with. *American Behavioral Scientist, 43*(5), 767–780.

Westbrook, R. B. (1991). *John Dewey and American Democracy.* Ithaca, NY: Cornell University Press.

Wilkinson, S. (2007). *Insights from study abroad for language programs.* Boston: Thomson/Heinle.

17

NARRATIVES OF INTERCULTURAL TRANSFORMATION

Student Perspective Transition

Ingrid Adams

> Come closer to the common mystery. Attend to the ordinary. There is nothing else to find. All the traveling of thought returns to the beginning and recognizes the obvious. It is wisdom that sees the ordinary with amazement.
>
> —Lao Tzu, Chinese philosopher, fourth century BCE

L ife is a collection of stories, narratives by which we codify our experiences, both internal and external. A study abroad experience offers a rich environment from which to collect such life stories. The salient cultural issues embodied in students' chronicles can reveal important information concerning adjustment to the study abroad situation. In this chapter we share students' stories with the hope that international educators will be able to use some of these student stories in their efforts to orient and inform students about what to expect on their study abroad adventure. Narratives in students' own words are usually more engaging than more abstract discussions of potential cultural clashes.

The stories reported here were selected from a total of 494 compositions written by 72 traditional university students (ages 19 to 25) in the context of an intercultural communications (ICC) class during their study abroad sojourn. See chapter 9 of this book to learn more about the research project that developed the selection criteria used to choose the stories reported here. The academic intention of the ICC class was to encourage students' attentiveness to and reflection about their host culture environment, and through this awareness to facilitate learning about the host culture and ultimately about the self.

The exploration for the students was process driven. Sojourners were asked to identify salient cultural issues and write about these topics in a prescribed format. While the format for writing about the chosen issue was fixed, students were entirely free in their choice of topics. This allowed the students to examine closely cultural differences with regard to their own experiences and perceptions. Thus students selected their stories on the basis of what Ward, Bochner, and Furnham (2001) describe as "critical incidents" or "an event that matters" (p. 5). Study abroad educators might gain understanding of their students by becoming aware of both the topics the students selected and the manner in which they reacted to those incidents.

Within the parameters set by the Description, Interpretation, and Evaluation (DIE) assignment, students relayed the salient event in objective terms in the description; the interpretation allowed sojourners to focus on the underlying aspects or values of the host culture that could be at play in causing the specific event; the evaluation gave students the liberty to focus on why, from their own viewpoint, they thought the event occurred and how they felt about it (Bennett, Bennett, & Stillings, 1977). The DIE format provides a rich source of insight into student adjustment.

The following three sections are based on the pattern of change in the salience of stories about intercultural adjustment topics over time: salience decreases, salience changes direction, salience increases. Each section includes four parts:

1. Introduction of the category of specific change over time and the associated salient topics in those categories
2. The category's fit with theories of intercultural adjustment
3. Narratives from students in their own words chosen for their representation of the specific topic, and for their layers of depth regarding cultural differences
4. Brief interpretation of student narrative in the context of
   a. the clash between U.S. and Austrian/German cultures;
   b. the cultural value(s) that are relevant; and

c. how the specific theory might explain change over time in that
value

Categories of Intercultural Adjustment That Decrease in Salience Over Time

Salient topics: Communication, Public Interaction, Social Contact
Applied intercultural theory: Anxiety/Uncertainty Management Theory

The personal adjustment version of the anxiety/uncertainty management
theory focuses on the reaction of sojourners entering new cultures and interacting with host nationals (Gudykunst, 2002). In the initial stages of cross-
cultural contact, sojourners are uncertain about host nationals' feelings, attitudes, and behaviors, thus attempts to predict how best to react are fraught
with anxiety. If this anxiety does not diminish, sojourners are unable to communicate effectively, and are more likely to process information in simplistic,
ethnocentric ways. This tends to perpetuate anxiety. Alternatively, if sojourners can be open to new information and creatively develop new ways
of thinking that take into account the perspectives of host nationals, then the
probability of successful interaction increases and anxiety is reduced. Over
repeated, successful encounters, sojourners continue to reduce anxiety. The
once foreign culture becomes more predictable, and navigating through it
less fraught with difficulty.

Communication

Definition
Usually the lack of accurate understanding communicated between students
and members of the host culture, often based on differing communication
styles, independent of knowledge of the host culture language.

Student narratives
1. I grew up in a small town and people knew each other through generations. At home, locals generally greet one another with "Hello how are
you?" or "How's it going today?" This custom was also extended to new
people in town though with perhaps a little more curiosity than heart.
When I first arrived in my host culture I extended those greetings to people
on the street, expecting the same interaction I was used to at home. Something like "I am great thanks for asking" or "good! How about you?" A

brief, but personal encounter. This is not custom here. People look at me weird, some stare at me, give a head nod, or, what I have come to learn, their customary obligatory hello and moved on. I suppose people in the cities need to find some way to have space. Once I was able to understand that need, I dropped my country greeting customs for the local ones. Though I still prefer that personal touch in greetings, I got used to the simple hellos and have learned to extend them in kind.

The first day-to-day communications after arriving in the host country are often the greetings sojourners exchange with host nationals encountered on neighborhood streets, while using public transportation, and so on. This student's narrative highlights the importance of these initial encounters. The home culture greeting ritual with which the sojourner hoped to fit in identifies him as an outsider without appropriate knowledge of local communication styles. Through critically thinking about the apparent cultural differences, the sojourner develops a cognitive understanding, thus managing anxiety. He demonstrates in his narrative that, although cultural adaptation took place, personal preference was acknowledged and retained. The sojourner's self-concept was not distorted in the process of cultural adaptation (Berger, 2001; Weiten & Lloyd, 2003).

> 2. Europe seems to be a cash-based society. In America practically no one carries cash and I never considered that using my credit card would be an issue. This week I went to the small grocery store in my host family's neighborhood. I tried to pay with my VISA card. To my surprise, the checkout clerk handed the card back to me shaking her head to say no, pointing to the picture of the EC-Card on the store window. I had no idea what the difference was between the EC-Card and my VISA. I felt like a total fool since I had no other way of paying for all the items with the cash I had in my pocket. Gravely disappointed I left the store without much of my food. I wish my language skills were better and I could have asked what the problem was, but I think language skills would have not changed the outcome.

Commerce in much of Europe is rooted in *Einzelhandel* (small business owners). Specialty shops such as bakeries, butcher shops, small grocery stores, coffee houses, etc., are frequented by locals, often daily, and as indicated in the narrative, are largely cash based. The communication struggle in this incident centers on the inability of the student to understand and to make himself understood. Both written cues (the unnoticed window sign) and oral communication (the clerk's explanation in an unintelligible language) create uncertainty of how to react. The knowledge gained from this encounter helped the student to reorient himself regarding how to pay for purchases. This understanding reduced future uncertainties and decreased anxiety through repeated successful interactions with shopkeepers.

Public Interactions

Definition

Differing expectations about where specific social events were most likely to take place, and the frequency of unexpected public behaviors.

Student narratives

1. It seems being American makes one a target in this city. I don't mean that negatively only. Sometimes people want to talk just to practice their English. For the most part I don't mind since my German skills improve in the process as well. What is bothersome is when people start yelling, "American go home," as was the case in the subway today. I wanted to talk with the guy and ask him about his hatred and how I became an outlet for that when he knows nothing about me as an individual. No one seemed to mind him yelling. Perhaps local people are used to it and any interference would only add fuel to the issues. From my peers I learned that my experience was not an isolated case. They too had been yelled at. Perhaps it is the same people yelling. Regardless, I found it disturbing. I felt like I had a responsibility as an American. I just did not quite know what that responsibility was.

The United States is a high-profile country with a wide-reaching political and economic agenda. Unfortunately, this U.S. visibility can be a motive for stereotyping Americans in various negative ways. One can ascertain that the host national's action described in the narrative construed the United States as an enemy of sorts and illustrated that cognitive perception in his behavior (Berger, 2001). A very basic explanation of the host national's action may be attributed to a mental illness. One can, of course, not be sure, and it would be a mistake to stereotype the host national's behavior, though such erratic behavior may be more common in a large city than a small town. In the narrative the student demonstrates a positive outcome of the interaction, through the inhibition of his own negative emotions toward the host national. Future such encounters may be upsetting, but not unexpected. The student's constructive way of dealing with the event and learning from peers having had the same experience predict the decrease in topic salience over time.

> 2. In the U.S. I go to the grocery store to shop for my produce, place them in the provided bags and proceed to the checkout counter. My produce is weighed, priced, bagged, and, if I have a lot, carried out to my car. After an anxiety laden checkout experience where I was rejected at the checkout counter, I learned that here, I have to weigh my own produce and glue the price sticker on the bag. Then I have to be sure to bring something to carry my groceries home with if I do not want to pay for a bag. I did not speak the language well enough to actually communicate with the clerk so I ended up being frustrated and embarrassed. I felt that I had shown to the world just how ignorant an American can be. The grocery store's clerk rolling her eyes at me did not help much. The good news is now I know those rules.

Academic sojourners are also ambassadors of their country (Ward et al., 2001), and this sojourner tells us that having failed in that mission made her feel incompetent. The story clearly narrates the expectations of the host culture when shopping for groceries and how that practice clashes with that of the home culture rules. This crisis at the grocery store surely facilitated a learning opportunity for the sojourner. Knowledge of the practices described in the story could ease students' stress levels associated with the responsibility students feel as ambassadors of their home culture.

Social Contact

Definition

Leisure time or socially oriented contact with others from the host culture, not related to the academic or homestay environments.

Student narratives

> 1. It seems Europeans spend a great deal of energy discussing politics. Last week I found myself sitting with a group of locals to enjoy a beer after a game of basketball. As the conversation went from basketball to politics their voices grew ever louder. At one point the conversation could be construed as a shouting match. I was sure a fist fight was imminent. But not

so. My German is by far not rich enough to participate in the kind of debate I was witnessing, nonetheless I stayed attentive. The majority of the conversation seemed to center around our President. Perhaps it was just as well that I could not understand everything that was said. This was an occasion where I was not really disappointed with my German skills. What amazed me was that at the end of the heated encounter we all engaged in the ritual of drinking "Bruedershaft" (Brotherhood).

This sojourner witnessed that for host nationals there are rules of engagement when discussing politics. Passion is allowed, and then friendships are reconfirmed. Discussions or arguments can even edge into name calling and personal attacks. U.S. students see such actions as excessive and an irretrievable insult. However, when the discussion is over, the underlying friendship is reasserted. The sojourner managed anxiety through basic observation. The cultural boundaries prevented the anticipated brawl. Regular witness to such passionate discussions certainly explains decrease in topic salience over time. In fact, students can learn to enjoy the "spiciness" of such discussions.

2. The dating scene here in Europe is somewhat perplexing. My friend and I had been introduced to a local, good looking, great sense of humor guy. Last week a group of us including this hot local went out to a dance club. As the night went on, this Austrian became very friendly and flirtatious with us girls. By the end of the night we (the girls) received kisses on the cheeks from him and his email address. He encouraged us to write so we could do this again another time. Before we separated we asked him what his plans were for the weekend. His response was that he "usually spends time with his girlfriend on the weekends." I felt somewhat used. How could he have such a good time with us, when his girlfriend was maybe sitting at home waiting for him to take her dancing? I had heard that here people go out to clubs as groups, dance with each other, have conversation, and then everyone goes home. This encounter confused me.

In early adulthood one of the prevailing needs is to learn about and engage in intimate relationships with an exclusive partner (Berger, 2001). The cultural norm in the United States is that, once formed, intimate relationships are exclusive. This restriction is not limited to sexual activities but also tends to span social activities. This is perhaps where the confusion for this sojourner is rooted. In Austria, particularly, the *bussi* (kiss on the cheek) is a socially accepted expression of affection. Lighthearted flirtatious behavior is usually not considered infidelity. From the sojourner's story it can be deduced that the young man was not sexually inappropriate and was rather forthright when asked about future engagements. Over repeated exposure, students learn more about host culture expectations concerning dating and relationship boundaries.

In summary, the topics illustrated in this section (Communication, Public Interaction, and Social Contact) typically provide a high level of uncertainty for students early in their sojourn but become more and more predictable with expanded exposure to the culture. International educators can predict that such issues will be prominent in the early days of study abroad.

Categories of Intercultural Adjustment That Change in Salience Over Time

Salient topics: Privacy, Health, Social Rules, Language
Applied intercultural theory: Culture Shock

The culture shock hypothesis proposes three phases of adjustment (Oberg, 1960) The first phase is dominated by the sojourners' feelings of anticipation that mask day-to-day difficulties. In the second segment of adjustment sojourners begin to notice the world around them in more objective terms. This attention produces crisis where a myriad of emotions can arise. The sojourner may become anxious or frustrated and feel inadequate, lonely, and angry about the circumstances presented. This is the "shock" of the culture shock. Awareness of circumstances has replaced the initial euphoria. The third and final phase of this U-shaped curve is the adjustment phase. Successful navigation of this final stage depends to some extent on the individuals' personality, coping mechanisms, education about the host culture, general attitude about life, willingness to address change, and of course on the sojourners' sense of adventure. With the exception of those in the category of Language, the following student stories show an elevated concern for these topics in the middle, rather than at the beginning or end, of the sojourn.

Privacy

Definition

Differing expectations concerning what types of behavior and events should be shared versus held private, and mechanisms by which privacy is maintained.

Student narratives

1. So—last week my host mother offered to do my laundry. I felt a little odd handing my underwear over to her to wash. But, well what can I say, I needed it done. A day later or so I walked into my host brother's room after school to use his computer. He is 15. When I entered the room I could not believe my eyes. I was shocked to find my underwear and other clothing hanging in his room to dry! I was mortified! Immediately I began to gather all the clothing I recognized to be mine and moved it into my room. Maybe my American view of the importance of privacy is dominating my feeling. Supposedly we care more about privacy. I think of my underwear as a very private thing. I cannot shake the vision of my host brother looking at my underwear and possibly closely investigating it. Fifteen year old boys, and strangers at that, should not have access to girls' panties. What did my host mother think when she put my underwear in her son's room to dry? How was she ok with the potential of him examining my underwear? I mean it would *not* be ok if he came and looked at them in my drawer, and this gave him easy access!

This is a beautiful example of a culture shock crisis facilitated by an innocent, common, European way of drying laundry in the winter. While this custom is a typical energy-saving practice in Western Europe, for an unsuspecting U.S. sojourner it was a dramatic invasion of privacy. The student is tormented by the possibility of the teenager examining her underwear. Most likely, the boy never noticed them because in his culture garments lose specificity when they hit the drying rack. What perhaps made this situation tense and exacerbated the crisis is the difference between American and Western European sensitivity to sexuality. The adjustments the sojourner made to ameliorate the initial culture shock crisis are well defined in the narrative. The young woman gathered her underwear and in doing so regained her sense of privacy and personal safety. This action implies an adjustment by the sojourner for the remaining time with the host family. The previous story details a situation that may indicate too little privacy, while the following story highlights situations in which the U.S. students' perception is that there is too much.

> 2. I was sitting in my room reading with the door open in case someone wanted to come in and visit. All of a sudden, my little host brother (he is 10) comes in, smiles at me, and shuts the door on his way out. I was confused about his motives for shutting my door. I feel strange about it. I think an open door welcomes people inside which is what I was trying to convey. A friend said that Austrians close doors, but I still don't feel right about. I sit in my room with my door closed. I feel like my family thinks I don't like them, or don't want to talk to them because my door is closed. Sometimes when I leave my room my family will all be in the living room with the door closed. I want to go in and talk with them. I was told that I should knock and go in. I find this most difficult. To me when a door is closed it means I would like my privacy, please go away.

Closed doors are strongly associated with privacy for U.S. sojourners as this story tells. In Austria, Germany, and other European countries closed doors to common living areas are generally matters of energy efficiency and are not associated with privacy. The custom is especially prevalent in older homes where main living areas are often separated by doors, a departure from America's open-space home architecture concepts. The sojourner speaks about the feelings of self-doubt that this custom evoked. This culture shock crisis challenges the sojourner to contemplate and balance several issues at once: the desire to interact with the host family, the need to assure personal privacy, and the courtesy to respect the privacy of the host family.

Health

Definition

Health-related incidents as well as the prevalence of smoking and the differing expectations and laws regarding drinking of alcoholic beverages.

Student narratives

> 1. This past Friday I came down with an ear ache. I wanted some aspirin or Tylenol to relieve the pain. Because it was already 7 pm and I knew the drugstore two blocks away would be closed, I went to *Interspar*, a supermarket/clothing store located in the railway station. There the clerk found someone who spoke better English than I did German. When I asked her

for aspirin, or other pain medications, she shook her head in disbelief. Her facial expressions made me feel like an idiot. My reaction was, lady, I am not asking for a narcotic, or antibiotics all I want is a simple aspirin. She proceeded to tell me that all the pharmacies were closed for the weekend and I would have to wait until Monday. Needless to say I was very upset when I left the store. I could not understand why I had to wait until Monday for what is in the U.S. an everyday over-the-counter medication available anywhere. I went home and luckily my host mother had some aspirin in her medicine cabinet she let me have.

Grocery stores in the United States offer a vast supply and variety of over-the-counter drugs. This custom is far removed from that in Austria and Germany, as this sojourner learned to her distress. Anger and frustration about this cultural difference provoked the sojourner as well as the host national. The student made a wise choice leaving the store. It may have been beneficial for this sojourner to know these rules about over-the-counter drugs in the host country, as well as the rules concerning opening hours of pharmacies. Beyond this knowledge, all sojourners could benefit from a well-stocked first-aid kit to take overseas.

2. So many people in Vienna smoke! Smoking is permitted almost everywhere and there are very few, if any, non-smoking partitions in restaurants and no smoking lounges in buildings. Vienna seems to be the place where the glamour of smoking is making its last stand. Unlike a lot of things, I will never get used to breathing this unhealthy air. But what can a person do? Stay home? Having my clothes smell like smoke is a pain. I guess if I smell bad all the time, then I have nothing with which to compare it. I will definitely not miss this offensive Austrian habit.

This is a tale of surrender. For an American nonsmoker this host culture practice is difficult to accept. In the United States, the ills of smoking rate among the highest priorities of health education in public schools. Knowing the risks associated with smoking, the sojourner has to make serious choices when the practice pervades in virtually all public spaces, as described in the narrative. This student deals with the issue through basic surrender. Intercultural adjustment is not always learning fun and positive things. Sometimes, it is simply about learning the wisdom of accepting what is, however disagreeable it may be.

Social Rules

Definition

Differences in expectations of the "rules" of social interaction, regarding things such as eye contact, personal space; especially differences in what was socially appropriate versus inappropriate.

Student narratives.

1. Austrians seem to be very private people until they stand in line. I went to the Opera tonight. The first time I stood in line there it was pretty crowded and people where standing immediately behind each other. At the U-Bahn and other crowed public places I have experienced the same. Generally I am getting used to it. I don't even mind people bumping into me as long as they aren't violent about it. This evening at the Opera however was down right irritating and made me feel uncomfortable. The place was not crowded but still the woman behind me seemed to think she was standing in a crowded line. I wanted to turn around and say AHHH, go away evil old thing!!! But, of course I just stood there completely accepting my fate. I am just glad we keep talking about the space bubble thing in class. Perhaps this woman is so used to standing in crowded lines, and standing close is so ingrained in her, that she is not aware when there is space to maybe stand a little less packed

Vienna proper together with the surrounding suburbs is home to about 2 million people, 25% of the total Austrian population. The writer comes from a significantly less populous area of the United States. The clash underlying the encounter described lies perhaps in the way this student thinks about being close and under what conditions the described proximity is acceptable. Social psychology teaches that our behavior is mostly consistent and that we tend toward social conformity most of the time (Baron & Byrne, 2003). Through this theoretical lens the clash between home culture and host culture acceptance of proximity can be understood. The student found comfort in her education about the space bubble (Hall, 1969) and the ability to bear one's lot in life. Both assisted in adjusting to host culture public interactions. Again, the adjustment to the host culture need not be comfortable in order to be predictable and to lower anxiety. At some point, the difference in the host culture and the student's personal space comfort zones will become routine and fall mostly out of awareness.

2. While riding home on the 13A bus one night I noticed a very attractive woman sitting in a nearby seat. After a short while we made eye contact for more that a few seconds. I looked away feeling uncomfortable making eye contact with someone I did not know for more than five seconds. I then looked at her through her reflection in the window and soon there after we made eye contact though the reflection for more than a few seconds. I found this amusing and a smile came to my face. She never smiled back. I felt happy that she kept staring at me, but disturbed when she never smiled back.

Dating host nationals while abroad invites an entirely different set of cross-cultural challenges for late-adolescent and young adult sojourners. Unfamiliarity with dating rules combined with linguistic difficulties may leave a young person confused, as this narrative tells us. Host culture social, societal, religious, and familial tenets may require a level of understanding by the sojourner beyond the knowledge base of day-to-day interactions with host nationals. Rules may vary across gender. The young man writing this narrative shares his confusion and feelings of rejection. Those challenges, though not entirely separate from issues a developing young person would have to deal with in the home culture, are exacerbated in the presence of culture shock (Ward et al., 2001). These feelings can amplify doubt in already-fragile self-esteems during late-adolescent and early adulthood years (Berger, 2001).

Language

Definition

Concerns with the use of the host culture language and feelings of inadequacy concerning use of a foreign language.

The Language category showed a change over time opposite of the previous categories in this section. It dipped in the middle of the sojourn but was higher at the beginning and the end.

Student narratives

1. It has been hard. Wherever I turn, language difficulties follow me like a dark shadow. My internal dialogue is my only familiar communication companion. Lately, it has been telling me that I don't fit in here. Before going abroad, my vision of isolation was always associated with spatial confinement. Not that I have changed my mind about that. I have however, added another perspective, an expanded definition of isolation to my

world. Wow, how we depend on language. It is the tool to confirm feelings, discuss events, or ask for help in finding places. Perhaps an artist can communicate with paintings or a pianist through the keys of his instrument, but in everyday life, language is the tool that opens doors of inclusion and forward motion. This morning I had to talk myself into getting up and out. My legs hit the floor powered by the lyrics of a song that goes something like this: take a shower and shine your shoes, you got no time to lose, you're a young man you must be living . . . Ok, I am up. *Guten Morgen!* A good start—what do you think? My friend internal dialogue.

Most (60%) of the authors of the DIEs used here did not speak the host culture language at the beginning of their sojourn. It can be assumed that this sojourner is one of the 60% who arrived in the host country with absent, or limited, host culture language skill. Sojourners generally rely less on host-national-supported social networks than on relationships with their compatriots (Ward et al., 2001). While relationships with host nationals may not be primary, they no doubt fill an important emotional need. The story of this sojourner paints a picture of isolation from the host culture rooted in poor language skills. That chasm is filled with unmet emotional needs fueling anxiety about fitting in. Often such doubts emerge early and fade slightly with a few functional phrases that allow a superficial connection with host nationals. Inherent in the narrative is the young man's strong internal locus of control (Baron & Byrne, 2003) and apparent sense of humor. Inspired by poetry he ushers himself out of bed and thus begins a positive adjustment phase.

2. This past weekend our host mother cooked dinner for a party of five. Earlier in the day she asked the two of us to eat in our rooms because the table was not large enough to accommodate us all. We understood the problem and agreed to eat in the rooms as requested. At dinner time we both came into the kitchen to get our food. By my standards, the table would have easily accommodated the two of us. While filling my plate, I thought for sure they would ask us to join them. But not so. I felt a little left out and unimportant. In addition, our host never introduced us to her guests. It was disappointing to not have an opportunity to practice the host language in a truly local social setting. We heard them visit for awhile after dinner as is customary here. Perhaps the guests were not ready to make that extra effort it takes to have conversation with people who are learning

the language. I know how much effort it has taken to effectively communicate with our host mother. I think we could have made a contribution to the evening. We both had worked very hard on our language skills. Perhaps this has less to do with language and more with personalities but I think language might have still been a decisive factor for the exclusion. It also made me contemplate how fluent is one expected to be in the host language to truly be included in the host culture.

Contrary to the young man in the previous narrative, whose distress was primarily rooted in poor linguistic skills, this sojourner's anguish seems to be fueled by language proficiency. The student speaks about the diligent commitment to language. Underlying that commitment are hopes, if not expectations, to fit in with the host family. Social integration is associated with positive psychological adjustment for the sojourner (Ward et al., 2001). As such, the student's desire to nurture a relationship with host nationals is not inappropriate. The narrative illustrates that a distressing experience related to language skills may not be circumvented even with excellent host culture linguistic skills.

In summary, changes in salience of topics discussed in this section (Privacy, Health, Social Rules) may follow the culture shock U-curve. At the midpoint of the adjustment process some topics ignored earlier emerge as important, and are resolved later. For the topic of Language, that pattern was reversed.

Categories of Intercultural Adjustment That Increase in Salience Over Time

> *Salient topics:* Cross-Cultural Comparison, General Environment, Social
>   Preferences
> *Applied intercultural theory:* Sociocultural Learning

The sociocultural learning theory suggests that the sojourner is initially overwhelmed with learning basic rules of engagement in the host culture. As the sojourner adjusts to the culture and he or she has learned some rudimentary skills associated with getting around town, interacting with locals, etc., the focus shifts and the worldview of the sojourner broadens. This initial adjustment leads to more learning, and increased exploration of skill and knowledge follow. While on the sojourn, students extend their travel to neighboring counties where cultural differences tend to be further illuminated not only with the home culture but also with the primary host culture.

Cross-Cultural Comparisons

Definition

A comparison of U.S. and host culture values and behaviors as compared with other foreign cultures that the students encountered during their travels.

Student narratives

1. Over the weekend a group of us visited Poland. It was refreshing! The Polish people were very friendly in Zakopane and Krakow. We found a local club, where, to our surprise, we encountered only Polish students. We were immediately included by the group. In the local bars in Vienna, everyone stared at us like outcasts. But in Krakow we were accepted right in. I was actually approached by a girl and later by a guy just to chat. Perhaps this friendliness can be attributed to the fact that Poland unlike Vienna sees very few American tourists and may still be fascinated by people from other parts of the world. Whatever the reason I felt comforted and really enjoyed the friendliness and acceptance of us. Not to put down Austrians but they keep to themselves quite a bit more. That German circle of close friends that stays the same forever plays into this concept I suppose.

European cultural rules, languages, and customs vary, sometimes more than others, depending on the country. Inclusion in various cultures and their groups therefore depends on many variables. This story highlights how study abroad host culture experiences facilitate comparative analysis, and supports the notion that, once rudimentary skills are learned, the sojourner's worldview can expand. Rehearsed in levels of inclusion or exclusion, as it may be, in the primary host culture, the sojourner has a reference from which to accept and enjoy the engaging positive encounter illustrated in the narrative. The student implies in the narrative that the experience with other groups increased understanding of the primary host culture, which no doubt leads to increased coping skills to deal with the perceived personal distance there.

2. On my first day in Rome I went to the Spanish steps and had not been sitting down for a minute yet when an Italian guy came up and started

talking to me. Conversely, I don't think that a random Austrian guy has talked to me in the two months that I have been there. Austrian people tend to mind their own business more. Plus our book says that they don't tend to want to make more friends. The opposite must be true for Italians. Either that or they think that American tourists are easy targets for their sexual exploits. At first I thought it was nice to be able to meet local people so easily—traveling I meet lots of backpackers and make lots of friends, but they are rarely from the country I am visiting. After a while though cat calls do get irritating. I might not know or talk to many Austrian guys, but at least I can feel safe walking around Vienna.

This sojourner's experience highlights gender-specific sociocultural learning needs while abroad. Attention to personal safety has to be weighed against the enthusiasm to engage in available cross-gender relationships. Exposure to the diverse European cultures offers a multitude of learning opportunities and thus salience of topic in this category. The student's story offers a well-defined example of how female sojourners learn the cultural norms expressed by males and learn to balance effectively social interactions, male attention, and personal safety over time.

General Environment

Definition

Differences with regard to environmental concerns (e.g., recycling), features of architecture, and civic actions with regard to environmental issues.

Student narratives

1. Recently I witnessed a mother carrying her son up countless flights of stairs. I was perplexed, and to be honest a bit judgmental, wondering why this woman carried a child that I thought should be walking up the stairs. The image imprinted in my mind. Later that day I learned that this was a handicapped child being carried. I began to realize that there is almost no handicapped accessibility in Vienna. I have seen few ramps for wheelchairs, and most buildings do not have elevators. Streetcars have no handicapped access. Bathrooms are rarely big enough for a wheelchair. There are special street crossings for the visually impaired, but virtually nothing for wheelchair bound people. When I asked my host about this she simply said that the Nazis killed the handicapped, so there are now fewer of them. I was shocked at such a matter of fact response. Her answer was too big to contemplate. Besides, it seemed to me that was not a good reason for not having handicapped access in the twenty-first century. And, further, what

about people who have had accidents since WWII? I know little about the social-cultural history of Vienna and how that fits in with the minimal handicapped accessibility. Growing up in the U.S., I find it hard to accept that everyone can't have the same opportunities. Vienna is a beautiful city, and because of these restrictions the city cannot be enjoyed by everyone. I think it is a shame that people are isolated.

The narrative is an excellent example of the layers and processes associated with sociocultural learning. One surprise leads to another. The student shows an ability to be aware of and regulate her emotional reactions. Seeds of personal and intellectual growth—primary reasons to study abroad (Ward et al., 2001)—are evident in this narrative.

2. When I first arrived in Vienna, using the public transportation system was very intimidating. Without familiar landmarks I took the bus as well as the subway in the wrong direction on several occasions. By the time I arrived at my destination I was late for the appointment or the party was over. I felt stupid and scared. What I wanted to do was scream. But I knew that no-one would care. This is a huge city and I have observed people screaming, and not a soul attending to their needs. Now that I have been here a few weeks I have come to love the system for all the reasons I hated it in the beginning. I now feel confident that I can get anywhere in the city without major crisis. After the weekend trip with my host in the car I was also happy to be back on the bus. That Autobahn is frightening!

Navigating the public transportation system in a large city requires tools, as this narrative demonstrates—tools such as which bus routes to take where, bus-stop protocol, deciphering arrival and departure timetables, personal time management, and so on. The narrative describes the space in between ignorance and proficiency, between fright and exhilaration, where these skill sets are learned. As the sociocultural theory suggests and this story demonstrates, once learned, the skills empower the individual to learn more or simply enjoy the personal freedom the knowledge facilitates.

Social Preferences

Definition
Differences in acceptable general behavior of daily living such as shopping, advertising, expectations concerning appropriate dress, etc.

Student narratives

1. Sexuality is a very often used advertising practice here in Vienna. Advertising for just about everything involves some form of sex, scantly clad, almost naked, beautiful people using their attractiveness to sell something. Even the U-Express (my favorite magazine) has a bare-breasted woman on page three every day! Though I am not prude, it was a bit shocking to see the nudity in magazines, newspapers and other advertising mediums here. I guess I don't know how I feel about it. On one hand if it's effective for advertising, well then that's good. But, I worry about the exploitation of the human body. The religious side of me hates to see sexuality reduced to economics.

Nudity and sexuality are dealt with more casually in Europe and other countries around the globe than in the United States. The advertising practice the sojourner describes in the host culture is fundamentally not a major departure from advertising practices in the home culture where models are more modest—barely. Nonetheless, the difference is significant and requires adaptation both intellectually and emotionally. Such exposure and the host nationals' reactions to it provoke an examination of values more in depth later in the sojourn rather than earlier.

2. In America I am used to really comfortable toilet paper. We have quilted, and double-ply and toilet paper so soft you could use it as a pillow. In Austria, the toilet paper is like using sandpaper. This stands in contrast to Prague, where the toilet paper is more like a piece of steel wool. In the grand scheme of things, the toilet paper issue is really minor. An adaptable person will do what is necessary at the time—adapt. At that point it isn't a cultural practice that is better or worse, just different and necessity governs acceptance.

While abroad, one of the most important personal attributes to nurture is a healthy sense of humor. The conclusion of this student narrative demonstrates that sense of humor. All's well that ends well.

In summary the topics in this section (Cross-Cultural Comparison, General Environment, Social Preferences) increase in salience over time as students learn and expand sociocultural skills and understandings. They pay attention to and appreciate aspects of the host culture based on these learnings.

Final Thoughts

There are many more stories that could have been included in this section, each unique in a sense and contributory to the preparation of future sojourners. Hopefully, the experiences presented encourage open and interesting dialogue pre-sojourn and ultimately enrich the interpersonal and intellectual growth of future sojourners.

While the stories were categorized and presented as salient topics within the categories, it is crucial to understand that intercultural adjustment is not just one or the other salient topic. Nor can intercultural adjustment be explained solely by one or the other theory of intercultural adjustment. The study abroad experience and the intercultural adjustment that is asked of the sojourner is an interconnected web of topics that weave the tapestry of the study abroad experience.

References

Baron, R. A., & Byrne, D. E. (2003). *Social psychology.* Boston, MA: Allyn and Bacon.

Bennett, J. M., Bennett, M. J., & Stillings, K. (1977). *Description, interpretation, and evaluation: Facilitators' guidelines.* Retrieved February 6, 2007 from http://www.intercultural.org/resources.html

Berger, K. S. (2001). *The developing person through the life span* (5th ed.). New York: Worth.

Gudykunst, W. B. (2002). Intercultural communication theories. In W. B. Gudykunst & B. Mody (Eds.), *Handbook of international and intercultural communication* (2nd ed., pp. 183–205). Thousand Oaks, CA: Sage.

Hall, E. T. (1969). *The hidden dimension.* Garden City, NY: Doubleday.

Oberg, K. (1960). Cultural shock: Adjustment to new cultural environments. *Practical Anthropology, 7,* 177–182.

Ward, C., Bochner, S., & Furnham, A. (2001). *The psychology of culture shock* (2nd ed.) London: Routledge.

Weiten, W., & Lloyd, M. A. (2003). *Psychology applied to modern life* (7th ed.). Belmot, CA: Wadsworth/Thompson Learning.

18

SYNTHESIS AND CONCLUSIONS

Victor Savicki and Robert Selby

G iven the scope of the preceding chapters, it is a monumental task to develop syntheses and draw conclusions from the work of the contributing authors. Some themes repeat as threads that run through the layers of theory, research, and application. Some aspects are unique to the person, place, and time of the chapter focus. However, it is our sense that, standing back a step or so from these consistent themes and unique aspects, one can see patterns emerging. The whole really can be greater than the sum of the parts. We will try to bring these patterns into focus.

Although there may be one grand unifying scheme that ties together all of the themes offered in this book, we will take a more modest approach by trying to clarify smaller chunks of the overarching synthesis. Our goal is to visualize patterns that may clarify our understanding of the international education enterprise as a whole, that yield implications for executing the role of international educator, that enhance the positive outcomes for our students. We will attempt, where possible, to address the interplay of theory, research, and application, since we believe that these layers support each other. The following sections, then, represent patterns that have presented themselves to us as we have reflected upon the information from this book. The content is a bit like one of those visual puzzles where a slight shift in alignment allows a new pattern to pop out where it was previously hidden. There may be additional patterns to be seen. We hope that the reader will find those as well.

Training for Affective and Cognitive Approaches

International educators, trainers, and coaches should be educated themselves in approaches that acknowledge and utilize both affective learning and critical thinking. Experience with these approaches is not common in most people's academic history. There is no reason to think that international educators will be able to "just do it" without training and support. The educational methodologies based on the theories of experiential and transformative education require both understanding of human learning and acknowledgement of and facility with affective aspects such as feelings, attitudes, and values.

From the affective perspective, we are often taught to ignore or gloss over feelings because they are "too personal" or "don't belong in the classroom." New rules/norms for what is desirable need to be instituted. This is not to say that we want psychotherapy groups in study abroad classrooms. Rather it is an acknowledgment of the "juiciness" of the study abroad experience. The autonomic nervous system pumps hormones from our endocrine glands into our system upon contact with provocative environmental events. These hormones linger in our bloodstream over a period of time. They do not turn on and off like a light switch. Students can be aroused about their experiences over a long period of time. To ignore or discount this arousal presents a barrier to students' learning, since they will not be fully attentive to class content while they are distracted. Just "get over it" is not helpful advice. Also, such arousal often provides a key opportunity to examine cultural issues from which the feelings flowed while student motivation to examine such issues is high.

From the cognitive perspective, critical thinking is a skill that can be developed in many domains of learning, such as math, literature, and social and physical sciences. We want students to apply or learn this mode of thinking in the domain of international education. Central to employing this strategy in the study abroad setting is the systematic processing of cultural encounters, as illustrated by several of the chapters in section three, the applications section of this book. International educators need to learn not only the mechanics of helping students to process their encounters but also their role as coach and supporter rather than dispenser of knowledge. Allowing students to struggle may be difficult, yet it is essential for them to practice critical thinking. It is not always a straightforward process, going directly from A to B. Tolerance for ambiguity and some confidence in students' abilities are necessary. Training for international educators is important in order to learn and apply these skills.

Values Examination

Training in methods of critical thinking will give international educators multiple tools to help students disentangle their thoughts, feelings, and behaviors related to cultural issues. The ability of students to stand aside from their reactions, to examine them from alternative perspectives, to reframe who they are within a new context are all skills that will hold them in good stead throughout their lives. In the language of Transformative Learning Theory, they develop the skill to reflect on the premises underlying their meaning making. The study abroad experience provides a "hot house" for such learning. Daily challenges to students' bedrock values provoke a reaction. We need to provide them with the tools and opportunities to scrutinize those values that have mostly gone unexamined and often unidentified.

Values tend to link abstract beliefs with emotional layers of like/dislike, control/chaos, strength/weakness. As the transformative learning approach indicates, challenges on either the belief or emotional level press the student to exercise their values and either to reassert the worldview that those values support or to question that worldview. From the point of view of becoming an interculturally competent person, it is less important that the values change in specific ways than that students come to recognize that there are viable alternative worldviews that are supported by distinct alternate values. The pedagogical methods to accomplish values examination are demonstrated in section three of this book. Again, there is no reason to presume that international educators have learned these tools in their academic careers. We must make training in the understanding and use of such methods available.

Islands of Multiculturalism

The failure of some study abroad students to develop an intercultural or multicultural perspective does not indicate they are dense or defective. Rather it may indicate a lack of adequate teaching and modeling by study abroad program personnel. As Berry (2005) indicates, for students to adopt an integrative strategy of acculturation (valuing both host and home cultures), it is helpful if the culture that they are living in promotes multicultual values.

International educators and administrators may not have much control over the larger culture in which they are working, but they do have control over their classrooms and study abroad programs. These programs and the people who populate them can create islands of multiculturalism even within seas of segregation or exclusion. The key is to set a tone of "constructive alternativism" that values difference, reflection, and discussion. What seems so obvious to host culture natives may seem opaque and inaccessible to students arriving from their home cultures. Every detail of daily life provides an opportunity to examine home and host cultures in an open and curious manner. The student narratives in section three of this book give examples of such examination. Therefore, we need international educators with a multicultural perspective. It is important to place students in contact with instructors and support personnel who are natives of the study abroad culture. Yet, host culture natives who do not support multicultural values may do more harm than good if they provoke a protective, super-patriotic response in their students. These issues are particularly salient when the cultural distance between the U.S. and the study abroad culture is large. Students may have limited recourse to support and cultural acceptance outside of the study abroad program. In settings such as these, creating a supportive environment in which culture clashes can be identified, investigated, and discussed becomes extremely important. Several of the research studies in this book indicate that "sink or swim" cultural immersion in such settings is not helpful.

Time and Time Again

There is no reason to believe that students will not benefit from short-term study abroad experiences. While students are more likely to have crucial intercultural experiences over a longer time span, and they will have more opportunities to process the cultural differences between cultures, longer-term programs that are unaccommodating may yield worse student outcomes than do shorter, better organized, more supportive ones. The key, as has been said many times in this book, is to develop study abroad programs by design, not chance. The theoretical principles, the research, and the examples of application illustrated in this book provide guidelines for such systematic design. It may be that shorter stays in a foreign culture will require greater emphasis on predeparture and reentry in order to maximize the effect of the shorter actual contact with the host culture. Of course, longer-term programs would benefit as well. Currently, predeparture orientations can be somewhat hit or miss, depending on the institution from which the student is sent. Even more uneven is the reentry support and affirmation. The field would benefit from a consistently applied approach to student education on either end of their study abroad sojourn, as illustrated by several of the chapters in section three of this book. If we postulate that contact with the foreign culture is the mechanism for enhanced intercultural competence, then we need to maximize the effect of that contact. For shorter-duration programs, predeparture preparation and reentry ratification help focus and deconstruct the brief yet potent study abroad sojourn. Shorter sojourns require that international educators work harder.

More Research Must Be Done

For struggling students writing research papers, the phrase "more research must be done" is a standard part of the concluding paragraph. This phrase is obviously very apt in international education as well. Systematic research on study abroad issues is growing, but it is still in its infancy. We know too little about what happens with students during their study abroad, and what the long-term effects may be. The move to outcomes assessment is a good one (Bolen, 2007). Programs should be able to document their effectiveness. Yet, many of those assessments do not focus on the "growth and transformation" aspects of study abroad as articulated in this book. It is clear that there are many roads to understanding with regard to study abroad: education, psychology, sociology, anthropology, language learning, etc. We believe that a key to more comprehensive understanding of study abroad lies in the study of intercultural competence, growth and transformation aspects.

Beyond necessary research, the adaptation of research findings into practice also needs to be highlighted. In some fields, there is a 10- to 15-year lag between the discovery of important research findings and their implementation in practice. Given the accelerating demands on international education, we cannot tolerate that time lag. It is crucial to form links between research-ers and practitioners, such as the ones illustrated in this book.

Cultural Distance

Not all study abroad opportunities are created equal. Not only must the readiness of the individual student be evaluated, but also the features of the host culture may dictate that certain programmatic components should be available. Clearly, cultural knowledge and language fluency will be helpful in helping students adjust to the host culture. But, some host cultures will be relatively impenetrable, especially given the short-term nature of the study abroad sojourn. In these situations, supportive contacts with study abroad program personnel and fellow students become extremely important. We want students to benefit from their study abroad experience, not spend most of their sojourn depressed, anxious, isolated, or otherwise impaired. Differ-ent students will show different levels of readiness for cross-cultural contact. As international educators, we cannot presume all students are alike. Like-wise, we cannot presume that all cultures are alike. Each program will have to be designed to take into account its unique cultural aspects. Each program will have to put in place opportunities for students of differing levels of readiness. It is a complicated business that we are in. The concept of cultural distance is an interesting place to start these considerations. The greater the cultural distance, the more rare or difficult the language for U.S. students, the more the study abroad program will have to respond. Total cultural im-mersion is a laudable goal but may be unrealistic. One last point on this topic: program personnel, besides teachers and host families, can also have important impacts on students. Office staff, custodial workers, bus drivers, neighboring business people with regular student contact can make a differ-ence in the student experience. It pays to think in a systemic fashion about program design.

Emerging Ethical Guidelines

Many of the chapters suggest "should's" of international education. These come from the authors' point of view, experience, and cultural context; yet there do seem to be some emerging guidelines given the emphasis on inter-cultural competence and transformation. Clearly, the unguided, "sink or swim" attitude toward intercultural experiences falls beyond the pale of ethical practice. At a minimum, we as international educators and administrators should "do no harm." Leaving students to serendipitous chance poses unacceptable risks. The outcome of advancing student knowledge, skill, and abilities along some scheme of intercultural development is mandatory. From the growth and transformation view, this movement will require attention to the whole student, not just cognitive-academic aspects. It will emphasize guided reflection of underlying premises that form student values and identity. It will take into consideration the full cycle of international experience: predeparture orientation, supported immersion, and reentry. These student-focused activities will take into account the specific cultural context, as well as the responsibilities of international educators and administrators to the host culture. A more detailed set of guidelines will touch upon additional issues. This book only suggests further consideration. With the recognition and encouragement of student growth and transformation as a central piece of international education outcomes comes a responsibility to attend to the needs and struggles of students facing such changes.

Intercultural Competence and Transformation

Finally, the major themes of this book are found in its title: *Developing Intercultural Competence and Transformation*. The major point found in many chapters of this book is that these are processes not traits; they are journeys not destinations. There may be many levels of intercultural competence depending on student readiness, the quality of the immersion experience, the penetrability of the host culture, and access to support before, during, and after the cultural immersion experience. Assessing cultural competence is, to some degree, a value-added enterprise. Not all students will end at the same place, to some degree because they do not all start at the same place. It is, rather, their movement that is important. Likewise, transformation is not a once-in-a-lifetime occurrence. Subtle shifts in one's frame of reference as a result of a study abroad experience can set the stage for more radical shifts later. The culturally competent student does not emerge fully formed through some miraculous transformation, never to change for the rest of his or her life. Rather, these changes, dear to the heart of international educators, are iterative processes. Repetitions in an ever-increasing upward spiral of change are more descriptive. Intercultural experience can help students learn how to learn in situations in which their core assumptions are challenged. One extremely beneficial result of increasing intercultural competence and transformation is the development of what George Kelly (cited in Maher, 1969) calls "permeable constructs." That is, the conceptions students have of themselves, others, and the world are not surrounded by thick, rigid barriers, but rather are amenable to shifts in perspective. Flexibility and openness to redefining one's identity is a prerequisite to continued personal growth.

Conclusions

Educators are familiar with the age-old debate regarding whether we teach math, art, and history or students. The overly facile, but in this context entirely appropriate, observation is that we do both. In most situations, unless students in fact learn, one may question whether any teaching occurs at all. In study abroad, students appear to learn considerably more than is explicitly planned, much of it related to their personal and intellectual maturation. The educational challenges, then, as the chapters of this text make abundantly clear, are different from campus instruction: How do we balance the specifically defined objectives of academic coursework with the intentional, albeit serendipitous, exploitation of the full range of stimuli from which students learn abroad, thereby enabling them to assess critically their personal and cultural comprehension of the world about them? A "bottom line" conclusion of this book is that, whatever else we intend for students to learn while abroad, they are in a heightened state of self-awareness, perceiving their experiences and relationships as the core of all that is important. In this context, as much attention must be given to pedagogical process as to course content.

As practitioner-educators, it is our responsibility to ensure that students derive as much benefit as possible from time abroad. At least four aspects of the learning process emerge from the chapters in this book, none of which should require an increased investment of resources:

1. *Observation and interpretation:* A basic requisite for intercultural learning is the ability to see and ascribe meaning to things in a "foreign" setting. We can focus students' attention on certain behaviors and interactions in the host culture and get them to challenge, perhaps even reinterpret, their perceptions of events through structured emic analysis.

2. *Sequencing experiences:* We can schedule and sequence student activities in a manner that corresponds to their readiness to experience and learn. Leading students into the shallow end of the pool and equipping them with survival skills is essential so they are not "drowned" in an overwhelming tide of bewildering stimuli.

3. *Sharing opportunities:* Students who choose to study abroad are motivated by largely relational aspirations, so building a learning community corresponds to already present motives. We can assist students to be realistic about relationships they are likely to form with locals, and to value their friendships with other Americans who, through natural interaction, become instrumental to exploration and comparison.

4. *Reflection and analysis:* Given students' heightened self-awareness in a strange new environment, and the intense, albeit temporary, relationships they form, study abroad presents a virtually continuous opportunity to engage them in conversations about what it means to be who they are in a world so unlike them in certain ways but so similar in others. We can create "safe" venues for students to process who they are becoming.

Self-aware professors who teach abroad generally emphasize two things when they encourage others to follow in their shoes. First, they cannot teach a course abroad the same way they teach it on campus. This does not mean, they are quick to underscore, that they "dumb-down" their classes. On the contrary, they must ensure that students are not so overwhelmed by the deluge of new stimuli that they cannot focus on the essential objectives of the course. Second, they must focus on students' emotional states, since the people in their class are so preoccupied with what is happening to them personally. Professors inevitably become counselors and confidants, whether they wish to or not. Teach-abroad faculty discover the need to adjust, sometimes reversing preconceived biases, and most make the necessary adaptations. Our challenge is to *prepare* them in advance so these necessary adjustments are planned ahead, not learned on the job.

Similarly, we can do a better job of preparing students, in spite of our near universal exasperation that they do not "get" orientations until they are already immersed in a new social situation. Dr. Ellen Summerfield (personal communication, March 24, 2006) conducted a survey of international programs offices among member campuses of the Northwest Council on Study Abroad, surely representative of a cross-section of campuses generally. Most offices admitted that they have to devote most of their time and attention to the strictly "hygienic" level of predeparture preparation: visas, security, health, conduct, etc. Many campuses lack resources to do more, although absolutely everyone contacted cited the desire to do so.

Dr. Summerfield has written a great deal about the use of cinema and other readily available activities to prepare students to "see" important details in the environments to which students will have to adapt overseas (Summerfield, 1993, 1997; Summerfeld & Lee, 2006). She has also developed (but not yet implemented as this is being written) a highly interactive online course designed to establish learning communities among students who will travel to the same destinations, with the objective of "predisposing" students to the kinds of intercultural and self-exploratory learning in which they will soon be immersed, and to convene the community in cyberspace well after students return, until the experience abroad can be integrated into life at home. Ellen's innovations, and many similar innovations in our field, suggest that our profession can do more to standardize how we prepare students, even if we have limited resources on our own campuses.

In order to invest needed time and effort in these innovations, international educators and administrators must first understand the experiential and affective dimensions of learning that accompany study abroad. These are not distractions from "real" learning but supply rich contextual motivation to the overall learning process and, in students' own words, contribute many of the substantive rewards of living in another culture. It does indeed change their lives.

References

Berry, J. W. (2005). Acculturation. In W. Friedlmeier, P. Chakkarath, & B. Schwarz (Eds.), *Culture and human development* (pp. 291–302). New York: Psychology Press.

Bolen, M. C. (Ed.). (2007). *A guide to outcomes assessment in education abroad.* Carlisle, PA: Forum on Education Abroad.

Maher, B. (Ed.). (1969). *Clinical psychology and personality: The selected papers of George Kelly.* New York: Wiley.

Summerfield, E. (1993). *Crossing cultures through film.* Boston: Intercultural Press.

Summerfield, E. (1997). *Survival kit for multicultural living.* Boston: Intercultural Press.

Summerfield, E., & Lee, S. (2006). *Seeing the big picture: A cinematic approach to understanding cultures in America.* Ann Arbor: University of Michigan Press.

Ingrid Adams received her MA in Health Education from Western Oregon University in 2006. She has taught health-related classes at the university level and is currently a Wellness Educator in private practice. Her commitment to health is grounded in mindful living through knowledge, self-inquiry, and relaxation in movement. In addition to her academic degrees, Ms. Adams is a licensed massage therapist and holds the rank of Sifu (teacher) in Yang style *t'ai chi ch'uan*. Herself an immigrant, she values cross-cultural exchanges and views the study abroad experience as an important pillar for cross-cultural dialogue and personal growth. She has coordinated language and culture immersion programs at the university level and is a volunteer English tutor.

Carmen Arrúe, born in Cuba and raised in the United States, received a BA from the University of Florida and an MA from the Catholic University of America, with concentration in the fields of applied and medical anthropology. She has conducted research and fieldwork in the Brazilian Amazon, South Florida, and Northern Spain. Ms. Arrúe has crossed cultures many times and finally established her home in Asturias, Spain, where she has lived for the last 25 years. In this corner of the world, coincidentally the land where her grandfather was from, she directs a study abroad program in Oviedo for American university students. Among her varied tasks as Site Director, Ms. Arrúe developed a site-specific intercultural communication course, and is currently developing a training course targeted toward members of the host culture (host families, teachers of "Spanish as a Foreign Language," business-people). She has also developed a general intercultural communication syllabus that can be adapted easily to any Spanish study abroad site, as well a "condensed/abridged" version of the same, appropriate for short-term faculty-led programs in Spain. Ms. Arrúe is an active participant in several international education professional organizations such as NCSA (Northwest Council on Study Abroad), NAFSA, and APUNE (Association of American University Programs in Spain).

Janet M. Bennett, PhD, is Executive Director of the Intercultural Communication Institute and Chair of the ICI/University of the Pacific Master of Arts in Intercultural Relations program. Her PhD is from the University of Minnesota, where she specialized in intercultural communication and anthropology. For 12 years, she was Chair of the Liberal Arts Division at Marylhurst College, where she developed innovative academic programs for adult degree students. As a trainer and consultant, she designs and conducts intercultural and diversity training for colleges and universities, corporations, and social service agencies. She teaches courses in the training and development program at Portland State University and has published several articles and chapters on the subjects of developmental "layered" intercultural training and adjustment processes. She recently coedited *The Handbook of Intercultural Training,* 3rd edition (Sage, 2004).

Frauke Binder is Program Coordinator with the foreign studies program of AHA International in Vienna. She teaches the Cross-Cultural Course for American Students and works as a German language instructor. For several summers she also worked as a language instructor and Goethe-examiner at the DsaP, German Summer School of the Pacific, Portland, Oregon. Frauke also holds a Breathworker Certificate and has done numerous trainings (e.g., Breath, Voice and Movement, Bodywork and Psychosomatics). She gives therapeutic seminars in Vienna. She organizes the education of new breathworkers and does the public relations for the Association of Breathworkers in Vienna (ATMAN) and is a member of the International Breathwork Foundation. She has an MA (Magister) in German language and literature, modern history, and social psychology from the University of Hanover, Germany, and holds a postgraduate certificate for German as a foreign language from the University of Kassel.

Gabriele W. Bosley is Director of International Programs, Chair of the Department of Foreign Languages and International Studies, and Associate Professor of Foreign Languages/German at Bellarmine University. Gabriele received her graduate degrees in foreign language education/ESL and German studies from the University of Paderborn and the University of Louisville. Her research interests include twentieth-century German women's literature, foreign language acquisition, curricular development, and intercultural education. She designed and implemented Bellarmine's transcurricular Foreign Languages and International Studies degree, a minor in

International Studies and has chaired the FLIS department since 1998. She is also the founding Director of Bellarmine's International Programs Office, and has served in that capacity since 1995. Gabriele is the recipient of several regional and national awards and grants, is a regular presenter at conferences and currently serves on the boards of the Association of International Education Administrators, the UCS Board of Trustees, the Cooperative Center for Study Abroad Board of Trustees, the Kentucky Institute for International Studies Board of Directors, the Center for Cross-cultural Study Board of Advisors, the Kentucky Department of Education Professional Standards Board, the Louisville Mayor's International Advisory Council, and until recently the International Student Exchange Programs Council of Advisors and as the American Association of Teachers of German State Testing Chair.

Anne Chambers and **Keith Chambers** are cultural anthropologists, both holding PhDs from UC Berkeley. Their recent research has focused on the study abroad experience of U.S. undergraduates in Siena, Italy. Keith was Director of International Programs at Southern Oregon University from 1989 through 2004 and is currently a consultant applying anthropological understandings and research methods to social and cultural issues. Anne is Professor of Anthropology at Southern Oregon University and teaches a wide range of courses exploring the complexity of cultural systems. Their research on student goals and motivations in study abroad combines their interest in the roles that overseas experience and cultural learning play in undergraduate education and their commitment to the applied utility of the anthropological approach to culture. In addition to work with the Siena program, where they also taught in 2007, Anne and Keith have taught and carried out research in Norway and New Zealand, and have conducted ethnographic research in the Polynesian nation of Tuvalu for over 30 years, maintaining close ties with the community of Nanumea in particular. Their book, *Unity of Heart: Culture and Change in a Polynesian Atoll Society*, was published in 2001 by Waveland Press (Prospect Heights, Illinois).

Eric Cooley completed a PhD in clinical psychology at University of Texas at Austin in 1976, following a BA in psychology at Claremont Men's College. He is a Professor of Psychology at Western Oregon University, where he has taught for 31 years. He is also a licensed psychologist in the State of Oregon. Dr. Cooley's research interests have focused on the emotional well-being and development of college students as well as burnout in a variety of helping professions. In the college-student line of research, topics explored have included stress and coping, depression, eating pathologies, attachment styles, and predictors of academic success and retention at the university. His burnout research has examined teachers, counselors, mental health workers, child protective service workers, and correctional officers.

Darla K. Deardorff is Executive Director of the Association of International Education Administrators, a national professional organization headquartered at Duke University, where she also teaches cross-cultural courses. She has held several national leadership positions within NAFSA and the Forum on Education Abroad, and has presented at national and international conferences over the past decade, as well as given invited talks and workshops within the United States and in other countries. She has worked in the international education field for over 15 years and previously held positions at North Carolina State University and the University of North Carolina at Chapel Hill, where she has had experience in study abroad, international student services, cultural programming, and ESL teaching/teacher training, as well as teaching graduate courses in international education and intercultural communication. Dr. Deardorff has authored numerous publications on international education assessment and intercultural competence and serves as a consultant in these areas to universities and nonprofit organizations. She received her MA and PhD from North Carolina State University. Her research interests include intercultural competence, outcomes assessment, internationalization, and teacher preparation.

Rosemary Donnelly received her BA and MA in English literature in the United States. She moved to Greece more than 30 years ago, and is a founder and codirector of the Athens Centre, an educational and cultural centre that sponsors programs in Greece in affiliation with American colleges and universities. The university programs include semesters in Greece, as well as shorter programs emphasizing classical, Byzantine, and modern Greek studies. The Centre's summer programs on the Greek island of Spetses bring creative people to live and study together while attending the Athens Centre's theatre, poetry, and art workshops. Participants of all nationalities join the year-round modern Greek language courses at the Centre. Rosemary is a member of Democrats Abroad and the Greek-Irish Society, and takes part in activities organized by Greek environmental organizations.

Lynne Heller holds an MA and PhD in history from the University of Vienna. She is the Director of the Archives of the University of Music and Performing Arts Vienna. She is the founding Site Director of the AHA International Vienna Program, which was initiated in 1986. She has functioned as a co-initiator and co-instructor of the first AHA course on intercultural communication, which became a role model for similar courses for other AHA programs. She presented at the 1995 NAFSA Annual Conference "The Resident Director: A Voice From the Other Side," and supported and coauthored research on study abroad students in Vienna.

Joseph G. Hoff holds a PhD in educational policy and administration in comparative and international development education from the University of Minnesota, an MA in international administration (program in intercultural management) from the School for International Training, and a BA and an MA in Spanish from Saint Louis University. He is currently the Director, International Degree and Education Abroad, and Academic Coordinator of International Degrees at Oregon State University. He studied abroad in Madrid, Spain, in 1980/1981; taught English on the JET program in Shizuoka, Japan, in 1986–1990; and volunteered in Tanzania in January 2004. He is currently a member on the Teaching, Learning, and Scholarship Knowledge Community, NAFSA, and a member of the Academic Consortium Board, CIEE. He served as Assistant Director of International Programs at Brown University from 1994 to 2001; at the University of Minnesota CARLA Summer Institute in Minneapolis in summer 2003; and as co-instructor of the CARLA Summer Institute course Maximizing Study Abroad: Teaching Strategies for Language and Culture Learning and Use. He has several publications concerning integrating intercultural training into study abroad. Additional interests are tennis, hiking, and travel.

Amy Hunter received her MA in adult education and a BA in English, both from Portland State University. She began her career as an instructor of outdoor education at Eastern Washington University before transitioning into study abroad with AHA International (AHA) and the University of Oregon.

She has designed and delivered training for Fulbright and facilitated numerous orientations for learners preparing to live and work internationally. She currently serves as a Communications Specialist in the Office of the President at Oregon Health and Science University (OHSU), where she's involved in the development of a newly established Global Health Center. When not working, Amy spends her free time tinkering, drinking coffee, and chasing nearly impossible dreams. She lives aboard her sailboat, outside the Portland, Oregon, city limits.

Kris H. Lou is the Director of International Education and Associate Professor of International Studies at Willamette University in Salem, Oregon. He holds a PhD in International Relations from the University of Oregon, which included study in Austria, Germany, and the former Soviet Union. He also holds a Graduate Certificate in Russian and East European studies, an MA in political science, and a BA in Russian, German, and political science. He has worked in the field of international education, both in the United States and Germany, for 12 years. He has taught international relations and intercultural studies in the United States and Austria for a total of 17 years. Kris currently serves on the Council of Advisors for the International Student Exchange Program (ISEP), the Board of Advisors for the Center for Cross-Cultural Study (CC-CS), and the Advisory Board for International Studies Abroad (ISA). Kris has presented at numerous national and international conferences and is a member of NAFSA, AIEA, and EAIE.

Martha Merrill holds a BA in Russian literature from the University of Michigan; an MLS in liberal studies and creative writing from Boston University; an MALS in Islamic culture studies from Columbia University; and an MA and PhD in higher education administration from the University of Michigan. Martha has worked in colleges and universities, as a teacher and as an administrator, for nearly 30 years, including 5 years in Central Asia, in the Kyrgyz Republic. She has designed, administered, written about, and presented on international education topics since 1982. Currently Dean of Academic Programs at the International Partnership for Service-Learning and Leadership, Martha previously taught international education and intercultural communication courses at the School for International Training and served as the Vice President for Academic Affairs at the American University–Central Asia. Her current research interests include intercultural aspects of university reform and international cooperation among universities; quality assessment and its different definitions in higher education internationally; the ways intercultural development theory and learning theories apply to intercultural service-learning; and international education's responses to a new era of globalization and technological change.

Silvia Minucci earned her BA in foreign languages and literature from the University of Siena in 1998. She also obtained her Advanced Specialization (Dottore) in literary translation (Russian) from the University of Siena in 2000. Silvia currently serves as the Site Director at the AHA International Siena Program, where she has been working in various roles since 1999. She holds an adjunct faculty appointment teaching the program's Cross-Cultural Communication/Cross-Cultural Perspectives course and providing Italian language tutoring assistance. She has also presented on the topic of intercultural communication at the NAFSA meeting in 2006. Having studied abroad herself in France, Great Britain, Ireland, and Russia, Silvia understands students' adjustment difficulties as they adapt to living in another country. She has a particular interest in sign language, and in fact she attended a 2-year course in Italian Sign Language, receiving certification as a Social Communication Assistant from the Italian National Organization of Deaf-Mutes.

Margaret D. (Peggy) Pusch is Associate Director of the Intercultural Communication Institute, Executive Director of SIETAR USA, and an active trainer in the United States and Europe. She cofounded and was president of Intercultural Press, Inc. Her recent publications include "Intercultural Training in Historical Perspective," for the third edition of the *Handbook of Intercultural Training*, and *Culture Matters: An International Educational Perspective*, with Jeanine Hermanns. She has been president of NAFSA and SIETAR USA, is currently Chair of the board of trustees of the International Partnership for Service-Learning and Leadership, and is a member of the board of directors of the Association for International Practical Training. In 2005 she received the Lifetime Achievement Award from SIETAR Europa and the Optime Merens de Collegis award from SIETAR USA.

Victor Savicki holds a PhD in psychology from the University of Massachusetts. He is currently a Professor of Psychology Emeritus from Western Oregon University, where he taught for 33 years. His courses spanned several areas of psychology including clinical, industrial/organizational, and cross-cultural. He has taught in study abroad settings many times and has several publications addressing intercultural adjustment, and stress and coping in cross-cultural contexts, including the book *Burnout Across Thirteen Cultures,* published in 2002 (Praeger). His current research interests focus on the psychological and educational processes study abroad students navigate during their encounters with a foreign culture. He is also interested in assessment of study abroad outcomes. When not engaged in academic pursuits, he sails, skis, and travels.

Robert Selby retired in 2007 as the Executive Director of AHA International. Before joining AHA (then known as American Heritage Association) in 1990, Bob served as Dean of Off-Campus Programs at Linfield College and Vice President for Academic Affairs at Marylhurst College. He led AHA International's merger and integration into the University of Oregon during the final 3 years of his career, a career begun after completing a PhD in anthropology at the University of Utah in 1979. He was instrumental in developing and nurturing a research emphasis at AHA International, and promoted intercultural communication classes for U.S. study abroad students, the fruition of which are reported in this book.

INDEX